Richard Bowdler Sharpe, Claude Wilmott Wyatt

A Monograph of the Hirundinidae

Or Family of Swallows. Vol. II

Richard Bowdler Sharpe, Claude Wilmott Wyatt

A Monograph of the Hirundinidae
Or Family of Swallows. Vol. II

ISBN/EAN: 9783744757836

Printed in Europe, USA, Canada, Australia, Japan

Cover: Foto ©ninafisch / pixelio.de

More available books at **www.hansebooks.com**

A MONOGRAPH

OF THE

HIRUNDINIDÆ

OR

FAMILY OF SWALLOWS.

BY

R. BOWDLER SHARPE, LL.D., F.L.S., F.Z.S., Etc.,
DEPARTMENT OF ZOOLOGY, BRITISH MUSEUM;
HOLDER OF THE GOLD MEDAL FOR SCIENCE FROM H.I.M. THE EMPEROR OF AUSTRIA;
M.A. (Hon.) BATES COLLEGE, U.S.A.; HON. MEMBER OF THE NEW-ZEALAND INSTITUTE;
FOREIGN MEMBER OF THE ROYAL ACADEMY OF SCIENCES OF LISBON; HON. MEMBER OF THE ROYAL ZOOLOGICAL SOCIETY
(NATURA ARTIS MAGISTRA) OF AMSTERDAM; FOREIGN MEMBER OF THE AMERICAN ORNITHOLOGISTS' UNION;
MEMBER OF THE ROYAL SOCIETY OF NATURALISTS OF MOSCOW; FOREIGN MEMBER OF THE ZOOLOGICAL SOCIETY OF FRANCE;
MEMBER OF THE BRITISH ORNITHOLOGISTS' UNION, ETC. ETC.

AND

CLAUDE W. WYATT,
MEMBER OF THE BRITISH ORNITHOLOGISTS' UNION.

VOLUME II.

LONDON:
PRINTED FOR THE AUTHORS.
1885-1894.

PRINTED BY TAYLOR AND FRANCIS,
RED LION COURT, FLEET STREET.

LIST OF CONTENTS.
VOL. II.

	Page
Hirundo daurica	357
,, striolata	361
,, nipalensis	365
,, erythropygia	371
,, melanocrissa	379
,, domicella	381
,, emini	383
Table of Geographical Distribution of the Genus HIRUNDO (continued)	386
Hirundo hyperythra	389
,, badia. [No Plate.]	393
,, semirufa	395
,, gordoni. [No Plate.]	397
,, senegalensis	399
,, monteiri	403
,, euchrysea	407
,, sclateri	409
Appendix to the Genus HIRUNDO	411
Table of Geographical Distribution of the Genus HIRUNDO (continued)	428
Genus CHERAMŒCA	431
Cheramœca leucosternum	433
Appendix to the Genus CHERAMŒCA	435
Genus PROGNE (with Key to Species)	437
Progne purpurea	439
,, hesperia	455
,, furcata	459

LIST OF CONTENTS.

		Page
Progne concolor		463
„ dominicensis		465
„ domestica. [No Plate.]		469
„ chalybea		473
„ tapera		479
Appendix to the Genus Progne		487
Table of Geographical Distribution of the Genera Chermaœca and Progne		490
Genus Atticora (with Key to Species)		493
Atticora fasciata		495
„ cinerea		499
„ tibialis		501
„ melanoleuca		503
„ cyanoleuca		505
„ pileata		513
„ fucata		515
Appendix to the Genus Atticora		517
Table of Geographical Distribution of the Genus Atticora		520
Genus Petrochelidon (with Key to Species)		523
Petrochelidon nigricans		525
„ timoriensis. [No Plate.]		529
„ pyrrhonota		531
„ swainsoni		555
„ swainsoni erythrogastra (hybrid)		559
„ fulva		561
„ ruficollaris		567
„ rufigula		571
„ spilodera		573
„ fluvicola		57
„ ariel		585
Appendix to the Genus Petrochelidon		589
Table of Geographical Distribution of the Genus Petrochelidon		598
Subfamily II. Psalidoprocninæ (with Key to Genera)		601
Genus Psalidoprocne (with Key to Species)		601
Psalidoprocne holomelæna		603

		Page
Psalidoprocne obscura		607
,,	chalybea. [No Plate.]	609
,,	nitens	611
,,	orientalis	613
,,	antinorii	615
	petiti	617
	fuliginosa	619
,,	pristoptera	621
	albiceps	623
Appendix to the Genus PSALIDOPROCNE		625
Table of Geographical Distribution of the Genus PSALIDOPROCNE		630
Genus STELGIDOPTERYX (with Key to Species)		633
Stelgidopteryx serripennis		635
,,	ruficollis	647
,,	uropygialis	651
Appendix to the Genus STELGIDOPTERYX		653
Table of Geographical Distribution of the Genus STELGIDOPTERYX		658
Index		661

LIST OF PLATES.
VOL. II.

PLATE 65. Hirundo daurica.
,, 66. ,, striolata.
,, 67. ,, nipalensis.
,, 68. ,, erythropygia.
,, 69. ,, melanocrissa.
,, 70. ,, domicella.
,, 71. ,, cuiní.
,, 72. ,, hyperythra.
,, 73. ,, semirufa.
,, 74. ,, senegalensis.
,, 75. ,, monteiri.
,, 76. ,, euchrysea.
,, 77. ,, sclateri.
,, 78. *Map of the Genus* Hirundo.
,, 79. ,, ,, ,,
,, 80. ,, *the Genera* Hirundo, Cheramœca, *and* Progne.
,, 81. ,, ,, Hirundo *and* Progne.
,, 82. ,, ,, Hirundo, Progne, *and* Atticora.
,, 83. ,, ,, Hirundo, Atticora, *and* Petrochelidon
,, 84. ,, ,, ,, ,, ,,
,, 85. ,, ,, ,, ,, ,,
,, 86. Cheramœca leucosternum.
,, 87. Progne purpurea.
,, 88. ,, hesperia.
,, 89. ,, furcata.
,, 90. ,, concolor.
,, 91. ,, dominicensis.
,, 92. ,, chalybea.
,, 93. ,, tapera.

LIST OF PLATES.

Plate	94.	*Map of the Genus* Progne.
„	95.	Atticora fasciata.
„	96.	„ cinerea.
„	97.	„ tibialis.
„	98.	„ melanoleuca.
„	99.	„ cyanoleuca.
„	100.	„ pileata.
„	101.	„ fucata.
„	102.	*Map of the Genera* Atticora *and* Petrochelidon.
„	103.	Petrochelidon nigricans.
„	104.	„ pyrrhonota.
„	105.	„ swainsoni.
„	106.	„ swainsoni erythrogastra.
„	107.	„ fulva.
„	108.	„ ruficollaris.
„	109.	„ rufigula.
„	110.	„ spilodera.
„	111.	„ fluvicola.
„	112.	„ ariel.
„	113.	*Map of the Genera* Petrochelidon *and* Psalidoprocne.
„	114.	Psalidoprocne holomelæna.
„	115.	„ obscura.
„	116.	„ nitens.
„	117.	„ orientalis.
„	118.	„ antinorii.
„	119.	„ petiti.
„	120.	„ fuliginosa.
„	121.	„ pristoptera.
„	122.	„ albiceps.
„	123.	*Map of the Genus* Psalidoprocne.
„	124.	„ „
„	125.	Stelgidopteryx serripennis.
„	126.	„ ruficollis.
„	127.	„ uropygialis.
„	128.	*Map of the Genus* Stelgidopteryx.
„	129.	„ „

HIRUNDO DAURICA, Linn.

DAURIAN MOSQUE-SWALLOW.

Hirundo daurica, Linn. Mantissa Plant. App. p. 528 (1771); Gm. S. N. i. p. 1024 (1788); Lath. Ind. Orn. ii. p. 576 (1790); Gray, Gen. B. i. p. 57 (1845); Bp. Consp. i. p. 338 (1850); Selys-Longch. Bull. Acad. R. Belg. xxii. pt. 2, p. 103 (1855); Sharpe, Cat. Birds in Brit. Mus. x. p. 159 (1885); Oates, Faun. Brit. Ind., Birds, ii. p. 282 (1890).

Hirundo alpestris, Pall. Reis. Russ. Reichs, ii. App. no. 19 (1771-76); id. Zoogr. Rosso-Asiat. i. p. 534, pl. 30 (1811); Blasius, Nachtr. Naum. Vög. Deutschl. xiii. p. 209, pl. 383, fig. 3 (1860); Radde, Reis. Sibir., Vög. p. 280 (1863); Finsch, Verh. z.-b. Ges. Wien, xxix. p. 150 (1879); Seebohm, Ibis, 1883, p. 169; Homeyer & Tancré, MT. orn. Ver. Wien, 1883, p. 83.

Daurian Swallow, Lath. Gen. Syn. ii. pt. 2, p. 570 (1783).

Cecropis daurica, Less. Compl. Buff. viii. p. 498 (1837); Boie, Isis, 1844, p. 174; Dybowski, J. f. O. 1876, p. 192; David & Oust. Ois. Chine, p. 125 (1877, pt.).

Cecropis alpestris, Boie, Isis, 1844, p. 174; Gould, B. Asia, i. pl. 28 (1860); Dybowski, J. f. O. 1868, 1872, p. 336, 1874, p. 352, 1874, p. 334, 1875, p. 244; Taczan. Bull. Soc. Zool. France, i. p. 133 (1876); Prjev. in Rowley's Orn. Misc. ii. p. 161 (1877); David & Oust. Ois. Chine, p. 125 (1878).

Lillia alpestris, Boie, J. f. O. 1858, p. 364.

Lillia intermedia, Hume, Str. F. v. p. 263 (1877).

Lillia substriolata, Hume, Str. F. v. p. 264 (1877).

Hirundo intermedia, Hume, Str. F. viii. p. 84 (1879).

Hirundo substriolata, Hume, Str. F. viii. p. 84 (1879).

H. uropygio rufo: pileo dorso concolore: subtùs pallidè rufescens, distinctè striolata.

Hab. in Siberiâ orientali, in terrâ Assamicâ hibernans.

Adult male. General colour above deep blue, the back much streaked with white when the feathers are disturbed; head like the back, and not separated by a nuchal collar from the mantle; lesser and median wing-coverts like the back, the greater coverts, bastard-wing, primary-coverts, and quills blackish, externally glossed with blue; lower back and rump cinnamon-rufous, with a few blackish shaft-lines, very indistinct; upper tail-coverts dark blue; tail-feathers blackish, glossed slightly with blue; lores blackish, whiter at base, and surmounted by a narrow line of rufous, forming a slight eyebrow, which expands into a broad neck-patch of cinnamon-rufous, behind the ear-coverts, which are dingy whitish washed with rufous and distinctly streaked with black shaft-streaks; cheeks and throat also dingy whitish, with broader blackish shaft-streaks; remainder of under surface pale rufous, everywhere streaked with dusky blackish shaft-lines, less marked on the vent and under tail-coverts, the long ones of which end in dark blue or blue-black like the upper tail-coverts; sides of body and flanks washed with a little deeper rufous; axillaries and under wing-coverts clear rufous, with scarcely any shaft-lines, the edge of the wing more distinctly streaked with the latter; quills dusky below. Total length 8·4 inches, culmen 0·4, wing 5·15, tail 4·7, tarsus 0·65.

Adult female. Similar to the male in plumage. Total length 7·5 inches, culmen 0·35, wing 4·75, tail 4·5, tarsus 0·55.

Young. Duller in colour than the adult, and easily distinguished by the rufescent margins to the tips of the wing-coverts and secondary quills; rump more coarsely striped than in the old birds; ear-coverts nearly uniform sooty brown; rufous colour on sides of hinder crown very dull and less developed than in the adults. Wing 4·35 inches.

Hab. Eastern Siberia, wintering in Tibet and Mongolia, and also in Assam.

The number of species of Asiatic Mosque-Swallows has been a subject of discussion for many years, and even now we cannot regard the present state of our knowledge with any great satisfaction. After several attempts on Mr. Swinhoe's part to define the Chinese species, Mr. Allan Hume wrote a capital article on the Indian species of the group, and Mr. Henry Seebohm, in 1883, made a further contribution to our knowledge of the subject. In 1885 we had to describe the species of the *H. daurica* section of Swallows in the 'Catalogue of Birds,' and our conclusions principally agreed with those of Mr. Seebohm. The year 1890 has been remarkable for a further exposition of the Indian species, and this took place in the Natural History Museum, when Mr. E. W. Oates was able to lay out on the table a goodly series of specimens from the Hume collection, such as had never before been available for any European naturalist to work with. To this series of skins Mr. Seebohm brought his Japanese and Chinese examples, and found that Mr. Oates's conclusions were correct, and they are in the main adopted by Mr. Seebohm in his 'Birds of the Japanese Empire.' We have also had the advantage of the loan of Mr. Seebohm's specimens, and, with some slight modifications, we have adopted the opinion of the two naturalists above mentioned, though we still maintain our conviction that to draw a hard-and-fast line between the four races of Oriental Mosque-Swallows is nearly impossible, so much do they grade towards each other both in size and colour.

Four races may, however, be recognized, of which two are large and two small, two rufescent underneath and two whitish. Mr. Oates fixes the length of wing in the two large forms, *H. striolata* and *H. daurica*, as from 4·9 to 5·3 inches, and in *H. nipalensis* and *H. erythropygia* as from 4·5 to 4·7 inches.

Mr. Seebohm divides the four races into two sections, relying on the coarseness or fineness of the streaks on the under surface, and the presence or absence of shaft-streaks to the rump-feathers. Thus in the first section of finely streaked birds he puts

H. daurica (which, as will be noticed, he calls *H. alpestris*), with a wing measuring 4·9 to 5·2 inches, and *H. erythropygia*, with a wing of from 4·2 to 4·5 inches. Then in his second section of coarsely streaked species he puts *H. striolata*, with a wing of from 4·9 to 5·4 inches, and *H. nipalensis*, with a wing of 4·4 to 4·8 inches. We find that in the British Museum series the wing varies between 4·75 and 5·15 inches.

The oldest known species of the group is undoubtedly *H. daurica*, which was described by Linnæus in the Appendix to his 'Mantissa,' from a specimen brought from Siberia by Laxman. There can be no doubt as to the bird intended, and Linnæus's name must be retained in preference to that of *alpestris* of Pallas, which has probably been resuscitated by Mr. Seebohm for the species as being better known, and therefore *auctorum plurimorum*.

Pallas described his *Hirundo alpestris* as nesting in rocks and in caves on the Altai Mountains and in the other Siberian Alps, being found but rarely building in deserted dwellings. In his 'Zoographia,' he again gives the habitat as the Altai Mountains and Dauria, and he states his belief that it occurs throughout the whole mountain-region to Tibet and China. He describes and figures the nest, which is depicted as fixed to a rock; but it was probably drawn from memory, as it does not coincide with the form of the nest as described by other authors.

Messrs. Homeyer and Tancré have recorded the species from the Altai Mountains, and, according to Dr. Otto Finsch, it was breeding in a large colony between Urdschar and Bakti on the 20th of May; he again met with the species on the Irtisch River, above Buchtarminsk, on the 16th of June.

Dr. Dybowski records it as common throughout the whole of Dauria, and found it on the Amoor and in the Ussuri country, but it was not met with near Lake Baikal. It breeds in Dauria, and it was also found nesting in the Ussuri delta by Dr. Grabowski. Radde's localities for the species were the Krimski Post, the eastern slope of the southern part of the Apple Mountains, and again at Argun and Blagowestchensk.

In the British Museum are two specimens of Dr. Severtzoff's, procured by him in N.W. Mongolia, one being marked as from the River Etyr. The following account is given by General Prjevalski:—

"The specimens obtained by us in S.E. Mongolia and Kan-su have hardly any black streaks on the rust-coloured rump, and these are scarcely perceivable. At the same time, the black streaks are much narrower on the underparts than is shown in Gould's plate, although they are somewhat wider than in *C. erythropygia*, Sykes, which also differs from the present species by the absence of all streaks on the rump and the wider rust-coloured patch on the nape.

"The Daurian Swallow is extremely common in S.E. Mongolia, Ordos, and Ala-shan. In Kan-su it inhabits the median and low mountain-circles, and hardly ever visits the Alpine zone. It breeds on rocks, as well as in summer-houses, and even in tents.

"The shape of the nest is elongated-oval, about 8 or 10 inches long; the front portion is occupied by a narrow entrance. The eggs are pure white, five or six in number, and are deposited in the wider part of the nest, which is lined with hair, wool, and feathers. The young leave the nest about the middle of summer; but in a single instance we found, on the 20th of September, in Din-juan-in, close to the Ala-shan Mountains, a nest with some unfledged young in it.

"It arrives in S.E. Mongolia much later than *Hirundo gutturalis* (*i. e.* about the 10th of May), although in the mountains of Kalgan we once observed it on the 23rd of April. The first birds in Kan-su were seen on the 14th of May. The autumnal migration takes place in the early part of September; and on the 12th of this month we saw a large flock about the river Tetunga, which occupied about two hours in passing us. In the Ussuri country we only once observed it."

As regards the winter habitat of this Swallow we do not know much. Mr. Seebohm says that it winters in Mongolia and Tibet, and we know that it goes to Assam and Cachar. It may even be resident here, as Mr. Hume's specimens of *H. intermedia* from Sadhyia, in Assam, were killed in June; but these were probably early winter arrivals, or laggards behind the main body of northward migrants. The type of *H. substriolata* of Hume came from Cachar, and is undoubtedly *H. daurica*. A slight error occurs in Mr. Oates's book, for he considers that "two specimens from Cachar, February (types of *Lillia substriolata*, Hume)," belong to *H. striolata*; but these cannot be the types of *L. substriolata*, as they were shot in February 1879, whereas Mr. Hume's bird was described in 1877. There was only one Cachar specimen in his collection at that date, and consequently it must be the typical one, which we refer without hesitation to *H. daurica*.

The descriptions are taken from specimens in the British Museum, and the figure is drawn from a Daurian specimen in Mr. Seebohm's collection.

HIRUNDO STRIOLATA
(KAREN-NEE)

HIRUNDO STRIOLATA, Temm. & Schl.

JAVAN MOSQUE-SWALLOW.

Cecropis striolata, Boie, Isis, 1844, p. 174 (ex Kuhl, MSS. : descr. nulla); Cass. Cat.
Hirund. Mus. Philad. Acad. p. 3 (1853); Swinh. P. Z. S. 1871, p. 346 ; Wald. in
Blyth's B. Burm. p. 127 (1875); David & Oust. Ois. Chine, p. 127 (1877. pt.).
Hirundo striolata, Gray, Gen. B. i. p. 58 (1845); Temm. & Schl. Faun. Jap. p. 33
(1850, descr. orig.); Bp. Consp. i. p. 340 (1850); Wall. P. Z. S. 1863, p. 485 ;
Blyth, Ibis, 1866, p. 337; Gray, Hand-l. B. i. p. 69, no. 801 (1869); Hume &
Davison, Str. F. vi. p. 44 (1878); Seebohm, Ibis, 1883, p. 169; Vorderm. Nat.
Tijdschr. Nederl. Ind. xlii. p. 210 (1883); Sharpe, Cat. Birds in Brit. Mus. x.
p. 161 (1885); Oates, Faun. Brit. Ind., Birds, ii. p. 281 (1890); Seebohm, Birds
Japan. Emp. p. 143 (1890); Steere, List B. Philippines, p. 16 (1890).
Hirundo daurica (nec L.), Swinh. Ibis, 1860, p. 48, 1863, p. 255.
Lillia striolata, Hume, Str. F. v. p. 261 (1877).
Hirundo japonica (nec T. & S.), Oates, Handb. B. Brit. Burm. i. p. 305 (1883).
Hirundo striolata, β. *substriolata* (nec Hume), Seebohm, Ibis, 1883, p. 169.

H. major; similis *H. dauricæ* et staturâ æquali, sed subtùs albescens, striis pectoralibus latioribus et
uropygio distinctè striatulato distinguenda.

Hab. in Chinâ meridionali et in insulâ " Formosa " dictâ : in terris Assamicis et Burmanicis usque ad
insulas Philippinas et ad eas " Java " et " Flores " dictas.

Adult male (type of species). General colour above dark purplish blue, the back perceptibly streaked
with white where the white bases to the feathers show through ; lesser and median wing-coverts
like the back; greater coverts, bastard-wing, primary-coverts, and quills black, washed with
purplish blue externally; lower back and rump light chestnut-rufous, with narrow blackish
shaft-lines, not very distinct ; upper tail-coverts purplish blue with rufous bases ; tail-feathers
black washed with purplish blue ; head like the back, with a few streaks of rufous on the hind
neck ; no rufous on base of forehead; loral plumes dusky with whitish bases, surrounded by a
narrow streak of rufous ; from behind the eye a triangular patch of dull chestnut, extending on
the sides of the neck, but not meeting behind the nape ; ear-coverts dingy fulvous, with blackish
shaft-streaks ; cheeks and under surface of body whitish, more silky white on the throat and
a little deeper buff on the sides of the body; all the under surface from the chin to the vent
streaked with distinct blackish centres to the feathers, broader on the throat and breast ; under
tail-coverts fulvescent, with broad and conspicuous tips of blue-black ; under wing-coverts and
axillaries pale fulvescent, with narrow shaft-lines of black, the outer coverts more strongly
mottled with blackish central markings ; quills dusky below, more ashy along the edge of the
inner web. Total length 7·6 inches, culmen 0·55, wing 5·05, tail 4, tarsus 0·6.

Adult female. Does not differ from the male in colour. Total length 7 inches, wing 5·1, tail 3·67, tarsus 0·65.

Hab. From Java and Flores, north to the Burmese countries, Southern China and Formosa.

THIS species is as large as *H. daurica*, having the wing from 4·65 to 5·3 inches, but it is much whiter below, more coarsely streaked, and has distinct black shaft-lines to the rufous feathers of the lower back and rump. It was originally described from Java, where we suspected that it would be only a winter visitant, but Dr. Vorderman states that it breeds at Batavia. Mr. Wallace also procured the species in the island of Flores. During the Steere Expedition to the Philippines, Mr. Moseley shot two specimens in the islands of Luzon and Masbate at the end of April. Our next habitat for the species is the island of Formosa, where, according to Mr. Swinhoe, it abounds in every homestead.

The species is doubtless found throughout Southern China, and it possibly migrates to Assam, as Mr. J. R. Cripps procured a specimen at Dibrughur in November. Two examples were procured in the Karen Hills in January, by Major Wardlaw Ramsay, at a height of 3000 feet, and the same naturalist also obtained a specimen at Karen-nee on the 29th of March, at a height of 2600 feet.

Swinhoe thus describes the nesting of the species in Formosa:—

"On taking possession of our native house at Tamsuy, I observed a nest of this Swallow under the rafters in the central hall. It was exteriorly built of specks of mud, like the nests of the Martin, but had a neck-like entrance, giving the whole the form of a French flask, flattened against the roof; the inside was lined amply with feathers. Pallas's figure gives a very good idea of its structure. The mouth, however, does not always point upwards, but is adapted in form and direction to the shape of the spot against which it is placed. At the close of March the pair to which the nest belonged returned, and in April began to repair the old nest. Towards the close of this month the female was sitting on three white, unspotted eggs. The male and female share the duties of incubation, the female usually taking the longest spell. For the sake of science, we let the birds have their own way, though they made a great mess about our small house, and nearly drove us wild with their loud discordant twittering.

"In a ramble one spring morning, at dawn, I saw large numbers of these Swallows perching on some high bamboos. The sun was fast dispelling the thick night-fog that still hung low and heavy, and the birds seemed in high spirits at the return of fine weather. They fluttered from branch to branch, and as they regained a footing, rocked backwards and forwards before recovering their balance. It was in April, and they were all paired, the male being always distinguishable by his larger size and longer tail. In pairs they sang, or rather twittered, their notes *kee-wee-keé*, like sounds that might be produced by some metal instrument sadly out of tune. The male loudly sang his bar, and the female followed in a lower key. The male then fluttered his wings and began again; the female followed suit. In this way the whole clump of tall, graceful bamboos looked alive with these birds, and resounded with their strange notes. Some pairs would start away and pursue one another, at first, with a smooth, skimming flight; then in an excited manner they would stagger along and, fluttering their wings, sing lustily their notes of love."

The description is copied from the British Museum 'Catalogue of Birds,' and is drawn up from the typical specimen in the Leyden Museum. The Plate represents a very strongly marked individual from Karen-nee in the Tweeddale collection. The majority of the specimens examined are whiter underneath, and have not such a pronounced black patch on the ear-coverts.

HIRUNDO NIPALENSIS

HIRUNDO NIPALENSIS, *Hodgs.*

HODGSON'S MOSQUE-SWALLOW.

Hirundo nipalensis, Hodgs. Icon. ined. in Brit. Mus., Passeres, pl. vi. fig. 1 (no. 329); id. J. A. S. Beng. v. p. 780 (1836); id. in Gray's Zool. Misc. p. 82 (1844); Hume & Davison, Str. F. vi. p. 44 (1878); Hume, Str. F. viii. p. 84 (1879); Scully, t. c. p. 233; Bingham, Str. F. ix. p. 118 (1880); Hume, t. c. p. 246; Oates, Handb. B. Br. Burm. i. p. 306 (1883); Sharpe, Cat. Birds in Brit. Mus. x. p. 160 (1885); Hume, Str. F. xi. p. 27 (1888); Salvad. Ann. Mus. Civ. Genov. (2) v. p. 576 (1888); Oates, ed. Hume's Nests & Eggs Ind. B. ii. p. 195 (1890); id. Faun. Brit. Ind., Birds, ii. p. 282 (1890).

Hirundo daurica (nec L.), Gray, Cat. Fissir. Brit. Mus. p. 23 (1848); Blyth, Cat. B. Mus. As. Soc. p. 198 (1849); Horsf. & Moore, Cat. B. Mus. E. I. Co. i. p. 92 (1854, pt.); Swinh. Ibis, 1861, p. 328; Jerd. B. Ind. i. p. 160 (1862, pt.); Swinh. Ibis, 1863, pp. 89, 255; id. P. Z. S. 1863, p. 287; id. Ibis, 1870, p. 90; Beavan. Ibis, 1865, p. 405; Tytler, Ibis, 1868, p. 196; Pelz. t. c. p. 307; Brooks, Ibis, 1869, p. 46; Beavan, t. c. p. 404; Hume, Str. F. ii. p. 168 (1874).

Hirundo alpestris japonica, Temm. & Schl. Faun. Japon., Aves, p. 33, pl. 11 (1850).

Hirundo japonica, Bp. Consp. i. p. 340 (1850); Gray, Hand-l. B. i. p. 69, no. 809 (1869); Sharpe, Cat. Birds in Brit. Mus. x. p. 162 (1885).

Cecropis japonica, Cass. Cat. Hirund. Philad. Mus. p. 4 (1853); Swinh. P. Z. S. 1871, p. 436; id. Ibis, 1874, p. 346; Blakist. Amended List B. Japan, pp. 25, 48 (1884); Tristr. Ibis, 1885, p. 194.

Hirundo erythropygia (nec Sykes), Gray, Hand-l. B. i. p. 69, no. 806 (1869, pt.); Cock & Marsh. Str. F. i. p. 350 (1873); Hume, Str. F. iii. p. 318 (1875); Godw.-Aust. J. A. S. Beng. xlv. pt. 2, p. 68 (1876); Cripps, Str. F. vii. p 76 (1878); Bingham, Str. F. viii. p. 192 (1879).

Cecropis daurica (nec L.), Jerd. Ibis, 1871, p. 352; Tacz. P. Z. S. 1887. p. 599, 1888, p. 462.

Cecropis arcticitta, Swinh. P. Z. S. 1871, p. 346.

Lillia daurica (nec L.), Hume, Nests & Eggs Ind. B. p. 78 (1873).

Cecropis nipalensis, Hume, Str. F. iii. p. 42 (1875).

Hirundo (Cecropis) nipalensis, Brooks, Str. F. iii. p. 230 (1875).

Cecropis erythropygia (nec Sykes), Blyth, B. Burm. p. 127 (1875); Blakist. & Pryer, B. Japan, p. 139 (1878).
Lillia arcticitta, Hume, Str. F. v. pp. 261, 266 (1877).
Lillia japonica, Hume, Str. F. v. p. 261 (1877).
Lillia nipalensis, Hume, Str. F. v. p. 262 (1877).
Hirundo arcticitta, Oates, Handb. B. Br. Burm. i. p. 306 (1883).
Hirundo alpestris, β. *nipalensis*, Seebohm, Ibis, 1883, p. 169.
Hirundo alpestris, Seebohm, Birds of Japan, Emp. p. 142 (1890).
Hirundo alpestris nipalensis, Seebohm, t. c. p. 143 (1890).

H. similis H. daurica et subtùs paullo rufescens, sed multo minor, alâ breviore : subtùs distinctè striata.

Hab. in insulis Japonicis et in Chinâ, in montibus Himalayanis: in peninsulâ Indicâ et in regione Indo-Burmanicâ totâ hibernans.

Adult male. General colour above dark purplish blue, streaked with white where the white bases show through; the wing-coverts like the back; bastard-wing, primary-coverts, and quills blackish, glossed externally with steel-blue; rump and upper tail-coverts cinnamon-rufous, with distinct narrow black shaft-lines, the long coverts dark purplish blue, with light rufous bases; tail-feathers black, glossed with steel-blue; crown of head dark purplish blue like the back; over the eye a few rufous feathers; sides of the hinder crown deep rufous, converging towards the nape, but not forming a distinct collar, the nape-plumes being blue edged with rufous; lores whitish, tipped with dusky; ear-coverts smoky brown, slightly tinged with rufous and broadly streaked with dusky brown; cheeks and throat dull white, broadly streaked with blackish, more distinctly on the latter; remainder of the under surface pale rufescent buff, very distinctly streaked with black; sides of upper breast purplish blue; thighs rather white; under tail-coverts like the abdomen, the lower ones blue-black with pale rufescent bases and black shaft-lines; lateral under tail-coverts white, with black shaft-lines and a distinct oval spot of blue-black near the tip; axillaries and under wing-coverts rufescent buff, all with distinct black shaft-lines, broader on the outer under wing-coverts; quills below dusky, paler along the inner web: "bill black; feet dusky; claws black; iris blackish brown" (*J. Scully*). Total length 7·4 inches, culmen 0·4, wing 1·55, tail 4, tarsus 0·65.

Adult female. Similar to the male in colour. Total length 7·3 inches, culmen 0·35, wing 4·5, tail 3·7, tarsus 0·6.

Young. Differs from the adult in its duller blue plumage, and in having narrow whitish edges to the inner secondaries: "bill black, the base of the lower mandible and gape fleshy yellow; feet dusky brownish; claws yellow; iris brownish black" (*J. Scully*).

Hab. Southern Islands of Japan, China, Himalaya Mountains. Wintering in the Peninsula of India and the Burmese countries.

In this species the length of the wing varies from 4·3 to 4·75 and even 4·8 inches, so that in this respect it attains to the dimensions of *H. daurica*, from which, indeed, it is difficult to separate the species specifically. The streakings of the underparts are sometimes almost as strongly indicated as those of *H. striolata*, while the slightly rufescent colouring of the under surface allies it to *H. daurica*. It can, indeed, only be considered a small race of the latter species, though some examples are as pale below as *H. striolata*.

It was first discovered by Mr. Hodgson in Nepal. He says that it is "the Swallow of the Central Region, a household creature, remaining for seven or eight months in the year." Dr. Scully also writes :—"This Swallow is even more common in the valley of Nepal than *H. rustica*, and is much more familiar in its habits than that species, constantly flying about houses and often entering into the room. It lives in the valley for about eight months in the year, migrating to lower levels in winter. It was not uncommon in the Nawakot district about the end of November.

"This species breeds in the valley from April to the end of July, some birds certainly producing two broods in the season. The nests are made of pellets of fine light-coloured clay, and are usually fixed between the rafters of verandahs or of rooms which are little used. The shape of the nest is a rather irregular half-retort; the entrance being long and narrow. The usual number of eggs laid is four, and these rest on a beautiful cushion of soft feathers—often those of the Chikore, Black Partridge, and Pigeon. The eggs are well known; pure delicate white, in shape long oval, smaller at one end."

It likewise occurs throughout the Western Himalayas, though Mr. Brooks did not observe it in Kashmir. At Murree it breeds, and, according to Colonel C. H. T. Marshall, it is the "House-Swallow" of the place. He found eggs in June. Stoliczka found it at Nachar in the Sutlej Valley, and Mr. Hume states that it is far from rare there. It nested regularly at Rothney Castle, Mr. Hume's beautiful house at Simla; and Captain Beavan writes :—" Noticed at Simla about the end of April, now and then about the house, as if in quest of a place to build in; but apparently it does not build until much later. I observed this species at Simla up to Sept. 15th, when I noticed that it was almost the only species visible, and still common."

Mr. Brooks records this Swallow as common both at Nynee Tal and Almora, as well as at Binsur, which is twelve miles further north than Almora. Specimens from Mussoorie are in the Hume collection, and Mr. Brooks records it as met with on the march from Mussoorie to Gangaotri. Between Simla and Mussoorie, Colonel Tytler also says that the species was common and at considerable heights.

In the winter it is met with in the plains of India, and Mr. Hume's collection contains specimens from Oudh and Etawah; it has been met with as far south as Manbhoom, where Captain Beavan found it "tolerably common."

Mandelli procured the species in the Bhutan Dooars in April, and there are specimens in the Hume collection from this locality, as well as others from Faridpur in Eastern Bengal, obtained by Mr. J. R. Cripps, while Mr. Inglis procured it at Dilkusha in Cachar. Colonel Godwin-Austen has specimens from the Dafla Hills. Mr. Hume writes :—" Though not common, I met with this occasionally both in the hills and plains of Manipur. I found this species about Karimganj in Sylhet, and have received it from N.E. Cachar, but (though it doubtless occurs) from no other place in the valley of Assam." Mr. Hume considered that he also obtained *H. japonica* and *H. substriolata* in Manipur, but all his specimens must be referred to *H. nipalensis*. Major Wardlaw Ramsay procured an example in the Karen Hills in March. Specimens from Pegu are in the British Museum, and Mr. Oates says that it is found in winter over the whole of British Burmah and is the only Swallow which is common. In Tenasserim it is sparingly distributed in suitable localities. Mr. Davison says:—" I only saw these Swallows in the extreme north and south of the province. They affect open grassy slopes, and these are not common elsewhere." Mr. Davison's localities for the species are:—Pahpoon, Moulmein, Pakchan, Bankasun, and Malewun. Feu met with it at Kaukaryit. According to Dr. Tiraud it is found also in Cochin China.

As far as we know, the present species is spread over the greater part of China. Dr. McKinlay has sent it from Shanghai, and Mr. Swinhoe has procured it at Amoy and Chefoo. He states that it breeds in China, and he believes that it inhabits Hainan also. The following is his note on the species:—"A few passing flocks spend a day or two in Amoy during winter. It is found in the extreme north of China as a resident only; but in the south, where the winter climate is more genial, it stays all the year, roaming about in small parties during the cool weather, and merely shifting its haunts from exposed to sheltered localities according to the severity of the season. In Southern China it is by no means so common as the Chimney-Swallow, and far more locally distributed." The Tweeddale collection has likewise two specimens from the Island of Pootoo.

Mr. Swinhoe separated the Pekin bird as *H. arctivitta*, but we cannot allow that this is different from *H. nipalensis*. It is a summer visitant to the north of China, but was frequently seen in flocks by Mr. Swinhoe in August and September.

In Japan it is, according to Mr. Seebohm, "a summer visitant to the southern islands, but has not yet been recorded from Yezo." There are four skins in the Pryer collection from Yokohama. Messrs. Blakiston and Pryer have given the following note in their 'Birds of Japan':—" It is common about Tokio, where it builds a long bottle-shaped nest under the eaves of buildings. Eggs six; white. Not yet found in Yezo. Specimen in Hakodate Museum from Tokio; specimens also in the museum there. It has only lately been discovered at Yokohama, although there have long been many suitable places for it to breed. The first was noticed in 1878." Captain Blakiston says that, to his surprise, he also once observed this Swallow on the 23rd of January. It has also been found in Corea by Dr. Kalinowski.

With regard to its nesting-habits in India, we quote the following from Mr. Oates's edition of Mr. Hume's well-known work on the 'Nests and Eggs of Indian Birds':—

"This, the larger of our Indian Mosque-Swallows, although visiting during the cold season the plains of India, breeds, so far as I know, exclusively in the Himalayas—I mean, of course, within our limits.

"It is very familiar about the houses of most of our hill-stations, but I think that it constructs its nest by preference under the eaves and in the verandahs of empty houses and staging bungalows, which are seldom in the hills occupied for many successive days in any month. At the same time its nest is often to be seen under projecting ledges of cliffs, and occasionally, where these occur, in ruined buildings.

"The breeding-time, according to my experience, is from April to August; but I have taken a dozen eggs in July to one in any other month. The nests are very similar to those of its plains congener, long and retort-shaped, very neatly built with clay pellets, as a rule very warmly lined first with grass or fibres and fine roots, and then with various-sized feathers, of which there is often quite a large bunch. They average, however, much larger than those of *H. erythropygia*, and one I recently measured had the tubular entrance 13 inches in length and the chamber more than 7 inches in diameter exteriorly.

"Mr. Brooks remarks :—'The nest is always a half-retort, fixed to the underside of an overhanging rock or cave, generally with only one entrance; but a friend of mine, Mr. Horne, gives me an account of one fixed to one of the verandah rafters of a house where the nest has two entrances.

"'In the hills about Almora I found the nest several times, sometimes in open exposed places, at other times where the rocks were overgrown with wood. The eggs resemble those I took in the plains. The plains bird does not breed till the hot winds are over, at the end of June or beginning of July; but in the hills I found eggs nearly hatched in May. Others at Binsar, Mr. Horne informs me, have only just laid in the middle of July, when I write. The hill-bird breeding in the verandahs of houses, as well as in caves, accords with the habit of the Chinese bird, which Mr. Swinhoe remarks 'breeds under the roof-tops.''

"Captain Hutton says :—'This is the common Swallow of the Doon and hills, arriving in the latter locality in March, and building its retort-shaped nest of mud beneath the eaves of houses, against window-frames, at the side of verandah beams, and other suitable situations; the lining is of feathers. Some eggs taken on the 20th of May were hard-set, but other broods were still earlier, as a nest placed against the window of my room had then contained young ones for some days previously. During the heavy mists of the rainy season these nests often fall by their own weight from the quantity of moisture imbibed.

"'When far removed from houses, these birds resort to lofty rocks, beneath the ledges of which the nest is placed. Its shape is flattish hemispherical, with some variation, being at times more globose, with a long neck forming the entrance passage, and thus giving the nest a retort shape. When the bird has selected the spot on which it intends to build, it usually deposits a white chalky substance, by way of cement, against the wall or beam as the case may be, as an adhesive foundation for the subsequent wall of mud. Without this precaution the weight of the material would cause it to part from its foundation. This same whitish earth may also be seen in the narrow neck of the nest, more especially at the mouth, where strength is required to resist the constant abrasion that would otherwise ensue from the frequent entrance and exit of the bird. Generally speaking, this chalky cement is applied to any part that may from circumstances appear to require strengthening, as it likewise gives consistency to the mud. Sometimes, if the situation affords sufficient room, the long neck projects in a straight line from the body of the nest, but where the space is confined, or an obstacle interposes, the neck is turned off at an angle, and in such cases there is pretty sure to be a layer of the chalky cement at the point of deviation from the previous direction. When, however, the material is of a sufficient consistency to be adhesive without the cement, none is applied. In the construction of the nest the mud is laid on in small rounded lumps, which gives a rude and knotty appearance to the surface. The lining is abundant and is composed of fine grass and feathers.

"'There are frequently two broods from the same nest in the same season, the first in the end of May and beginning of June, the other in July and August. The birds that built against my window reared one brood in June, and, as soon as the young were able to fly, they were escorted by the old birds during the day and were initiated in the art of fly-catching, returning to the nest about sunset or earlier if the rain was heavy. This continued for about ten days, when the young birds disappeared, and the old ones laid again in the same nest towards the end of July.'

"The late Captain Beavan mentions that he 'found a nest which was built in the verandah of the dâk bungalow at Fagoo on the 2nd August, 1866. It was then but just finished, and the female had not yet begun to lay her eggs. The nest is like that of *H. rustica*, made of mud, but has a funnel-shaped entrance, some 4 or 5 inches in length, continued from the top of the nest along the angle caused by the meeting of the wall and the roof. The female keeps inside the nest, and from the continued twittering which she made when visited by the male, I thought at first that the nest contained young; and it was not until I drove her out that I discovered my mistake.'

"The eggs of this species are similar to those of *H. erythropygia*, except that they are slightly larger. They are long ovals, slightly compressed towards one end, pure white, the shell of exquisite fineness, and somewhat, but not very, glossy.

"In length they vary from 0·81 to 0·89 inch, and in breadth from 0·55 to 0·6 inch, but the average is 0·85 to 0·55 inch."

The descriptions are copied from the British Museum 'Catalogue.' The specimen figured is in the Hume collection. The drawing, taken by Mr. Wyatt during his visit to the Himalayas, represents the snows of Nepal and Mount Everest.

HIRUNDO ERYTHROPYGIA, *Sykes.*

SYKES'S MOSQUE-SWALLOW.

Hirundo erythropygia, Sykes, P. Z. S. 1832, p. 83; Jerd. Madr. Journ. xi. p. 237 (1840); Blyth, Ibis, 1866, pp. 237, 337; G. King, J. A. S. Beng. xxxvii. pt. 2, p. 215 (1868); Gray, Hand-l. B. i. p. 69, no. 806 (1869); Brooks, Ibis, 1869, p. 16; Blanf. J. A. S. Beng. xxxviii. p. 172 (1869); Blyth, Ibis, 1870, p. 161; Blanf. J. A. S. Beng. xl. p. 27 (1871); Stoliczka, op. cit. xli. p. 231 (1872); Adam, Str. F. i. p. 370 (1873); Brooks, J. A. S. Beng. xliii. pt. 2, p. 243 (1874); id. Str. F. iii. p. 230 (1875); Aitken, t. c. p. 212; Hume, t. c. p. 318; Butler, t. c. p. 451; Wald. Ibis, 1876, p. 338; Butler, Str. F. v. p. 226 (1877); Davidson & Wenden, Str. F. vii. p. 76 (1878); Murray, t. c. p. 113; Legge, B. Ceylon, p. 594 (1879); Hume, Str. F. viii. p. 84 (1879); Butler, Cat. B. Sind, &c. p. 10 (1879); id. Cat. B. S. Bomb. Pres. p. 14 (1880); Wardlaw Ramsay, Ibis, 1880, p. 18; Vidal, Str. F. ix. p. 43 (1880); Butler, t. c. p. 377; Reid, Str. F. x. p. 18 (1881); Davidson, t. c. p. 292 (1882); Davison, t. c. p. 345 (1883); Seebohm, Ibis, 1883, p. 169; Sharpe, Cat. Birds in Brit. Mus. x. p. 164 (1885); Taylor, Str. F. x. p. 457 (1887); Terry, t. c. p. 469; Oates, ed. Hume's Nests & Eggs Ind. B. ii. p. 197 (1890); id. Faun. Brit. Ind., Birds, ii. p. 283 (1890); Seebohm, B. Japan. Emp. p. 143 (1890).

Hirundo daurica (nec Pall.), Blyth, Cat. B. Mus. As. Soc. p. 198 (1849, pt.); Layard, Ann. & Mag. Nat. Hist. xii. p. 170 (1853); id. & Kelaart, Prodr. Cat. App. p. 58 (1853); Cass. Cat. Hirund. Mus. Philad. Acad. p. 4 (1853); Horsf. & Moore, Cat. B. E.I. Co. Mus. i. p. 92 (1854, pt.); Jerd. B. Ind. i. p. 160 (1862, pt.); Bulger, P. Z. S. 1866, p. 568; Holdsw. P. Z. S. 1872, p. 419; Murray, Vertebr. Faun. Sind, p. 103 (1884).

Cecropis daurica, Cass. Cat. Hirund. Mus. Philad. Acad. p. 4 (1853).

Cecropis erythropygia, Gould, B. Asia, i. pl. 29 (1868); Jerd. Ibis, 1871, p. 352; Blyth, B. Burm. p. 127 (1875); Fairb. Str. F. iv. p. 254 (1876).

Lillia erythropygia, Hume, Nests & Eggs Ind. B. p. 76 (1873); id. Str. F. v. p. 255 (1877).

H. similis H. dauricæ, sed multo minor: subtus albicans; striis pectoralibus obsoletis distinguenda.

Hab. in peninsula Indicâ.

Adult male. General colour above deep purplish blue, with white striations where the bases of the feathers show through; the wing-coverts like the back; quills blackish, externally glossed with dull blue; rump and upper tail-coverts deep ferruginous, the longer coverts deep purplish blue;

tail-feathers blackish glossed with dull blue; crown of head like the back, from which it is almost separated by a nuchal collar of deep ferruginous, the sides of the hinder crown and sides of the neck being of the latter colour and converging on to the nape, the nuchal collar being only interrupted by a few dark-blue plumes in the form of spots; a narrow frontal line and a streak over the eye deep ferruginous; lores whitish, tipped with dusky; ear-coverts pale rufous with dusky shaft-streaks; cheeks, throat, and under surface of body whitish, slightly marked with fulvous on the breast and flanks; the whole of the underparts narrowly streaked with dusky blackish shaft-lines, disappearing on the under tail-coverts, the long ones of which are deep blue-black with whitish bases; under wing-coverts and axillaries rather deeper fulvous than the breast, with nearly obsolete dusky shaft-lines, which are, however, more plainly developed on the small wing-coverts near the edge of the wing; quills dusky below, paler along the edge of the inner web: " bill, legs, and feet black; iris brown" (*W. V. Legge*). Total length 6·2 inches, culmen 0·35, wing 4·45, tail 3·1, tarsus 0·5.

Adult female. Similar to the male in colour. Total length 6·0 inches, culmen 0·4, wing 4·25, tail 2·95, tarsus 0·5.

Hab. The greater part of the Indian Peninsula and Ceylon.

THIS is the smallest of the four Indian Mosque-Swallows, and is distinguished not only by its lesser dimensions, the wing not exceeding 4·5 inches, but by its pale under surface and the narrow striations of the breast, which, as Mr. Oates remarks, are hardly broader than the shafts of the feathers themselves.

It is the Swallow of the plains of India, and does not extend its range into the Himalayas, where its place is taken by *H. nipalensis*. Mr. Brooks says that in Kashmir he found it as far up as Chungus on the Tami River. A specimen from Naoshera, obtained on the 6th of May, is in the Hume collection. According to Colonel Butler it is found in Sind, Cutch, Káthiáwár, Gujarát, and Mount Aboo. " Rare in the plains in the hot weather. Common in the cold weather throughout the region, except Sind, where it is rare." A specimen procured by Mr. Murray at Sehwan on the 15th of December is in the Hume collection, and he also procured it at Lakki. In Cutch it is very common, according to Dr. Stoliczka. "A few birds," writes Colonel Butler, "remain in Deesa the whole year, but most of them retire to the hills during the hot weather, leaving about the 30th of April, and returning about the 25th of June. It is not very common near the Southern Lake, but breeds there."

He also observes:—"Very abundant at Aboo, where it breeds during the rains in June and July, fixing its curious retort-shaped nest usually to the roof of a cave, and laying two or three pure white eggs. I am doubtful whether it occurs in the plains during the hot weather, but I am inclined to think it does not. My opinion is that most of them pass the hot weather on the hills, where they abound at that season, and breed in the rains, returning to the low country again about the end of September, soon after which they disappear entirely on the hills, and become very common all over the plains."

In the Hume collection are specimens from Agra (June), Bundelkund (Dec. 8), and Etawah (December), and the Tweeddale collection contains an example from Dehra Doon. Dr. King also met with it in Kumaun Bhabur on the 2nd of March.

Mr. George Reid writes in his paper on the birds of the Lucknow Civil Division:— "The Red-rumped or Mosque Swallow is probably a permanent resident, though it is only in the cold weather that it is at all abundant, the majority migrating to breed either in the hills or in suitable localities in the plains, though I do not see why Lucknow should not suit it as well as most places. A few most likely do breed in the old mosques and minarets about the city, but on every occasion I have either failed to find their nests or to see the birds.

"During the cold weather, as already remarked, it is, however, very common about Lucknow, frequenting the deep cutting known as Hyder Ali's Canal, as well as the mosques and minarets in the city, in vast numbers. In the district I have occasionally come across great flocks basking in the sun on the ground, generally in ploughed fields, and sanding themselves like Sparrows; while at other times I have seen them on the telegraph wires, sitting in rows and keeping up an incessant chattering or twittering. They occasionally perch on bare trees, and probably pass the night in mango topes in the absence of more suitable nesting-places. In no other way can I account for their presence in localities, remote even from villages, where I have seen them often in great numbers at the break of day."

Mr. B. H. Hodgson procured this species in Behar. Mr. Brooks has the following note:—"*H. erythropygia* breeds near Chunar, and in most places in the North-west Provinces where there are old buildings or quarries suitable. The eggs are laid at the commencement of the rains." The Hume collection contains specimens from Mogulserai (November) and Dinapur (December), obtained by Mr. Brooks, and another from the neighbourhood of Calcutta. Mr. W. T. Blanford noticed it in the Wardha Valley, and he also writes:—

"On February 23, close to Wún, in South-eastern Berar, I saw an immense flock of these Swallows flying about one spot on the ground and constantly alighting. There was no flight of winged ants or termites to attract them, and they might have been preparing to migrate, or resting during migration. I frequently met with this species near Nagpur."

Dr. Jerdon's note is as follows:—"This Swallow in general prefers the proximity of jungles. I saw it in Goomsoor, in the jungles round the Neilgherries, and also on the summit of the hills, in various other parts of the west coast and in the Carnatic, at the Tapoor pass. In the northern part of the tableland, however, I have seen it occasionally in the cold weather only, both in the neighbourhood of water and on dry open plains."

In Western Khandesh Mr. Davidson records this species as a permanent resident, common throughout the district and breeding in the rains; and, according to Messrs. Davidson and Wenden, it is common and breeds in the Deccan.

The species was first named by Colonel Sykes, who writes:—"This species appeared in millions in two successive years in the month of March on the parade-ground at Poona; they rested a day or two only, and were never seen in the same numbers afterwards."

Colonel Butler states that it is a resident throughout the Southern Bombay Presidency and common throughout the region.

In the South Konkan, according to Mr. Vidal, it is common and generally distributed, breeding in the hot weather on the cliffs and under eaves of houses.

The Rev. S. B. Fairbank procured the present species near Ahmednuggur in November, and Mr. Taylor says that he found it fairly common in the hill tracts of Manzeerabad in Mysore.

Mr. W. Davison states that this species is abundant on the Nilghiris, and is a resident, breeding in the same places as *Hirundo javanica*, fixing its nest against the roof of some deserted building or under some shelving rock, the nest, of course, being retort-shaped. They generally breed several together, but not always, and sometimes three or four nests are joined together.

This species is common not only on the Nilghiris and their slopes, but also occurs commonly through the Wynaad and the Mysore country abutting on the Nilghiris. Captain Terry states that it was noticed by him at Pulungi in the Palani Hills in April.

Colonel Vincent Legge writes:—"This little Swallow only finds a place in the avifauna of Ceylon as a straggler, and but two instances of its occurrence in the island have been brought to my notice. Layard, the first to get it in Ceylon, writes thus concerning it:—' I found one of these birds in the village of Pt. Pedro in December; it had probably been driven over from the opposite coast by stress of weather; it was hawking about the street. I fired at and wounded it, but it flew away. Next day it was again in the same place, and I succeeded in killing it.' At this season of the year the north wind, styled at Colombo the 'longshore wind,' brings many Indian birds to our shores, and doubtless was the means of driving the present species southward of its natural habitat; but as it is an inhabitant of the Nilghiris and other parts of the south of India, it is strange that it does not more frequently visit Ceylon. In the second instance it was procured by Mr. Bligh on the Catton Estate in April 1877."

The following account of the nesting-habits of the present species is copied from Mr. Oates's edition of Hume's 'Nests and Eggs of Indian Birds':—

"Sykes's Striated Swallow, which is, as a rule, a permanent resident of the plains, breeds, according to my experience, from April to August.

"Typically the nest, which is usually affixed to the under surface of some ledge of rock, or the roof of some cave or building, and which is constructed of fine pellets of mud or clay, consists of a narrow tubular passage, like a white-ant gallery on a large scale, say some 2 inches in diameter, and from 4 to 10 inches in length, terminating in a bulb-like chamber from 1½ to 7 inches in diameter externally. These nests have been aptly described as retort-shaped, and I do not think any lengthy description will convey a clearer idea of the typical shape. They are not always, however, of this shape. Indeed (though I am bound to say I cannot agree with him) Mr. F. R. Blewitt, who has probably taken more of their nests than any one else in India, is disposed to believe that the long retort-shaped nests are commonly built as residences, and the less-developed ones as breeding-places. He says:—'Eccentric to a degree is this Swallow in the selection of a suitable place for its nest. I have obtained it on the ground, at the base of a rock, having for protection just a small overhanging ledge; in a hole in any old wall; affixed to the roof-top of a pucka house; to the under ledge of a high rock; the arch of a culvert or bridge, &c.; but never, though they *may* occur there, 'in mosques and pagodas;' and 'twenty and thirty together,' as stated in Jerdon. I have always found the nest single. The form and material of the nest depend mainly on the locality chosen for it. Sometimes a simple collection of feathers answers the purpose; at others, as when attached to a roof-top, ledge of rock, &c., it is more or less domes-shaped, the exterior of fine clay, the inside lined with feathers. The opening for egress and ingress is invariably made above the centre of the nest. Frequently have I seen the 'spherical or oval-shaped mud nest with the long neck or tubular entrance,' described by Jerdon, but only *once* with eggs in it. This peculiar-shaped nest is also constructed at times by *H. filifera*, and from frequent observations I have sometimes fancied that it is intended more for a winter residence than for breeding purposes. I have recently observed many of both species actively employed in the construction of these nests, long after the breeding-season was well over. In the beginning of August I robbed a nest of *H. erythropygia*, found attached to the roof of an outhouse; and in the identical place from whence I had removed the former nest, the same pair of birds have now nearly completed a new nest, 'oval-shaped, with the tubular entrance,' for, as I suppose, a winter retreat. The birds only occupy it at night. The eggs are pure white, and four appears to be the greatest number.'

"During the breeding-season the old birds fly round about their nest, morning and evening, uttering quite a variety of rather pretty, somewhat musical notes. During the day they remain near, and one of them generally in the nest, or the pair may be seen perched on some stone below the nest, sitting for an hour at a time preening their feathers, the male every now and then singing a few notes. Old quarries, like those near Futtehpore Sikri and Chunar, are favourite breeding-haunts of this species; and so are the old Moslem ruins that abound so in Upper India.

"The nest-chamber is lined, sometimes thickly, sometimes thinly, with feathers only, as a rule, but occasionally with a mixture of these and fine grass.

"They are not easily driven away once they have made a nest. I have broken into nests twice running, to see if any eggs were laid, and each time the birds have repaired the nest, in which, despite these repeated burglaries, they have finally laid.

"Major C. T. Bingham remarks:—'Breeds at Allahabad in March, April, May, and

June, and at Delhi I have found their nests also in September. They build long retort-shaped nests made of pellets of mud, plastering them against the roof of culverts underneath, against the top of caves, in banks of rivers, and in ruins, against the roof of any deserted mosque. Three, I think, is the ordinary number of eggs laid; these are pure white, and rather cylindrical in shape.'

"Colonel Butler writes :—'The Red-rumped Swallow breeds in the neighbourhood of Deesa in June and July. The nest is usually stuck to the roof of caves or holes in rocks, and, like that of other Swallows, is built of mud externally, and lined with dry grass and feathers. It is of a peculiar form, being completely closed up, of an oval shape, terminating at one end with a tubular passage about 7 or 8 inches long, by which the birds enter. During the period of incubation, the female sits very closely, suffering a great noise to be made without flying off the nest. It is not uncommon to find both birds in the nest during the time the hen is sitting. I have taken nests in April at Mount Aboo, but these were exceptional instances, as they do not as a rule commence building before the middle or end of May. In the plains they often build under bridges, archways across nullah culverts, &c.'

"Mr. Benjamin Aitken mentions that 'Between the 20th and 31st May, 1871, Jerdon's Red-rumped Swallow was observed to be in possession of nests, in similar places to those of *Cotile concolor*, at Khandálla, a hill-station on the top of the Bhore Ghat.'

"Mr. James Aitken says :— 'This is one of those birds which seem highly to appreciate the advantages of civilization, and to think, like Cowper's cat, that men take a great deal of trouble to please them. In Berar they have almost discarded the mosques which gave them their name, and have betaken themselves to the culverts of the roads, which are now being constructed all over the country. Wherever a road is made some of the culverts are sure to be taken possession of, as soon as the rains commence, by pairs of these Swallows, which may be seen darting in at one end and out at the other, or hawking about for flies over the pools of water at the road-side; their flight has, however, nothing of the extreme rapidity of that of the Swifts or Wire-tailed Swallows. During the cold season the young often assemble in large flocks, but these all disperse, or perhaps migrate, as the weather gets warmer, and only a few pairs remain to breed during the monsoon. The nest is of mud, with a prolonged entrance running along the wall, and is lined with coarse grass and feathers. The eggs are long shaped and pure white, without spot of any kind. In the subterraneous situation in which the nest is so often placed, and with the air still further excluded by the long neck, it is a marvel how the young escape suffocation.'

"Mr. Davison remarks :—'This species breeds on the Nilghiris about the commencement of April. The nest, as usual with Swallows, is composed externally of mud, and thickly lined with feathers; it is shaped like the half of a Florence flask. It is placed generally against the roof of a cave or overhanging rock. The eggs are generally three in number, pure white, and of rather an elongated form. Several nests are often placed close together, and often some favourite site is apparently the bone of contention between several pairs.

"'I once found, a few miles out of Ooty, several nests of this bird placed on the underside of a large overhanging rock, and although the breeding-season had long passed (it was, I think, in the early part of November that I found these nests), I nevertheless climbed up to where they were, to see if there were any addled eggs. After examining a few of the nests, I came to one which had the tubular entrance walled up, and the mud perfectly hard and dry. On breaking away a part of the nest I found a dead bird in it, which had come quite to the sealed end of the tubular neck, and had there died; the nest contained three old eggs, of which the contents had partially dried up. I can only account for this bricking, or, I should say, walling up of the entrance to the nest, by supposing that some of the other birds had coveted and failed to obtain this site for their nests. It is only natural to suppose that more than one pair were concerned in the business, as it would have taken at least one bird to keep the bird from leaving its nest, and another to keep its mate away from the nest, and probably another, or several other pairs, to close the entrance.'

"Dr. Jerdon (who, however, did not discriminate this and the preceding species) states that 'a few couples, at all events, breed in the south of India; for I have seen their nests on a rock at the Dinahutty waterfall on the Nilghiris, twenty or thirty together. I have found one or two nests in deserted outhouses in Mysore; and they are said to breed very constantly on large buildings, old mosques, pagodas, and such like; hence the native name of Mosque-Swallow in the south of India; but I rather think there is a considerable increase of their numbers during the cold weather, and it was no doubt at the time of their northward migration that Colonel Sykes saw them in such vast numbers at Poona. The nest, as figured by Pallas and observed by myself, is a spherical or oval-shaped mud nest, with a long neck or tubular entrance, of the kind which is called a retort nest, and the eggs are white, faintly marked with rusty-coloured spots.'

"Miss Cockburn, writing from Kotagherry, says:—'I only once found a nest, and this was on the 9th April. It was constructed under a shelving rock, raised so high from the ground as to allow of my walking under it. The cave, if I may so call it, was in a wild, lonely locality, suggestive more of bears than Swallows.

"'The nest, which was built of clay, was about $\frac{1}{2}$ foot long, the entrance being at one end. It was warmly lined with feathers, and contained three pure white eggs, very long in shape. As I wished to know if the number would be increased, they were left for a couple of days. On visiting the spot again, I found the length of the nest had been *increased* considerably, the eggs being left at the far end; but as there were no more than three, they were taken possession of.'

"I also have noticed the birds (or one of them) still building, and yet found eggs more or less incubated within.

"The eggs are pure white, with scarcely any perceptible gloss; generally a long oval, occasionally somewhat pyriform in shape, and rarely very long and narrow like those of our Indian Swift. They are perfectly spotless, and so far as shape and size go the egg of *H. daurica* figured by Bree sufficiently correctly represents an average specimen. Many eggs, however, are longer and narrower than that figure, and while all are, as in the figure, somewhat pointed towards the end, some are conspicuously so.

"The eggs vary from 0·75 to 0·83 inch in length, and from 0·52 to 0·6 inch in breadth; but they average about 0·78 by 0·55 inch."

The descriptions are taken from specimens in the British Museum. The figure is drawn from a bird in Mr. Wyatt's collection, procured by him on Mount Abu, and a view is given of one of the corners of the Fort at Agra.

MELANOCRISSA

HIRUNDO MELANOCRISSA, Rüpp.

ABYSSINIAN MOSQUE-SWALLOW.

Cecropis melanocrissus, Rüpp. Syst. Uebers. pp. 17, 22 (1845); Des Murs in Lefebvr. Voy. Abyss., Zool. p. 79 (1849); Heugl. Syst. Uebers. p. 16 (1856).
Hirundo rufula (pt.), Bp. Consp. i. p. 339 (1850).
Hirundo melanocrissa, Gray, Hand-l. B. i. p. 69, no. 807 (1869); Heugl. Orn. N.O.-Afr. i. p. 159 (1869); Sharpe, P. Z. S. 1870, p. 315; Blauf. Geol. & Zool. Abyss. p. 346 (1870); Finsch, Trans. Z. S. vii. p. 319 (1870); Heugl. Orn. N.O.-Afr. iv. App. p. lvii (1874); Rochebr. Faun. Sénég., Ois. p. 218 (1884); Salvad. Ann. Mus. Civic. Genov. (2) i. p. 121 (1884); Sharpe, Cat. Birds in Brit. Mus. x. p. 165 (1885).
Lillia melanocrissa, Hume, Str. F. 1877, p. 258.

H. uropygio rufo; pileo dorso concolori; subtùs fulvescens, vix striolata, gutture et praepectore tantum striis linearibus obsoletè notatis.

Hab. in Africâ septentrionali-orientali et in provinciâ Gambensi interiore.

Adult. Above deep indigo-blue glossed with purple, with the usual white lines on the upper part of the back; feathers in front of the eye black; a narrow line of feathers from the base of the bill extending backwards over the eye, sides of the neck, and round the nape, and forming an interrupted nuchal collar, deep sienna; rump paler sienna; quills brownish black, glossed with greenish steel-blue; upper tail-coverts deep steel-blue; tail-feathers brownish black, glossed with greenish above; cheeks and throat pale buffy white, the shafts of the feathers marked by small black lines; rest of the body buff, with faint streaks; the apical end of the under tail-coverts glossy blue-black, having the appearance of a black patch; bill black; feet dark brown. Total length 7 inches; culmen 0·4, wing 4·7, tail 3·6, tarsus 0·6.

Hab. North-eastern Africa generally, and the interior of Senegambia.

This Swallow belongs to the rufous-rumped section of the genus *Hirundo*, with the head blue like the back. The under surface of the body is streaked, but very faintly, the dusky shaft-lines being confined to the throat and chest.

Dr. Rüppell, who discovered the species in Abyssinia, states that he found it on the high plateau of Tembeu and in the lake-country of the province of Semien. He met with it in summer from July to October, and he describes it as placing its nest against walls of rock, its habits being those of the common Chimney-Swallow.

Von Heuglin writes:—"This Swallow is generally found in pairs throughout the rainy season until the month of February in Central Abyssinia, both in the mountains and plains, and appears to depart between March and June. It has a powerful flight, and whirls in a whistling stream round the highest peaks of the rocks, and sometimes, like its allies, utters a piping, melancholy, and yet somewhat sweet-sounding note. It is in motion all day, and we have never seen it settle on trees or rocks."

Mr. W. T. Blanford procured a specimen at Undel Wells in April, but states that it was only seen by him at low or moderate elevations, and he does not recollect to have ever noticed it on the tableland. Brehm believes that he saw this Swallow at Mensa, in the Bogos country, in April, but Von Heuglin suggests that *Hirundo senegalensis* may have been the species actually observed. During his last expedition to Shoa, the late Marquis Antinori procured the present species at Denz, Let-Marafià, and Mahal-Uonz. It was very common near the latter village from April to September, nesting in June and August on rocks.

Dr. de Rochebrune states that it is rare in Senegambia and was found at the following places—Kita, Bakel, Fonta-Koro, Gangaran, Bakoy, and Bafing; he also says that it inhabits Upper Senegambia, whence examples have been sent by Dr. Colin. The smaller race, *H. domicella*, replaces it apparently in certain parts of Senegambia, the localities mentioned by Dr. de Rochebrune being different for the two forms.

Von Heuglin states that there is a specimen of the present bird in the Stuttgardt Museum from South Africa, but there can be little doubt that the locality is erroneously given.

The figure in the Plate has been drawn from Mr. Blanford's specimen in the British Museum, from which also the description has been taken.

HIRUNDO DOMICELLA

HIRUNDO DOMICELLA, F. & H.

SMALL AFRICAN MOSQUE-SWALLOW.

Hirundo melanocrissa (non Rüpp.), Hartl. Orn. W.-Afr. p. 27 (1857); Heugl. J. f. O. 1863, p. 168 (var.).
Hirundo domicella, Finsch & Hartl. Vög. Ostafr. p. 143 (1870); Heugl. Orn. N.O.-Afr. i. p. 159 (1869–70); Sharpe, P. Z. S. 1870, p. 315; id. Cat. Afr. B. p. 16 (1871); Forbes, Ibis, 1883, p. 547; Shelley, t. c. p. 547; De Rochebr. Faun. Sénég., Ois. p. 219 (1884); Sharpe, Cat. Birds in Brit. Mus. x. p. 165 (1885).
Lillia domicella, Hume, Str. F. 1877, p. 269.

H. pileo dorso concolore; uropygio rufo; subtùs sericeo-alba vix fusco striolata; subalaribus pectori concoloribus, sericeo-albis; alâ 4·4.

Hab. in regione Æthiopicâ cis-equatoriali.

Adult male. General colour above deep purplish blue, the mantle streaked with the white bases to the feathers; rump pale cinnamon; wing-coverts like the back; greater coverts, bastard-wing, primary-coverts, and quills dusky brown, externally glossed with deep purple, duller on the primaries; upper tail-coverts purplish blue; tail-feathers blackish, externally washed with purplish blue; crown of head like the back, from which it is separated by a collar of rich cinnamon on the hind neck, interrupted in the middle; lores blackish, surmounted by a thin line of rufous; feathers below the eye pale cinnamon, deepening towards the ear-coverts, which are deep cinnamon-rufous, as also the sides of the neck; cheeks and under surface of body silky white; the throat, fore neck, and sides of the upper breast showing thin hair-like striations, scarcely visible; sides of body slightly washed with buff, deepening on the lower flanks; thighs silky white; under tail-coverts purplish black, those near the vent buffy white; under wing-coverts and axillaries silky white like the breast; quills below dusky, ashy along the inner edge: "iris brown" (*W. A. Forbes*). Total length 7 inches, culmen 0·35, wing 4·4, tail 4·6 (longest feather 3·7), tarsus 0·5.

The *adult female* does not differ in colour from the male, but shows the narrow striations on the chest a little more strongly than in the male. Total length 7 inches, culmen 0·35, wing 4·4, tail 4·6 (longest feather 3·45), tarsus 0·5.

Dr. von Heuglin mentions that a young specimen in the Stuttgardt Museum collected by Schimper, probably in Eastern Abyssinia, has the under surface sullied white, and marked with fine blackish striæ to the feathers; these shaft-streaks are also visible on the rump.

Hab. West Africa, from Senegambia to the Niger; Gazelle River in Equatorial Africa.

THIS can only be regarded as a small form of *H. melanocrissa* of Abyssinia, as it differs merely in its smaller size, rather whiter under surface, and in the nearly obsolete character of the dusky striations on the throat and breast. Although known for a long time to occur in Western Africa, it was generally confounded with *H. melanocrissa*, and it was only in 1870 that Drs. Finsch and Hartlaub discriminated it clearly and bestowed on it a separate specific name.

The typical specimens came from Casamence, and we have ourselves seen several examples from the same locality. It is not common in any part of Senegambia, according to Dr. de Rochebrune, who states that he met with it at the following localities—Gambia, Casamence, Mélacorée, Zekinkior, Sedhiou, and Bathurst.

The late Mr. W. A. Forbes met with the species at Shonga, on the river Niger, and the pair of birds obtained by him are now in the British Museum, with the collection bequeathed to the nation by that admirable and much-regretted naturalist.

In North-eastern Africa Von Heuglin observed this Swallow in the marshy districts of the Gazelle River in the month of February, where it was living in small communities. According to the same observer, it is probably a migratory bird in those districts. He describes it as having a swift and elegant flight, in the course of which it makes a hovering movement without any apparent vibration of the wings. They may often be observed flying off the bare branches at the tops of high trees, generally three or more together. The note is a plaintive whistle, "*ter-ter.*"

The figure in the Plate is drawn from a specimen in Capt. Shelley's collection. The descriptions are taken from a pair of birds collected by the late Mr. W. A. Forbes on the river Niger.

HIRUNDO EMINI

HIRUNDO EMINI, Reichenow.

EMIN'S SWALLOW.

Hirundo melanocrissa (nec Rüppell), Emin, J. f. O. 1891, pp. 340, 345.
Hirundo emini, Reichen. Ber. Allg. deutsch. orn. Ges. xi. p. 2 (Jan. 1892); id. J. f. O. 1892, p. 30.
Hirundo astigma, Shelley, Ibis, 1893, p. 19.

H. uropygio rufo; pileo chalybeo-nigro; subtùs minimè striolata; caudà minimè albo maculatà.

Hab. in Africâ centrali-orientali.

Adult male. General colour above blue-black, with whitish bases and margins to the feathers of the mantle, producing a striped appearance, the lower back and rump cinnamon-rufous; upper tail-coverts and tail blue-black, the latter without any white spots; wing-coverts like the back, the greater coverts and quills blackish glossed with blue-black, the innermost greater coverts tawny isabelline, forming a patch; crown of head and nape blue-black like the back; a loral spot of isabelline buff; feathers below the eye and ear-coverts dusky blackish, washed with chestnut; from behind the eye a very distinct patch of chestnut extending backwards to the sides of the nape, but not sufficiently to cause a nuchal collar, though the blue feathers of the nape are slightly tinged with chestnut; cheeks, throat, and sides of neck isabelline, the rest of the under surface from the lower throat downwards a little deeper in colour and a little more tawny, deepening on the under tail-coverts, all of which have the terminal half blue-black, the long coverts entirely of the latter colour; under wing-coverts and axillaries like the breast. Total length 7·5 inches, culmen 0·35, wing 4·9, tail 1·75, outer tail-feathers 3·9, tarsus 0·6.

Hab. Vicinity of Victoria Nyanza, and occurring again in the Shiré Highlands.

Dr. REICHENOW first described this species from Emin Pasha's collection made on the Victoria Nyanza, when two specimens were forwarded to the Berlin Museum from Bussisi and Bukoba; the first of these was procured in October and the second in November. Dr. Reichenow compared the new species, which he named in honour of Emin Pasha, with *H. melanocrissa*, and it is undoubtedly very closely allied to the latter bird, but is deeper cinnamon-coloured below, and has no sign of any shaft-streaks.

Captain Shelley, in describing the collections sent by Mr. H. H. Johnston, C.B., from the Shiré Highlands, named a Swallow *Hirundo astigma*, and compared it with *H. semirufa*, to which it certainly bears some resemblance by reason of its unstriped under surface. The type of *H. astigma* was procured by Mr. Alexander Whyte, who collected Natural History specimens for Mr. Johnston, at an elevation of 6000 feet, on the Milanji Plateau, on the 29th of October, 1891.

The British Museum has received in exchange from the Berlin Museum one of the typical specimens of *H. emini* from Bussisi, and we at once saw that *H. astigma* is identical with it. Its nearest ally is certainly *H. melanocrissa* rather than *H. semirufa*, and it differs from the former species in its darker cinnamon-coloured under surface, while it is further distinguished by its more dusky ear-coverts and by the rufous collar on the hind neck not being complete, as appears to be sometimes the case in *H. melanocrissa*.

The description is taken from the Bussisi specimen, now in the British Museum, and the figure in the Plate is drawn from the typical specimen of *H. astigma*, also in the same Museum.

For the geographical distribution of this species, *vide infrà*, Plate 79 [Map].

	Migratory.		Acclima[tised]
→/→	Bird of passage.	○	Perman[ent]
→⊖→	Remains locally during the winter.	(X)	Changi[ng]
→△→	Transplanted.	~	Visitor.
→•→	Winter resident.		Acciden[tal]

	Nearctic Region.			Neotropical Region.			Palæ[arctic]
	Arctic Sub-Region.	Cold Temperate Sub-Region.	Warm Temperate Sub-Region.		Central American Sub-Region.		Eurasian Sub-Region.
	Arctic Province. / Alaskan Arctic Province.	Hudsonian Province. / Canadian Province. / St. Lau. Province. / Aleutian Province.	Humid Province. Appalachian Sub-Province. / Austro-Riparian Sub-Province.	Arid Province. Campestrian Sub-Province. / Sonoran Sub-Province. / Antillean Sub-Region.	Mexican Province. / Indosian Province.	Sub-Andean Sub-Region. / Amazonian Sub-Region. / Brazilian Sub-Region. / Patagonian Sub-Region. / Arctic Sub-Region.	European Province. / Central Siberian Province. / East Siberian Province.
25. H. dauricus	..	.. ..					..
26. H. striolata	..	.. ..					
27. H. nipalensis		.. ..					
28. H. erythropygia		.. ..					..
29. H. melanocrissa							
30. H. domicella		.. ..					
31. H. cairui	..	.. ..		..			

∨ Guest.
† Wanderer.
☐ Rarely ⎫
☐ Generally ⎬ nesting.
☐ In colonies ⎭

	Ethiopian Region.								Indian Region.				Australian Region.				

HIRUNDO HYPERYTHRA

HIRUNDO HYPERYTHRA, *Blyth*.

CEYLONESE CHESTNUT MOSQUE-SWALLOW.

Hirundo hyperythra, Blyth, J. A. S. Beng. xviii. p. 814 (1849); id. Cat. B. Mus. As.
    Soc. p. 198 (1849); Kelaart, Prodr. Cat. p. 118 (1852); Layard, Ann. & Mag.
    Nat. Hist. xii. p. 170 (1853); Blyth, Ibis, 1867, p. 306; Gray, Hand-l. B. i. p. 69,
    no. 798 (1869); Holdsw. P. Z. S. 1872, p. 419; Legge, B. Ceylon, p. 592 (1879);
    Hume, Str. F. 1879, p. 84; Sharpe, Cat. Birds in Brit. Mus. x. p. 167 (1885).
Herse hyperythra, Bp. Consp. i. p. 340 (1850).
Cecropis hyperythra, Gould, B. Asia, i. pl. 30 (1868); Jerd. Ibis, 1871, p. 352;
    Hume, Str. F. 1877, p. 266.

H. similis H. badiæ, sed minor, et subtùs magis distincte nigro lineata.

Hab. in insulâ Ceylonensi.

Adult. General colour above purplish blue or deep steel-blue, a little streaked on the hind neck and mantle with fulvous, the feathers having a concealed fulvous edging, which becomes evident when they are disarranged; wing-coverts like the back; bastard-wing, primary-coverts, and quills blackish, externally glossed with steel-blue; feathers of lower back steel-blue, tipped with rufous like the adjoining rump and upper tail-coverts, the longest of the latter being steel-blue; tail-feathers blackish glossed with steel-blue; crown of head like the back; lores dusky, surmounted by a narrow line of rufous from the base of the forehead, extending over the eye, and forming a scarcely perceptible eyebrow; sides of hinder crown, ear-coverts, cheeks, sides of neck, and entire under surface of body deep chestnut, very plainly marked with narrow blackish shaft-lines, a little broader on the ear-coverts and on the throat; thighs and under tail-coverts chestnut, the longer under tail-coverts tipped or subterminally spotted with blue, the longest entirely blue; the under wing-coverts and axillaries chestnut, with distinct blackish shaft-lines near the edge of the wing; quills below dusky black: " bill deep brown, in some specimens blackish, the base of the lower mandible reddish; legs and feet vinous brown; iris sepia-brown " (*W. V. Legge*). Total length 6·4 inches, culmen 0·4, wing 4·55, tail 2·95, tarsus 0·55.

    Sexes alike in plumage.

    Immature birds have the hue of the under surface paler than the adults and the shaft-streaks not so clear (*W. V. Legge*).

Hab. Ceylon.

THE present species and its ally, *H. badia*, constitute quite a peculiar section of the genus *Hirundo*, having the rufous band across the lower back and rump like the Mosque-Swallows, but having at the same time a deep chestnut under surface, with little or no indications of streaks.

This Swallow is a permanent resident in Ceylon, where it was first found by Mr. E. L. Layard, and he has given the following account of the species:—

"I first discovered this species in November, 1849, at Ambepussa, on the road to Kandy. I have since then seen them at Putlam, up the central road as far as the hills extend, at Ambeganuoa, and up the Caltura river from Perth sugar-estate to Ratnapoora and Adam's Peak. They breed in caverns and under bridges, and build a nest of mud attached to the roof. The general shape and size is that of a small basin, with a round entrance-hole at the top. The lining is composed of fine hay and feathers, and the eggs are laid in March. The late Dr. Gardner informed me that a pair built their nest on a ring supporting a hanging lamp, nightly used in his sitting-room. They securely hatched their eggs, unscared by the cleaning or lighting of his lamp, and the young birds returned to the nest every night for about a month after being fully fledged."

Colonel Vincent Legge has given an exhaustive account of the species in his 'Birds of Ceylon,' which we transcribe herewith:—

"*Distribution.*—This fine Swallow was discovered by Layard, who met with it in 1849, near Ambepussa. It is widely distributed throughout all the low country, with the exception of the extreme north, where I have not noticed it. In the forest-districts lying between Dambulla and the latitude of Manaar it is local, being chiefly confined to small tracts of cultivation in the vicinity of tanks; in the Eastern Province, which is equally wild, it is restricted to similar localities, and in the Western Province is found principally in the interior. So plentiful is it, however, in the south-west of the island, that it is the common Swallow of the town of Galle, and seems to affect the sea-coast quite as readily as the interior, except during the wet windy weather of the south-west monsoon, when it retires for shelter to the secluded vales away from the sea-board. About Kandy, and in the Central Province generally up to 3000 feet, it is common, and in Uva and Haputale is found much higher than that elevation, for I have known it to breed at 4000 feet in the latter district. Mr. Bligh has seen it once at Nuwara Elliya; but it is rare on that elevated plateau, although in many of the coffee-districts it may be seen hawking at higher altitudes than that of the Sanatarium. In the Morowak-Korale district it is not uncommon.

"*Habits.*—Our Ceylon Swallow frequents towns and villages alike with the country. In the latter, marshes and paddy-fields, open glades in secluded valleys, and lonely tanks in the wilds of the jungle are the places to which it is partial. It is found in the Central Province about estate-stores and bungalows, and often consorts there with the little Bungalow-Swallow, breeding in cattle-sheds and outhouses and permanently frequenting their vicinity. It is a characteristic bird of the wild village tanks in the Vanni, and its cheerful chirrup is often one of the first bird-sounds which meets the ear, on the sportsman suddenly emerging from the forest and finding himself standing at the brink of one of those interesting places. Several have perhaps been resting on a dead log, half covered with weeds and water, or sitting on the dried mud of the bed of one of these small reservoirs, and finding the solitude of their retreat suddenly invaded, glide off on the wing, uttering their curious guttural notes, at the same time that, from the same cause, half a dozen lazy-looking but watchful crocodiles rush, with a mighty splash, into the muddy pool. Such haunts as these literally teem with insect-life; and I have seen scores of these Swallows hawking about a small water-hole of about half an acre in extent, which was all that remained of what was, in the wet season, a fine sheet of water. Its flight is slower than that of most Swallows, and it often sails along on outstretched wings, now and then making a sort of circle in its course. In the south it is fond of frequenting paddy-fields made in the narrow glades lying between the low wooded hills characteristic of that part.

"*Nidification.*—The Red-bellied Swallow breeds in the north, west, south, and centre of the island from March until June, constructing a Martin-like nest in outhouses, open dwellings, or under culverts and bridges. The nest is composed externally of mud and lined with feathers; it is large, and the entrance is situated usually at the end of a spout, running from 3 to 6 inches along the planks at the top of the nest; some have merely a circular orifice at the top. One which I frequently observed during the course of its construction was built in a merchant's office in Galle, the familiar little architects taking no notice whatever of the clerks who wrote at their desks just beneath; it was completed in about three weeks, the spout being added last, and after this was finished, one of the pair took up its position inside the nest and received the feathers brought by its mate to the entrance. The eggs are either two or three in number, and some brought to me as belonging to this bird were pure white and pointed lengthy ovals in shape, much resembling those of *Cypselus affinis*; they measure 0·85 inch by 0·56 inch. I have not taken the eggs myself."

The descriptions are taken from specimens in the British Museum, and the figure in the Plate from one procured by Mr. Wyatt near Kandy.

HIRUNDO BADIA (Cass.).

MALAYAN CHESTNUT MOSQUE-SWALLOW.

Cecropis badia, Cass. Proc. Philad. Acad. 1853, p. 371 ; id. Cat. Hirund. Mus. Philad. Acad. p. 4 (1853).
Hirundo badia, Gray, Hand-l. B. i. p. 69, no. 804 (1869) ; Sharpe, Cat. Birds in Brit. Mus. x. p. 166 (1885).
Cecropis archetes, Hume, Str. F. 1877, p. 266.
Hirundo archetes, Hume, Str. F. 1879, p. 47 ; Legge, B. Ceylon, p. 592 (1879).

H. uropygio rufo : capite dorso concolore ; subtùs castanea.

Hab. in peninsulâ Malayensi.

Adult. General colour above glossy steel-blue ; hind neck and mantle slightly streaked with reddish on disturbing the feathers ; lesser and median wing-coverts like the back ; greater coverts, bastard-wing, primary-coverts, and quills blackish, externally washed with steel-blue ; rump and upper tail-coverts deep chestnut, the long upper tail-coverts steel-blue ; tail-feathers black glossed with steel-blue ; crown of head like the back ; lores dusky ; a narrow line of red commencing at the base of the forehead and extending over the eye, forming a narrow and scarcely perceptible eye-brow ; sides of hinder crown, ear-coverts, cheeks, and under surface of body deep chestnut, with indistinct blackish streaks, very tiny on the ear-coverts and throat, but a little larger on the breast, abdomen, and flanks ; a patch of steel-blue feathers on the sides of the upper breast ; thighs and under tail-coverts chestnut, the long ones of the latter with steel-blue ends, the longest entirely steel-blue ; under wing-coverts and axillaries chestnut, the latter slightly mottled with dusky bases and narrow blackish shaft-lines ; quills below dusky brown : "bill black, fleshy white at gape ; legs and feet black or purplish black ; claws black ; iris deep brown" (*W. Davison*). Total length 6 inches, culmen 0·4, wing 4·95, tail 2·7, tarsus 0·6.

The following are the measurements of the series in the British Museum :—

	Total length. in.	Wing. in.	Tail. in.
a–c. ♂ ad. Kureo	7·4–7·8	4·8–5·3	3·6–3·9
d. ♀ ad. ,, ...	7·2	5·1	3·5
e. ♂ ad. Selangore	7·2	5·25	3·8
f–l. ♀ ad. ,, ...	6·8–7·2	5·0–5·2	3·5–3·9
m. ♂ juv. Kossoum	6·2	5·05	3·1
n, o. ♂ ad. Poongyah	7·5–7·7	5·2	3·8
p. ♀ ad. ,, ...	7·0	5·1	3·5
q, r. ♂ ad. Girbu	6·0 (moulting)	5·1–5·2	(moulting)

The *adult female* is similar in colour to the male.

A *young male* from Kossoum is much duller and more purplish black above, and has rufous tips to the upper tail-coverts and inner secondaries; underneath the rufous is not of so deep a chestnut as in the adult, and the chest and sides of the breast are mottled with dusky black spots.

Hab. Malayan Peninsula.

This beautiful Swallow takes the place in the Malayan Peninsula of *Hirundo hyperythra* of Ceylon, to which it is very closely allied. It is, however, a much larger and finer bird, and has scarcely any indication of black streaks on the under surface.

The present species appears to be confined to the Malayan Peninsula, the first example having been described by Cassin from a Malaccan specimen in the Philadelphia Museum. A specimen in the Tweeddale collection, and another in the British Museum, were all the specimens recorded as existing in collections, until Mr. Davison procured the types of *Cecropis archetes* of Hume.

The Hume collection contains a fine series of this Swallow, showing that its range is pretty extensive. From Malacca itself specimens shot in March and July are represented, and four examples were obtained in October, 1875, by Mr. Davison in Kuroo, a native State 26 miles distant from Malacca. Several specimens were procured by Mr. Davison in Selangore in March and August, and it extends as high as the Tonka district, for in the Hume collection are specimens collected by Mr. Darling at Kossoum in May, Poongyah in August, and Girbu in September.

No notes have been published on the habits of this species.

The descriptions are taken from the series in the British Museum, but we have not figured the species, as it so closely resembles the Ceylonese *H. hyperythra*.

HIRUNDO SEMIRUFA

HIRUNDO SEMIRUFA, Sund.

RED-BREASTED SWALLOW.

Hirundo semirufa, Sunder. Œfv. K. Vet.-Akad. Förh. Stockh. 1850, p. 107; Sharpe. Ibis, 1869, p. 188; Ayres, t. c. p. 290; Gray, Hand-l. B. i. p. 69, no. 802 (1869): Sharpe, P. Z. S. 1870, p. 317; id. Cat. Afr. B. p. 16 (1871); Ayres, Ibis, 1880, p. 260; Sharpe, in Oates's Matabele Land, App. p. 312; id. ed. Layard's B. S. Afr. p. 370, pl. ix. fig. 1 (1882); Shelley, Ibis, 1882, p. 260; Ayres, Ibis, 1884, p. 227; Sharpe, Cat. Birds in Brit. Mus. x. p. 167 (1885).

H. uropygio rufo; pileo dorso concolore; subtùs unicolor, haud striata; gulâ albâ.

Hab. in Africâ meridionali.

Adult. Above dark blue, inclining to indigo; rump chestnut; upper tail-coverts dark blue; wing-coverts like the back, the inner greater coverts fulvous on their inner web, forming a spot; quills black, brownish underneath, glossed above with dark blue; tail black, glossed with blue above, every feather, except the two centre ones, having a very large white spot on the inner web; space between the bill and the eye velvety black; cheeks and ear-coverts deep blue-black; entire under surface chestnut, very deep on the flanks and abdomen, the under tail-coverts paler rufous-buff; under wing-coverts isabelline buff; edge of wing fulvous mottled with black: "bill black; legs dusky; iris dusky" (*T. Ayres*). Total length 8·8 inches, culmen 0·7, wing 5·2, tail 5·3, tarsus 0·55.

Mr. Gurney describes a supposed immature specimen as being "paler rufous below, with the upper surface brownish black instead of dark blue with a metallic lustre as in the old bird." This description better suits the worn breeding-dress of the adult than that of the immature bird, which ought to show rufous tips to the inner secondaries.

Hab. South Africa; from Natal through the Transvaal and Matabele country to Mashoona Land.

THIS is a large species, entirely confined to the southern province of the Ethiopian Region. In the 'Catalogue' we were inclined to separate the present bird from the West-African *H. gordoni* on account of the paler under tail-coverts; but a further examination of the series in the British Museum and in Capt. Shelley's collection convinces us that this character is not a constant one, and there is scarcely any specific difference between these two Swallows. *H. semirufa* is merely a large deeply-coloured race of the West-African species with a perceptibly longer wing; but both in intensity of coloration and in size the Congo and Gaboon specimens of *H. gordoni* are intermediate. In Natal and Transvaal examples the wing measures 4·95–5·25 inches, a Congo specimen (immature) 4·5, a

Gaboon bird 47, and the Fantee and Senegal specimens 45-46. The South-African specimens are rather paler under the wing, on the under wing-coverts and axillaries, but even in this respect they only differ to a slight extent from *H. gordoni*.

But little has been recorded of the habits and nidification of this species. It was discovered by the late Prof. Wahlberg in Natal, and was afterwards obtained by Mr. T. Ayres in the Transvaal, where, however, it is scarce. It appears near Potchefstroom in the spring of the year, in September, and remains throughout the summer. It was found by Mr. Ayres to be "much more plentiful in the warmer Rustenberg district than in the open and colder country around Potchefstroom." A specimen in the British Museum was obtained by Mr. F. A. Barratt between Pretoria and Lydenburg; and the late Mr. Frank Oates met with the species at Tati in the Matabili country in October, and further north at Inchlangin in December. It was seen during Mr. Jameson's expedition by Mr. Ayres in the Mashoona country in September, October, and December.

Mr. T. Ayres found the nest of the present species in an old brick-kiln on the outskirts of the village of Rustenberg, and he says that it much resembled that of *H. cucullata*. Mr. Frank Oates found many small beetles in the stomach of one which he shot at Inchlangin.

The figure in the Plate has been drawn from a specimen in Capt. Shelley's collection, the description being copied from the British-Museum 'Catalogue.'

HIRUNDO GORDONI, Jard.

GORDON'S SWALLOW.

Hirundo melanocrissa (nec Rüpp.), Jard. Contr. Orn. 1849, p. 4.
Hirundo gordoni, Jard. Contr. Orn. 1851, p. 141, 1852, p. 17; Hartl. Orn. W.-Afr.
p. 27 (1857); id. J. f. O. 1861, p. 103; Gray, Hand-l. B. i. p. 69, no. 799 (1869);
Sharpe, Ibis, 1869, p. 188; id. P. Z. S. 1870, p. 317; id. Cat. Afr. B. p. 46 (1871);
Shelley & Buckley, Ibis, 1872, p. 288; Ussher, Ibis, 1874, p. 63; Reichen. J. f. O.
1875, p. 21; Bocage, Orn. Angola, p. 182 (1881); De Rochebr. Faun. Séneg.. Ois.
p. 219 (1884); Sharpe, Cat. Birds in Brit. Mus. x. p. 168 (1885).
Cecropis gordoni, Cass. Proc. Philad. Acad. 1859, p. 33.

H. similis *H. semirufa*, sed minor.

Hab. in Africâ occidentali.

Adult. Above glossy indigo-blue, duller on the wing-coverts; quills brownish black, glossed above, especially on the secondaries, with dark blue; rump sienna-rufous; upper tail-coverts dark indigo; tail brownish black, washed with dull indigo above, the inner webs of all but the six central feathers having a large white patch; entire under surface of body sienna-rufous, a little paler on the throat, thighs, and under wing-coverts; bill black; feet dark brown. Total length 6·5 inches, culmen 0·35, wing 1·5, tail 4, tarsus 0·55.

Hab. West Africa, from Senegambia to Angola.

We have already, under the heading of *H. semirufa*, given our reasons for regarding Gordon's Swallow as a small race of the latter species, which it represents in West Africa. Its range is rather extensive, as it is found from Angola northwards to Senegambia; but how far it ranges in the interior, we are at present uninformed.

In Senegambia, according to Dr. de Rochebrune, it is not common, but he records it from the following localities:—Gambia, Casamence, Méhicorée, Zeikinklor, Sedhiou, Sainte-Marie, and Albreda. Mr. Büttikofer did not meet with the species in Liberia, but on the Gold Coast, where it was originally obtained by Dr. Gordon. Capt. Shelley and Mr. T. E. Buckley state that it was "plentiful throughout the district, and generally met with in pairs perched on the top of some low bush or on the coarse grass of the plains." The late Governor Ussher writes as follows:—"Tolerably common in the eastern or Accra district of the Gold Coast, and now and then met with in the Fantee districts. It is a bold handsome bird, fond of building about houses, and much resembling *H. rustica* in its habits, especially in its low swooping flights over level open ground. It is frequently to be found basking in the open roads and rolling itself in the dust, or, as the natives express it, 'washing itself.'"

The late Mr. L. Fraser obtained this Swallow at Abomey, and MM. Verreaux received specimens from Gaboon, where Mr. DuChaillu met with it on the Ogowè River. Dr. Lucan procured one specimen on the Congo; and in the Lisbon Museum there is a single example from Angola, collected by Dr. Welwitsch. Prof. Barboza du Bocage thinks that although no ticket is attached to the specimen, there can be no doubt of its authenticity, and that it was doubtless obtained to the north of the Quanza.

The description is copied from the British-Museum 'Catalogue of Birds,' and is taken from a specimen in the national collection.

HIRUNDO SENEGALENSIS, L.

GREAT AFRICAN MOSQUE-SWALLOW.

Hirondelle à ventre roux de Sénégal, Daubent. Pl. Enl. vii. pl. 310.
Hirundo senegalensis, Linn. Syst. Nat. i. p. 345 (1766); Swains. B. W. Afr. ii. p. 72, pl. 6 (1837); Gray, Gen. B. i. p. 58 (1845); id. Cat. Fissir. Brit. Mus. p. 23 (1848); Jard. Contr. Orn. 1849, p. 4; Bp. Consp. i. p. 339 (1850); Hartl. Orn. Westafr. p. 27 (1857); Dubois, Ois. Eur. pl. 35 (1862); Hartl. J. f. O. 1869, p. 103; Gray, Hand-l. B. i. p. 69, no. 796 (1869); Heugl. Orn. N.O.-Afr. i. p. 156 (1869); Sharpe, P. Z. S. 1870, p. 316; Sharpe, Ibis, 1872, p. 71; Shelley & Buckley, t. c. p. 288; Heugl. Orn. N.O.-Afr. iv. App. p. lvii (1874); Ussher, Ibis, 1874, p. 62; Reichen. Corresp. Afrik. Gesellsch. Berlin, 1875, no. 178; id. J. f. O. 1875, p. 21; Sharpe & Bouv. Bull. Soc. Zool. France, i. p. 37 (1876); De Rochebr. Faun. Sénég., Ois. p. 219 (1884); Salvad. Ann. Mus. Civic. Genov. (2), i. p. 120 (1884); Sharpe, Cat. Birds in Brit. Mus. x. p. 168 (1885).
Hirundo rufula, Gould, B. Eur. ii. pl. 55 (1837, nec Temm.).
Cecropis senegalensis, Less. Compl. Buff. viii. p. 498 (1837); Boie, Isis, 1844, p. 174; Rüpp. Syst. Uebers. p. 22 (1845); Cass. Cat. Hirund. Mus. Philad. Acad. p. 3 (1853); Heugl. Syst. Uebers. p. 16 (1856); Bouvier, Cat. Ois. Marche &c. p. 9.
Hirundo melanocrissus (nec Rüpp.), Heugl. J. f. O. 1862, p. 297.
Cecropis melanocrissus, Antin. Cat. descr. Ucc. p. 25 (1865); Salvad. Atti R. Accad. Torino, 1870, p. 728.

H. uropygio rufo; pileo dorso concolori; subtùs unicolor, gulâ albidâ; rectricibus non minimè albo maculatis.

Hab. in Africâ occidentali et in Africâ septentrionali-orientali.

Above purplish blue; sides of the head and back of the neck, almost forming a nuchal collar, as well as the entire rump, deep sienna; quills dull black slightly glossed with blue; upper tail-coverts dull purplish blue; tail-feathers black, unspotted; throat and cheeks buffy white, as also are the under wing-coverts; rest of the underparts deep chestnut; bill black; feet very dark brown. Total length 9 inches, wing 5·7, tail 4·2.

We have not seen any indications of an approach to *H. monteiri*, though both this species and *H. senegalensis* occur on the Congo. The specimen of *H. senegalensis* from Landana, in Capt. Shelley's collection, is rather whiter on the throat than others from the Gold Coast, and thus somewhat resembles *H. monteiri*, but there is not a sign of the white spots on the tail which are so strongly characteristic of the latter species.

Hab. West Africa; occurring in suitable localities from Senegambia to the Congo. North-east Africa; Central Abyssinia and Kordofan, Shoa, and the sources of the Gazelle River.

THIS large Swallow belongs to the red-rumped section of the genus *Hirundo*. It is distinguished by its large size from all its allies in this section, as well as by its uniform under surface, without any dark striations.

It was originally described from Senegal, and we have seen several specimens from this part of Africa. Dr. de Rochebrune states that it is common there, and enumerates the following localities where he has met with it—Saldé, Dagana, Podor, Thiouk, Sorres, M'Bao, Ponte, Albreda, and Bathurst. It was not seen by Mr. Büttikofer in Liberia, but it reappears on the Gold Coast. Mr. Blissett sent us a specimen from Ekraful, and Capt. Shelley and Mr. T. E. Buckley found it near Accra, and more especially at Quamin-flo. The birds " were paired in February, and probably breeding in the large hollow trees, the topmost boughs of which they usually frequented."

The following note is from the pen of the late Governor Ussher :—" This handsome Swallow has only been observed by me on the plains of Accra, in the eastern districts of the Gold Coast. I never saw it in the forest. They are generally to be found in small companies of eight or ten perched on the tops of high decayed or leafless trees, and occasionally leave their posts for food, uttering a peculiar and pretty cry. Waterpools attract them much in this sparsely watered district. Their flight is powerful and graceful beyond that of other Swallows. The natives hold them in some veneration, and call them ' God's children,' and appeared scandalized at my shooting them, although they were satisfied when I explained the purpose for which I was collecting their skins, and that I was not impelled to do so from any wanton or inhumane motive."

A specimen was obtained by Mr. Petit at Landana on the Congo, and is now in Capt. Shelley's collection. This seems to be its southern limit on the west coast.

Dr. von Heuglin writes as follows :—" *H. senegalensis* is a migratory bird in North-eastern Africa. We found it from May to January in Kordofan and Central Abyssinia, at a height of from 5000 to 9000 feet ; but near the sources of the Gazelle River only towards the end of the rainy season. Rüppell also received it from Shoa. These Swallows are often seen in large flocks settling on the bare tops of trees, or flying backwards and forwards, both high and low, in the meadows and grass-land, especially after thunder-storms. The call is very loud and strong, and sounds plaintive and whistling, like *té-ér*, or *hüed, hüed*. According to Brehm it is even found on the Red Sea.

" Verreaux's statement that this Swallow occurs in Nubia is probably incorrect, as in North-eastern Africa it does not seem to cross the 14th meridian."

The late Marquis Antinori mentions this species under the name of *Cecropis melano-crissus*, and states that it arrives in the Djur country towards the end of March, but does not stay after the first few days of April. After this time it appears to go both to the east and west into the mountainous parts of the White Nile. He noticed that it arrived at the same time as *Eurystomus afer*, the African Roller, and frequented the same marshy places. At sunrise they settle on the tops of the trees, after a few short turns, and there remain motionless for some time, when one will suddenly start off afresh, upsetting the resting-place; and as they are accustomed to sit close together on a branch, there is great contention for a place, those that are driven off having to find another perch. From the trees they descend to the water, over the surface of which they hunt for insects; but after about an hour's exercise, they rise into the air and disappear, not returning to the place till the next morning. The same naturalist met with the species in the Adda Galla country during the late Italian expedition to Shoa, where the native name was "*Tobbisa*."

The description is taken from an adult bird in the British Museum, the figure in the Plate being drawn from a specimen in Capt. Shelley's collection.

HIRUNDO MONTEIRI

HIRUNDO MONTEIRI, *Hartl.*

MONTEIRO'S SWALLOW.

Hirundo monteiri, Hartl. Ibis, 1862, p. 340, pl. ii.; Gurney, Ibis, 1863, p. 116; Kirk, Ibis, 1864, p. 320; Gray, Handl. B. i. p. 69, no. 803 (1869); Bocage, Jorn. Lisb. 1868, p. 40, 1869, p. 339; Finsch & Hartl. Vög. Ostafr. p. 139 (1870); Sharpe, P. Z. S. 1870, p. 316; id. Cat. Afr. B. p. 46 (1871); Gurney in Anderss. B. Dam. Ld. p. 49 (1872); Sharpe, P. Z. S. 1873, p. 713; id. & Bouvier, Bull. Soc. Zool. France, i. p. 38 (1876); Reichen. J. f. O. 1877, p. 24; Cab. J. f. O. 1878, p. 222; Fischer & Reichen. t. c. p. 257; Fischer, t. c. p. 280; id. J. f. O. 1879, p. 344; Bocage, Orn. Angola. p. 181 (1881); Shelley, P. Z. S. 1881, p. 565; Böhm, J. f. O. 1883, p. 178; Schalow, t. c. p. 352; Sharpe, ed. Layard's B. S. Afr. p. 368 (1883); Fischer, Zeitschr. ges. Orn. i. p. 358 (1884); Sharpe, Cat. Birds in Brit. Mus. x. p. 169 (1885); Fischer, J. f. O. 1885, p. 128; Matschie, J. f. O. 1887, p. 152.

H. major: uropygio rufo; pileo dorso concolore; subtùs fere unicolor, minimè striata; gulâ albicante; rectricibus albo notatis.

Hab. in Africâ orientali (a prov. Zanzibaricâ usque ad fl. Zambesianum), in Africâ occidentali in prov. Congensi usque ad terram Damarensem septentrionalem.

Male. Above glossy blue-black, the head capped and united to the nape by a broad interrupted band of blue-black feathers, a narrow line of feathers from the base of the nostrils to the eye dusky; the sides of the neck very bright rufous; shoulders and sides of the chest dark blue-black like the back; breast and under tail-coverts deep rufous, with a black spot near the tip of the longest feathers of the latter; thighs white; bill and feet black; iris brown; "inside of mouth yellow" (*Fischer*). Total length 8·5 inches, culmen 0·45, wing 5·75, tail 4·75, tarsus 0·65.

Young. Above blue-black, but not so rich or so glossy as in the adult; quills and tail dusky brown, with scarcely any perceptible gloss on the upper surface; lower part of the back pale rufous; throat, cheeks, and under wing-coverts pure white; sides of the neck and breast rufous, but not so rich as in the adult; under tail-coverts rufous, the basal half of the longer feathers black.

Dr. Reichenow, writing about specimens of this Swallow from the Loango Coast, and Dr. Cabanis, in his account of the late Dr. Hildebrandt's collection, both refer to the variability of the amount of white marking on the tail-feathers, and they are inclined to regard *H. monteiri* as nothing more than a race of *H. senegalensis*. Dr. Reichenow remarks:—"The white spot on the tail-feathers, which Dr. Hartlaub considered to be characteristic of the species, is sometimes strongly, sometimes feebly developed. One specimen, moreover, in spite of its white tail-spot, shows a reddish-brown nape-band, which should by rights be a character of *H. senegalensis*; and, lastly, in one specimen with entirely black tail-feathers, the reddish-brown nape-band is altogether wanting; so that it would be possible to establish four varieties." Our experience of the specimens in English museums has not confirmed the variations in character detailed by Dr. Reichenow, and at present we keep the two species distinct. From the observations given by the above-named naturalist it is evident, however, that, on the northern limits of its range, *H. monteiri* shows a tendency to coalesce with *H. senegalensis*, and the two forms may interbreed on the Congo.

Hab. West Africa from the Loango Coast to Ondonga; East Africa from the Zanzibar district to the Shiré river.

THIS fine Swallow, as big as *H. senegalensis*, and therefore one of the largest members of the family, is confined to Africa, where it occupies a more southern area in that continent than its near ally. It was described by Dr. Hartlaub from a specimen brought from Angola by the late Mr. J. J. Monteiro, one of the many true naturalists who have lost their lives in the Dark Continent. It appears to extend along the west coast of Africa as far as the Congo region, for Dr. Falkenstein sent specimens from the Loango coast, which Dr. Reichenow has described as showing a great tendency to develop the characters of *H. senegalensis*. Both species have been procured by Dr. Lucan and M. Louis Petit at Landana, on the Congo, and it is quite possible that they interbreed in this locality.

Monteiro's Swallow also extends its range into the provinces of Benguela and Mossamedes, where it has been procured by Senhor Anchieta at Biballa and Capangombe, and the same explorer has procured it on the River Cunene. The late Mr. C. J. Andersson met with the species at Ondonga in Ovampo Land, and a specimen in the British Museum was shot by him at Elephant Vley. He observes:—" To the best of my knowledge this fine Swallow (of which I first obtained a few individuals on the river Okavango in 1859) never extends its migration so far south as Damara Land proper; and, indeed, very few individuals come much further south than the Okavango."

On the eastern side of the continent this Swallow probably does not cross the Zambesi. Sir John Kirk observed it "on the banks of the river Shiré, away from dwellings, flying near the water, and alighting on the clay banks, where it was observed entering holes; but whether these had originally been formed by Bee-eaters was not ascertained."

It would appear to be more plentiful to the northward. The late Dr. Böhm says that it was common in the neighbourhood of Kakoma. He procured it in December, February, and March, at this place, and specimens were in his last collection from Qua Mpara, where he met with it in July in the mountain-forests, and also at Marungu, to the westward of Lake Tanganyika.

Sir John Kirk has procured it at Pangani and in the Usambara Hills, and it goes as far north as Mombasa, having been met with here by the Rev. Mr. Wakefield. Dr. Fischer states that he often saw it in the neighbourhood of Mombasa, mostly in pairs. In the beginning of August he fell in with eight specimens sitting on a dead tree, some of them being young birds. Dr. Hildebrandt found the species rarer near Mombasa and in Ukamba than *H. puella*. Dr. Fischer notes its occurrence near Malindi in May and June, breeding there in the latter month. In December some were seen at the mouth of the Tana, and he likewise states that he collected this Swallow in small numbers near Pangani in December, and near Little Arascha Lake in March. He also obtained a specimen at Komboko, in the Kilima Njaro district, on the 1st of April. His other locality for the species is Bagamoyo. The late Dr. Böhm also mentions having shot a Swallow, which he believed to be this species, at Konko in Ugogo.

Mr. Andersson observes:—"Those that came under my notice were always found in large open forests, flying high above the tree-tops in pursuit of their insect prey, or occasionally perching on lofty, isolated, and aged trees, and they were in consequence by no means easy to procure." Dr. Böhm states that it is more often found in the clearings of the forests and open spaces, and he has often noticed it flying over the swamps, like our European Swallow, with its wings touching the water. In the latter half of February the birds were in great numbers, in pairs, frequenting the bare trees and stumps, especially in the vicinity of the low-lying wet rice-fields. Twice, on the 9th and 22nd of February, he shot a female bird with some small lumps of earth in her mouth, and he fancied that they must nest on the trees. Dr. Fischer also noticed a curious habit of this Swallow, that they would descend suddenly from a great height, and rest on a dead bough, a favourite position, which they appeared to affect for a long time.

The descriptions are taken from specimens in the British Museum, and the figure is drawn from one in Captain Shelley's collection.

HIRUNDO EUCHRYSEA.

HIRUNDO EUCHRYSEA, Gosse.

JAMAICAN SWALLOW.

Hirundo euchrysea, Gosse, B. Jamaica, p. 68. pl. 12 (1847); Gray, Cat. Fissir. Brit. Mus. p. 26 (1848); March, Proc. Philad. Acad. 1863, p. 295; Gray, Hand-l. B. i. p. 72, no. 849 (1869); Scl. & Salv. Nomencl. Av. Neotr. p. 14 (1873); Sharpe, Cat. Birds in Brit. Mus. x. p. 170 (1885).

Herse euchrysea, Bp. Consp. i. p. 34 (1850).

Petrochelidon euchrysea, Sclater, P. Z. S. 1861, p. 72; id. Cat. Amer. B. p. 39 (1862).

Callichelidon euchrysea, Baird, Review Amer. B. p. 304 (1865); A. & E. Newt. Handb. Jamaica, 1881, p. 107.

Tachycineta euchrysea, Cory, Auk. iii. p. 58 (1886); id. B. West Indies, p. 72 (1889).

H. metallicè aureo-viridis: uropygio dorso concolore: subtùs alba.

Hab. in insulâ " Jamaica " dictâ.

Adult. General colour above metallic golden green, greener on the head; wing-coverts like the back; greater coverts, bastard-wing, and primary-coverts blackish, externally washed with golden bronze; quills black, with a slight bronzy shade on the outer edge; tail-feathers blackish washed with golden bronze; lores velvety black; ear-coverts, fore part of cheeks, and base of chin metallic golden green like the upper surface; throat and remainder of under surface of body pure white; thighs black; under tail-coverts pure white; axillaries and under wing-coverts metallic golden green, with dusky bases; quills sooty black below: "bill black; feet purplish black" (*Gosse*). Total length 5 inches, culmen 0·3, wing 4·2, tail 2·2, tarsus 0·4.

Young. Differs from the adult in having the feathers of the throat and breast obscured with dusky subterminal bars. The metallic plumage is also duller and greener, with not such a strong golden lustre.

Hab. Jamaica.

This is one of the most distinct of all the Swallows, being remarkable for its metallic plumage. Although it is to be seen in many Museums, it is by no means common in collections, and little has been recorded of its habits. In fact we have not been able to find any record since the date of Mr. Gosse's well-known work on the 'Birds of Jamaica.' There he writes:—

" This exceedingly lovely little Swallow, whose plumage reflects the radiance of the

Humming-birds, is found, as I am informed by Mr. Hill, in the higher mountains formed by the limestone range of the very centre of the island, as in Manchester and St. Ann's. It is not until we ascend this central chain that we meet with this sweet bird, occasionally in the more open dells, but principally confined to the singular little glens called cockpits."

The figure is taken from a specimen in the Salvin-Godman collection, and the descriptions are copied from the British Museum 'Catalogue of Birds.'

HIRUNDO SCLATERI, Cory.

SCLATER'S SWALLOW.

Hirundo euchrysea, var. *dominicensis*, Bryant, Proc. Bost. Soc. N. H. xi. p. 95 (1866).
Hirundo sclateri, Cory, Auk, 1884, p. 2; id. B. S. Domingo, p. 45, pl. 5 (1884); Sharpe, Cat. Birds in Brit. Mus. x. p. 171 (1885).

H. suprà metallicè viridis, chalybeo nitens, vix cuprescens : fronte chalybeo lavatâ : subtùs alba.

Hab. in insulâ Dominicensi maris Caribbæi.

Adult male. General colour above glossy steel-blue, with a very little reflexion of golden-green under certain lights; lesser wing-coverts like the back; median and greater coverts black, edged with the glossy shade of the back; bastard-wing, primary-coverts, and quills black, externally edged with golden green, the secondaries with purplish blue, the primaries with dull green; upper tail-coverts glossy steel-blue with golden reflexions; tail-feathers black, edged with steel-blue or dull green; crown of head golden green with steel-blue reflexions, the forehead decidedly steel-blue; lores black; sides of face and ear-coverts like the head, as also a spot on the chin; cheeks, throat, sides of neck, and under surface of body pure white; some of the flank-feathers internally golden green; thighs blackish; under tail-coverts white; under wing-coverts and axillaries dull steel-blue, edged with glossy green; quills below dusky, more ashy along the inner webs. Total length 5 inches, culmen 0·25, wing 4·45, tail 2·0, tarsus 0·35.

The sexes are alike, according to Mr. Cory.

Hab. San Domingo.

WE are indebted to our friend Mr. C. B. Cory for the loan of a skin of this beautiful Swallow, described by him from San Domingo. In its brilliant glossy plumage it approaches *H. euchrysea* of Jamaica, but the prevailing colour is green instead of golden bronze, and there is a pronounced gloss of steel-blue, of which there is no trace in the Jamaican bird.

Mr. Cory writes :—"This species was quite abundant in the vicinity of La Vega, San Domingo, during July and August; none were taken elsewhere, although a small flock of Swallows were observed a few miles east of Gonaives, which I believe were the present species."

The description and figure are both taken from the above-mentioned specimen, lent to us by Mr. Cory.

APPENDIX
TO THE
GENUS HIRUNDO.

HIRUNDO SAVIGNII [*anteà*, p. 237].
Add :—

Chelidon sacignii, Stejn. Proc. U.S. Nat. Mus. v. p. 31 (1882).
Hirundo sacignii, E. C. Taylor, Ibis, 1886, p. 379; Sharpe & Wyatt, Monogr. Hirund. pt. xi. (1889).
Hirundo rustica sacignii, Hartert, Kat. Vogels. Senck. Mus. p. 99 (1891).
Hirundo cahirica, Gätke, Vogelw. Helgol. p. 135 (1891); Seebohm, Ibis, 1892, p. 19.

Supposed to have been seen on Heligoland on the 20th and 21st of May, 1891, but doubtless only a fine-coloured *H. rustica*.

For the geographical distribution of this species, *vide infrà*, Plate 44 [Map].

HIRUNDO GUTTURALIS [*anteà*, p. 241].
Add :—

For the geographical distribution of this species, *vide infrà*, Plate 45 [Map].

HIRUNDO TAHITICA [*anteà*, p. 275].
Add :—

Hirundo tahitica, Sharpe & Wyatt, Monogr. Hirund. pt. xv. (1892).

For the geographical distribution of this species, *vide supra*, Plate 44 [Map].

HIRUNDO JAVANICA [*anteà*, p. 279].
Add :—

Hirundo javanica, Hartert, J. f. O. 1889, p. 354; Sharpe, Ibis, 1890, p. 280; id. & Wyatt, Monogr. Hirund. pt. xv. (1892); Hose, Ibis, 1893, p. 399.

Mr. C. Hose says that this is the common Swallow of the Baram district, building under the eaves and floors of the bungalows, which, we must remind the reader, are raised off the ground on piles.

On page 285, line 17, *for* "Sulu" Islands *read* "Sulu." Mr. A. H. Everett has procured the species on Sibutu Island.

Mr. Hartert informs us that the species is apparently not rare in Deli and Lankat in N.E. Sumatra, where the birds were also seen building nests under the houses.

For the geographical distribution of this species, *vide supra*, Plate 44 [Map].

HIRUNDO NAMIYEI [anteà p. 287].

Add :—

Hirundo namiyei, Sharpe & Wyatt, Monogr. Hirund. pt. xv. (1892).

For the geographical distribution of this species, *vide suprà*, Plate 44 [Map].

HIRUNDO NEOXENA [anteà, p. 289].

Add :—

Hirundo neoxena, Sharpe & Wyatt, Monogr. Hirund. pt. vi. (1887); North. Cat. Nests & Eggs Austr. B. p. 30 (1889); W. J. Campbell, Proc. Austr. Assoc. Sc. 1890. p. 193.

Mr. North writes:—"A set of the eggs of this species in the Australian Museum collection measure as follows:—Length (A) 0·73 × 0·5 inch; (B) 0·74 × 0·59 inch; (C) 0·72 × 0·58 inch; (D) 0·76 × 0·6 inch; (E) 0·73 × 0·58 inch." Noticed by Mr. Campbell on Houtman's Abrolhos, flying near Pelsart Island.

For the geographical distribution of this species, *vide suprà*, Plate 44 [Map].

HIRUNDO ANGOLENSIS [anteà. p. 293].

Add :—

Hirundo angolensis, Sharpe & Wyatt, Monogr. Hirund. pt. i. (1885); Bocage, Jorn. Sc. Lisb. (2) no. viii. p. 258 (1892).

Senhor Anchieta procured this species at Quissange, and Quibula in Benguela.

For the geographical distribution of this species, *vide suprà*, Plate 45 [Map].

HIRUNDO ARCTICINCTA [anteà, p. 295].

Add :—

Hirundo rustica (nec L.), Emin, J. f. O. 1891, p. 340.
Hirundo angolensis (nec Bocage), Reichen. J. f. O. 1892, p. 31.
Hirundo arcticincta, Sharpe & Wyatt, Monogr. Hirund. pt. xv. (1892).

Found by Emin Pasha on the Victoria Nyanza, at Bussisi in October, and at Bukoba in December; and by Dr. Stuhlmann on Sesse Island in December.

For the geographical distribution of this species, *vide suprà*, Plate 45 [Map].

HIRUNDO LUCIDA [antea, p. 297].

Add:—

Hirundo lucida, Büttik. Notes Leyd. Mus. vii. p. 159 (1885); Sharpe & Wyatt, Monogr. Hirund. pt. i. (1885); Büttik. Notes Leyd. Mus. viii. p. 218 (1886); id. Reiseb. Liberia, ii. p. 473 (1890); Rendall, Ibis, 1892, p. 218.

OBTAINED by Mr. Stampfli about fifteen miles from Monrovia, in Liberia, on the Messurado River, in October. Mr. Büttikofer found a nest on the 2nd of April, on an old window-seat of the Dutch factory at Monrovia; it was constructed in the same way as the nests of *Hirundo rustica*, and contained three half-fledged nestlings.

On the River Gambia, Dr. Rendall says it is "common and fearless of man; its low sweet song is sustained for a minute or more, and bears a resemblance to that of a Canary, but is always subdued in tone. Its builds a cupshaped nest of mud, lined with fine grass and feathers, and lays from three to five eggs."

For the geographical distribution of this species, *vide supra*, Plate 45 [Map].

HIRUNDO ALBIGULARIS [antea, p. 303].

Add:—

Hirundo albigularis, Fischer, J. f. O. 1885, p. 128; Sharpe & Wyatt, Monogr. Hirund. pt. x. (1889); Bocage, Jorn. Sc. Lisb. (2) viii. p. 258 (1892).

BESIDES the Malindi record, Dr. Fischer also notices this species from Bagamoyo.

For the geographical distribution of this species, *vide infra*, Plate 78 [Map].

HIRUNDO ÆTHIOPICA [antea, p. 307].

Add:—

Hirundo æthiopica, Sharpe & Wyatt, Monogr. Hirund. pt. ii. (1885); Fischer, J. f. O. 1885, p. 128; Oustalet, Bibl. Ecole Hautes-Etudes, xxxi. art. x. p. 5 (1886); Hartert, J. f. O. 1886, p. 580; Salvad. Ann. Mus. Genov. (2) vi. p. 230 (1888).

THE present species was not met with by the Marquis Antinori in Shoa, but Dr. Ragazzi procured a young bird at Gasciä Mulu on July 31st.

Dr. Fischer's localities for the species, as observed by him in East Africa, are as follows:—Mombasa, Malindi, Pangani, Maurui, Little Aruscha, Komboko, and Mussiro.

Dr. Oustalet records this Swallow as found by M. Révoil in Somali Land.

Mr. Hartert found it common at Loko on the Benue River, in July. It was breeding in the houses of the negroes, at the highest point of the roof.

For the geographical distribution of this species, *vide infra*, Plate 78 [Map].

HIRUNDO LEUCOSOMA [anteà, p. 311].

Add :—

Hirundo leucosoma, Sharpe & Wyatt, Monogr. Hirund. pt. i. (1885); Reichen. J. f. O. 1891, p. 382.

SENT from Togo Land by Dr. Büttner.

For the geographical distribution of this species, *vide infrà*, Plate 78 [Map].

HIRUNDO DIMIDIATA [anteà, p. 313].

Add :—

Hirundo dimidiata, Sharpe & Wyatt, Monogr. Hirund. pt. xi. (1889); Bocage, Jorn. Sc. Lisb. (2) viii. p. 258 (1892).

For the geographical distribution of this species, *vide infrà*, Plate 79 [Map].

HIRUNDO NIGRITA [anteà, p. 317].

Add :—

Hirundo nigrita, Sharpe & Wyatt, Monogr. Hirund. pt. iv. (1886); Büttik. Notes Leyd. Mus. x. p. 68 (1888), xi. p. 130 (1889); Shelley, Ibis, 1890, p. 163; Reichen. J. f. O. 1890, p. 117; Büttik. Reiseb. Liber. ii. p. 100, cum fig. (1891).

Waldenia nigrita, Reichen. J. f. O. 1875, p. 21; Hartert, J. f. O. 1886, p. 590.

DR. REICHENOW found the present species common on the Lower Wuri and Camaroons. In Liberia Mr. Büttikofer obtained the eggs. He gives a picture of the nest, built of mud and attached to the bough of a tree overhanging the river. He gives the following interesting note:—" Frequently found in pairs with nest and eggs on the Du Queah, from its mouth upwards to the first falls, and on all other rivers I happened to visit on my journey to Cape Palmas. The beautiful River-Swallow is not easily got to leave the place which it once has chosen as nesting-place, and will always keep within some hundred yards from it. On one of my first trips up the Du Queah, on the 3rd of January, I found a nest with two fresh eggs in a hollow of a log, projecting about six feet above high water. The nest consisted of small stems of grass, small pieces of bark, and a few feathers, without any earthy substances, and contained two eggs. As it was a very fine nesting-place I sawed the end of the log down when passing a few days afterwards and carried it off with nest and eggs, which were then four in number. About two weeks afterwards I happened to pass the same spot again and found a new nest in the remaining part of the hollow, probably built by the same pair of Swallows, but this time constructed of clay and mud in the way of our House-Martin, and stuck to the wall of the hollow. It was lined with some stems of grass and other soft materials, and a few feathers of a Pigeon, and contained three eggs. I again carried off the nest and eggs without troubling the birds, which had disappeared for a moment. Some time afterwards I visited this spot and was not a little astonished to find a new nest, built like the last one, and containing one single egg; but this time I found it too cruel to carry off the nest again, and therefore ordered my boys to pull on and leave to the twice-tormented birds the pleasure of their breeding business. The eggs are thickly spotted and speckled with reddish brown, on a rosy-white ground. Their shape is oviform, the size 19 mm. in length and 13 mm. in width."

According to Dr. Hartert, this Swallow was not rare on the Lower Niger, building its nest on the huge dead trees in the stream. Mr. Jameson procured it at Yambuya, on the Aruwhimi River.

For the geographical distribution of this species, *vide infrà*, Plate 79 [Map].

HIRUNDO ATROCÆRULEA [*anteà*, p. 319].

Add :—

Hirundo atrocærulea, Sharpe & Wyatt, Monogr. Hirund. pt. iii. (1886); Seebohm, Ibis, 1887, p. 310.

In his paper on the Birds of Natal, Mr. Seebohm writes as follows :—" By far the most interesting of the Swallows that came under my notice in Natal was the Blue Swallow (*Hirundo atrocærulea*). A few pairs of these charming little birds were almost always to be seen hawking diligently for flies over a small field which led from the garden of my friend Mr. Mark Hutchinson's house down to a little stream that flowed at the foot of the bush. Graham Hutchinson told me that they were seldom seen in the open veldt, and always chose sheltered nooks near bush and water. Early in the morning they often used to perch on the wire fence that enclosed the garden. He told me that they were never seen in winter. They associated freely with the other species, but were often alone."

For the geographical distribution of this species, *vide supra*, Plate 15 [Map].

Add :—
HIRUNDO NIGRORUFA [*anteà*, p. 325].

Hirundo nigrorufa, Sharpe & Wyatt, Monogr. Hirund. pt. iii. (1886); Bocage, Jorn. Sc. Lisb. (2) viii. pp. 257, 258 (1892).

For the geographical distribution of this species, *vide infrà*, Plate 78 [Map].

Add :—
HIRUNDO SMITHII [*anteà*, p. 327].

Hirundo filifera, Fischer, J. f. O. 1885, p. 128; Matschie, J. f. O. 1887, p. 141; St. John, Ibis, 1889, p. 155; Reichen. J. f. O. 1891, p. 153; Rendall, Ibis, 1892, p. 219.

Hirundo smithii, Sharpe & Wyatt, Monogr. Hirund. pt. iii. (1886); Shelley, P. Z. S. 1888, p. 40; Salvad. Ann. Mus. Gen. (2) vi. p. 231 (1888); Oates, ed. Hume's Nest & Eggs Ind. B. ii. p. 188 (1890); id. Faun. Brit. Ind., Birds, ii. p. 280 (1890); Emin, J. f. O. 1891, p. 59; Sharpe, Ibis, 1892, p. 305; Bocage, Jorn. Sc. Lisb. (2) viii. p. 258 (1892); Reichen. Jahrb. Hamb. Wiss. Anst. x. p. 16 (1893).

COUNT SALVADORI records a fine adult male of this species obtained at Malcogebdù, in Shoa, by Dr. Ragazzi, on the 19th of February. It was procured by Emin Pasha at Wadelai in September. Mr. F. J. Jackson met with it in the Kikuyu country in August. Dr. Fischer's localities for the species are the town of Zanzibar in August, Lindi, Tschara, and Wapokomoland. Dr. Stuhlmann met with the species at Zanzibar in November, Emin Pasha at Mrogoro in Ugogo in May. Dr. Böhm has sent specimens from Karema.

According to Dr. Rendall, the species is rare on the Gambia. He found a nest with three eggs on the 7th of November, 1889, the nest being exactly like that of *Hirundo lucida*.

The late Sir Oliver St. John, in his paper on the birds of Southern Afghanistan and Kelat, remarked :—" Somewhat to my surprise I found this bird on several occasions in the Arghandab valley, and on one occasion near Kelát-i-Ghilzai, 5000 feet above the sea. It was not common, and I observed it nowhere else. Mr. Murray notices its occurrence at Quetta, but I have not seen it there."

The following additional notes on the nesting of the species have appeared in Mr. Oates's edition of Mr. Hume's 'Nest and Eggs of Indian Birds' :—" Major C. T. Bingham says :—' I have found many nests of this beautiful Swallow under the bridges on both the eastern and western Jumna canals at Delhi. They are half-saucers of mud lined with straw and a few soft feathers. On the 27th May eleven nests that I took contained three eggs each, and more than half of them hard-set, so that I should say the bird breeds about Delhi in April and May.'

"Mr. Benjamin Aitken tells us that he has 'observed the nidification of the Wire-tailed Swallow only on the river at Akola. One pair had a nest on the 23rd December, 1869, but I did not examine it. On the 7th of January (1870) another pair were building a nest. Three eggs were taken from a nest in the beginning of February, 1870. The birds at once began a new nest against a rock a few yards off from the first place, and successfully reared three young. On the 26th July, 1870, I made a note that the Wire-tailed Swallow had almost disappeared from Akola; they had been common on the river in the dry season.'

"Colonel Butler says:—' I found a nest of the Wire-tailed Swallow at Deesa on the 10th August, 1875, fastened to the brickwork of a well, but could not ascertain its contents, as I could not induce any of my coolies to go down and take it. I took another nest out of the same well on the 11th August the following year (1876) containing two eggs very slightly incubated. It was a half-cup, built of mud and thickly lined with feathers, and fastened to the brickwork under an overhanging ledge of stone. I have often found the nest under bridges overhanging the water, and in holes of rocks with a similar aspect.' Writing subsequently from Sind, he further says:—'*Hyderabad, Sind, 9th June,* 1878. A nest under an archway over a canal, containing two fresh eggs. Another nest in a well on the 12th June, containing three fresh eggs. Two more nests under archways over canals on the 20th, each containing three fresh eggs; and any number of other nests in the same neighbourhood, and in the Eastern Narra in similar situations.'

"Messrs. Davidson and Wenden, writing from the Deccan, remark:—' Common and breeds.'

"Lieut. H. E. Barnes, writing of Rajputana in general, says:—"The Wire-tailed Swallow, to my mind the handsomest of the Hirundines, breeds from the latter part of February to April, and again in August and September.'"

For the geographical distribution of this species, *vide infrà*, Plate 80 [Map].

HIRUNDO GRISEOPYGA [*antea*, p. 335].

Add:—

Hirundo griseopyga, Sharpe & Wyatt, Monogr. Hirund. pt. iv. (1886); Reichen. J. f. O. 1887, p. 62; Emin, J. f. O. 1891, p. 340; Bocage, Jorn. Sc. Lisb. (2) viii. p. 258 (1892); Reichen. J. f. O. 1892, p. 31.

Dr. Fischer, on his last journey to the Victoria Nyanza, procured this species at Waschi, on the east side of the lake, on the 20th of January. Emin Pasha also met with it at Bussisi in October.

For the geographical distribution of this species, *vide infrà*, Plate 81 [Map].

HIRUNDO CUCULLATA [anteà, p. 337].

Add:—

Hirundo cucullata, Sharpe & Wyatt, Monogr. Hirund. pt. iii. (1886); Bocage, Jorn. Sc. Lisb. (2) viii. p. 258 (1892).

For the geographical distribution of this species, *vide infrà*, Plate 80 [Map].

HIRUNDO PUELLA [anteà, p. 341].

Add:—

Hirundo puella, Reichen. J. f. O. 1887, p. 62; Sharpe & Wyatt, Monogr. Hirund. pt. xi. (1889); Shelley, Ibis, 1890, p. 163; Emin, J. f. O. 1891, p. 59; Reichen. J. f. O. 1891, p. 153; Emin, t. c. p. 345; Hartl. Abhandl. nat. Ver. Bremen, 1891, p. 30; Bocage, Jorn. Sc. Lisb. (2) viii. p. 258 (1892); Reichen. Jahrb. Hamb. Wiss. Anst. x. p. 16 (1893).

PROCURED by Dr. Fischer, during his last journey to the Victoria Nyanza, at Msinguissua. Emin Pasha procured the species at Bukoba in November. Dr. Stuhlmann obtained a nestling near Mbusiné in Usegua, on the 28th of August, and Emin met with the species at Tabora, in Uniauembe, in August.

The present bird was represented in a collection from the Quanza River, received by Mr. Henry Whitely of Woolwich; and Anchieta has collected specimens at Quissangue, Quibula, Quindumbo, Caconda, and Humbe. Mr. Jameson procured it on the Lower Congo.

For the geographical distribution of this species, *vide infrà*, Plate 82 [Map].

HIRUNDO RUFULA [anteà, p. 347].

Add:—

Hirundo rufula, Giglioli, Avif. Ital. p. 184 (1886); id. 1. Resoc. p. 312 (1889); id. op. cit. ii. p. 653 (1890); id. op. cit. iii. p. 512 (1891); Pleske, Mém. Acad. Imp. St. Pétersb. (7) xxxvi. n. 41 (1888); Guillem. Ibis, 1888, pp. 100, 112, 116; Sharpe & Wyatt, Monogr. Hirund. pt. x. (1899); Lilford, Ibis, 1889, p. 329; Brusina, Orn. Croat. p. 58 (1890); Oates, Faun. Brit. Ind., Birds, ii. p. 284 (1890); Gätke, Vogelw. Helgol. p. 436 (1891); Seebohm, Ibis, 1892, p. 19; Koenig, J. f. O. 1892, p. 365.

PROCURED by the late Mr. Russow at Tschinas in Central Asia.

According to Dr. Koenig the present species is a very rare visitor to Tunis, and he has only heard of two examples having been obtained in that country.

Dr. Guillemard, in his account of the birds of Cyprus, writes as follows : —" At one place I noticed a solitary *Hirundo rufula*, a species which I did not again come across until long afterwards. Although it is, perhaps, to be found in each of the Districts of the island, it is very local. It occurs at Famagusta, at the ruins of Bellapais, at Kyrenia, in the pass above Lanarka tou Lapethou, and near the village of Poli; but at all these places it seemed to frequent the immediate neighbourhood of its home, and never go far a-field.... On the battlements of the fortress of Famagusta I shot *Hirundo rufula*, and found its nest in a rock-hewn cavern, attached to the smooth flat roof. In general this is the situation adopted, but sometimes the back of the nest is built against a beam, or against a wall where it joins the ceiling. The entrance is a short tunnel, with a slightly covered lip. The eggs are pure white, and, in this case, were six in number."

He further observes:—" I camped below the ruins of Bellapais, a magnificent semimonastic building of the Lusignan period, with a great part of the beautiful cloisters still standing, and spent most of the following day in photographing it. *Hirundo rufula* was in great abundance here, and in a large hall, which was doubtless the refectory, there were many nests. Most of them were inaccessible, but from one I took some eggs, no doubt of a second clutch. The Commissioner of the Kyrenia district, with whom I was staying later, informed me that a pair had raised three broods of young ones in one season in a nest built in his bedroom."

Lord Lilford also noticed the species in Cyprus, and writes as follows:—" Very common in certain localities and, as Guillemard states, seldom to be met with at any considerable distance from its breeding-haunts. I only met with this very beautiful and conspicuous Swallow at a certain spot amongst the hills not far from the south coast of the Horn of Cyprus and at Famagusta; but Guillemard found it in many other localities, notably at the ruins of Bellapais; he mentions having noticed a solitary individual of this bird on March 6th, 1887, between Pera-Khorio and Tochui."

For the geographical distribution of this species, *vide infrà*, Plate 81 [Map].

HIRUNDO DAURICA [*antea*, p. 357].

Add:—
Hirundo daurica, Sharpe & Wyatt, Monogr. Hirund. pt. xiv. (1890).
Cecropis daurica, Tacz. P. Z. S. 1887, p. 599, 1888, p. 462; id. Mém. Acad. Imp. Sci. St. Pétersb. (7) xxxix. p. 182 (1891).

Dr. Taczanowski says that this species is widely spread over Western Siberia, from the Irtisch river in Dauria, through the Amoor and Ussuri countries as far as the sea of Japan. Mr. Godlewski states that directly it arrives in Dauria it at once begins to construct its nest, over which it spends a great deal of trouble, as it is large in proportion to the size of the bird and is composed of mud; it is fixed to the roofs of verandahs of houses and other buildings, or on rocks which have protuberances similar to a ceiling. In July it lays five or six eggs, and in August the young leave the nest, and quit the country in September.

In Corea, according to Mr. Kalinowski, it is rare in summer, and does not seem to come every year. In 1888 it nested, but in 1889 not one was seen.

For the geographical distribution of this species, *vide infrà*, Plate 78 [Map].

HIRUNDO STRIOLATA [*anteà*, p. 361].

Add :—

Hirundo striolata, Sharpe & Wyatt, Monogr. Hirund. pt. i. (1885).

For the geographical distribution of this species, *vide infrà*, Plate 79 [Map].

HIRUNDO NIPALENSIS [*anteà*, p. 365].

Add :—

Hirundo nipalensis, Sharpe & Wyatt, Monogr. Hirund. pt. xiv. (1890); Sclater, Ibis, 1891, p. 44; De la Touche, Ibis, 1892, p. 108.

? *Hirundo daurica*, St. John, Ibis, 1889, p. 155.

Hirundo alpestris (nec Pall.), Styan, Ibis, 1891, pp. 323, 351.

It is probably to this species that the following note by the late Sir Oliver St. John refers :—"In 1881 I saw a small flock of Red-rumped Swallows near Kach, but failed to procure a specimen. Which of the many forms of *H. daurica* they belonged to I cannot therefore say."

Mr. Styan says that in the Lower Yangtse Basin it arrives rather later than *H. gutturalis*, and leaves about the same time; it is not nearly so common as the latter, but still is numerous enough; it also breeds in the natives' houses. He adds :—"I can throw no light on the vexed question of the various subspecies of this group, and all the specimens I have examined appear to be of one species."

Mr. De la Touche writes :—"At Swatow both *H. gutturalis* and *H. nipalensis* are residents, the former being of course far more abundant in summer than in winter. At Foochow the Swallows are migratory or else summer visitants. On one or two occasions only in winter I noticed there a stray House-Swallow."

For the geographical distribution of this species, *vide infrà*, Plate 81 [Map].

HIRUNDO ERYTHROPYGIA [anteà, p. 371].

Add:—

Hirundo erythropygia, Sharpe & Wyatt, Monogr. Hirund. pt. xiv. (1890).

For the geographical distribution of this species, *vide infrà*, Plate 82 [Map].

HIRUNDO MELANOCRISSA [anteà, p. 379].

Add:—

Hirundo melanocrissa, Sharpe & Wyatt, Monogr. Hirund. pt. iv. (1886); Salvad. Ann. Mus. Civic. Genov. (2) vi. p. 231 (1888).

PROCURED by Dr. Ragazzi in Shoa, at Gasciamulà in April, at Let-Maratla in May and November, at Buscoftù in June, and at Dens in July. In the latter month young birds were obtained, which Count Salvadori describes for the first time. He says that the three specimens had only just left the nest; they were much smaller than the adults, with the black of the upper parts less intense and having a greenish reflection, the inner secondaries having a reddish tip, the rump of a duller rufous than the adults, but the under surface of the body brighter, more or less variegated on the breast with blackish.

For the geographical distribution of this species, *vide infrà*, Plate 79 [Map].

HIRUNDO DOMICELLA [anteà, p. 381].

Add:—

Hirundo domicella, Sharpe & Wyatt, Monogr. Hirund. pt. ii. (1885).
Hirundo rufula togoensis, Reichenow, J. f. O. 1891. p. 382.

H. togoensis was discovered by Dr. Büttner in Togo Land, in February. Two specimens were obtained on the 16th and 21st of that month, and Dr. Reichenow points out that the species is very like *H. rufula*, but is distinguished by its smaller size, shorter wings, by the entire absence of stripes underneath, and by the deeper chestnut-red colour of the nape.

Dr. Reichenow, in answer to our inquiries, tells us that he was at first inclined to refer the Togo-Land specimens to *H. domicella*, but he points out that in this species the under tail-coverts are described as "glossy steel-blue" in the 'Catalogue of Birds.' In his examples of *H. togoensis*, he says, the under tail-coverts have only the tips blue, but the base pale, as in *H. rufula*, of which he considers *H. togoensis* to be a race. The rump, however, is described by him as uniform rufous, not shading off paler as in

H. rufula. We find, however, that our description of the under tail-coverts in *H. domicella* is wrong, and that recent specimens in the British Museum with more perfect feathering show that the under tail-coverts are blue at the ends, with whitish bases, so that there can be little doubt that *H. togoensis* is *H. domicella*, and we must apologize to Dr. Reichenow for having misled him.

For the geographical distribution of this species, *vide infrà*, Plate 83 [Map].

HIRUNDO HYPERYTHRA [*anteà*, p. 389].

Add :—

Hirundo hyperythra, Sharpe & Wyatt, Monogr. Hirund. pt. xi. (1889); Oates, ed. Hume's Nest & Eggs Ind. B. ii. p. 201 (1890); id. Faun. Brit. Ind., Birds, ii. p. 284 (1890).

For the geographical distribution of this species, *vide infrà*, Plate 81 [Map].

HIRUNDO BADIA [*anteà*, p. 393].

Add :—

Hirundo badia, Sharpe & Wyatt, Monogr. Hirund. pt. xi. (1889); Hartert, J. f. O. 1889, p. 354; Oates, ed. Hume's Nest & Eggs Ind. B. ii. p. 186, note (1890).

Mr. HARTERT states that the Berlin Museum possesses a specimen of this Swallow from Sumatra. He found it breeding in Perak, and has given us the accompanying interesting account of the nesting-habits as observed by him :—" I myself have never seen this species in Sumatra, and do not think that it occurred in those parts of the island which I have visited : it is such a striking species that it could scarcely have escaped my notice.

"In the stomachs of those which I procured in Perak were some somewhat large *Cicadæ*, flies, and mosquitoes. It was near the Kampong 'Padang Ringas,' in the interior of Perak, that I first saw this fine Swallow, as I was hunting for butterflies and beetles in the burning mid-day sun. It was flying over the rice-fields, catching insects, and soon disappeared ; but I could not make out where the birds came from or whither they went, and, having no gun in my hand at the time, I could not procure a specimen, though I at once recognized that it was a Swallow I had not seen before. I met with the species again, however, some weeks after, further in the interior in the district of Kinta, where it was breeding in the beginning of July, as I found the nests under one of the houses erected, as usual, on piles. The nests were very peculiar, and were constructed in the same way as those of our Common Martin, and lined with feathers.

The nests were very large, being quite a foot or more in length. The two under the house were constructed in the interval between two beams, so that they rested on the lower beam. In the middle they were more slender, for each consisted of two nests, as it were, connected by a broad passage about two inches long. There was an entrance to one nest only. One of them contained two eggs, but the other was empty.

"Later on I became acquainted with what I suppose to be their original mode of nesting. I noticed several birds flying above the trees in the dense primæval forests in Kinta, and saw them entering the caves which are to be found in the limestone hills which are scattered about in this district. In one of these limestone caves, which was very damp, I found a number of the nests; but all were empty, so that I suppose that the proper laying time would be in May and June, and that I had happened upon a late breeding pair, when I discovered the before-mentioned eggs under the house, as narrated above.

"The nests in the cave were less distinctly divided into two portions. The further they were in the cave, the broader and longer were the nests, while those nearer to the entrance varied in shape according to the accommodation afforded by the crevices or shelves of the rocks. All these empty nests were soft and friable, and easily broken, while those I found beneath the house, and indeed all those recently constructed, were very strong.

"The eggs were longish ovals, pure white, with little gloss. They are larger than those of *H. daurica*, to unspotted specimens of which they are very similar. The grain, however, is much coarser in the eggs of *H. badia*, and shows very distinctly the rough cross-lines which are characteristic of the eggs of many Swallows. They measured 23·0 mm. × 15·6, and 23·9 mm. × 15·9. Weight 17 cgs."

The following note occurs in Mr. Oates's edition of Mr. Hume's 'Nests and Eggs of Indian Birds':—"Mr. J. Darling, Jun., records the following note regarding the nidification of *Hirundo badia*: 'The first bird of this species I shot in Kossoom was one of a flock that appeared from the east and flew straight away westwards. I afterwards found them in considerable numbers in a large limestone cave, in which they were breeding later on.

"'Again, in Poongah, I saw numbers flying about the limestone hills that surround the town. Their habits and voice are almost similar to those of *H. javanica*. The nest is built of pellets of mud stuck to the under surface of some rock in the shape of a half-goblet with a very long neck, and is lined with coarse grass-roots and feathers.'"

For the geographical distribution of this species, *vide infrà*, Plate 81 [Map].

HIRUNDO SEMIRUFA [anteà, p. 395].

Add:—

Hirundo semirufa, Sharpe & Wyatt, Monogr. Hirund. pt. i. (1885); Reichen. J. f. O. 1887, pp. 308, 309; Shelley, P. Z. S. 1888, p. 40.

The differences between *H. semirufa* and *H. gordoni* are so slight that it will probably be found that the two forms intergrade, and will have to be treated as one species, of which *H. semirufa* is the larger southern form. The specimens procured by Emin Pasha at Wadelai on the 12th of October have been referred to the latter by Captain Shelley.

Mr. Bohndorff procured this race at Kassongo, on the Upper Congo, about 4° 30′ S. lat., and at Kibongo, between Kassongo and Lake Tanganyika.

For the geographical distribution of this species, *vide infrà*, Plate 84 [Map].

HIRUNDO GORDONI [anteà, p. 397].

Add:—

Hirundo gordoni, Sharpe & Wyatt, Monogr. Hirund. pt. ii. (1885); Hartert, J. f. O. 1886, p. 590; Shelley, Ibis, 1890, p. 163; Reichen. J. f. O. 1891, p. 382; Bocage, Jorn. Sc. Lisb. (2) viii. p. 258 (1892).
Hirundo semirufa, Reichen. J. f. O. 1887, pp. 308, 309.

Dr. Reichenow records the present species from Togo Land. Mr. Hartert observed it at Loko, on the Benue. It was not seen in the villages but on the edges of the forests, and was not very common. The late Mr. Jameson procured it at Yambuya, on the Aruwhimi River.

A mistake has occurred in our account of the present species, where it appears that Mr. Büttikofer had found this Swallow on the Gold Coast, which he has never visited. The sentence (line 26) should read as follows:—"On the Gold Coast it was originally obtained by Dr. Gordon, &c., &c."

For the geographical distribution of this species, *vide infrà*, Plate 84 [Map].

HIRUNDO SENEGALENSIS [anteà, p. 399].

Add :—

Hirundo senegalensis, Sharpe & Wyatt, Monogr. Hirund. pt. ii. (1885); Hartert. J. f. O. 1886, p. 590; Reichen. J. f. O. 1887, p. 62; id. J. f. O. 1890, p. 117; Rendall, Ibis, 1892, p. 218.

Dr. RENDALL states that he only procured this species at Combo, on the River Gambia. Dr. Hartert, during his expedition up the Niger and Benue Rivers, only found it at the King's Kraal, at Anassawara. It was apparently breeding in the neighbouring rocks. Dr. Reichenow noticed it on the Camaroons and Wari Rivers.

Dr. Fischer, during his last journey to the Victoria Nyanza, procured this Swallow at Kawanga, to the north-east of the lake, on the 15th of January. He also noticed it in Ussuri and Usukuma. Mr. F. J. Jackson states that it was plentiful in Uganda in May, and was evidently about to breed there, as one of the birds he shot was carrying a feather in its bill.

For the geographical distribution of this species, *vide infrà*, Plate 85 [Map].

HIRUNDO MONTEIRI [anteà, p. 403].

Add :—

Hirundo monteiri, Sharpe & Wyatt, Monogr. Hirund. pt. x. (1889); Emin, J. f. O. 1891, p. 59; Reichen. J. f. O. 1891, p. 153; Hartl. Abhandl. nat. Ver. Bremen, 1891, p. 31; Bocage, Jorn. Sc. Lisb. (2) viii. p. 258 (1892); Reichen. J. f. O. 1891, p. 153, 1892, p. 30; Sharpe, Ibis, 1892, p. 305.

Hirundo senegalensis (nec L.), Böhm, J. f. O. 1882, p. 134, 1883, p. 178, 1885, pp. 47, 58; Emin, J. f. O. 1891, p. 310.

SENHOR ANCHIETA has obtained this species in many localities in Angola and Benguela, at Ambaca, Quissangue, Quindumbo, Galanga, and Cacouda.

Mr. F. J. Jackson also met with it in the Teita district.

Emin Pasha sent specimens from Niangala and Mssanga in Ugogo, procured in June.

Dr. Stuhlmann met with Monteiro's Swallow on the Victoria Nyanza at Njakamaga and Buanga, in October.

For the geographical distribution of this species, *vide infrà*, Plate 85 [Map].

HIRUNDO EUCHRYSEA [anteà, p. 407].

Add :—

Hirundo euchrysea, Sharpe & Wyatt, Monogr. Hirund. pt. xiv. (1890); Cory, Cat. West Ind. B. p. 115 (1892).
Tachycineta euchrysea, Scott, Auk, x. p. 181 (1893).

"This species," says Mr. Scott, " seems to be of very local distribution. During the months spent by me in Jamaica it was not even noted. From all that can be learned it is confined to the higher altitudes, where it is resident and only common locally."

For the geographical distribution of this species, *vide infrà*, Plate 80 [Map].

HIRUNDO SCLATERI [anteà, p. 409].

Add:—

Hirundo sclateri, Sharpe & Wyatt, Monogr. Hirund. pt. vii. (1888); Cory, Cat. West Ind. B. p. 115 (1892).

For the geographical distribution of this species, *vide infrà*, Plate 80 [Map].

		Nearctic Region.						Neotropical Region.						Pala...		
	Arctic Sub-Region.	Cold Temperate Sub-Region.			Warm Temperate Sub-Region.				Central American Sub-Region						European Sub-Region.		
	Arctic Province.	Alaskan Arctic Province.	Hudsonian Province.	Canadian Province.	Sitkan Province.	Alleghanian Province.	Humid Province.		Arid Province.			Antillean Sub-Region.	Mexican Province.	Isthmian Province.	Sub-Andean Sub-Region.	Amazonian Sub-Region.	Brazilian Sub-Region.	Patagonian Sub-Region.	Arctic Sub-Region.	European Province.	Central Siberian Province.	East Siberian Province.
						Appalachian Sub-Province.	Texto-Riparian Sub-Province.	Campestrian Sub-Province.	Sonoran Sub-Province.											
32. H. hyperytha			..	..	..	..	..					..	..	..	..		
33. H. ludi...			..	..	..	..	..					..	..	..	..		
34. H. amicuja			..	..	..	..	..					..	..	..	..		
35. H. gyelani			..	..	..	..	..					..	..	..	..		
36. H. ...			..	..	..	..	..					..	..	..	..		
37. H. ...			..	..	..	..	..					..	..	..	..		
38. H. ...			..	..	..	..	○					..	..	..	..		
39. H. ...			..	..	..	..	○					..	..	..	..		

Legend:
→ Migratory.
-→ Bird of passage.
-⊖- Remains locally during the winter.
-△- Transplanted.
-+- Winter resident.
△ Acclim...
○ Perma...
⚭ Changi...
∼ Visitor
🐾 Accid...

GENUS HIRUNDO (continued).

∨ Guest.
† Wanderer.
☐ Rarely
🔲 Generally } nesting.
🔳 In colonies

	Ethiopian Region.							Indian Region.						Australian Region.				
Saharan Sub-Region.	Soudanese Sub-Region.	West-African Sub-Region.	Abyssinian Sub-Region.	East-African Sub-Region.	South-African Sub-Region.	Cape Province.	Natalese Province.	Cauensean Sub-Region.	Eremian Sub-Region.	Indian Peninsular Sub-Region.	Indo-Malayan Sub-Region.	Himalo-Malayan Sub-Region.	Himalayan Sunon Sub-Region.	Celebean Sub-Region.	Moluccan Sub-Region.	Papuan Sub-Region.	Australian Sub-Region.	New Zealand Sub-Region.	Fijian Sub-Region.	Hawaian Sub-Region.
..	..	..	..	..	..	..	..	..	..	..	○									
..	..	..	..	..	..	..	..	..	..	..	○									
..	..	..	○	..	..	○														
..	..	○																		
..	○	○	○	..	..	..	..	○												
..	..	..	○	..	..	..	○													

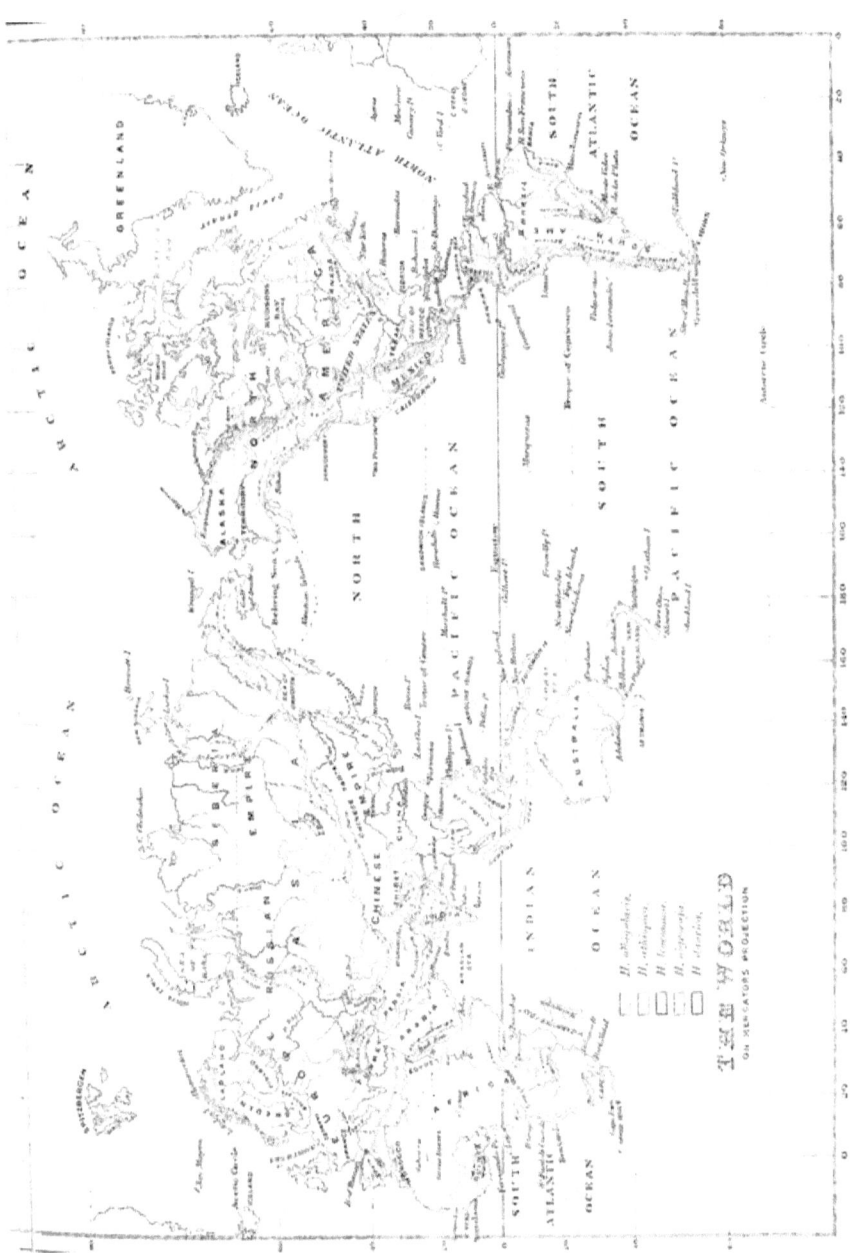

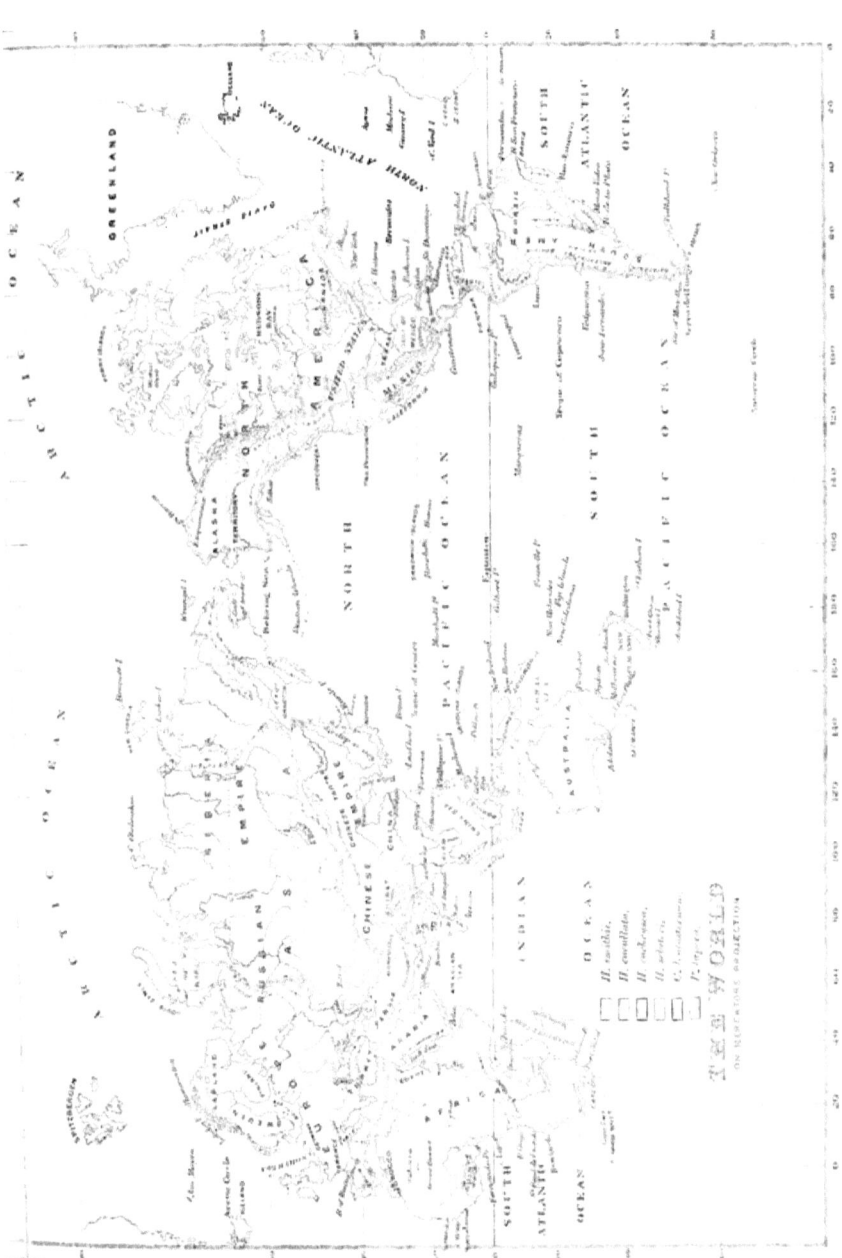

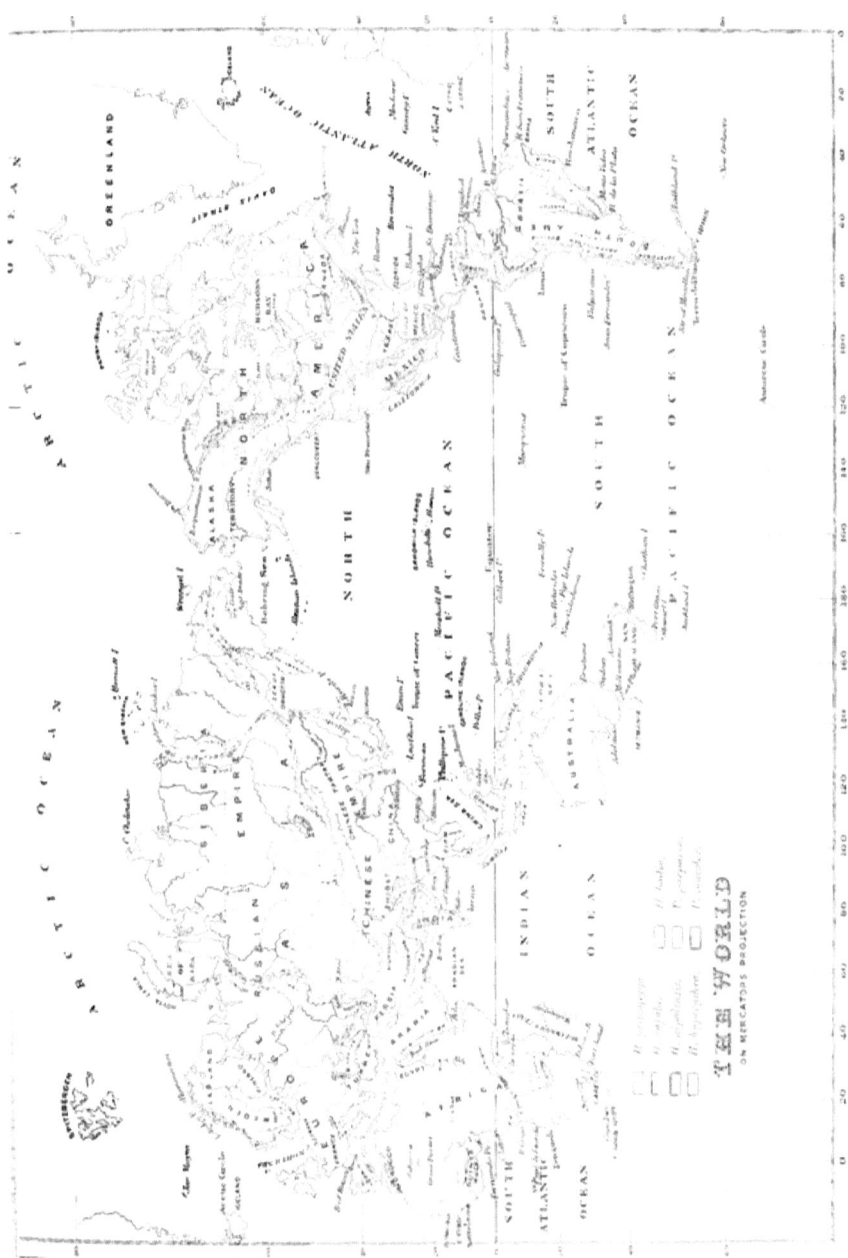

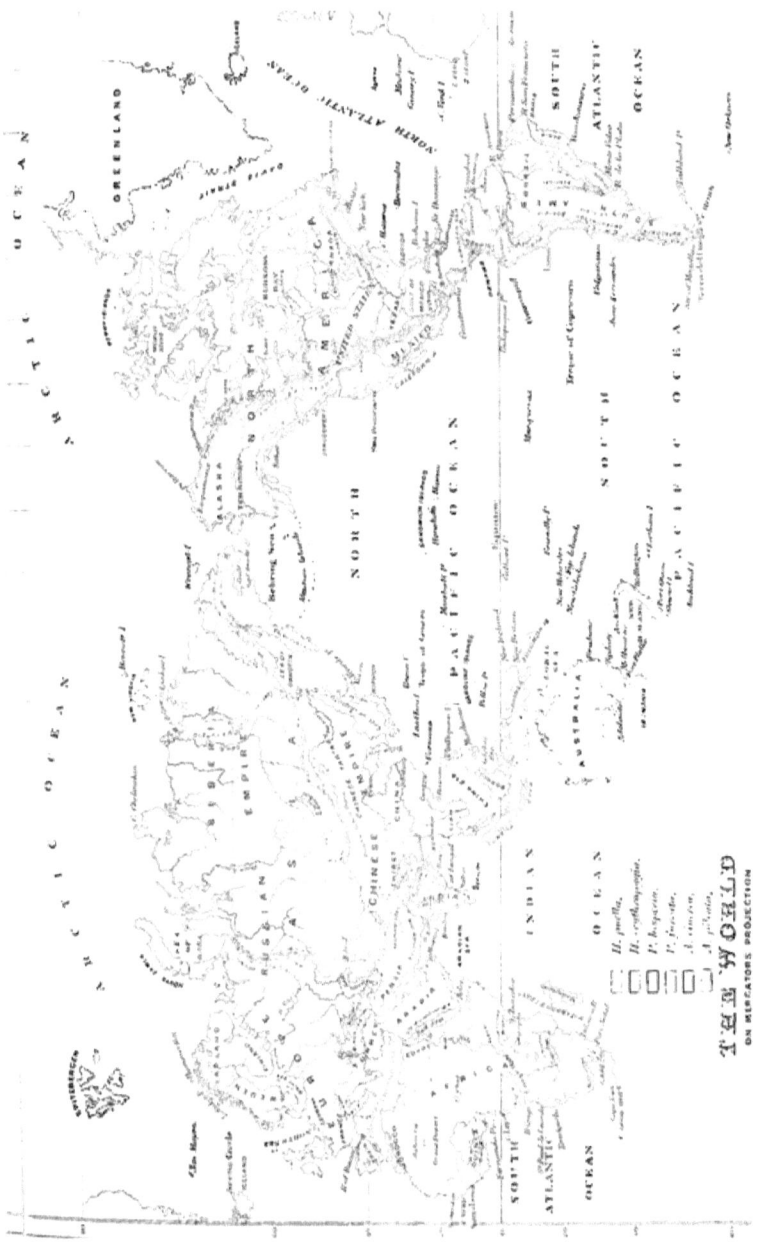

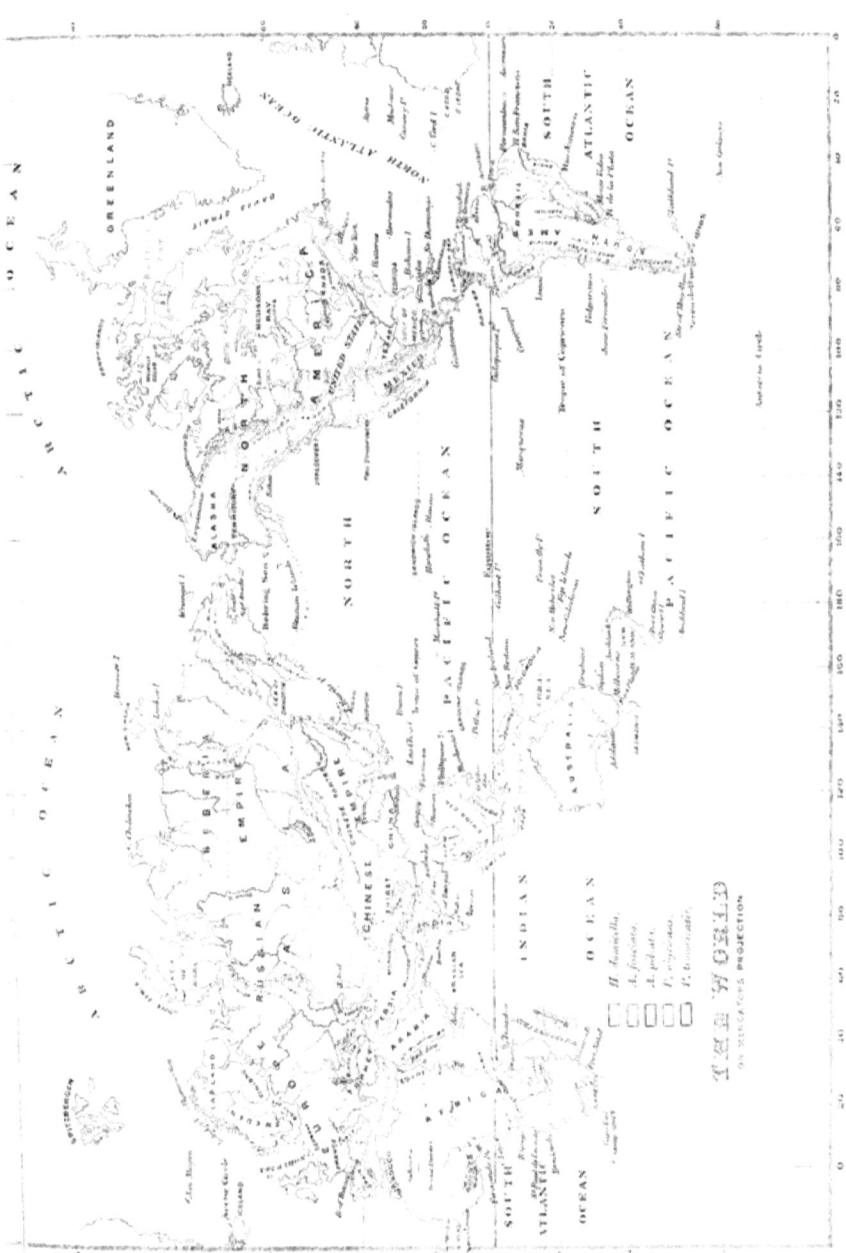

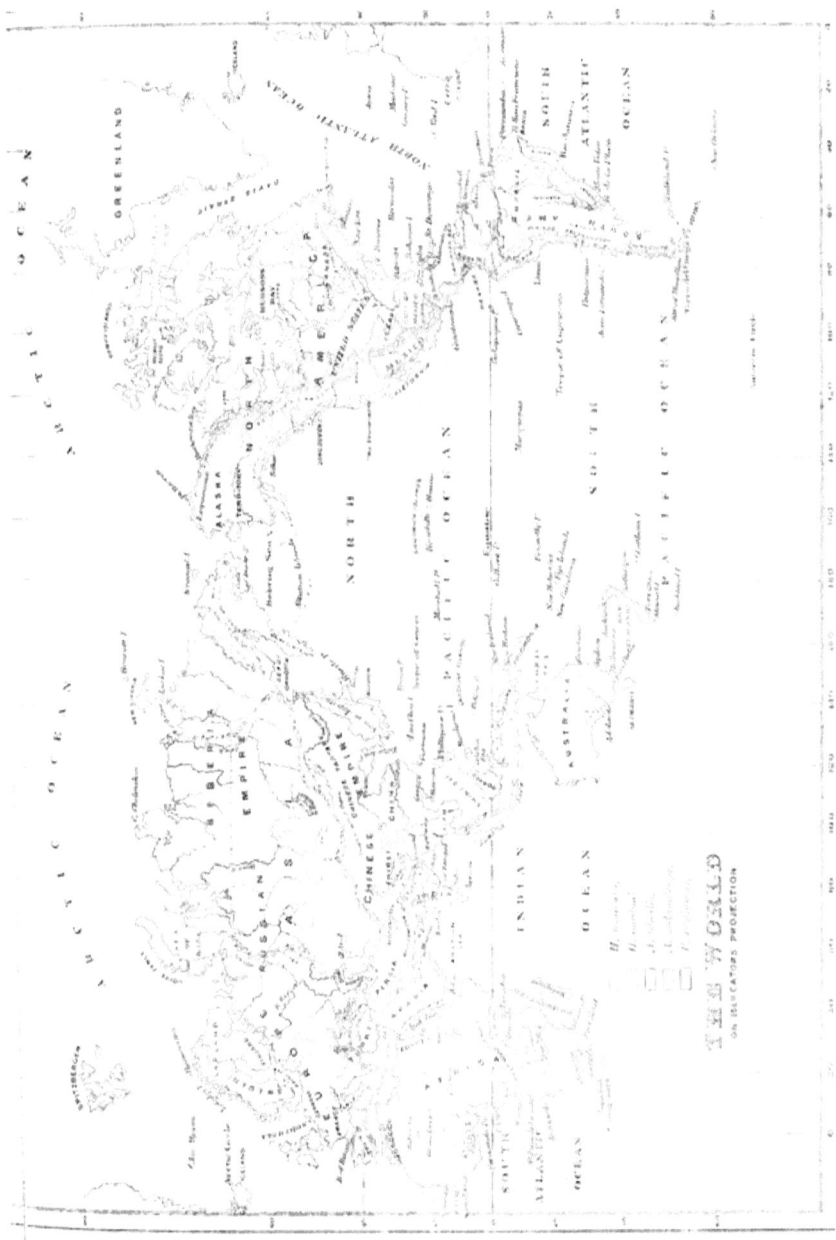

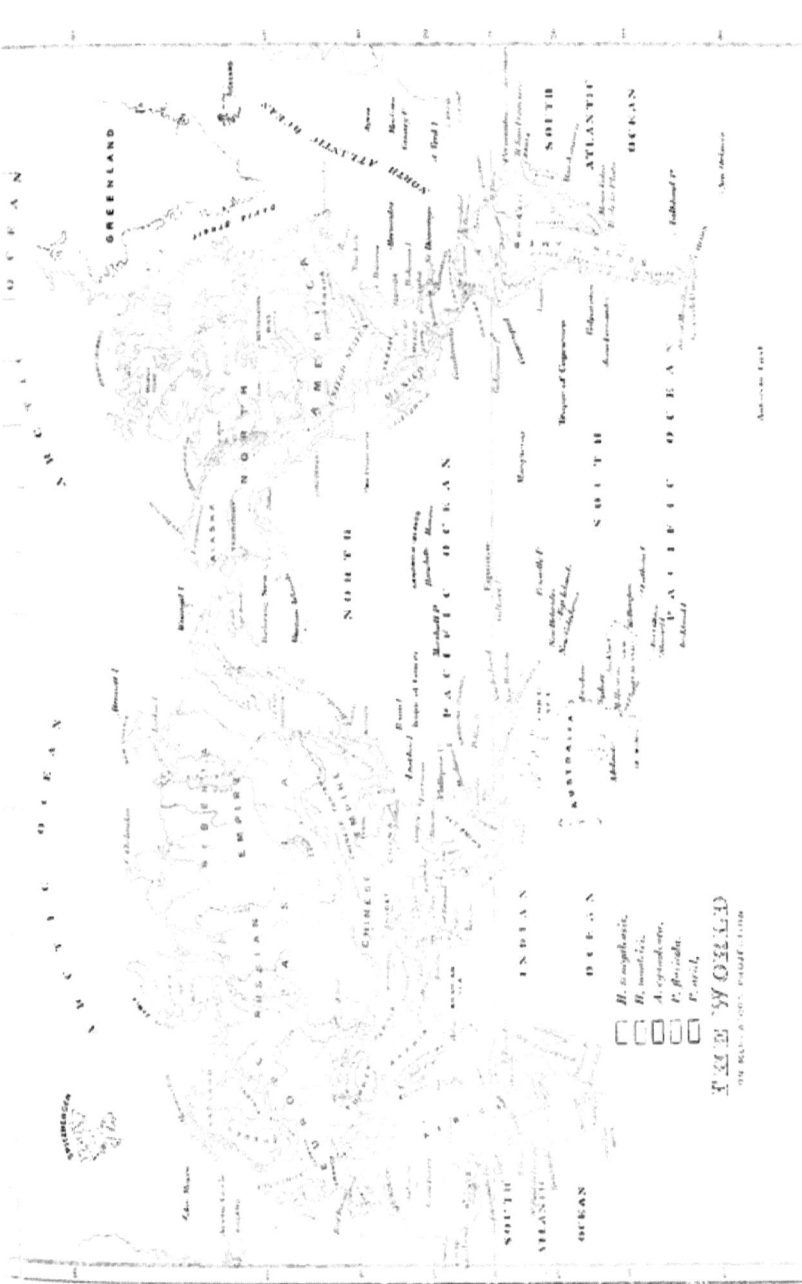

Genus VII. CHERAMŒCA.

Cheramœca, Cab. Mus. Hein. Th. i. p. 49 (1850)

Type
C. leucosternon.

Range. Confined to Australia.

CHERAMŒCA LEUCOSTERNUM (Gould).

WHITE-BREASTED SWALLOW.

Hirundo leucosternus, Gould, P. Z. S. 1840, p. 172.
Atticora leucosternon, Gray, Gen. B. i. p. 58 (1845); Gould, B. Austr. fol. pl. 12 (1848); Cass. Cat. Hirund. Mus. Philad. Acad. p. 6 (1853); Diggles, Orn. Austr. pl. 21. fig. 2; Gray, Hand-l. B. i. p. 73, no. 863 (1869).
Atticora leucosterna, Bp. Consp. i. p. 337 (1850).
Cheramœca leucosterna, Cab. Mus. Hein. Th. i. p. 49 (1850); Gould, Handb. B. Austr. i. p. 115 (1865).
Cheramœca leucosternon, Ramsay, Proc. Linn. Soc. N. S. W. ii. p. 179 (1878).
Cheramœca leucosternum, Sharpe, Cat. Birds in Brit. Mus. x. p. 171 (1885); Ramsay, Tab. List Austr. B. p. 3 (1888).

C. pileo albo, plumis basaliter brunneo variegatis: subtùs alba.

Hab. in Australiâ.

Adult. Upper surface particoloured; crown of head white, with brown centres to the feathers; nape and hind neck as well as the sides of the neck brown; mantle and upper back white, the lateral feathers blackish along the outer web; scapulars, lower back, rump, and upper tail-coverts blue-black; least wing-coverts brown; remainder of the wing-coverts, bastard-wing, primary-coverts, and quills blue-black, browner on the inner webs of the feathers; tail-feathers blackish; lores blackish brown; ear-coverts brown; cheeks, throat, fore neck, and breast white, extending slightly down the flanks; centre of lower breast, abdomen, and under tail-coverts blue-black; thighs white; axillaries and under wing-coverts white, with a slight wash of smoky brown; quills dusky brown: "bill blackish brown; legs and feet greenish grey; iris dark reddish brown" (*J. Gould*). Total length 5·5 inches, culmen 0·25, wing 3·95, tail 3, tarsus 0·5.

Young. Differs from the adult in having the whole head brown, with only a streak of white across the forehead extending backwards above the eye; the quills edged with white. Total length 4·6 inches, wing 3·8, tail 2·15, tarsus 0·5.

Hab. Confined to the Southern, Interior, and South-western portions of Australia.

This peculiar species of Swallow was first discovered by Mr. Charles Coxen, who sent a specimen shot on the banks of the Namoi to Mr. Gould in 1840. Dr. E. P. Ramsay gives its habitat as New South Wales, the interior of the Continent, Victoria, South Australia, West and South-west Australia. It appears occasionally in collections from the Swan River, but is by no means a common species in museums.

Mr. Gould has given the following account of the species in his 'Handbook,' and we cannot find that any additional information respecting it has been published since that date:—

"The White-breasted Swallow is a very wandering species, never very numerous, and is generally seen in small flocks of from ten to twenty in number, sometimes in company with the other Swallows. It usually flies very high, a circumstance which renders it very difficult to procure specimens. In Western Australia this bird chooses for its nest the deserted hole of either the Dalgyte (*Perugulea lagotis*) or the Boodee (a species of *Bettongia*), but more generally drills holes in the sides of banks, like the Sand-Martin of Europe. The holes are perfectly round, about two inches in diameter, run horizontally for three feet from the entrance, and then expand into a chamber or receptacle for the nest, which is constructed of the broad portions of dried grasses and the dry dead leaves of trees. Mr. Johnson Drummond informed Gilbert that he had frequently found seven, eight, or nine eggs in a single nest, from which he inferred that more than one female lays in the same nest: the eggs are white, somewhat lengthened, and pointed in form. It would seem that the holes are not constructed exclusively for the purpose of nidification, for upon Gilbert's inserting a long grass-stalk into one of them, five birds made their way out, all of which he succeeded in catching; upon his digging to the extremity, in the hope of procuring their eggs, no nest was found, and hence he concludes that their holes are also used as places of resort for the night.

"Since this information was transmitted, I have received notices of this bird from many other sources, which enable me to state with tolerable certainty that it is spread during summer at least over the whole of the southern portion of the interior, from Queensland to Swan River. Strange to say, however, I have never seen examples of this species in any collection formed out of Australia; yet the occurrence of a bird whose wing-powers are so great might naturally be expected in New Guinea or some of the adjacent islands."

The figure of the bird is drawn from a specimen in the Tweeddale collection, and the descriptions are taken from examples in the British Museum.

APPENDIX

TO THE

GENUS CHERAMŒCA.

CHERAMŒCA LEUCOSTERNUM [antea. p. 433].

Add:—
Cheramœca leucosternum, Sharpe & Wyatt, Monogr. Hirund. pt. xi. (1889); North, Nests & Eggs Austr. B. p. 38 (1889).

MR. NORTH writes:—"This species of Swallow is the only one with which I am acquainted that is not migratory, being found in this locality (Mossgiel, New South Wales) and to the same extent as regards numbers all the year round. It is widely distributed throughout the timbered or 'back' country, but is never found on the plains, and is generally seen in small flocks of five or six in number. It breeds here during the month of October, in holes in the sides of the entrances to the burrows of either the *Bettongia* or *Peragalea*, whether inhabited by these animals or not. I have never found more than four eggs in a nest.

"Three eggs taken by Mr. Bennett on October 19th, 1885, at Mossgiel, are pure white, and measure as follows:—(A) 0.64×0.48 inch; (B) 0.63×0.48 inch; (C) 0.64×0.47 inch.

"Specimens in my possession, taken by Mr. Gardner in South Australia, give the same measurements."

For the geographical distribution of this species, *vide supra*. Plate 80 [Map].

Genus VIII. PROGNE.

	Type
Progne, Boie, Isis, 1826, p. 971	*P. purpurea.*
Phæoprogne, Baird, Review Amer. B. p. 283 (1864) .	*P. tapera.*

Range. The greater part of North and South America; Antilles; Galapagos.

Clavis specierum.

a. Suprà purpurascenti-nigræ.
   a'. Subtùs purpurascenti-nigræ.
      a''. Fascia celata alba ad latera dorsi postici posita: fascia altera alba celata ad latera hypochondriarum posita . . . .
          { 1. *purpurea*, p. 139.
          { 2. *hesperia*, p. 155.
      b''. Fascia unica ad latera dorsi postici posita: fascia altera hypochondriaca nulla . . . . 3. *furcata*, p. 159.
      c''. Fascia alba dorsalis et fascia alba hypochondriaca nullæ . . . . 4. *concolor*, p. 163.
   b'. Pectus et abdomen alba.
      d''. Guttur et præpectus purpurascenti-nigra, notæo concoloria . . . 5. *dominicensis*, p. 165.
      e''. Subtùs albæ.
         a'''. Major: cauda 3·3 poll. . . . . 6. *domestica*, p. 169.
         b'''. Minor: cauda 2·4–2·7 poll. . . . . 7. *chalybea*, p. 173.
b. Suprà brunnea: subtùs alba: fascia longitudinalis brunnea in medio pectoris posita . . . . 8. *tapera*, p. 179.

PROGNE PURPUREA, L.

PURPLE MARTIN.

Purple Martin, Catesby, Nat. Hist. Carol. i. pl. 51 (1731).
The Great American Martin, Edwards, Nat. Hist. B. iii. pl. 120 (1750).
Le Martinet de la Caroline, Briss. Orn. ii. p. 515 (1760).
Hirundo purpurea, Linn. Syst. Nat. i. p. 344 (1766, ex Catesby); Wilson, Amer. Orn. v. p. 58, pl. 39. figs. 2, 3 (1812); Audub. B. Amer. pl. 22 (c. 1830); Swains. & Rich. Faun. Bor.-Amer., Aves, p. 335 (1831); Audub. Orn. Biogr. i. p. 115 (1831); id. B. Amer. i. p. 170, pl. 45 (1839); D'Orb. in Ramon de la Sagra's Cuba, Ois. p. 94 (1840); Yarr. Brit. B. ii. p. 232 (1843); Jones, Nat. Bermuda, p. 34 (1859).
Hirundo subis, Linn. Syst. Nat. i. p. 344 (1766, ex Edwards); Maynard, B. Florida, p. 71 (1874)
Hiroadelle de la Louisiane, Daubent. Pl. Enl. vii. pl. 722.
Purple Swift, Pennant, Arctic Zool. p. 431 (1785).
Purple Swallow, Lath. Gen. Syn. ii. pt. 2. p. 575 (1783).
Canada Swallow, Lath. tom. cit. p. 575 (1783).
Violet Swallow, Lath. tom. cit. p. 574 (1783).
Hirundo violacea, Gm. Syst. Nat. i. p. 1026 (1788).
Hirundo cærulea, Vieill. Ois. Amér. Sept. i. p. 27, pls. 26, 27 (1807).
Hirundo versicolor, Vieill. N. Dict. d'Hist. Nat. xiv. p. 509 (1817).
Hirundo ludoviciana, Cuv. Règne Anim. i. p. 374 (1817).
Progne purpurea, Boie, Isis, 1826, p. 971; Bp. Comp. List B. Eur. & N. Amer. p. 8 (1838); Gray, Gen. B. i. p. 59 (1845); id. Cat. Fissir. Brit. Mus. p. 27 (1848); Bp. Consp. i. p. 337 (1850); Cab. Mus. Hein. i. p. 50 (1850); id. J. f. O. 1856, p. 3; Burm. Th. Bras. iii. p. 140 (1856); Cass. Ill. B. Calif. p. 245 (1856); Brewer, N. Amer. Ool. i. p. 103, pl. iv. fig. 47 (1857); Baird, in Baird, Cass., & Lawr. B. N. Amer. p. 314 (1860); Gundl. J. f. O. 1861, p. 328; Sclater, Cat. Amer. B. p. 38 (1862); Blakist. Ibis, 1862, p. 4, 1863, p. 65; Gray, Cat. Brit. B. p. 34 (1863); Degl. et Gerbe, Orn. Eur. i. p. 594 (1867); Gray, Handl. B. i. p. 74. no. 886 (1869); Cooper, B. Calif. p. 113 (1870, pt.); Pelz. Orn. Bras. pp. 16, 102 (1871); Coues, Key N.-Amer. B. p. 114 (1872); Scl. & Salv. Nomencl. Av. Neotr. p. 14 (1873); Coues, B. N.-West, p. 91 (1874); Newt. ed. Yarr. Brit. B. ii. p. 361 (1880); A. & E. Newton, Handb. Jamaica, 1881, p. 107; Salvin, Cat. Strickl. Coll. p. 153 (1882); id. & Godm. Biol. Centr.-Amer., Aves, i. p. 223

(1883); B. O. U. List Brit. B. p. 45 (1883); Sharpe, Cat. B. in Brit. Mus. x. p. 173 (1885); Salvin, Ibis, 1885, p. 205; id. Ibis, 1888, p. 255.

Progne subis, Baird, Review Amer. B. p. 274 (1864); Sumichr. Mem. Bost. Soc. N. H. i. p. 547 (1869); Lawr. op. cit. ii. p. 271 (1874); Baird, Brewer, & Ridgw. Hist. N.-Amer. B. i. p. 329, pl. 16. figs. 7-10 (1874); Heush. Rep. Expl. 100th Mer. p. 213 (1875); Ridgw. U. S. Geol. Surv. 40th Par. pt. iii. Orn. p. 439 (1877); Merrill, Proc. U. S. Nat. Mus. i. p. 125 (1878); Coues, B. Color. Vall. p. 445 (1878); id. Bull. U. S. Geol. Surv. iv. p. 572 (1878); Cooper, Proc. U. S. Nat. Mus. ii. p. 247 (1880, pt.); Ridgw. op. cit. iii. p. 175 (1880); Stearns, New Engl. Bird-Life, i. p. 189 (1881); Hoffman, Bull. U. S. Geol. Surv. vi. p. 222 (1881); Coues, Key N. Amer. B. 2nd ed. p. 325 (1884); Drew, Auk, ii. p. 15 (1885); Merriam, t. c. p. 57; Agersborg, t. c. p. 279; Cory, Auk, iii. p. 56 (1886); Brewster, t. c. p. 111; Anthony, t. c. p. 169; Everm. t. c. p. 183; Fox, t. c. p. 317; Seton, t. c. p. 324; A. O. U. Check-l. p. 292 (1886); Towns. Proc. U. S. Nat. Mus. x. pp. 221, 236 (1887); Ridgw. Man. N. Amer. B. p. 459 (1887); Beckh. Proc. U. S. Nat. Mus. x. pp. 638, 640 (1887); Langdon, Auk, iv. p. 131 (1887); Lloyd, t. c. p. 291; Beckh. t. c. p. 302; Richm. Auk, v. p. 23 (1888); Scott, t. c. p. 31; Faxon & Allen, t. c. pp. 150, 152; Chapm. t. c. p. 275; Brewst. t. c. p. 389; Cory, B. W. Ind. p. 70 (1889); Everm. Auk, vi. p. 25 (1889); Rives, t. c. p. 53; F. H. Allen, t. c. pp. 77, 78; Pindar, t. c. p. 315; Kimball, t. c. p. 339; Loomis, Auk, vii. p. 125 (1890); Mearns, t. c. p. 261; Thompson, Proc. U. S. Nat. Mus. xiii. p. 608 (1890); Brewst. & Chapm. Auk, viii. p. 138 (1891); Dwight, Auk, ix. p. 138 (1892); Coombs, t. c. p. 205; Scott, t. c. p. 213; Ridgw. t. c. p. 307; Attwater, t. c. p. 340; Lawr. t. c. p. 356; Hatch, B. Minnesota, p. 350 (1892); Rhoads, Auk, x. p. 17 (1893); White, t. c. p. 226.

Progne elegans, ad., Baird, Review Amer. B. p. 275, note (1864).

Progne cryptoleuca, Baird, t. c. p. 277 (1864); Gray, Hand-l. B. i. p. 75, no. 894 (1869); Ridgw. Man. N. Amer. B. p. 459 (1887); Scott, Auk, ix. p. 213 (1892).

Progne subis, var. *cryptoleuca*, Baird, Brewer, & Ridgw. Hist. N.-Amer. B. i. p. 332 (1874).

Progne subis cryptoleuca, Ridgw. Proc. U. S. Nat. Mus. iii. p. 175 (1880), iv. p. 210 (1881); Scott, Auk, vi. p. 325 (1889).

Cecropis ciolurea, Boie, Isis, 1828, p. 316; Less. Compl. Buff. viii. p. 498 (1837).

Cecropis subis, Less. Compl. Buff. viii. p. 498 (1837).

P. purpurascenti-nigra; fasciis albis celatis binis, unâ ad latera dorsi, alterâ ad latera hypochondriarum positis.

Hab. in Americâ septentrionali æstivans, in Americâ meridionali hibernans.

Adult male. General colour above glossy dark purplish blue, with a concealed spot of silky white on the sides of the lower back; lesser and median wing-coverts like the back but rather duller; greater coverts, bastard-wing, primary-coverts, and quills blackish, externally glossed with dull blue; tail-feathers also blackish with a dull blue gloss; lores blackish; sides of face, ear-coverts, cheeks, and entire under surface of body dark purplish blue like the back, with a second patch of silky white feathers on the sides of the flanks; axillaries and under wing-coverts like the breast; quills ashy black below, rather lighter along the inner web: " bill deep brownish black; feet purplish black; iris dark brown " (*Audubon*). Total length 7·5 inches, culmen 0·55, wing 5·85, tail 3·05, tarsus 0·55.

Adult female. Differs from the male in not being blue below. General colour above dark purplish blue, not so brilliant as in the male; the head like the back, the forehead browner, the feathers slightly mottled with purplish-blue centres; lesser and median wing-coverts like the back; greater coverts, bastard-wing, primary-coverts, quills, and tail-feathers black, glossed externally with dull blue; lores black; ear-coverts dull blue; cheeks, throat, and breast light ashy brown, extending on to the sides of the neck; feathers of the throat with narrow dusky shaft-lines, those of the fore neck blacker, obscured with hoary whitish tips; sides of upper breast with a few feathers tipped with purplish blue like the back; centre of breast and abdomen whitish, the feathers with more or less distinct dusky shaft-lines; in the centre of the breast a longitudinal spot of dusky blackish; sides of body and flanks dark smoky brown, with ashy-whitish margins to the feathers; thighs brown externally, white internally; under tail-coverts white, with dusky centres to the feathers, becoming darker before the tips; axillaries and under wing-coverts dark sooty brown or blackish, the coverts near the edge of the wing glossed with steel-blue and distinctly edged with white; quills dusky below, more ashy along the inner web. Total length 7·5 inches, culmen 0·55, wing 5·65, tail 2·85, tarsus 0·55.

Young. Resembles the old female, but is browner above, with scarcely any blue gloss, excepting on the head; the secondaries narrowly fringed with white near the ends; sides of neck brown, with an ill-defined crescent of ashy white; throat, breast, and under surface of body brown, with hoary margins to all the feathers; lower breast, abdomen, and under tail-coverts pure white, with a few brown shaft-streaks on the former; under wing-coverts dark brown, those near the edge of the wing with white edges.

A young bird from Sing Sing shows scarcely any dusky shaft-streaks on the under tail-coverts. Such a specimen is very difficult to distinguish from *P. chalybea*, as the dusky centres to the under tail-coverts of the immature of *P. purpurea* are the chief character by which the latter may be distinguished from *P. chalybea*.

The male in the second year still greatly resembles the adult female, but is whiter below, with very distinct shaft-streaks of dark brown on the breast and abdomen; a few bright blue feathers are observable on the throat and chest; mesial under tail-coverts streaked with brown, the lateral ones externally brown.

A male in the second year from Washington, D.C., in the Henshaw collection has the dusky centres to the under tail-coverts well marked, but has the grey on the forehead and on the sides of the neck, reminding one of *P. hesperia*, as we have remarked in our account of the latter species.

With regard to *P. cryptoleuca*, Mr. Ridgway says (Manual, p. 159) that it is smaller than *P. purpurea*, with narrower tail-feathers and, relatively, a more deeply forked tail. The adult male is said by him to have the feathers of the ventral region marked, beneath the surface, with a broad spot, or bar, of white. The adult female and immature male have the whole under portion, and the sides of the head and neck, chest, sides, and flanks, uniform sooty greyish brown, in marked contrast to the white of the belly, anal region, and under tail-coverts. He adds: "Six Cuban and two Floridan specimens of this well-marked species are before me. The adult females and immature males (of which there are four from Cuba and two from Florida in the N. M. collection—the latter from Cape Florida and Clearwater) are exceedingly distinct in plumage from those of *P. subis* [i. e., *P. purpurea*]. In fact, they resemble so closely corresponding plumages of *P. dominicensis*, that I am unable to state how they can be distinguished." In the face of this strong testimony from the pen of so great an authority as Mr. Ridgway, we can only suppose that we have not yet had a specimen of the true *P. cryptoleuca* before us. A specimen sent by Mr. Scott as the hen of *P. cryptoleuca* from Tarpon Springs, and procured by him on the 17th of April, is identical with the female bird from Halfday, Illinois, in the British Museum.

Hab. North America, not ranging into the extreme north, but generally distributed. Wintering in South America.

THE Purple Martin is widely distributed over North America, but does not go so far north as some of the other Swallows. It does not find a place in the different works on the ornithology of Alaska. Professor Coues says that "The breeding-range of the species coincides with the whole distribution in North America wherever suitable nesting-places can be found, and the bird is, moreover, resident in some portions. Our birds are known to come over the border very early in the spring or in February, and gradually spread over the country, reaching the highest latitudes by the middle or latter part of May. Such early appearance subjects them to painful vicissitudes of the weather, large numbers having been known to perish in sudden storms or cold snaps."

Dr. C. Hart Merriam, writing on the migration of birds in the spring of 1884, refers to the present species as follows:—"The common Purple Martin is a species by which to trace migration, for it is well known and widely distributed, and its habit of occupying boxes erected for its use in towns and villages renders its movements far easier of observation than in the case of forest-dwelling birds. In winter the Martin visits South America, but the last of the fall migrants rarely leave our southern border before December. Returning, the advance guard usually enters the Gulf States towards the latter part of February. During March, the great army arrives and spreads over the whole of the Southern States, the van appearing in many parts of Virginia, Kentucky, Southern Illinois, Missouri, and Kansas, some enterprising individuals reaching even as far north as latitude 40°. If not retarded by cold, the first week of April finds them pushing swiftly northward, and by the end of the month they have distributed themselves over nearly the whole of the United States east of the Rocky Mountains, and are already common in some parts of Canada. The exact time of their appearance at any given locality in the Northern States varies as much as two weeks from year to year. During the spring of 1884 they were recorded from Water Valley, Miss., March 1; Gainesville, Texas, March 5; Caddo, Indian Territory, and Newport, Arkansas, March 9; St. Louis, Mo., March 24; Manhattan, Kansas, March 25; Southern Iowa, March 30. During April they move through Northern Illinois and parts of Wisconsin and Minnesota, arriving at latitude 45° about the end of the month. May 19 they reached Portage la

Prairie, in Manitoba. East of the Mississippi Valley they were seen in Jessamine County, Kentucky, March 18; at Buffalo, West Virginia, March 22; Camden, Indiana, March 28; New Lexington, Pa., April 16; Columbus, Ohio, April 15; Niagara Falls, April 18; Auburn, New York, April 20; Belleville, Ontario, April 22; Ottawa, Canada, April 27. In New England the returns show them at Saybrook, Conn., April 19; Greenfield, Mass., April 27; Moosehead Lake, Maine. April 23. They were seen at St. Johns, New Brunswick, May 2; Chatham, N.B. (Mirimichi Bay, facing the Gulf of St. Lawrence), May 10; and at Cape Breton Island, north of Nova Scotia, June 1.

"Turning now to the other side of the Continent, their progress is found to have been much affected by the unfavourable weather. In California Mr. L. Belding has records from San Diego, April 28; Stockton, March 1; Marysville, March 17; Poway, May 1; San José, May 3; Olema, May 8; and Chico, May 22."

Sir John Richardson states that the Purple Martin arrives within the Arctic Circle earlier than any other of its tribe; it makes its first appearance at Great Bear Lake on the 17th of May, at which time the snow still partially covers the ground, and the rivers and lakes are still fast bound in ice. The late Captain Blakiston records the species from the Forks of the Saskatchewan on the 11th of May, 1858.

Mr. Ernest Thompson sends us the following note:—"The Purple Martin arrives in Manitoba about the 15th of May, frequenting the half-open country in much the same degree as the White-breasted Swallows, but also manifesting a strong liking for town-life, for in Winnipeg and Portage la Prairie it is a very abundant bird. When it nests thus in towns it selects for occupation any convenient crevice or cavity about a building, caring only that it be well away from the ground, but the majority of those we see during the summer have their homes in some deserted Woodpecker-hole. On the banks of the Pembina River, near Pelican Lake, I found a small colony of Martins inhabiting a scattered grove of old and dying scrub oaks. In most instances the Martins were indebted to the friendly offices of the Golden-winged Woodpecker for their homesteads. This was on the 17th of May, and the birds had apparently arrived but recently. By the third week in August the species usually has disappeared from the 'Big Plain.'"

The same gentleman has also kindly sent the following note on the distribution of the species in Canada:—

"*Distribution in Ontario*:
  "*London and vicinity*. Common in every city, town, and generally every village through Western Ontario. A few pairs breeding and scattered through the country, probably in hollow trees, as I find old and young together hanging about some dead trees (*W. E. Saunders*).
  "*Hyde Park*. Summer resident (*John A. Morden*).
  "*Listowel*. Common in town (*W. L. Kells*).
  "*Hatchley*. Occurs (*W. Yates*).
  "*Hamilton*. The Purple Martin arrives in Southern Ontario about the 10th of

May, and, though generally distributed, is nowhere abundant (*T. McIlwraith* in 'Birds of Ontario').

"*Toronto*. Common and breeding about here.
 "April 16, 1887. Purple Martins arrived.
 "April 20, 1888. Purple Martins arrived.
"*Elora*. Summer visitant in some localities (*Hon. Chas. Clarke*).
"*Bruce Co.*, central region. Summer resident (*W. A. Schoenau*).
"*Galt*. I found this species very abundant here in 1878.
"*Millbrook*. Summer resident, tolerably common; noted first arrival 15th April, 1885 (*G. Sootheran*).
"*Cobocouk*. Noted by myself as common there in June 1885.
"*Peterboro'*. Common (*Rev. Vincent Clementi*).
"*Yarker*. Summer resident, common April 8th to May 1st (*John G. Ewart*).
"*Kingston*. Common (*Dr. C. K. Clarke*).

"*Distribution in Province of Quebec*:
 "*Montreal*. Summer resident, tolerably common (*W. W. Dunlop*).
 "*County of Quebec and north to Lake St. John*. Summer resident, rare (*John Neilson*).

"*Distribution in Manitoba and the North-west*:
 "*Carberry*. Common, breeding; noted only where there is large dead timber.
 "*Winnipeg*. Summer resident, common (*R. H. Hunter*).
 "*Portage la Prairie*. Somewhat common (*C. W. Nash*).
 "*Lake Manitoba*. Occurs (*Prof. J. Macoun*).
 "*Pembina River in Southern Manitoba*. Here on 17th May, 1882, I found a hollow tree about which several pairs were flying."

Professor Coues writes:—"I was rather surprised to find Martins breeding on Turtle Mountain, having observed none at Pembina. In this locality, where there is, of course, no artificial convenience for the purpose, they must nest in Woodpeckers' holes and similar cavities of trees, as they do in other parts of the West where I have observed them. This was the only locality where the species was observed, though it is known to extend to the Saskatchewan region."

In South-eastern Dakota Mr. Agersborg says: "Common every summer; it is found only in our towns, and not met with in the country."

Mr. Rhoads has included the present species as an inhabitant of British Columbia, but it does not occur in Mr. Chapman's paper, nor does Mr. J. K. Lord appear to have met with it. Mr. Fannin states that the Purple Martin is a summer resident to the east of the Cascade Mountains. Mr. Belding believes that the bird referred to is *Progne hesperia* and not *P. purpurea*. It would therefore probably be *P. hesperia*, which is recorded by Mr. Lawrence in his paper on the birds of Gray's Harbour, in Washington County, as breeding at Olympia, but the range of *P. hesperia*, in relation to *P. purpurea*, is not yet sufficiently worked out.

Dr. P. L. Hatch gives the following note on the present bird in Minnesota:—"When the long winters of Minnesota have gone, so that the snows have disappeared from the thickets and corners of the fences, and tiny Coleopterous insects begin to appear in the air, even then still chilly, the Purple Martin may appear any forenoon approaching twelve o'clock. It usually does so in company with greater numbers of the White-bellied Swallows. In 1870 they both came on the 17th of April, and after skirmishing vigorously about for an hour, and finding no food along the river, departed as abruptly as they came. On the 22nd they returned in augmented numbers, and went no more away for that season. The species is nearly universally distributed over the State. It leaves the whole country almost simultaneously between the 20th and 25th of August, in company with the White-bellied Swallows. Years of record show that they have left the vicinity of Minneapolis either on the 23rd or 24th of that month."

Mr. Washburn, when referring to this species in his notes gathered on his second trip to the Red River Valley, says:—"This species occurs about Mille Lacs, where the farmers provide boxes for them. The great majority, however, nest with the Gulls on an island called Spirit Island by the Indians, lying about two miles from the south-eastern shore of Lake Mille Lacs. Here large numbers lay their eggs in the sand—in the crevices and fissures of the rocks, and serve as allies in driving away the Ravens and other birds disposed to prey upon the eggs and young of the Gulls."

Throughout Illinois and Indiana it is plentiful in summer, and the same may be said of all the New England States. Mr. Stearns, in his 'New England Bird-Life,' writes as follows:—"A common summer resident, almost universally nesting nowadays in the boxes provided for its accommodation, or equivalent retreats about buildings. The distribution of the species, though in nowise dependent upon faunal considerations, is influenced by other conditions which cause the bird to be irregularly dispersed in New England, and rare or even wanting in many localities where one would expect to find it. I am inclined to think that here and elsewhere in the United States the Martin is not, on the whole, so very numerous as we suppose. Wherever it occurs, the size of the bird, its striking colour, the noise it makes, and its activity and domesticity conspire to render it an object so conspicuous that we unconsciously acquire an exaggerated idea of its general abundance. It, moreover, appears to be somewhat on the decrease in New England, from some cause not well understood. Its loquacity is an annoyance to many persons, and hospitality is frequently denied; though the bird is certainly a serviceable one in the work of holding insects in check—vastly more so than its inveterate enemy, the European Sparrow. The Martin originally built in hollows of trees, as the White-bellied Swallow still does, but is now seldom, if ever, known to nest except in artificial receptacles. It reaches us late in April or early in May, and leaves early in September. Two broods are commonly reared, the first set of eggs being laid in

May, the other in July. The nest is built of hay, sometimes with twigs intermixed, and is lined with feathers."

In the District of Columbia Mr. Richmond says it is rather common. There are several nesting-sites where the Martins still "hold the fort," despite the English Sparrows, notably the Masonic Temple and the Post Office Department building. In his paper on the summer birds of the Pennsylvania Alleghanies, Mr. Dwight says that some of these birds were nesting at Altoona, and there is every likelihood of its being found on the mountains. In Poulton County, Kentucky, according to Mr. Pindar, it is a common summer resident, and the same is recorded of Roane County, Tennessee, by Mr. Fox. Mr. Langdon says that in the Chilhowel Mountains, of Tennessee, he only noticed it at Knoxville and Marysville in August.

Mr. Brewster says that in Western North Carolina the present species is common in most of the towns and villages, building chiefly, if not wholly, in the Martin-boxes; and Mr. Loomis states that in the parts of South Carolina he visited, the birds nested wherever gourds were put up for their accommodation.

Mr. Coombs, writing from the Calumet plantation, in the parish of St. Mary's, Louisiana, says that the Purple Martin was common from April to August, breeding wherever gourds or boxes were prepared for the birds. He states that they generally disappeared quite early in the autumn, the last brood being usually fledged by the middle of August. Writing of the birds of Bayou Sara, Mr. Beckham says that the Purple Martin was abundant in the towns, but was seen nowhere else.

Many of the western localities for the species will require verification, as the distribution of *Progne purpurea* and *P. hesperia* is by no means satisfactorily determined, and the whole subject requires strict examination. Mr. Mearns says that in the Arizona mountains the Purple Martin is "an abundant summer resident throughout this high region, especially near water. It usually builds its nest in holes in the largest dead pines, several pairs living in the same tree. The Martin of this region, while differing somewhat from the Eastern bird, is not the subspecies *P. hesperia* recently described by Mr. Brewster, to whom I am indebted for the means of making the comparison." Mr. Scott states that it was rather uncommon about Tucson. In Colorado, according to Mr. Drew, it breeds from 6000 to 8000 feet.

Mr. Henshaw, in his 'Report of the Exploration of the 100th Meridian,' writes as follows:—

"This species is universally distributed throughout the United States, and in the West its abundance is fully as great as in the East. It occurs throughout Utah, being found in the vicinity of towns, and breeding plentifully in boxes placed for its convenience, as at Salt Lake City, or retiring in large colonies to the solitudes of the mountains, where it rears its young in the abandoned Woodpeckers' holes. Wherever found, it is never content to remain isolated in pairs, but associates together in colonies of greater or less number. Farther south, in New Mexico and Arizona, they are of no less common occurrence, but seemingly are more confined to the mountains, though this, perhaps, is due to the lack of timber in the lowlands, and a consequent want of the necessary facilities for rearing the young, rather than to any natural preference for high regions. About the middle of August, while in extreme South-eastern Arizona, I noticed each evening immense numbers of these birds and the Cliff-Swallows flying swiftly overhead, their course leading them directly south. They only paused now and then to catch an insect, immediately resuming their onward flight. All the actions of these birds seem to indicate that the migration at this early date had begun, yet I have found in quite a number of instances the parents feeding the just-fledged young as late as August 22nd."

A specimen from Mount Shasta, in the British Museum, seems to us to be true *P. purpurea*, and the following note by Mr. Townsend appears to refer to this species:— "Martins were not common in the localities where I collected. A few were noticed about some buildings at the west base of Mount Shasta in midsummer. A colony of a dozen or more was found established in a large dead pine on the edge of the forest at the eastern base of Mount Lassen, on June 6. The only nest I could reach occupied a large decayed cavity twenty feet from the ground. It contained four fresh eggs. There were other nests higher up."

In Western Texas Mr. Lloyd says that the Purple Martin is plentiful in summer in suitable places. It breeds in colonies, arriving towards the end of February and departing about the 1st of November. At San Antonio it is common in summer, according to Mr. Attwater. At Fort Brown, in Southern Texas, Dr. Merrill only observed the species during migration, but he noticed their arrival as early as the 20th of January.

In Florida the resident species is supposed to be *Progne cryptoleuca*. Mr. Scott has forwarded several specimens from Tarpon Springs, but after a careful examination we have been unable to discover any specific characters for the recognition of this supposed species. We add Mr. Scott's note on the Purple Martins :—

"It seems to me probable that all Martins found *breeding* on the Gulf Coast of Florida, at least as far north as Tarpon Springs, are referable to *P. cryptoleuca*, and though the material that I have before me is limited, yet one of the male birds is fairly intermediate between *P. subis* proper and what I think will ultimately have to be considered as the subspecies *P. subis cryptoleuca*, though the latter is now given specific rank. I have submitted material collected in the vicinity of Tarpon Springs to Mr. J. A. Allen, who concurs in the above views and from whose letters on the subject I quote as follows:—'The Martins I should refer to *Progne subis cryptoleuca*, of which the single female and two of the males are fairly typical. The other male I should consider *as intermediate* between *P. subis* and *P. subis cryptoleuca*, which latter I believe at least only a geographical race of *P. subis*.' As the birds are abundant in the breeding-season in the town of Tarpon Springs, and as I am expecting additional representatives from at least two points of the south on the Gulf Coast, as well as from Key West, I hope at an early date with more abundant material to deal conclusively with the subject. At

Tarpon Springs it is difficult to obtain birds, as they are almost confined to the town limits, where shooting of all birds at any season is prohibited. At this point the first Martins to arrive are seen as early as the first week in March, but I suspect these are representatives of true *P. subis* on their way north, as the birds that frequent the Martin-boxes in the town do not seem at all common until the first week in April, and do not nest until the middle or last of that month. Mr. Atkins noticed the first Martins at Punta Rassa on March 20, 1886, and saw them frequently during the summer 'at a point on the beach near the pine-trees. Evidently breeds.' He has also noted Martins as rather common migrants at Key West, but has not found them breeding at that point."

Mr. Chapman states that at Gainsville, Florida, the Purple Martins arrived on the 3rd of March. The species was a common summer resident, breeding where boxes and gourds were erected for their accommodation. Messrs. Brewster and Chapman record the ordinary Purple Martin from the Suwanee River, so that they apparently do not recognize the distinctness of *P. cryptoleuca*, which Mr. Scott believes to be the resident species in Florida. The latter gentleman states that in the Caloosahatchie Region *P. cryptoleuca* is a migrant and breeds, while *P. purpurea* is a migrant only. Mr. Maynard gives the following note:—

"The first time I ever met with the Martins in Florida was on Biscayonne Bay. I was rowing along the shore north of Miami, in company with Mr. Henshaw, when we observed two of these birds flying about a dead stub in the pine woods, which at this point came down to the shore uninterrupted by a hummock. This was in April, and they were evidently searching for a breeding-place. In May 1872, Mr. E. C. Greenwood found them nesting abundantly on the western bank of Indian River, near Fort Capron. This style of building appears to be usual with these birds while in the wilderness, but in the more settled portions of the South, as well as in the North, they prefer boxes erected for their benefit."

The Purple Martin occurs in the Bermudas on migration, as Mr. Jones mentions that, like *Tachycineta bicolor*, they were numerous during the great flight of Swallows in September, 1849.

The late Colonel Grayson writes:—"I found it breeding in Tepic, in the month of May, also in Guadalajara; they were nesting under the eaves of houses or in water-spouts. It is seldom seen in the locality of Mazatlan, and then only accidental and migratory, flying very high."

Professor Sumichrast says that the species is resident in the alpine region of Vera Cruz.

In the 'Biologia Centrali-Americana,' Messrs. Salvin and Godman have the following remark:—"Referring to its Mexican range, it seems not improbable that this is merely an extension of the area it inhabits during the summer months in North America, and that the Mexican birds accompany the more northern ones in their winter migration. Against this theory is Professor Sumichrast's observation that the bird is resident in the higher parts of Vera Cruz."

Several specimens were procured by Mr. Gaumer in the Island of Cozumel in May, and Messrs. Salvin and Godman state that they have received a specimen from British Honduras from Mr. Blancaneaux. They did not procure the species in Guatemala, and we believe that the above records constitute all the occurrences in Central America. Nor does it appear to visit the Antilles, unless we except the island of Cuba, where, according to Mr. Cory, *P. cryptoleuca* is found. We have, however, never ourselves seen a specimen from this island.

The Purple Martin of North America winters in the continent of South America, apparently in Brazil. It has never been found in British Guiana, but specimens are in the British Museum from Bahia and Para, while Natterer met with the species at Barra do Rio Negro, from December to February, again at Manaqueri in December, and also at Pernambuco and Rio de Janeiro.

What the species recorded by Tschudi as common on the coast of Peru (*cf.* Tacz. Orn. Pérou, i. p. 236) can be, we are unable to say.

The following is Dr. Brewer's account of the habits of the Purple Martin, as given by him in the 'History of North-American Birds':—

"The Purple Martin is emphatically a bird common to the whole of North America. It breeds from Florida to high northern latitudes, and from the Atlantic to the Pacific. It is very abundant in Florida, as it is in various other parts of the country further north, and the large flocks of migrating birds of this species which pass through Eastern Massachusetts the last of September attest its equal abundance north of the latter State. It occurs in Bermuda, is resident in the Alpine region of Mexico, and is also found at Cape St. Lucas. Accidental specimens have been detected in England and in Ireland. It is abundant on the Saskatchewan. Burmeister states that this species is common in the vicinity of Rio de Janeiro, and that it is distributed in moderate abundance through the whole of tropical South America. Von Pelzeln also cites it as occurring on the Rio Negro and at Manaqueri through the three winter months, nesting in old buildings and in holes in the rocks. It is, however, quite possible that he refers to an allied but distinct species.

"In a wild state the natural resort of this species, for nesting and shelter, was to hollow trees and crevasses in rocks. The introduction of civilized life, and with it other safer and more convenient places, better adapted to their wants, has wrought an entire change in its habits. It is now very rarely known to resort to a hollow tree, though it will do so where better provision is not to be had. Comfortable and convenient boxes, of various devices in our cities and large towns, attract them to build in small communities around the dwellings of men, where their social, familiar, and confiding disposition makes them general favourites. There they find abundance of insect food, and repay their benefactors by the destruction of numerous injurious and noxious kinds, and there, too, they are also comparatively safe from their own enemies. These conveniences vary from the elegant Martin-houses that adorn private grounds in our Eastern cities to the ruder gourds and calabashes which are said to be frequently placed near the humbler cabins of the southern negroes. In Washington the columns of the public buildings, and the eaves and sheltered portions of the piazzas, afford a convenient protection to large numbers around the Patent Office and the Post Office buildings. The abundance of this species varies in different parts of the country, from causes not always apparent. In the vicinity of Boston it is quite unusual, though said to have been forty years since quite common. There its place is taken by the *H. bicolor*, which occupies almost exclusively the Martin-houses, and very rarely builds in hollow trees.

"Sir John Richardson states that it arrives within the Arctic Circle earlier than any other of its family. It made its first appearance at Great Bear Lake as early as the 17th of May, when the ground was covered with snow, and the rivers and lakes were all ice-bound.

"In the Southern States it is said to raise three broods in a season; in its more northern distribution it raises but one. Their early migrations expose the Martins to severe exposure and suffering from changes of weather, in which large numbers have been known to perish. An occurrence of this kind is said to have taken place in Eastern Massachusetts, where nearly all the birds of this species were destroyed, and where to this day their places have never been supplied.

"Within its selected compartment the Martin prepares a loose and irregular nest. This is composed of various materials, such as fine dry leaves, straws, stems of grasses, fine twigs, bits of string, rags, &c. These are carelessly thrown together, and the whole is usually warmly lined with feathers or other soft materials. This nest is occupied year after year by the same pair, but after each new brood the nest is thoroughly repaired, and often increased in size by the accumulation of new materials.

"The Martins do not winter in the United States, but enter the extreme southern portions early in February. Audubon states that they arrive often in prodigious flocks. On the Ohio their advent is about the 15th of March, and in Missouri, Ohio, and Pennsylvania about the 10th of April. About Boston their appearance is from the 25th of April to the middle of May. Mr. Audubon states they all return to the Southern States about the 20th of August, but this is hardly correct. Their departure varies very much with the season. In the fall of 1870 they were to be found in large flocks, slowly moving southward, but often remaining several days at a time at the same place, and then proceeding to their next halt. Their favourite places for such spots are usually a high and uninhabited hillside near the sea.

"The Martin is a bold and courageous bird, prompt to meet and repel dangers, especially when threatened by winged enemies, never hesitating to attack and drive them away from its neighbourhood. It is therefore a valuable protection to the barnyard. Its food is the larger kind of insects, especially beetles, in destroying which it does good service to the husbandman. The song of the Martin is a succession of twitters, which, without being musical, are far from being unpleasant; they begin with the earliest dawn, and during the earlier periods of incubation are almost incessantly repeated.

The eggs of the Purple Martin measure ·94 of an inch in length by ·79 in breadth. They are of an oblong-oval shape, are pointed one end, are of an uniform creamy-white, and are never spotted. They are quite uniform in size and shape. Eggs from Florida are proportionally smaller than those from Northern States."

Dr. Hatch's notes from Minnesota are as follows:—"These birds soon build their nests in various places, but manifest a strong preference to have them near dwellings. Their readiness to occupy boxes, artificial houses placed on poles, on the eaves of out-houses, is a matter of the commonest observation, doubtless from no sentiment toward our species, but because our habits and our habitations attract the larger quantities of insects upon which they feed; yet, like the Chimney-Swallow, they frequent the forests, and employ holes in old dead trees in many places familiar to me. They habitually enter the State at the southern border early in April, as Dr. Hvoslef of Lanesboro' has the 3rd of that month in his record for several years in succession. He also observed the circumstances of their disappearing again for a few days—once eleven—and then invariably remaining upon their return. The nest consists of fine straw, hay, dried leaves, and feathers which are employed to line it. They lay four pure white eggs, that are almost indistinguishable from those of the White-bellied Swallow. The first brood is brought out by the 10th of June and another one late in July.

"As a fighter, the courage of this bird has but one approximation, and that is the Kingbird. Crows, Ravens, Hawks, and Eagles are instantly put to flight by them, and, in the words of Wilson, ' so well known is this to the lesser birds, that as soon as they hear the Martin's voice engaged in fight, all is alarm and consternation. To observe with what spirit and audacity this bird dives and sweeps upon and around the Hawk, or the Eagle, is astonishing. He also bestows an occasional bastinadoing on the Kingbird, when he finds him too near his premises, though he will at any time instantly co-operate with him in attacking the common enemy.' The value of the Purple Martin to the general or the special agriculturist is so well understood and so universally accepted on account of their destruction of noxious insects, that, for an exception, no argument is needed with that class of producers to defend it."

For the following account we are indebted to the kindness of our friend Mr. Ernest Thompson:—"Its nest is usually placed in situations similar to those selected by the White-breasted Swallow, a favourite location being the joist-holes left in the end of a house, when it is intended that at some future period another building will be conjoined. The material of the nest proper is, as in most of the Swallows, straw and the large curling feathers from the flanks of Geese or other barn-fowl.

"My friend Mr. C. W. Nash communicates some interesting observations on this species, as follows:—'I take the following extract from an unpublished paper of mine on this bird, written in 1878: From my notes on migration kept from the year 1873 I find that this bird usually arrives in the Province of Ontario about the middle of April, the earliest date I have recorded being April the 15th and the latest May 4th, dependent somewhat, I presume, upon the season, although, from observations made in the county of Wentworth in 1874, the birds can take care of themselves even when caught by the most severe weather after their arrival here. In this year (1874) the birds arrived in the town of Dundas on the 15th day of April and took possession of their usual nesting-places in boxes which had been put up for and used by them for some years, and in certain holes under eaves that they also were in the habit of occupying, and they devoted themselves as usual to hawking for insects about the streets. The weather on this day was mild, but that night it turned cold and we had hard frosts and snow until the 22nd of April, when it became warm and the birds reappeared, having been in the meantime six days closely huddled up in their old nests—not torpid, for they chirped and would slightly move if their box was touched or opened. They, however, lived through this, and on this 22nd of April came out and flew about as hungry and lively as usual for a day or two, when another cold snap occurred and they again betook themselves to their boxes until after the 27th of April, when they again came out and were not further troubled by the weather for that year.'

"I will only remark on this account that it appears to have been accurately made and that it unites with a class of circumstances which give rise to the exploded theory of the hibernation of Swallows to indicate that they are possessed of some habits and powers of which we have as yet but slight knowledge, and which are deserving of a careful investigation."

The accompanying note is from the pen of Mr. Maynard:—"They invariably flock to places where accommodations are provided for them and avoid all others. The offspring of those which have inhabited a certain locality will also return and take up their abode there, so that a number of apartments in one box will be constantly occupied. If other domiciles are erected quite near the same spot they will be inhabited, but it is extremely difficult to induce these birds to enter a new house if it stands a mile or more from those occupied by the colony; they, therefore, are extremely local in their distribution. I know of localities where Martins have bred for years, while they could never be induced to remain in another section which was but a mile distant, although I erected houses in suitable situations. They frequently appeared there in spring, but after examining the place and flying about for a day or two, invariably returned to the old locality. Although fond of any particular spot they may be easily driven from it. If a few birds are shot in early spring upon their arrival, the survivors will disappear and cannot be persuaded to reinhabit the house from which they have been expelled, even after the lapse of many years. Accidents occurring, which are detrimental to them, although not caused through the agency of man, appear to produce the same effect. Some years ago the Purple Martins, which bred in many boxes in Cambridge, arrived from the south quite early, induced by unusually warm weather, and took possession of their respective domiciles, but unfortunately the instincts which prompted them to come north so soon were at fault, for they were scarcely established in their summer houses when a prolonged cold snap came on and many of the poor Martins were frozen to death in their houses. The remainder left at once and there have been no birds of this kind found nesting in that section of Cambridge since.

"The Purple Martin is the only Swallow with which I am acquainted that will readily perch on trees which are covered with foliage, alighting amid the leaves after the manner of nearly all the Passerine birds, but they never hop from twig to twig. The song of the Martin is loud and cheerful; in autumn, when they are more generally distributed than at other times, these clear notes frequently reach the ear when the birds are almost invisible, as they sail high in the air with a strong and graceful flight. Early in September these birds migrate south, but do not remain in Florida all winter, and not one is to be seen in the State after the 1st of November."

The figures in the Plate have been drawn from specimens in the Salvin-Godman collection, and the descriptions are taken from examples in the British Museum.

For the geographical distribution of this species, *vide supra*, Plate 81 [Map].

PROGNE HESPERIA, Brewster.

WESTERN PURPLE MARTIN.

Progne purpurea et *Progne subis*, auct. ex California.
Progne subis (nec L.), Belding, Proc. U. S. Nat. Mus. i. pp. 391, 394 (1878); id. op. cit. v. p. 517 (1882).
Progne subis hesperia, Brewster, Auk, vi. pp. 92, 93 (1889); A. O. U. Check-l. 2nd Suppl. Auk, vii. p. 63 (1890); Belding, Occ. Papers Calif. Acad. Sci. ii. p. 183 (1890); Fisher, N. Amer. Fauna, no. 7, pt. 2. p. 109 (1893).

Mas similis mari *P. purpurea*. Fœm. tamen a fœmina *P. purpureæ*, fronte et collo postico canescentibus distinguenda.

Hab. in America boreali occidentali.

Adult male. Not to be distinguished from the male of *P. purpurea*. Total length 7 inches, culmen 0·5, wing 6·65, tail 2·9, tarsus 0·55. (*Mus. W. Brewster.*)

Adult female. Similar to the female of *P. purpurea*, but differing in the hoary white shade on the forehead and hind neck; the sides of the neck silvery white like the throat; entire underparts hoary white, faintly mottled with brown bases to the feathers of the throat and chest; under tail-coverts pure white like the abdomen. Total length 7 inches, culmen 0·5, wing 5·4, tail 2·75, tarsus 0·6. (*Mus. W. Brewster.*)

Hab. California, and probably the whole Pacific coast of the United States and British Columbia.

THIS western race of *P. purpurea* was described in 1889 by Mr. William Brewster, from specimens procured by Mr. M. Abbott Frazar in the Sierra de la Laguna in Lower California. The males are not to be told apart from those of *Progne purpurea*, and the distinctness of the race depends upon the characters of the female bird. Mr. Brewster thus summarizes the differences:—" Described in general terms, the female of *P. hesperia* may be said to have the forehead, fore part of crown, nuchal collar, and entire underparts ashy white, the darker markings and shades being only apparent on a critical examination."

He has very kindly lent us a pair of this new race for purposes of examination, and we find that they bear out the title to separation which he claims for the Purple Martin of Lower California; at the same time it should be noted that in certain stages of plumage the true *P. purpurea* approaches very closely to the female of *P. hesperia*, and an example from Bahia in Brazil shows the characteristic hoary forehead and whitish sides of neck which are among the chief features of *P. hesperia*. A male in the second year from Washington, killed on the 30th of May (Henshaw collection), also closely approaches *P. hesperia* in the above-named particulars. Both these specimens, however, are true *P. purpurea*, as they are not so white on the throat, are more dingy on the breast and abdomen, and have the long under tail-coverts very distinctly centred with brown; this last character seems to be a very well-marked one for distinguishing *P. purpurea*.

Besides the typical specimens from the Sierra de la Laguna, Mr. Brewster says that he has seen others in Mr. Batchelder's collection from the Ojai Valley, in California, and Mr. Xantus's birds from Cape St. Lucas are also *P. hesperia*, as is shown by a specimen in the British Museum.

It is extremely difficult for us to determine the exact range of this western race of Purple Martin owing to lack of specimens, but we have some doubts whether the distinctive characters of *P. hesperia* will be upheld by future observers. Judging from the small series at our disposal, *P. purpurea* is at certain seasons very similar to *P. hesperia*, and the latter can be nothing but a western race, which, indeed, is all the status that Mr. Brewster claims for it. The British Museum possesses a young male from Big Trees, obtained by Mr. Forrer, which is certainly referable to *P. hesperia*, but amongst the series in the Museum there are several birds which seem to connect the two races entirely.

Mr. L. Belding, in his paper on the Birds of the Pacific District, claims for the western race a range reaching even into British Columbia, but we believe that the Purple Martin from several of his more northern localities must be *P. purpurea*. This, however, is a question which the American ornithologists alone can settle. We subjoin Mr. Belding's note:—

"A dozen or more of both sexes were temporarily sojourning at San Diego, April 28, during a cool rain-storm. It does not appear to breed on the coast about San Diego (*L. B.*).

"Poway, twelve miles from the coast. First seen May 1, 1884, a few only; common in the spring of 1883 (*Blaisdell*).

"Little Santa Maria Valley, April 4, 1884, one only (*Emerson*).

"Julian, April 4, 1884 (*N. S. Goss*).

"San Bernardino. Rare summer resident in the mountains; rare migrant in the Valley (*F. Stephens*).

"Santa Cruz, common (*Joseph Skirm*).

"San José. First seen May 3, 1884, two or three; they did not remain. Arrived April 9, 1885 (*A. L. Parkhurst*).

"Contra Costa County. Rare summer resident (*W. E. Bryant*).

"Olema. First seen May 8, 1884; breeds (*A. M. Ingersoll*).

"Stockton. Common summer resident here and in many localities in Central California below fir-forest, where it is very rare (*L. B.*).

"Marysville. Arrive in March (*W. F. Peacock*; *Frank Manning*).

"Chico. First seen May 22, 1884 (*W. Proud*).

"I never saw this bird in Washington Territory (*Cooper*).

"I obtained at Fort Steilacoom a specimen of *Progne* (*Suckley*).

"Colonies encountered at numerous localities among the pine-woods of the mountains, where they are quite local (*Henshaw*).

"Rare, east of the Sierra Nevada. In Carson it was common, while in Virginia City but a single individual was seen June 18, 1868 (*Ridgway*).

"Stockton, March, common (*J. J. Snyder*)

"Murphys, March and April (*J. P. Snyder*).

"Sebastopol. First seen in April ; rare; breeds (*F. H. Holmes*).

"Marysville, March ; common and breeds (*W. F. Peacock*).

"Sierra Valley, June 18–21, common, breeding ; several little Martin-houses recently erected for their use ; not known to do so elsewhere on the Pacific coast.

"British Columbia. Summer resident east of Cascades (*J. Fannin*).

"Camp Harney. One of the most abundant summer residents (*Bendire*).

"Hoffman. Usually abundant in the vicinity of rivers, streams, and even large springs.

"Ridgway. Noticed along every portion of our route across the Great Basin, especially in the vicinity of rivers or lakes, or at settlements whether great or small.

"Cooper, 1870. In June I saw a flock of these birds busily catching young grasshoppers on the dry hillside, where these insects were swarming.

"Salt Spring Valley (Calaveras County). Sept. 13, a few about the reservoir (*L. B*)."

In the account of the birds obtained during the Death Valley Expedition, Dr. A. K. Fisher writes:—"A colony of Martins was found breeding at Old Fort Tejon, in the Cañada de las Uras, California, June 28, 1891, by Dr. Merriam and Mr. Palmer. They were nesting in Woodpeckers' holes in large oaks in front of the old fort, where three were killed. Mr. Belding noted the species at Crocker's, 21 miles north-west of the Yosemite Valley, in May."

Dr. Cooper has given the following interesting note on the Purple Martin in his 'Ornithology of California,' and it no doubt refers principally to *P. hesperia*:—" I have not seen the beautiful and sociable Martins in the Colorado Valley, nor observed them along the coast earlier than April 20th, when they were migrating through San Francisco, perching for a few hours on lofty flag-staffs during the warm morning, but disappearing when the sea breeze began to blow. They resort chiefly to the warm valleys of the interior, nesting in holes of large trees from near San Diego to Puget's Sound. I also found them nesting on the summits of the Coast Range, in company with the *Hirundo thalassina* and *H. bicolor*, but preferring the dead tops of the loftiest red woods for their domiciles. They are numerous at Sacramento in summer, and probably through most of the Sierra Nevada, but retire to the south in August.

"They have not yet attracted so much attention among our movable and busy people as in the East, where almost every country-house, and even some in large cities, furnish them with a residence, usually a neat little hotel with many apartments, each opening on to a porch, and all mounted together on a high pole. Like Pigeons, the Martins live in perfect harmony with their neighbours; while our other house-loving pets, the Bluebirds and Wrens, must have a large range of territory, and drive away intruders too near their homes. Yet the Martins have courage enough, as is shown by their occasionally driving away the smaller birds, and even Pigeons, to appropriate their quarters. They also drive away every Hawk or Crow that shows itself near their nest, and thus protect poultry.

"The loud and twittering song of the Martin, though mixed with some harsh notes, is remarkably pleasing, and continues during its whole stay with us, beginning at dawn, and heard at intervals during the day as they pursue their prey through the higher air, generally far above the smaller Swallows, though they sweep occasionally along the ground. Their nest is made of leaves, straw, hay, and feathers in large quantities, and their eggs, from four to six, are pure white. They probably raise two broods here, as in the East. They prey on the larger flying insects that appear during the day, and none are so swift as to escape them."

The specimens figured in the accompanying Plate are two of the typical examples kindly lent to us by Mr. Brewster, and the descriptions have been taken from the same birds.

For the geographical distribution of this species, *vide suprà*, Plate 82 [Map].

PROGNE FURCATA, Baird.

PATAGONIAN PURPLE MARTIN.

Progne purpurea (nec L.), Gould, Voy. 'Beagle,' Birds, p. 38 (1841); Scl. P. Z. S. 1872, p. 548; Hudson, t. c. p. 606; Durnford, Ibis, 1877, p. 32, 1878, p. 392; White, P. Z. S. 1882, p. 595.

Progne modesta (nec Gould), Gray, Cat. Fissir. Brit. Mus. p. 28 (1848).

Progne furcata, Baird, Review Amer. B. p. 278 (1864); Sclater, P. Z. S. 1867, pp. 321, 337; id. P. Z. S. 1868, p. 531; Gray, Hand-l. B. i. p. 74, no. 890 (1869); Sharpe, Auk, i. p. 368 (1884); id. Cat. Birds in Brit. Mus. x. p. 175 (1885); Sclater & Hudson, Argent. Orn. i. p. 24 (1888).

Progne elegans (juv.), Baird, Review Amer. B. p. 275 (1864); id. in Baird, Brewer, & Ridgw. Hist. N. Amer. B. i. p. 328 (1874); Barrows, Bull. Nutt. Orn. Club, viii. p. 89 (1883).

P. purpurascenti-nigra ; fasciâ albâ unicâ sericeâ ad latera dorsi infimi positâ.

Hab. in Americâ meridionali, in Patagoniâ usque ad Brasiliam meridionalem et provinciam Mendozanam.

Adult male. General colour purplish blue above and below ; the lesser and median wing-coverts like the back ; greater coverts, bastard-wing, primary-coverts, and quills black, glossed externally with blue ; tail-feathers black, washed with blue ; on the sides of the back a small tuft of silky white feathers. Total length 7·7 inches, culmen 0·5, wing 5·55, tail 3·3, tarsus 0·6.

Adult female. General colour above dull blue, with a brown shade on the forehead and hinder neck ; wing-coverts like the back, the greater and primary-coverts and quills blackish, glossed externally with dull blue, browner on the inner webs; tail-feathers blackish glossed with blue ; lores dusky blackish; sides of face and ear-coverts dull smoky brown, with a slight blue gloss ; cheeks and throat dull smoky brown ; remainder of under surface of body dark smoky brown, with blackish shaft-streaks, and obscured with broad whity-brown edges to the feathers; the under tail-coverts coloured like the breast, the long ones dull brown, with whity-brown edges and a distinct subterminal shade of purplish black ; sides of body nearly uniform dark brown, with a purplish gloss; axillaries and under wing-coverts uniform smoky brown, the coverts near the edge of the wing edged with whity brown; quills smoky brown below. Total length 7·8 inches, culmen 0·55, wing 5·5, tail 3·3, tarsus 0·55.

Obs. The types of *Progne elegans* of Baird were lent to us by the U.S. National Museum. The specimen no. 21009 agrees with the female birds in the British Museum: it is marked " ♂ juv.," and may be a male of the second year. The second specimen (no. 21011) is undoubtedly quite young, judging from the light margins to the feathers of the upper surface, these being very distinct on the wing-coverts and secondaries. The under surface is nearly uniform sooty brown, with ashy margins, more distinct on the breast and abdomen, the under tail-coverts rather broadly tipped with white.

The series in the British Museum measures :—

	Total length. in.	Wing. in.	Tail. in.	Tarsus. in.
a. ♂ ad. Rio Negro (*Hudson*)	8·3	5·6	3·35	0·55
b. ♂ ad. ,, ,,	7·8	5·5	3·15	0·55
c. ♀ imm. Chupat (*Durnford*)	7·8	5·45	3·2	0·6
d. ♂ ad. Chili (*Bridges*)	7·8	5·45	3·2	0·6
e. ♂ ad. Mendoza (*Weisshaupt*)	7·4	5·55	3·15	0·6
f. ♂ ad. ,, ,,	7·7	5·45	3·25	0·6
g. ♀ ad. Rio Negro (*Hudson*)	7·7	5·3	2·9	0·55
h. ♀ ad. Mendoza (*Weisshaupt*)	7·2	5·3	2·6	0·6
i. ♀ ad. ,, ,,	7·7	5·3	3·0	0·55
k. ? ad. ,, ,,	7·7	5·6	3·15	0·55

Hab. Patagonia, northwards, apparently to the Argentine Republic, and westwards as far as Mendoza.

THE details of the range of this species are by no means satisfactorily recorded, and more information is desirable. The series of skins in the British Museum indicates that it is an inhabitant of Patagonia, and that it extends as far as Mendoza. All the other records are involved in great obscurity, and without the evidence of specimens they must all be received with more or less suspicion, the more so that until quite recently the species was confounded, even by authors of repute, with *P. purpurea*, and in all probability with *P. domestica* also. The latter is a large form of *P. chalybea*, resident in South-eastern Brazil, while *P. purpurea* is only a winter visitor to South America.

The following note is given by Mr. Darwin in his account of the Voyage of the 'Beagle' :—

"My specimens were obtained at Monte Video (November), and Bahia Blanca, 39° S. (September). At the latter place the females were beginning to lay in September (corresponding to our March); they had excavated deep holes in a cliff of compact earth, close by the side of the larger burrows inhabited by the Ground Parrot of Patagonia (*Psittacara patagonica*). I noticed several times a small flock of these birds, pursuing each other, in a rapid and direct course, flying low, and screaming in the manner so characteristic of the English Swift."

Not a single specimen of *Progne* collected by Mr. Darwin appears to have passed to the British Museum, and consequently we are unable to state whether the species obtained by him at Monte Video was the same as the one met with at Bahia Blanca, which was, of course, the true *P. furcata*.

The late Mr. Henry Durnford, writing on the birds observed by him in Central Patagonia, says that this species was a spring and summer visitor. "Observed commonly throughout our journey wherever there were steep cliffs or rocks. I took eggs near Tombo Point on the 30th of December. They had all left Chupat by the 1st of March." It was "pretty common about the Tosca cliff, up the Chupat valley, in the crevices of the rocks in which they were breeding. The male is uniform glossy steel-blue, and easily distinguishable from the female, whose underparts are speckled with grey, lightest about the vent. Both sexes uttered harsh screams whilst we were sitting under the cliff. A few seen at Ninfas Point." Although he spoke of the species as *Progne purpurea*, we know by a specimen from the Chupat valley in the British Museum, collected by Mr. Durnford on the 9th of November, 1875, that the species is really *P. furcata*.

Mr. Barrows gives the following note:—

"Specimens were taken at Bahia Blanca, where the birds were abundant, and they were frequently seen in the Sierra de la Ventana. While at Carhué and Puan (March 21st to April 9th, 1881) none were seen, but the weather was so cold that doubtless they had gone north. At Concepcion this species was never observed."

The following is Mr. W. H. Hudson's account (Arg. Orn.) of the species:—

"This Purple Martin is occasionally seen in the eastern provinces of La Plata when migrating, but has not been found nesting anywhere so far north as Buenos Ayres. I met with it breeding at Bahia Blanca on the Atlantic coast, and on the Rio Negro, where it is very common. It arrives in Patagonia late in September, and leaves before the middle of February. On the 11th of that month I saw one flock flying north, but it was the last. It breeds in holes under the eaves of houses or in walls, and its nest is like that of *P. chalybea*; but many also breed in holes in the steep banks of the Rio Negro. They do not, however, excavate holes for themselves, but take possession of natural crevices and old forsaken burrows of the Burrowing Parrot (*Conurus patachonicus*). In size, flight, manners, and appearance the Purple Martin closely resembles *Progne chalybea*, the only difference being in the dark plumage of the under surface. The language of the two birds is also identical; the loud excited scream when the nest is approached, the various other notes when the birds sweep about in the air, and the agreeably modulated and leisurely-uttered song are all possessed by the two species without the slightest difference in strength or intonation. This circumstance appears very remarkable to me, because, though two species do sometimes possess a few notes alike, the greater part of their language is generally different; also because birds of the same species in different localities vary more in language than in any other particular. This last observation, however, applies more to resident than to migratory species."

The notes on *P. purpurea* given by Mr. Durnford ('Ibis,' 1877, p. 168) and Mr. Gibson ('Ibis,' 1880, p. 22), in which they speak of that species as nesting near Buenos Ayres, must belong to *P. domestica*. In the 'Catalogue of Birds' they have been placed under the heading of the present species, and this is probably a mistake.

The specimen which the late Mr. White stated that he had obtained at Fuerte de Andalgala, Catamarca, on the 28th of September, 1880, determined by Dr. Sclater as

2 C 2

P. purpurea, may have been that species. Dr. Sclater gives Mr. White's locality as "Buenos Ayres" in the 'Argentine Ornithology' (p. 25).

Numerous specimens have been obtained in Mendoza, and a series from this province is contained in the collection of the British Museum. The occurrence of the species in Chili is very doubtful, and Dr. Philippi expressly names *P. furcata* as one of the species which has been wrongly recorded from that country. The only authority for its capture in Chili appears to be a specimen in the British Museum, said to have been obtained there by Mr. Bridges; but the exact locality is not attached to the specimen, and, in the days when Mr. Bridges collected, "Chili" would be considered quite exact for a bird which may have been obtained in Mendoza.

The specimens described and figured in the present work are in the British Museum.

PROGNE CONCOLOR.

PROGNE CONCOLOR (*Gould*).

DARWIN'S PURPLE MARTIN.

Hirundo concolor, Gould, P. Z. S. 1837, p. 22.
Progne modesta, Gould in Voy. 'Beagle,' Birds, p. 39, pl. v. (1841); Gray, Gen. B. i. p. 59 (1845); Bp. Consp. i. p. 337 (1850); Prév. et Des Murs, Voy. 'Venus,' v. p. 182 (1855).
Progne concolor, Baird, Review Amer. B. p. 278 (1864); Gray, Hand-l. B. i. p. 74, no. 888 (1869); Salvin, Trans. Z. S. ix. p. 476 (1876).
Hirundo modesta, Néboux, Rev. Zool. 1840, p. 291; Sundev. P. Z. S. 1871, p. 125.

P. minor: unicolor: fasciis albis ad latera dorsi imi sitis absentibus.

Hab. in insulis Galapagensibus.

Adult. Similar to *P. purpurea*, but smaller, and having no silky white feathers either on the sides of the back or sides of the flanks. Total length 6·5 inches, culmen 0·45, wing 4·95, tail 2·7, tarsus 0·45.

The *female* is described by Dr. Néboux as being smaller than the male, and of a greyish-brown colour.

Hab. Galapagos Islands.

This species is apparently confined to the Galapagos Islands, where it was discovered by the late Mr. Charles Darwin. He found it on James Island, and, during the expedition of the 'Venus,' Dr. Néboux met with it on Charles Island. Dr. Habel, according to Mr. Salvin, saw the species on Indefatigable Island, but did not bring home any specimens.

Mr. Darwin's note on the species is as follows:—

"This bird was observed only on this one island of the group, and it was there very far from common. It frequented a bold cliff of lava overhanging the sea. Had not Mr. Gould characterized it as a distinct species, I should have considered it only as a small variety, produced by an uncongenial site, of the *Progne purpurea*. I can perceive no difference whatever from that bird, excepting in its less size, slenderness of limbs, and less deeply forked tail; and the latter difference may perhaps be owing to youth."

The figure and description are taken from the type specimen in the British Museum.

PROGNE DOMINICENSIS.

PROGNE DOMINICENSIS (Gm.).

CARIBBEAN PURPLE MARTIN.

Hirondelle de S. Domingue, Briss. Orn. ii. p. 493 (1760).
Hirondelle d'Amérique, Daubent. Pl. Enl. vii. pl. 545. fig. 1.
Le Grand Martinet noir à ventre blanc, Montb. Hist. Nat. Ois. vi. p. 669 (1799).
St. Domingo Swallow, Lath. Gen. Syn. ii. pt. 2, p. 573 (1783).
Hirundo dominicensis, Gm. Syst. Nat. i. p. 1025 (1788); Vieill. Ois. Amér. Sept. p. 59, pls. 28, 29 (1807); E. C. Taylor, Ibis, 1864, p. 166.
Hirundo albiventris, Vieill. N. Dict. d'Hist. Nat. xiv. p. 533 (1817).
Progne dominicensis, Gray, Gen. B. i. p. 59 (1845); Jard. Ann. & Mag. Nat. Hist. xviii. p. 120 (1846); Gosse, B. Jamaica, p. 69 (1847); Bp. Consp. i. p. 337 (1850); Sclater, P. Z. S. 1857, p. 232; March, Pr. Philad. Acad. 1863, p. 295; Baird, Review Amer. B. p. 279 (1864); Bryant, Proc. Bost. Soc. N. H. x. p. 252, xi. p. 94 (1866); Gray, Hand-l. B. i. p. 74, no. 891 (1869); Scl. & Salv. Nomencl. Av. Neotr. p. 14 (1873); Scl. P. Z. S. 1876, p. 14; Lawr. Proc. U. S. Nat. Mus. i. pp. 56, 269, 187 (1878); Gundl. J. f. O. 1874, p. 311; A. & E. Newt. Handb. Jamaica, 1881, p. 107; Salv. Cat. Strickl. Coll. p. 153 (1882); Cory, B. Haiti and St. Domingo, p. 14 (1884); Sharpe, Cat. Birds in Brit. Mus. x. p. 176 (1885); Cory, List B. West Indies, p. 10 (1886); id. B. West Ind. p. 70 (1889).

P. pectore et abdomine albis: gutture toto et praepectore late purpureis dorso concoloribus.

Hab. in insulis maris Caribbaei.

Adult male. General colour above glossy purplish blue; the scapulars and lesser wing-coverts like the back; median and greater wing-coverts, bastard-wing, primary-coverts, and quills blackish, externally glossed with dull blue, the inner webs of the quills internally brown; tail-feathers blue-black, browner on the inner webs; lores velvety black; sides of face, ear-coverts, cheeks, throat, chest, and sides of body and flanks glossy purplish blue like the back; centre of breast, abdomen, and under tail-coverts pure white, the lateral under tail-coverts with a shade of dusky slate-colour towards the end of the outer web; the blue breast-feathers adjoining the white centre of the body either edged with white, or else white on the outer web and blue on the inner; thighs dusky brown; on the sides of the breast a few concealed silky-white plumes, adjoining which on the sides of the back is another patch of silky white, which is entirely hidden by the closed wings; axillaries and under wing-coverts glossed with blue; quills dusky blackish below: "iris dark hazel" (*Gosse*). Total length 7 inches, culmen 0·5, wing 5·65, tail 3·25, tarsus 0·55.

Adult female. Duller in colour than the male, but having the same white belly and under tail-coverts. General colour of the upper surface brown, glossed with purplish blue or dull purplish blue, with brown bases to the feathers; throat, chest, and sides of body brown. Total length 7 inches, culmen 0·45, wing 5·45, tail 2·9, tarsus 0·6.

Young. Much browner than the adults, with only a slight blue gloss; quills fringed with whity brown; bill yellow at gape.

The following measurements are taken from the series of specimens in the British Museum:—

				Total length.	Wing.	Tail.	Tarsus.
				in.	in.	in.	in.
a.	♂ ad.	Spanishtown (*W. T. March*)	. . . .	6·9	5·7	2·8	0·5
b.	♂ ad.	Jamaica	,, ...	7·2	5·6	2·8	0·55
c.	♂ ad.	,, (*Mus. Salvin & Godman*)	. . . . .	7·0	5·7	2·8	0·55
d.	Juv.	,, ,, ...		6·8	5·45	2·75	0·55
e.	♀ ad.	,, (*W. T. March*)	. . . .	7·3	5·6	2·8	0·5
f.	♂ ad.	Porto Rico (*H. Bryant*)	. . . .	6·8	5·6	2·8	0·55
g.	♂ ad.	,, ,, ...		6·8	5·8	2·9	0·55
h.	♂ ad.	,, ,, ...		6·9	5·55	2·8	0·5
i.	♀ ad.	,, ,, ...		7·3	5·65	2·8	0·55
k.	♀ ad.	,, ,, ...		6·8	5·5	2·75	0·55
l.	♀ ad.	,, (*Dr. Gundlach*)	. . . .	7·0	5·5	2·55	0·55
m.	Juv.	,, (*Swift*)	. . . .	7·3	5·4	2·6	0·55
n.	Juv.	,, ,, ...		7·3	5·25	2·7	0·55
o.	♀ ad.	,, (*G. Latimer*)	. . . .	7·0	5·5	2·55	0·55
p.	♂ juv.	S. Domingo (*C. G. MacGregor*)	. . . .	6·5	5·55	2·6	0·55
q.	♂ ad.	Dominica (*F. A. Ober*)	. . . .	7·3	5·7	2·8	0·5
r.	♀ ad.	S. Lucia (*Semper*)	. . . .	6·7	5·15	2·45	0·5

The female of *P. dominicensis* and the young birds are very difficult to distinguish from *Progne chalybea*, and, indeed, the young of the two species are quite inseparable. The old female of *P. dominicensis* appears to have the throat more ashy brown than the same sex of *P. chalybea*, which is decidedly duller brown. There are generally also some small dusky shaft-streaks on the throat and breast in *P. chalybea*, of which we can find no trace in *P. dominicensis*.

Hab. S. Domingo, Jamaica, and the Lesser Antilles.

THIS beautiful species is confined to the West-Indian Islands, and is a well-known inhabitant of Jamaica. It also occurs in San Domingo. Mr. Cory found it not uncommon near Samana, and states that although none were taken elsewhere, it is probably abundant in some localities. We have seen several specimens from Porto Rico, where it was found to be very plentiful by Mr. E. C. Taylor in 1863.

In Dominica, Mr. F. Ober writes, "the first seen was shot at Mountain Lake, 2300 feet above the sea-level, on the 23rd of March; later in the season I found a few on the Atlantic side, in June, breeding in the cliffs at Batalie, on the Caribbean shore." The same traveller also met with the species in the islands of Martinique and Grenada. One specimen only was observed on the latter island, and it is probably rarer on the southern islands of the Lesser Antilles. The late Sir William Jardine (Ann. & Mag.

Nat. Hist. xviii. 1846, p. 120) gives an account of *Progne dominicensis* in the island of Tobago, from the notes of Mr. Kirk; but we believe that the species of Purple Martin inhabiting that island will turn out to be *Progne chalybea*, with which *P. dominicensis* was confounded by naturalists for a great many years.

Mr. Gosse gives the following account of the species:—

"In Jamaica it is very common, at least in the lowlands and inferior mountain-ranges, during the summer; some remain with us during the winter, but as there is a very marked diminution of their numbers, I conclude that a large body of them migrate on the approach of that season, probably to Central America. About the end of March we see them in great numbers, assembled early in the morning on the topmost branches of the lofty cotton-trees, which at that season are leafless. On these they crowd so closely, side by side, that I have known five to be killed at one discharge. In the autumn we observe exactly the same habit, and perhaps we may trace some analogy here to those periodical congregations of other species which are known to be connected with migration. . . . .

" . . . . . . The Blue Swallow has the same propensity to bring up his family in darkness as his purple brother. The stipe of an old palm, whose porous centre decays, while the iron fibres of the exterior remain strong, is his ordinary resort. At the beginning of April, I observed several pairs flying in and out of holes, bored, I suppose, by the Woodpecker, in the stipe of a dead cocoanut still tall and erect, but a mere leafless post, tottering in the breeze and ready to fall. At the middle of May, Sam observed several pairs flying in and out of holes, about two inches in diameter, beneath the eaves of Belmont house.

"Near the end of June, when on my way in a coasting-boat from Bluefields to Kingston, I was lying wind-bound in Starvegut Bay. There the inhospitable shore is strewn with immense fragments of limestone rock, honeycombed and fretted into holes, through which the surf breaking furiously, finds vent in perpendicular jets and spouts of water, or in columns of spray resembling steam from an engine-pipe, accompanied with a crashing roar. Yet I observed with interest that the Blue Swallows were frequenting these rocks, and I noticed one repeatedly going in and out of a small hole near the summit of a rugged mass, separated from the shore, and completely isolated from the boiling surf. Lansdown Guilding, in some notes on the Zoology of the Caribbean Islands (Zool. Journ. iii. p. 408), observes: 'We have but few of this family in St. Vincent: among them is a Swallow, which roosts and, I believe, builds in the rock of the sea-shore.' 'It is curious,' he adds, 'to observe the bird in calm weather skimming patiently along the sea in search of insects, evidently ignorant of the fact that they are confined to fresh water, and do not sport on the surface of salt waters.' I cannot agree, however, with this accomplished naturalist here: that the Swallows do occasionally skim over the sea. is undeniable; and that gnats and other minute insects are also in the habit of frequenting the salt water, though not in such numbers as over the fresh ponds and rivers, is no less certain, at least in Jamaica."

Mr. W. T. March has also published the accompanying note on the species in Jamaica:—

"Though sometimes met with domiciled in buildings, the *Progne* still manifests its peculiar predilection for dark places. In the office of the Island Secretary, in Spanish Town, they resort to the ceiled roofs of the upper story, entering through holes found under the eaves, where they live and carry on the work of incubation in total darkness. At each end of the House of Assembly is a hole drilled through the brick wall for the insertion of a pipe for carrying off the surplus water from the drip and water-jars; in consequence of some alterations made in this respect, the pipes were removed and the holes stopped up from within, but left open outwardly; in each of these holes the *Progne* builds every year. In the mountains, caves and hollow trees are chosen for the nesting-places. The nest is composed of an odd mixture of shreds of cloth, silk, paper, leaves, grass, twigs, etc., all loosely put together with a lining of down and feathers. In Spanish Town the nest is composed principally of the soft, flexible portion of the seed-pods of the *Catalpa longissima*. The eggs are round, oval, clear white, 15-16ths by 11-16ths of an inch. The species is musical. It is one of the phases of the naturalist's barometer, as whenever, though the atmosphere be clear and dry, the *Progne* perches on the weather-cock or lightning-rod, on the highest points of the house top, or on the topmost twigs of some lofty tree, chanting its incantation, cloudy weather and rain will surely follow within 24 hours. I believe stragglers of this species remain during the winter months. Several species of the migratory *Hirundines* traverse the island from north to south in the autumn, and from south to north in the spring. They pass in considerable numbers high overhead. Sometimes in squally weather their flight is lower, skimming rapidly along, rarely alighting, and then only for a few seconds. I have on several occasions had some passing glimpses of some alighting for a moment at some water puddle in the road or street, but these opportunities are rare. On one occasion I saw distinctly some large Martins with ashy-blue backs, and others were black Swallows. I observed and heard several flocks pass over in September of 1862, but they were too high to recognize."

The descriptions are from birds in the British Museum, and the figures have been taken from specimens in the Salvin-Godman collection.

PROGNE DOMESTICA (*Vieill.*).

AZARA'S PURPLE MARTIN.

Golondrina domestica, Azara, Apunt. ii. p. 502, no. 300 (1805).
Hirundo domestica, Vieill. N. Dict. d'Hist. Nat. xiv. p. 520 (1817).
Progne domestica, Gray, Gen. B. i. p. 59 (1845); id. Cat. Fissir. Brit. Mus. p. 28 (1848); Bp. Consp. i. p. 337 (1850); Cab. Mus. Hein. Th. i. p. 51 (1850); Burm. La-Plata Reis. ii. p. 477 (1861); Baird, Review Amer. B. p. 282, note (1864); Gray, Hand-l. B. i. p. 75, no. 893 (1869); Scl. & Salv. P. Z. S. 1869, p. 159; Pelz. Orn. Bras. pp. 17, 402 (1871); Sharpe, Cat. Birds in Brit. Mus. x. p. 177 (1885).
Progne dominicensis (nec Gm.), Burm. Th. Bras. iii. p. 141 (1856).
Progne elegans, Gray, Hand-l. B. i. p. 74, no. 888 (1869).
Progne chalybea (nec Gm.), Hudson, P. Z. S. 1872, p. 606; Scl. & Salv. P. Z. S. 1873, p. 258, 1879, p. 495; White, P. Z. S. 1882, p. 595; Barrows, Bull. Nutt. Orn. Club, viii. p. 88 (1883); Scl. & Hudson, Argent. Orn. i. p. 25 (1888).
Progne purpurea (nec L.), Durnford, Ibis, 1877, p. 168; Gibson, Ibis, 1880, p. 22.
Progne chalybea domestica, Berlepsch & Ihering, Zeitschr. ges. Orn. ii. p. 116 (1885).

P. similis *P. chalybeæ*, sed major.

Hab. in Brasiliâ meridionali-orientali et in republicâ Argentinâ.

Adult male. General colour above bright purplish blue, the lesser and median wing-coverts like the back; greater wing-coverts, bastard-wing, primary-coverts, quills, and tail-feathers black, with a gloss of steel-blue externally; lores blackish; ear-coverts and sides of neck glossy purplish blue like the upper parts; cheeks dark smoky brown, tipped minutely with purplish blue; throat and fore neck and chest pale ashy, with minute dusky shaft-lines, and obscured with margins of ashy whitish, broader on the chest where they join the white breast; sides of the upper breast with crescentic tips of purplish blue; breast and abdomen and under tail-coverts pure white; thighs white, with dusky bases; flanks and sides of the body pale smoky brown, with dusky shaft-streaks; a patch of silky-white feathers on the sides of the lower back; feathers on the sides of the rump white with blue centres; axillaries smoky brown washed with blue; under wing-coverts smoky brown, with blackish shaft-stripes, the outer ones edged with white. Total length 8 inches, culmen 0·5, wing 5·75, tail 3·2, tarsus 0·55.

Hab. South-eastern Brazil, Argentine Republic.

This is a large race of the common South-American *Progne chalybea*, and it has usually been considered by naturalists to be identical with that species, but is decidedly worthy of recognition as a race. It is the bird spoken of by Azara as the *Golondrina domestica* of Paraguay, and it is apparently plentiful in the neighbourhood of Buenos Ayres. Dr. von Ihering has procured it at Taquara, in the province of Rio Grande do Sul, and specimens from Santa Catarina are in the Salvin and Godman collection. The examples obtained by Natterer in the neighbourhood of Ypanema and Rio de Janeiro may belong in all probability to this large race of *P. chalybea*.

Dr. Burmeister states that it is common throughout the whole of the La Plata region, and Mr. Hudson states that the extreme limit of its range is about 250 miles south of the city of Buenos Ayres. He observes:—"It was well called '*Golondrina domestica*' by Azara, being pre-eminently a domestic bird in its habits. It never breeds in banks, as the Patagonian Purple Martin often does, or in the domed nests of other birds in trees, a situation always resorted to by the Tree-Martin, and occasionally by our Common Swallow; but is so accustomed to the companionship of man, as to make its home in populous towns as well as in country-houses. It arrives in Buenos Ayres about the middle of September, and apparently resorts to the same breeding-place every year. A hole under the eaves is usually selected, and the nest is roughly built of dry grass, hair, feathers, and other materials. When the entrance to its breeding-hole is too large, it closes it up with mud mixed with straw; if there be two entrances, it stops up one altogether. The bird does not often require to use mud in building; it is the only one of our Swallows that uses such a material at all. The eggs are white, long, pointed, and five in number.

"In the season of courtship this Martin is a noisy, pugnacious bird, and always, when quitting its nest, utters an exceedingly loud startling cry, several times repeated. It also has a song, uttered both when resting and when on the wing, composed of several agreeable modulated notes, and in a thick rolling intonation peculiar to our Swallows. This song does not sound loud when near, yet it can be distinctly heard when the bird appears but a speck in the distance. I may here remark that, with the exception of the *Petrochelidon pyrrhonota*, which possesses a sharp squeaky voice, like the Swallows of Europe, all our Hirundines have soft voices: their usual twittering when they are circling about resembles somewhat the chirping of the English House-Sparrow in tone, but besides these notes they possess a song more pleasing to the ear. Before leaving in February, these birds congregate in parties of from twenty to four or five hundred, usually on the broad leafy top of an old ombú tree."

This is doubtless the species spoken of by Mr. Durnford and Mr. Gibson under the name of *P. purpurea*, as nesting near Buenos Ayres. In the 'Catalogue of Birds' we referred their notices to *Progne furcata*, but Mr. Hudson expressly states that this species does not breed in the above-mentioned locality. Mr. Durnford says:—

"The dates of arrival and departure of this bird are about the same as those of *P. tapera*. The young are on the wing early in February. Common both in the town and country, breeding freely in chinks in walls, under the eaves of houses, and holes in trees. Pre-eminently a homely bird. During the summer its loud harsh notes, uttered whilst on the wing, may be constantly heard, but when resting on a telegraph-wire or twig of a tree it has quite a pretty little song."

Mr. Gibson's note is as follows:—

"Abundant near Buenos Ayres; coming in the first week of September, and leaving about the end of March. Immediately on their arrival they begin to examine their old nesting-sites; but the eggs do not seem to be laid till much later, and I have taken fresh ones towards the end of November. These sites are crannies in the eaves or gables of any building, or various similar situations; but the nest is never so isolated from one contiguous beam or wall as to necessitate its being entirely built of mud, that material being only used to close up the open sides and leave but one entrance-hole. The mud is very coarsely mixed, sometimes with a good deal of grass in it. The lining consists merely of some dry grass. One of their favourite localities is a beam underneath the eaves of our large wool-store, just at the doorway. It says much for their familiarity that the constant traffic does not deter them from building there. The eggs are of a beautiful white, pear-shaped, and average $\frac{31}{10} \times \frac{24}{100}$; six is the largest clutch I have taken."

He likewise observes:—"There were two entirely black specimens which used to appear annually at the head station; but I have not seen them for the last year or two." These were probably *P. purpurea* on a winter visit from North America, but they may well have been *P. furcata*. At any rate the mere fact that such a careful observer as Mr. Gibson thinks it worth while to allude to these wholly Black Martins as distinct from the ordinary species of Buenos Ayres seems to prove that one of the above-named species occasionally visits Buenos Ayres.

Mr. Barrows, in his account of the Birds of Lower Uruguay, writes as follows:—

"All the Swallows are known as '*Golondrinas*,' and when it is desired to indicate a particular species an appropriate adjective is used. The present species arrives at Concepcion from the north somewhat later than the smaller Swallows, and is not so abundant, though its voice is usually heard at any hour of the day during the breeding-season. During October and November the nests are built—usually in hollows—beneath the eaves of houses and sheds. On October 22nd, 1880, I spent nearly the whole afternoon in watching several hundreds of this species and *P. tapera*, catching dragon-flies. A high, cold, south wind ('pampero') was blowing, and the dragon-flies were massed by thousands on the leeward sides of the bushes near the top of a bluff. Benumbed with the cold they only flew when hard pressed, and were then almost inevitably swept by the wind directly into the waiting mouths of the birds. Selecting a bush on which a peck or two of the insects were clinging, I would dislodge them by a sudden shake, and in an instant they became the centre of a flock of voracious birds, which seemed to have lost all fear, and were intent only on the helpless insects, which were snapped up often within a foot or two of my face.

"The dragon-flies were of a medium size, having a spread of perhaps 2½ to 3 inches. They did not cling to each other like bees or locusts, but simply crowded as near as possible, clinging so thickly to twigs and leaves as to hide entirely the colour of the foliage, and transform green mimosas into shapeless masses of grey and brown."

This species so closely resembles *Progne chalybea* that we do not consider it worth while to figure it.

PROGNE CHALYBEA

PROGNE CHALYBEA (Gm.).

WHITE-BELLIED PURPLE MARTIN.

Hirondelle de Cayenne, Briss. Orn. ii. p. 495, pl. xlv. fig. 1 (1760).
Chalybeate Swallow, Lath. Gen. Syn. ii. pt. 2, p. 574 (1783).
Hirundo chalybea, Gm. Syst. Nat. i. p. 1026 (1788); Neuwied, Beitr. Naturg. Bras. iii. p. 354 (1830).
Cecropis chalybea, Less. Compl. Buff. viii. p. 498 (1837).
Progne chalybea, Gray, Gen. B. i. p. 59 (1845); id. Cat. Fissir. Brit. Mus. p. 28 (1848); Bp. Consp. i. p. 337 (1850); Cab. Mus. Hein. Th. i. p. 51 (1850); Cass. Ill. B. Calif. p. 246 (1850); Cab. J. f. O. 1860, p. 402; Cass. Proc. Philad. Acad. 1860, p. 133; Lawr. Ann. Lyc. N. Y. vii. p. 318 (1861); Baird, Review Amer. B. p. 282, note (1864); Scl. & Salv. P. Z. S. 1864, p. 348; Gray, Hand-l. B. i. p. 74, no. 887 (1869); Layard, Ibis, 1873, pp. 375, 377; Scl. & Salv. Nomencl. Av. Neotr. p. 14 (1873); iid. P. Z. S. 1873, p. 258, 1879, p. 495; Salv. Cat. Strickl. Coll. p. 154 (1882); id. & Godm. Biol. Centr.-Amer., Aves, i. p. 224 (1883); Tacz. Orn. Pérou, i. p. 237 (1884); Sharpe, Cat. Birds in Brit. Mus. x. p. 178 (1885); Salvin, Ibis, 1885, p. 205.
Progne domestica (non V.), Gray, Cat. Fissir. Brit. Mus. p. 28 (1848).
Progne dominicensis (non L.), Gray, Cat. Fissir. Brit. Mus. p. 28 (1848); Cab. Mus. Hein. Th. i. p. 51 (1850); Cass. Cat. Hirund. Mus. Philad. Acad. p. 10 (1853); Sclater, P. Z. S. 1857, p. 201, 1859, p. 364, 1860, p. 292; Scl. & Salv. Ibis, 1859, p. 13; Salv. Ibis, 1859, p. 466; G. C. Taylor, Ibis, 1860, p. 110; Owen, Ibis, 1861, p. 61; Sclater, Cat. Amer. B. p. 38 (1862); Salvin, Ibis, 1866, p. 203; Von Frantz. J. f. O. 1869, p. 294; Sclater, P. Z. S. 1872, p. 606, note.
Progne purpurea (non L.), Cab. in Schomb. Reis. Guian. iii. p. 671 (1848).
Progne leucogastra, Baird, Review Amer. B. p. 280 (1864); Scl. & Salv. P. Z. S. 1867, pp. 569, 749, 754; Lawr. Ann. Lyc. N. Y. ix. p. 96 (1868); Gray, Hand-l. B. i. p. 75, no. 892 (1869); Sumichr. Mem. Bost. Soc. N. H. i. p. 547 (1869); Scl. & Salv. P. Z. S. 1870, p. 836; Wyatt, Ibis, 1871, p. 323; Lawr. Bull. U. S. Nat. Mus. no. 4, p. 17 (1876); Ridgw. Pr. U. S. Nat. Mus. iii. p. 175 (1880); Nutting, op. cit. v. p. 391 (1882).

P. suprà nitide chalybeo-nigra: subtùs alba, gutture et præpectore fumoso-brunneis lateraliter purpureo mixtis.

Hab. in Americâ centrali et in Americâ meridionali usque ad Boliviam et Brasiliam meridionalem.

Adult male. General colour above glossy dark purple, with a concealed spot of white on the sides of the lower back, the feathers composing this spot being white, with more or less purple towards the tip of the inner web; lesser and median wing-coverts like the back; greater coverts, bastard-wing, primary-coverts, and quills black, externally dull blue; upper tail-coverts like the back; tail-feathers blackish glossed with blue; lores velvety black; cheeks and ear-coverts black washed with purplish blue; throat and chest dark smoky brown, the fore neck and chest with hoary grey margins to the feathers, the throat rather darker and having dusky blackish shaft-stripes; sides of the upper breast more or less purplish blue, the feathers tipped with the latter colour, which extends some way down the sides of the body; entire abdomen, flanks, and under tail-coverts white; the white feathers of the lower breast where they adjoin the brown throat washed with smoky brown and having blackish shaft-streaks; axillaries dark purplish blue with brown bases; under wing-coverts dark sooty brown washed with blue; quills dusky below, lighter brown along their inner face: "bill brownish horn-black; legs dark fleshy brown; iris dark greyish brown" (*Neuwied*). Total length 6·6 inches, culmen 0·55, wing 5, tail 2·75, tarsus 0·5.

The *female* differs from the male in being duller blue and not so purple, but is otherwise similarly coloured. On the sides of the upper breast the blue ends to the feathers are less conspicuous and duller blue.

Young. Much more dingily coloured than the adults. Above sooty-brown slightly glossed with blue, the feathers having more or less obsolete pale margins; wing-coverts also dull blue with pale brown edges; quills and tail-feathers blackish glossed with steel-blue or greenish; lores dusky; cheeks, ear-coverts, and sides of neck brown, as well as the sides of the breast and flanks; throat and chest pale brown, the feathers of the latter edged with white; breast, abdomen, and under tail-coverts pure white; axillaries smoky brown; under wing-coverts brown edged with white. Tail less forked than in the adult.

Sometimes the under tail-coverts exhibit a brown shaft-streak, and still more rarely a pale shade of brown in the centre, but never to the extent of *P. purpurea* or *P. furcata.* The white belly and under tail-coverts in both the old and young birds are generally sufficient to distinguish the species.

The wing varies somewhat in specimens from different localities, as will be seen from the following list:—

Those from	Mexico		have the wing			5·45	inches.
,,	,,	Yucatan	,,	,,	,,	5·15	,,
,,	,,	Guatemala	,,	,,	,,	5·1–5·65	,,
,,	,,	Honduras	,,	,,	,,	5·3	,,
,,	,,	Costa Rica	,,	,,	,,	5·0–5·3	,,
,,	,,	Panama	,,	,,	,,	5·05–5·45	,,
,,	,,	Colombia	,,	,,	,,	5·0	,,
,,	,,	Ecuador	,,	,,	,,	5·3	,,
,,	,,	Trinidad	,,	,,	,,	5·0	,,
,,	,,	Guiana	,,	,,	,,	4·9–5·15	,,
,,	,,	Upper Amazons	,,	,,	,,	4·7–5·0	,,
,,	,,	Para	,,	,,	,,	5·0–5·3	,,
,,	,,	Bolivia	,,	,,	,,	5·4	,,

Thus it appears that the Central-American specimens are, on the whole, a little larger than those from South America.

The changes of plumage in this species are not properly understood, and whether seasonal differences exist we have not been able to make out. The young birds are brown with scarcely any gloss, and whatever lustre there be is of a greenish tint. There seems to be nothing of the pale-edged feathers which are found in the young of *P. purpurea*, and in most specimens of the latter there are distinct purple spots on the upper throat.

In the breeding-season the throat becomes extremely dark, and there are distinct blue-tipped feathers on the sides of the fore neck and chest. In the winter plumage adults apparently have ashy margins to the feathers of these parts, but we have not been able to trace the changes at different seasons with any degree of certainty. At one period of its life *P. purpurea* has a white breast, and is very similar to *P. chalybea*. It has, however, always a longer wing (5·15–5·9), and has the breast more coarsely streaked with blackish shaft-lines. There are generally also some blue feathers on the chin or throat, which proclaim the species.

Hab. Throughout Central America and the greater part of South America, as far as Southern Brazil and Bolivia.

BRISSON appears to have been the first naturalist to describe this Purple Martin, calling it 'L'Hirondelle de Cayenne.' Neither his description nor his figure are sufficiently accurate to determine for a certainty that they were intended for *P. chalybea*, and not for a young individual of *P. purpurea*, a species which also visits Cayenne in its migrations.

The references to Montbeillard (Hist. Nat. Ois. vi. p. 675) and to Daubenton (Pl. Enl. vii. pl. 545. fig. 2), made by us in the 'Catalogue of Birds,' do not seem really to refer to the present species, though they are considered by both Latham and Gmelin so to do. Latham's description, however, of the 'Chalybeate Swallow' answers tolerably to our bird, and this name Gmelin latinized into *Hirundo chalybea*, by which title the species is now widely known and recognized by the best authorities.

Mr. Cassin included this species in his 'Birds of California,' where, he says, it was first met with by Mr. John Bell of New York, but he himself subsequently saw several examples from that country. Mr. Ridgway (Proc. U. S. Nat. Mus. iii. p. 236) has very properly placed the species amongst those whose claim to be considered North-American is doubtful, and there can be no question that Cassin mistook a stage of *P. purpurea* for *P. chalybea*.

The records of most observers in the field are very similar with regard to the habits of this species, and it appears to breed throughout the wide extent of country recorded below. In Mexico it has been met with by Sallé at S. Andres Tuxtla, at Jalapa by De Oca, and in the Isthmus of Tehuantepec by the late Colonel Grayson. Professor Sumichrast states that it inhabits the hot and temperate region, and is found on the shores of both oceans, but does not extend into the department of Vera Cruz, further than to the height of 1200 metres. It nests at Orizaba in the steeples of churches and old buildings.

In Guatemala it was noticed in many places by Messrs. Salvin and Godman, but principally in the low-lying districts, the greatest height at which the travellers observed it being Dueñas, nearly 5000 feet above the sea. Mr. R. Owen forwarded the eggs from San Gerónimo. Capt. Dow procured it at Acajutla in the State of San Salvador, and Mr. Salvin noticed the species at La Union.

Mr. Dyson forwarded specimens from Honduras, where also Mr. G. Whitely met with it. Mr. G. C. Taylor writes from the same country:—"Swallows were common, especially at Comayagua and in the neighbourhood of churches. I shot one on the wing, while standing in the Plaza, in front of the Cathedral in Comayagua, to the great astonishment of many of the inhabitants, who had evidently never before seen anything shot while in motion. It measured 7 inches in length, and 13½ in extent." In Costa Rica it has been sent from San José by Hoffmann, and Von Frantzius states that it occurs mostly in the towns. Arcé sent specimens from Nicoya, where Mr. Nutting also found it abundant. M'Leannan procured it near Lion Hill Station in Panama, and Arcé on the Volcano of Chiriqui.

In Colombia Mr. Wyatt states that he shot immature specimens at Catamucho, in the Magdalena valley. Mr. Salvin met with it at Remedios, in Antioquia, and a specimen procured by Mr. L. Fraser at Esmeraldas, in Ecuador, is in the Sclater Collection. We have not seen any examples from Venezuela, though the species doubtless occurs in that country, and a specimen from Trinidad is in the British Museum. Throughout Guiana it is also dispersed, Mr. C. Bartlett having procured it at Albina, in Surinam, and Mr. Whitely having sent a considerable series from Bartica Grove, in British Guiana.

Mr. Wallace's collection contained specimens from the island of Mexiana and from Pará. Writing from the latter place, Mr. E. L. Layard says:—"I first saw this large Swallow on Christmas-day. A little flock of them were flying to and out of a hole in a hollow tree in the square near my house; some of them carried dry grass bents, apparently, and portions of soft lichens gathered from trees. On the 28th I shot one, a female, with the ovaries much distended. No others were about that day; but I subsequently procured them in the same locality, and at a farm-house near Pará. They perch readily and habitually on trees."

Mr. Edward Bartlett met with this species in many places in Eastern Peru, viz. at Xeberos, Urimaguas, Chyavetas, and Camicuros, and he says that it "breeds like a Woodpecker, in holes and trunks of trees."

Prince Maximilian does not apparently distinguish between the ordinary *P. chalybea* and the larger race, *P. domestica*. He says "it is the commonest Swallow in Brazil, where it affects human habitations, after the manner of the House-Martin and Swallow of Europe. Like these, it has a swift and graceful flight, and they are fond of perching on lofty buildings and the crosses on the churches, where whole rows of them may be seen. In the districts away from mankind, and on the remote sea-coast, as, for instance, between the estuaries of the rivers Doçe and Riacho and other places, where there are rocks in the sea, these Swallows doubtless nest in the clefts of some of the ledges; but whether they do so in the holes of the clay-built walls, I cannot affirm for certain.

They are everywhere known by the name of *Andorinha*, like the rest of the Swallows." The remarks made by the author about the changes of plumage show that the Prince confounded this species and *P. purpurea* together, as he speaks of the full-plumaged birds as being entirely blue.

The localities given by Herr von Pelzeln for the Swallows collected by Natterer show that he also did not regard *P. domestica* as a distinct race. The specimens obtained by Natterer at Caiçara were probably *P. chalybea*, while those from Ypanema and Rio de Janeiro were in all likelihood *P. domestica*. One specimen collected by Mr. Bridges in Bolivia is in the British Museum.

The eggs of this species sent from Guatemala by Mr. R. Owen were white and measured: axis ·85, diam. ·65 inch.

The description of the plumage is taken from the series in the National Collection, while the figures are drawn from specimens in the Salvin-Godman Collection.

PROGNE TAPERA

PROGNE TAPERA (*L.*).

TREE-MARTIN.

L'Hirondelle de l'Amérique, Briss. Orn. ii. p. 502, pl. 15. fig. 3 (1760).
Hirundo tapera, Linn. Syst. Nat. i. p. 345 (1766).
Golondrina de la Parda, Azara, Apunt. ii. p. 505 (1805).
Hirundo fusca, Vieill. N. Dict. d'Hist. Nat. xiv. p. 510 (1817); Baird, Review Amer. B. p. 285.
Hirundo pascuum, Neuwied, Beitr. Naturg. Bras. iii. p. 360 (1830).
Cecropis tapera, Less. Compl. Buff. viii. p. 498 (1837).
Progne fusca, Gray, Gen. B. i. p. 59 (1845); id. Cat. Fissir. Brit. Mus. p. 28 (1848); Bp. Consp. i. p. 337 (1850); Cab. Mus. Hein. Th. i. p. 51 (1850); Cass. Cat. Hirund. Mus. Philad. Acad. p. 10 (1853); Gray, Hand-l. B. i. p. 75, no. 895 (1869).
Progne tapera, Cab. in Schomb. Reis. Guian. iii. p. 672 (1848); id. Mus. Hein. Th. i. p. 51 (1850); Cass. Cat. Hirund. Mus. Philad. Acad. p. 10 (1853); Sclater, Cat. Amer. B. p. 38 (1862); id. & Salv. P. Z. S. 1866, p. 178, 1867, pp. 569, 749, 1868, pp. 139, 627; Wyatt, Ibis, 1871, p. 323; Scl. P. Z. S. 1872, p. 606; id. & Salv. Nomencl. Av. Neotr. p. 14 (1873); iid. P. Z. S. 1873, p. 258, 1879, p. 595; Tacz. P. Z. S. 1877, p. 320; Durnford, Ibis, 1877, p. 168; Gibson, Ibis, 1880, p. 23; White, P. Z. S. 1882, p. 595; Salv. Cat. Strickl. Coll. p. 154 (1882); Barrows, Bull. Nutt. Orn. Club, viii. p. 89 (1883); Tacz. Orn. Pérou, i. p. 236 (1884); Sharpe, Cat. Birds in Brit. Mus. x. pp. 180, 633 (1885); Scl. & Hudson, Argent. Orn. i. p. 26 (1888).
Progne pascuum, Bp. Consp. i. p. 337 (1850); Gray, Hand-l. B. i. p. 75, no. 896 (1869).
Cotyle tapera, Burm. Th. Bras. iii. p. 143 (1856); id. Reis. La-Plata, ii. p. 477 (1861).
Progne (*Phæoprogne*) *tapera*, Baird, Review Amer. B. p. 286 (1864).
Progne (*Phæoprogne*) *fusca*, Baird, t. c. p. 285 (1864).
Petrochelidon tapera, Pelz. Orn. Bras. p. 17 (1871).
Cotyle tapera, Burm. Th. Bras. iii. p. 143 (1856).
Progne (*Phæoprogne*) *tapera*, Baird, Review Amer. B. p. 286 (1864).
Progne (*Phæoprogne*) *fusca*, Baird, t. c. p. 285 (1864).
Petrochelidon tapera, Pelz. Orn. Bras. p. 17 (1871).

P. brunnea, præpectore dorso concolore: gulâ et corpore subtùs albis, pectore medio brunneo ovatim maculato.

Hab. in regione Neotropicâ.

Adult. General colour above glossy brown; the wing-coverts dark brown, edged with whity brown; bastard-wing, primary-coverts, and quills blackish brown, with scarcely any paler margins, excepting on the secondaries, the innermost of which are paler brown externally, with whity-brown margins near the tips; upper tail-coverts like the back, with slight indications of paler edges, more or less obsolete; tail-feathers blackish brown, with a narrow fringe of whity brown along the edge towards the tip of the inner web; crown of head brown, the forehead blackish, the rest of the crown slightly mottled with blackish centres to the feathers; lores dusky brown; ear-coverts uniform brown; cheeks paler and more ashy brown; throat ashy white; fore neck and chest ashy brown in the centre, darker brown on the sides as well as on the sides of the body and flanks, the feathers on the lower flanks being white externally, brown internally; breast, abdomen, thighs, and under tail-coverts white; in the centre of the breast a longitudinal streak of dark brown, the feathers forming which are dark brown on the inner and whitish on the outer webs; axillaries and under wing-coverts brown, with whitish tips to the feathers; quills dusky brown below, more ashy brown along the inner face of the quills: "legs blackish brown; bill dark horn greyish brown; iris dark" (*Neuwied*). Total length 7 inches, culmen 0·5, wing 5·5, tail 2·65, tarsus 0·55.

The sexes are alike in plumage, and the following are the dimensions of the series in the British Museum :—

		Total length. in.	Wing. in.	Tail. in.	Tarsus. in.
a. Ad.	Rio Grande (*Plant*)	7·0	5·5	2·7	0·6
b. Ad.	La Plata (*W. H. Hudson*)	7·0	5·35	2·55	0·5
c. ♀ ad.	Buenos Ayres (*E. W. White*)	6·7	4·9	2·5	0·5
d. ♂ ♀ ad.	Oran, Salta (*E. W. White*)	6·7	5·4	2·5	0·5
e. ♀ ad.	,, ,,	6·3	4·75	2·3	0·5
f. Ad.	Bolivia (*Bridges*)	7·0	5·45	2·7	0·5
g, h. ♂ ad.	Matto Grosso (*H. Smith*)	6·5	5·8	2·1–2·7	0·5
i. ♀ ad.	,, ,,	6·5	5·05	2·5	0·5
k. ♀ ad.	Carityba (*J. Notterer*)	6·0	5·0	2·2	0·45
l, m, n. Ad.	Bahia	6·5	5·0–5·3	2·5	0·5
o, p. Ad.	Pernambuco (*W. A. Forbes*)	6·0	4·8	2·1–2·3	0·5
q. Ad.	Rio Tocantins (*A. R. Wallace*)	6·1	5·2	2·5	0·5
r, s. ♂ ad.	Upper Ucayali (*E. Bartlett*)	6·2–6·7	5·2–5·4	2·5	0·5
t. ♀ ad.	,, ,,	6·3	4·8	2·4	0·5
u, v, w, x. ♂ ad.	Yquitos (*H. Whitely*)	6·5	4·9–5·2	2·3–2·6	0·45–0·5
y, z, a'. ♀ ad.	,, ,,	6·0	4·8–4·9	2·35	0·5
b', c'. Ad.	Santa Rita, Ecuador (*Villagomez*)	6·5	4·9–5·1	2·6	0·5
d'. ♀ ad.	Puerto Cabello (*A. Goering*)	5·8	4·75	2·2	0·5
e'. Ad.	Corentyn River (*E. im Thurn*)	5·2	4·7	2·1	0·5

A young bird, recognizable by its swollen yellow gape, differs from the adult in having distinct whitish fringes to the end of the quills and in being much paler brown. The tail is perfectly square, and the whole of the lower throat, fore neck, chest, and sides of breast are almost uniform brown, leaving the chin and upper throat, breast, abdomen, and under tail-coverts white. One immature specimen in the Museum, from Bahia, has a yellowish tinge on the abdomen.

The ovate drops of dark brown colour on the breast are developed to a greater extent during the breeding-season, if indeed they are not the principal evidences of nuptial plumage. They are never seen in young birds, and there are many specimens in the British Museum which have no trace whatever of these spots on the breast, being, moreover, almost entirely uniform hoary white underneath, excepting for a brownish shade on the fore neck and chest. The irregularity which characterizes the brown spots on the chest in these hoary specimens confirms our opinion that they are only developed when the nesting-season approaches.

At first we were inclined to think that the absence of these brown spots on the breast was only noticeable in specimens from northern localities, and certainly in a series from some places, such as Bahia, whence there are several specimens in the British Museum, not a single one has a trace of spots on the breast, whereas every one from the neighbourhood of Buenos Ayres (where the bird breeds) has these spots extremely well developed and the entire plumage very dark. All these specimens, however, are adult, and it is much to be desired that the young from the nest should be examined by a competent observer and the first plumage carefully described.

Hab. The greater part of South America.

The habits of this species, as detailed below, and the totally different style of plumage, present such a variation from the purple appearance of the ordinary members of the genus *Progne*, that there is a good deal to be said in favour of its separation under the subgeneric heading of *Phæoprogne*.

Our chief knowledge of the Tree-Martin is derived from observers in the Argentine Republic, and excellent notes on the species will be found below. The late Mr. Henry Durnford states that it arrives in the neighbourhood of Buenos Ayres in September, nests, and leaves about the first week in April. Mr. Hudson has collected many specimens near Conchitas, and Mr. E. W. White sent some from Oran in the Salta district, Monte Grande, and Pacheco. Prof. Burmeister met with it in the eastern La Plata districts, and states that it was not rare near Parana. In Uruguay, Mr. Barrows notices its arrival about the same time as *Progne purpurea*, viz. about the middle of September. The Smithsonian Institution possesses examples from the Rio Vermejo.

It extends to Bolivia, where d'Orbigny met with it in the province of Chiquitos, and a specimen obtained in that country by Mr. Bridges is in the British Museum. In Brazil, writes Prof. Burmeister, it is an inhabitant of the Campos districts in the interior, but is nowhere very common. It does not live in the woods there, but frequents the scattered bushes on the Campos, hunting for insects, nesting in old trees, and avoiding the neighbourhood of man. The localities where Natterer observed the species were the following:—Porto do Rio Araguay (October); Eugenho do Cap. Ant. Correia (December); Cuyaba (July, September); Caiçara (January, October, and November); Maribatanas, (April); Barra do Rio Negro (February). He states that it was common in Cuyaba, living in the deserted nests of *Furnarius rufus*, and that it goes away at the beginning of winter. Several specimens were procured by Mr. and Mrs. Herbert Smith at Chapada, in the province of Matto Grosso, in September and October. The specimens from this expedition in the Salvin-Godman collection are three in number, and they are quite pale, but show the spots on the breast very plainly. All the brown pectoral spots are edged with hoary white like the rest of the under surface, and we believe that it is by the wearing off of these pale edges that the spots are developed in the breeding-plumage.

The late Mr. W. A. Forbes met with the species near Pernambuco during his stay there from July to September. Several specimens collected by Wucherer and other naturalists near Bahia are in the Museum collection, and the late Prince Neuwied found the species on the Campos Geraes in the interior of the province of Bahia.

In Amazonia the species was procured by Mr. Wallace on the Rio Tocantins. We have already referred to its occurrence on the Rio Negro, as reported by Natterer, who found it common on the right bank in December. Mr. Henry Whitely procured a large series at Yquitos on the Upper Amazons in June, July, and August. Scarcely any of these specimens show a trace of the pectoral spots, and a good many have whitish edges to the feathers of the upper surface. Mr. E. Bartlett found it at Xeberos and on the Upper and Lower Ucayali, where, he states, "it is common, and breeds in large numbers in all the country visited." Three specimens from the Upper Ucayali, now in the British Museum, were procured in May, August, and September respectively. Mr. Stolzmann found this Martin very common at Tumbez, and nesting; it was not observed south of this place.

In the Salvin-Godman collection are two specimens from the Santa Rita mountains in Ecuador, received from Mr. Villagomez, and the Sclater collection contains examples from Bogotà. In the Magdalena Valley Mr. Wyatt found this species ascending the Cordillera to some 4000 or 5000 feet; they were nesting at the end of January. Mr. A. Goering procured an example at Puerto Cabello, in Venezuela, in June.

In the Sclater collection is a specimen from British Guiana, obtained on the Corentyn River by Mr. im Thurn.

The record of localities does not explain where is the winter home of all the individuals which breed in Southern Brazil and the Argentine Republic.

Mr. W. H. Hudson gives a very interesting notice of the species in 'Argentine Ornithology':—

"The Tree-Martin is a very garrulous bird, and no sooner arrives, early in September, than we are apprised of the circumstance by the notes which the male and female incessantly sing in concert, fluttering and waving their wings the while, and seeming quite beside themselves with joy at their safe arrival; for invariably they arrive already mated. Their language is more varied, the intonation bolder and freer than that of our other Swallows. The length of the notes can be varied at pleasure; some are almost harsh, others silvery or liquid, as of trickling drops of water; they all have a glad sound; and many have that peculiar character of some bird-notes of shaping themselves into words.

"This Martin is never seen to alight on the ground or on the roofs of houses, but solely on trees; and when engaged in collecting materials for its nest, it sweeps down and snatches up a feather or straw without touching the surface. It breeds only in the clay-ovens of the Oven-bird (*Furnarius rufus*). I, at least, have never seen them breed in any other situation after observing them for a great many summers. An extraordinary habit! for, many as are the species that possess the parasitical tendency of breeding in other birds' nests, none of them confine themselves to the nest of a single species excepting the bird I am describing. It must, however, be understood that my knowledge of this bird has been acquired in Buenos Ayres, where I have observed it; and as this Martin possesses a wider range in South America than the Oven-birds, it is more than probable that in other districts it builds in different situations.

"On arriving in spring each pair takes up its position on some tree, and usually on a particular branch; a dead branch extending beyond the foliage is a favourite perch. Here they spend much of their time, never appearing to remain long absent from it, and often, when singing their notes together, fluttering about it with a tremulous uncertain flight, like that of a hovering butterfly. About three weeks after first arriving they begin to make advances towards the Oven-bird's nest that stands on the nearest post or tree; and if it be still occupied by the rightful owners, after much time has been spent in sporting about and reconnoitring it, a feud begins which is often exceedingly violent and protracted for many days.

"In seasons favourable to them the Oven-birds build in autumn and winter, and breed early in spring; so that their broods are out of their clay-houses by the end of October or earlier; when this happens, the Swallow that breeds in November quietly takes possession of the forsaken fortress. But accidents will happen, even to the wonderful fabric of the Oven-bird. It is sometimes destroyed and must be rebuilt; or its completion has perhaps been retarded for months by drought, or by the poor condition of the birds in severe weather; or the first brood has perhaps perished, destroyed by an opossum or other enemy. November, and even December, may thus arrive before some pairs have hatched their eggs; and it is these unfortunate late breeders that suffer from the violence of the marauding Swallows. I have often witnessed the wars of these birds with the deepest interest; and in many ovens that I have opened I have found the eggs of the Oven-birds buried under the nests of the Swallows. After the Swallows have taken up a position near the coveted oven, they occasionally fly towards and hover about it, returning again to their stand. By-and-by, instead of returning as at first, they take to alighting at the entrance of the coveted home; this is a sort of declaration of war, and marks the beginning of hostilities. The Oven-birds, full of alarm and anger, rush upon and repel them as often as they approach; they retire before this furious onset, but not discomfited, and only warbling out their gay, seemingly derisive, notes in answer to the outrageous indignant screams of their enemies. Soon they return; the scene is repeated; and this desultory skirmishing is often continued for many days.

"But at length the lawless invaders, grown bolder, and familiar with their strength and resources, will no longer fly from the master of the house; desperate struggles now frequently take place at the entrance, the birds again and again dropping to the ground clutched fiercely together, and again hurrying up only to resume the combat. Victory at last declares itself for the aggressors, and they busy themselves carrying in materials for their nest, screaming their jubilant notes all the time as if in token of triumph.

"The brave and industrious Oven-birds, dispossessed of their home, retire to spend their childless summer together, for the male and female never separate; and when the autumn rains have supplied them with wet clay, and the sense of defeat is worn off, they cheerfully begin their building-operations afresh. This is not, however, the invariable result of the conflict. To the superior swiftness of the Martin the Oven-bird opposes greater strength, and, it might be added, a greater degree of zeal and fury than can animate its adversary. The contest is thus nearly an equal one; and the Oven-bird, particularly when its young are already hatched, is often able to maintain its own. But the Martins never suffer defeat; for when unable to take the citadel by storm, they fall back on their dribbling system of warfare, which they keep up till the young leave the nest, when they take possession before it has grown cold.

"The Martin makes its own nest chiefly of large feathers, and lays four eggs, long, pointed, and pure white.

"It will be remarked that in all its habits above mentioned this bird differs widely from the preceding species. It also differs greatly from them in its manner of flight. The Purple Martins move with surprising grace and celerity, the wings extended to their utmost; they also love to sail in circles high up in the air, or about the summits of tall trees, and particularly during a high wind. At such times several individuals are usually seen together, and all seem striving to outvie each other in the beauty of their evolutions.

"The Tree-Martin is never seen to soar about in circles; and though when hawking after flies and moths it sweeps the surface of the grass with amazing swiftness, at other times it has a flight strangely slow and of a fashion peculiar to itself: the long wings are depressed as much as those of a Wild Duck when dropping on to the water, and are constantly agitated with tremulous flutterings, short and rapid as those of a butterfly.

"Neither is this bird gregarious like all its congeners, though occasionally an individual associates for a while with Swallows of another species; but this only when they are resting on fences or trees, for as soon as they take flight it leaves them. Once or twice, when for some mysterious cause the autumnal migration has been delayed long past its usual time, I have seen them unite in small flocks; but this is very rare. As a rule they have no meetings preparatory to migration, but skim about the fields and open plains in un-Swallow-like solitude, and suddenly disappear without having warned us of their intended departure."

Mr. Durnford and Mr. Gibson have also given interesting accounts of the habits of this species near Buenos Ayres. The former gentleman observes:—"It has a peculiar habit of raising its wings over its back in the midst of its aerial evolutions, and then dropping some distance through the air before taking flight again. In the summer these birds congregate in large parties, and seem never tired of circling about the topmost branches of some wide-spreading ombo-tree, which is their favourite resort."

Mr. Gibson has likewise only found it breeding in the Oven-bird's nest, which, he says, "it lines with a pile of feathers formed into a nest. Grass, wool, and hair are sometimes added; but the feathers are the principal material, and the amount is usually sufficient to fill up the interior of the Oven-bird's nest. The eggs, so far as I know, never exceed five in number, are pure white, and average $\frac{10}{10} \times \frac{13}{16}$."

He believes it to be as abundant near Buenos Ayres as *P. purpurea**, but says that, owing to its frequenting the woods and from the nature of its nidification, it is more diffused and appears scarcer. "It is also about a month later in coming, appearing in the first week in October, though it leaves at the same time as *P. purpurea**, the end of March. As it arrives after the last-named species, it is proportionately later in breeding, while, from being parasitical on *Furnarius rufus*, the date of its nesting varies greatly. Eggs are most generally taken in December; but I once found a nestful of young birds (full-fledged, it is true) as late as the beginning of March."

Mr. White fancied that this Martin was not particular as to the locality in which it breeds; and in Uruguay Mr. Barrows thinks that they may nest in natural hollows of trees, as he noticed several hovering about Woodpeckers' holes in a tall dead tree, though he also found it appropriating the deserted nest of *F. rufus*.

In Brazil, Natterer also noticed that the species was parasitic on the Oven-bird; but in Upper Amazonia Mr. E. Bartlett found it nesting in September in holes in sandy banks, the nest being made of fine dried grass or fibres; the holes were sometimes two feet in depth.

In the Campos of Brazil it is recorded by Burmeister as breeding in holes of trees; and in Peru, according to Mr. Stolzmann, it nests under the roofs of houses, and Mr. Wyatt also observed it similarly nesting at Ocaña in the Magdalena Valley.

The figure in the Plate is drawn from a specimen procured by Mr. Wyatt during his visit to Colombia, and the descriptions are founded on the series of skins in the British Museum.

* [*P. domestica* or *P. fecunda*?]

APPENDIX

TO THE

GENUS PROGNE.

PROGNE FURCATA [antea, p. 159].

Add :—

Progne furcata, Sharpe & Wyatt, Monogr. Hirund. pt. ix. (1889).

For the geographical distribution of this species, *vide suprà*, Plate 82 [Map].

PROGNE CONCOLOR [antea, p. 163].

Add :—

Progne concolor, Sharpe & Wyatt, Monogr. Hirund. pt. ix. (1889) ; Ridgw. Proc. U. S. Nat. Mus. xii. pp. 105, 119, 122, 123 (1889).

Mr. Townsend met with the present species in Indefatigable Island.

For the geographical distribution of this species, *vide suprà*, Plate 81 [Map].

PROGNE DOMINICENSIS [antea, p. 165].

Add :—

Progne dominicensis, Feilden, Ibis, 1889, p. 483 ; Sharpe & Wyatt, Monogr. Hirund. pt. ix. (1889) ; Cory, Auk, viii. pp. 47, 48 (1891) ; id. t. c. p. 294 ; id. Cat. West Ind. B. p. 114 (1892) ; Scott, Auk, x. p. 186 (1893).

Recorded from the Island of Barbadoes by Schomburgk. Colonel Feilden did not meet with the species himself in the island, but remarks that there is no reason to doubt Schomburgk's statement, as the species is abundant and resident in Granada and St. Vincent.

In Jamaica, says Mr. Scott, it is a migrant and summer resident, a few wintering.

He observed it only once himself, at Priestman's River on February 5th, when a large number of birds unquestionably of this species appeared in company with many *Hemiprocne zonaris*.

For the geographical distribution of this species, *vide infrà*, Plate 94 [Map].

PROGNE DOMESTICA [antcà, p. 469].

Add :—

Progne domestica, Sharpe & Wyatt, Monogr. Hirund. pt. ix. (1889).
Progne chalybea domestica, Berl. J. f. O. 1887, p. 5.

COUNT VON BERLEPSCH records the species from Lambaré, in Paraguay, on the 5th of December.

For the geographical distribution of this species, *vide infrà*, Plate 94 [Map].

PROGNE CHALYBEA [antcà, p. 473].

Add :—

Progne chalybea, Sharpe & Wyatt, Monogr. Hirund. pt. vi. (1887); Cherrie, Auk, ix. p. 22 (1892).
Progne leucogastra, Ferrari-Perez, Proc. U. S. Nat. Mus. ix. p. 139 (1886).

RECORDED by Prof. Ferrari-Perez from Jalapa in August. Mr. A. K. Cherrie writes from Costa Rica :—"A resident species about San José, but most abundant during the breeding-season from May to the last of July. A favourite nesting-site is in the hoods of the arc electric street-lamps. The young do not differ from the adult bird except in having softer plumage."

N.B.—P. 476, line 15 from top, *for* "Salvin" *read* "Salmon."

For the geographical distribution of this species, *vide infrà*, Plate 94 [Map].

PROGNE TAPERA [antcà. p. 479].

Add :—

Progne tapera, Berlepsch & Ihering, Zeitschr. ges. Orn. ii. p. 20 (1885); Sharpe & Wyatt, Monogr. Hirund. pt. xii. (1889).

RECORDED by Dr. Ihering from Taquara, Rio Grande do Sul, from October to December.

For the geographical distribution of this species, *vide suprà*, Plate 80 [Map].

	Migratory.	△
	Bird of passage.	○
	Remains locally during the winter.	⊗
	Transplanted.	~
	Winter resident.	

Nearctic Region. Neotropical Region. Pala...

V Guest.
† Wanderer.

Rarely }
Generally } nesting.
In colonies }

Ethiopian Region.   Indian Region.   Australian Region.

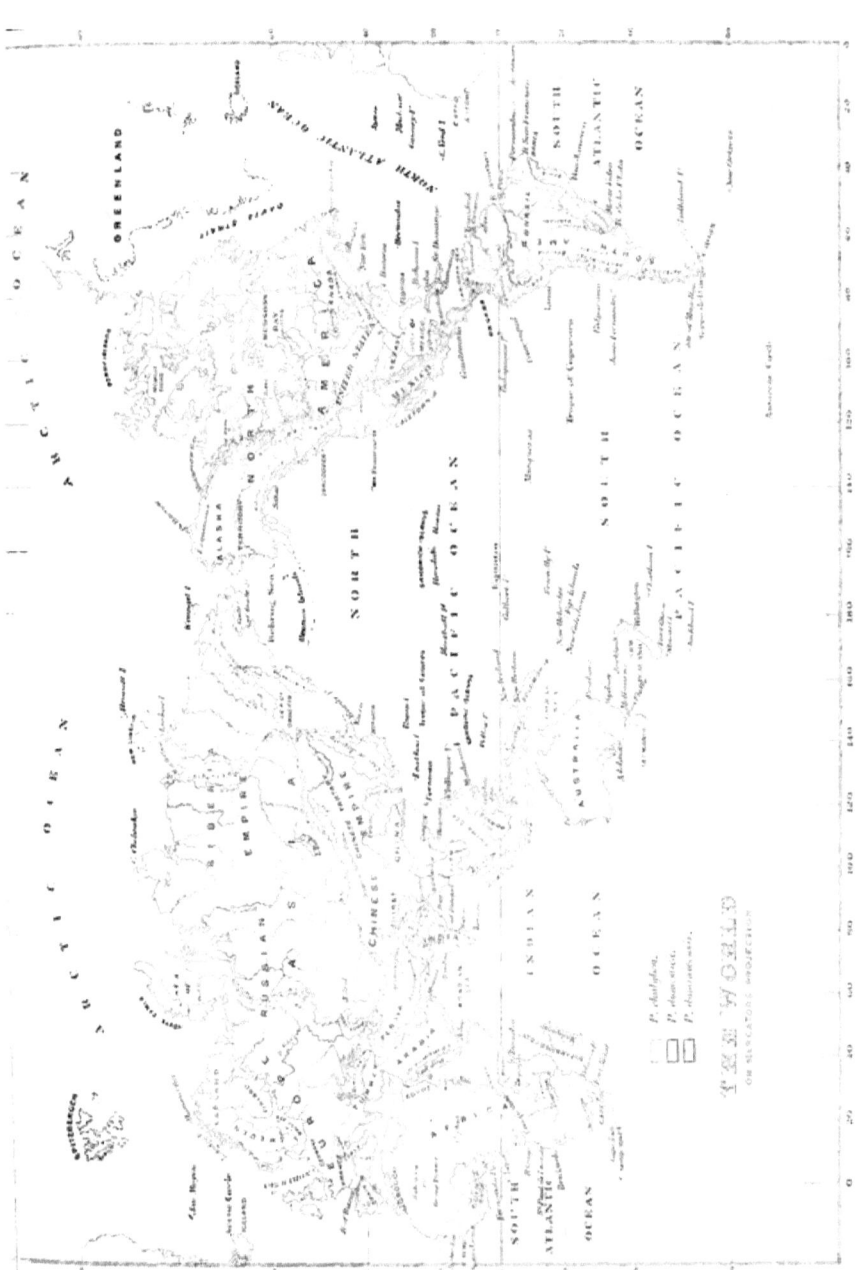

Genus IX. ATTICORA.

	Type.
Atticora, Boie, Isis, 1844, p. 172	*A. fasciata*.
Microchelidon (nec Reichenb.), Sclater, Cat. Amer. B. p. 39 (1862)	*A. tibialis*.
Neochelidon, Sclater, t. c. p. xvi (1862)	*A. tibialis*.
Notiochelidon, Baird, Review Amer. B. p. 306 (1865)	*A. pileata*.
Pygochelidon, Baird, t. c. p. 308 (1865)	*A. cyanoleuca*.

Range. The whole of South America, extending into Central America as far as Guatemala.

Clavis specierum.

a. Notaeum et gastraeum caerulescenti-nigra ; fascia lata pectoralis alba   1. *fasciata*, p. 495.
b. Gastraeum chocolatinum aut brunneum.
    a'. Tibiae brunneae, gastraeo reliquo concolores .   2. *cinerea*, p. 499.
    b'. Tibiae albae . . . .   3. *tibialis*, p. 501.
c. Gastraeum album.
    c'. Notaeum totum caerulescenti-nigrum ; hypochondriae albae.
        a''. Fascia praepectoralis caerulescenti-nigra .   4. *melanoleuca*, p. 503.
        b''. Fascia praepectoralis nulla . . . .   5. *cyanoleuca*, p. 505.
    d'. Interscapulium brunneum ; pileum caerulescenti-nigrum ; hypochondriae brunneae . .   6. *pileata*, p. 513.
d. Gastraeum album ; guttur et praepectus cervina ; pileum quoque cervinum.   7. *fucata*, p. 515.

ATTICORA FASCIATA

ATTICORA FASCIATA (Gm.).

WHITE-BANDED SWALLOW.

Hirondelle de Cayenne à bande blanche sur le ventre, Daubent. Pl. Enl. vii. pl. 724. fig. 2.
Hirondelle à ceinture blanche, Month. Hist. Nat. Ois. vi. p. 611 (1779).
White-bellied Swallow, Lath. Gen. Syn. ii. pt. 2, p. 567 (1783).
Hirundo fasciata, Gm. Syst. Nat. i. p. 1022 (1788); Swains. Zool. Illustr. 2nd ser. i. pl. 17 (1829).
Cecropis fasciata, Less. Compl. Buff. viii. p. 499 (1837).
Atticora fasciata, Boie, Isis, 1844, p. 172; Cab. in Schomb. Reis. Guian. iii. p. 672 (1848); Bp. Consp. i. p. 337 (1850); Cass. Cat. Hirund. Mus. Philad. Acad. p. 7 (1853); Burm. Th. Bras. iii. p. 146 (1856); Sclater, Cat. Amer. B. p. 39 (1862); Baird, Review Amer. B. p. 306 (1865); Scl. & Salv. P. Z. S. 1866, p. 178, 1867, pp. 569, 749; Gray, Hand-l. B. i. p. 72, no. 857 (1869); Pelz. Orn. Bras. pp. 18, 102 (1871); Scl. & Salv. P. Z. S. 1873, p. 258; iid. Nomencl. Av. Neotr. p. 14 (1873); Taczan. P. Z. S. 1882, p. 8; Salv. Cat. Strickl. Coll. p. 152 (1882); id. & Godm. Biol. Centr.-Amer., Aves, i. p. 229 (1883); Taczan. Orn. Pérou, p. 244 (1884); Sharpe, Cat. Birds in Brit. Mus. x. pp. 183, 634 (1885); Salvin, Ibis, 1885, p. 205.

A. suprà indigotico-nigra: corpore subtùs dorso unicolore: fasciâ latâ præpectorali albâ.

Hab. in provinciâ Guianensi et Amazoniâ usque ad Peruviam, Boliviam, et terram Equatorialem.

Nestling. Distinguished by the yellow gape, brown throat and chest and abdomen, the feathers of which are edged with whity brown; upper surface duller blue than in the adult bird, the rump and upper tail-coverts brown, with paler brown edges.

Young. Duller blue than the adult, or brown glossed with blue, with narrow edgings of whity brown to the feathers, more distinct on the greater series of wing-coverts; throat and fore neck brown glossed with blue; the entire chest and breast white; the abdomen and sides of lower flanks brown mixed with dull white; under tail-coverts brown, slightly washed with blue, the shorter ones having paler brown edges; axillaries and under wing-coverts brown, margined with white near the carpal bend of the wing.

Adult male. General colour above glossy blue-black; wing-coverts and quills black externally, edged with the colour of the back; tail very much forked, the feathers blue-black, glossy on their edges; lores and base of forehead velvety black; sides of face, ear-coverts, cheeks, and entire under surface of body glossy blue-black, including the under tail-coverts; across the breast a very broad band of white, extending a little way down the flanks; thighs white; under wing-coverts and axillaries brown, glossed with blue; quills dusky brown below, paler along the edge of the inner web. Total length 6 inches, culmen 0·35, wing 4·15, tail 3·1, tarsus 0·45.

Adult female. Similar to the male in colour. Total length 5·5 inches, culmen 0·35, wing 4·1, tail 2·8, tarsus 0·4.

The following notes refer to the series of specimens in the British Museum :—

Cayenne. Plumage dull and worn, almost bronzy, with the wings and tail in full moult (*Sclater Coll.*). Another (*Tweeddale Coll.*) is in brighter plumage, apparently just emerging from the moult, the long first primaries not yet replaced. A third male (*Salvin-Godman Coll.*) is also in complete plumage, excepting as regards the long primaries and secondaries, which are not yet moulted.

British Guiana. Three males (wing 4·0–4·1) and a female (wing 4·1) from the Atapurau River (*H. Whitely*), procured towards the end of January, are all in slightly worn plumage; but in a pair obtained by Whitely on the Merumè Mountains, the male (wing 4·15) is in full bright plumage, having apparently just completed its moult, while the female is still moulting the long primaries. The contrast between the bright plumage of the Merumè specimens and the rather bronzed appearance of those from the Atapurau River is very marked, and shows that the new feathering is acquired by the beginning of July, and becomes much worn by the end of the following January.

Amazonia. An adult bird from the Rio Negro (*A. R. Wallace*) is in slightly worn plumage (wing 4·05). An adult bird from Pebas (*J. Hauxwell*) is moulting the wings and tail. A young bird from the Upper Ucayali (*E. Bartlett*) has a nearly square tail; and an adult from Yurimaguas, March (*E. Bartlett*), is also moulting the long primaries.

Ecuador. An adult (*Sclater Coll.*) has the wing 3·9 inches, and a pair from the Copataza River (*C. Buckley*) also both measure 3·9 inches in the wing, which is slightly less than in Guiana examples. At Sarayacu Buckley also procured a nestling.

Peru. A female from Chanchamayo (*H. Whitely*) is in decidedly worn plumage, and has the wing 4 inches. It has a narrow white breast-band.

Bolivia. Of three adult specimens procured by Buckley at Yuyo, two are moulting their quills and tail-feathers. The third is in worn plumage, and has the wing 4 inches in length. A very young bird was obtained by Buckley at Cangalli.

We have gone somewhat into detail over the Museum series, in order to try and find out whether there is any confirmation of the difference in the width of the white breast-band, which is undoubtedly well-marked in the series in question. The broader breast-band, which we fancied (Cat. B. *l. c.*) to be a sign of immaturity, seems rather to be characteristic of more southern birds; and we should be able to differentiate two races with well-defined ranges, were it not for the Chanchamayo specimen in the Sclater Collection, which has as narrow a breast-band as the Guiana skins. The narrow breast-band, however, with this exception, is characteristic of the birds from Guiana and the Rio Negro; while those from Upper Amazonia, Ecuador, and Bolivia have all of them very broad white bands.

Hab. Guiana, Rio Negro district of Brazil, Upper Amazonia, Ecuador, Bolivia.

The blue-black plumage with the white thighs and the white band across the breast render this species easy to recognize. It was first described from Cayenne, and is apparently not rare in British Guiana. Sir R. Schomburgk found it to be the commonest species on the Barima and Baruma rivers, but he did not notice it breeding. Mr. Henry Whitely procured adult individuals at the end of January on the Atapurau River, and in July in the Merumè Mountains, but no young birds were in his collections. We should suppose, however, that the species is a resident in Guiana and breeds there.

Mr. A. R. Wallace found it common on the banks of the lower and middle Rio Negro; and the late Johann Natterer procured it on the Rio Guaporé in July, and on the Rio Negro in December. On the right bank of the latter river he found it common along with *Progne tapera*.

The late Mr. C. Buckley obtained specimens on the Copataza River, and a nestling at Sarayacu, showing that the species breeds in Ecuador; and that it does so on the Upper Ucayali is related by Mr. E. Bartlett, who also procured specimens at Yurimaguas and on the lakes of Santa Cruz. He writes :—" Breeds in banks along with *Stelgidopteryx ruficollis*, and lays four or five white eggs. The nest is rather more complete in structure than that of the latter, the grass-fibres and bents being finer. Nest taken in July." Mr. Stolzmann also procured this Swallow at Yurimaguas in February. A specimen obtained by Mr. J. Hauxwell at Pebas on the Upper Amazons is in the British Museum; and in August Mr. Henry Whitely shot a specimen at Chanchamayo in Peru. This record does not appear to have been published by Messrs. Sclater and Salvin, and is omitted in Dr. Taczanowski's work on the birds of that country. Specimens were obtained by Buckley at Yuyo in Bolivia, and a young bird from Cangalli, also procured by Buckley, is in the Salvin-Godman collection.

The above notes prove the species to be in British Guiana in January and July, and on the Rio Negro in July and December, nesting on the Upper Amazons in July, and occurring at Yurimaguas in February, and at Chanchamayo in August. The moulting of the Guiana specimens in July, as noticed above, proves that they could not be nesting at that time, as they were found to be doing on the Ucayali by Mr. Bartlett during that month, and therefore the habits of the species in different districts of South America appear to vary. It is much to be regretted that so little information is really available for the study of this and other species of South-American Swallows.

The Plate is drawn from a specimen in the Tweeddale collection, now in the British Museum.

ATTICORA CINEREA (Gm.).

ANDEAN SWALLOW.

L'Hirondelle du Pérou, Briss. Orn. ii. p. 498 (1760).
La Petite Hirondelle noire à ventre cendré, Month. Hist. Nat. Ois. vi. p. 673 (1779).
Ash-bellied Swallow, Lath. Gen. Syn. ii. pt. 2, p. 573 (1783).
Hirundo cinerea, Gm. Syst. Nat. i. p. 1026 (1788); Gray, Gen. B. i. p. 58 (1845).
Hirundo andecola, D'Orb. & Lafr. Syn. Av. p. 69 (1837); Tschudi & Cab. Faun. Peruan. p. 132 (1845–46); Scl. & Salv. P. Z. S. 1867, p. 981, 1868, p. 569, 1869. p. 151; Gray, Hand-l. B. i. p. 72, no. 853 (1869); Scl. & Salv. Nomencl. Av. Neotr. p. 14 (1873); Tacz. P. Z. S. 1874, p. 510; Scl. & Salv. P. Z. S. 1879, p. 595; Tacz. Orn. Pérou, i. p. 242 (1884).
Petrochelidon murina, Cass. Proc. Philad. Acad. 1853, p. 370; id. Cat. Hirund. Mus. Philad. Acad. p. 6 (1853); Sclater, P. Z. S. 1860, p. 74.
Atticora cinerea, Sclater, Cat. Amer. B. p. 39 (1862); Baird, Review Amer. B. p. 312 (1865); Scl. & Salv. P. Z. S. 1869, p. 599; iid. Nomencl. Av. Neotr. p. 14 (1873); Tacz. P. Z. S. 1874, p. 510, 1882, p. 8; Salvin & Godm. Biol. Centr.-Amer., Aves, i. p. 229 (1883); Tacz. Orn. Pérou, i. p. 243 (1884); Sharpe, Cat. Birds in Brit. Mus. x. p. 184 (1885).
Hirundo murina, Gray, Hand-l. B. i. p. 72, no. 852 (1869).
Atticora murina, Berlepsch & Tacz. P. Z. S. 1884, p. 287.

A. subtùs brunnea, tibiis brunneis pectore concoloribus.

Hab. in montibus Andeanis Americæ meridionalis.

Adult male. General colour above glossy greenish black, the lesser wing-coverts and scapulars like the back; median and greater wing-coverts and quills blackish brown, with a slight steel-green gloss; tail-feathers blackish brown, with dusky cross bars under certain lights; lores velvety black; ear-coverts and sides of neck glossy greenish black; cheeks and under surface of body clear earthy brown, including the thighs; under tail-coverts blackish brown, with glossy greenish-black edges; axillaries and under wing-coverts earthy brown like the breast; quills dusky, more ashy brown along the inner web: "bill black; feet brownish flesh-colour; iris dark brown" (*Stolzmann*). Total length 5·4 inches, culmen 0·3, wing 3·4, tail 2·4, tarsus 0·45.

Adult female. Similar to the male in plumage. Total length 5·8 inches, culmen 0·25, wing 4·4, tail 1·25, tarsus 0·45.

The shade of colour on the upper parts varies between steel-blue and steel-green, as is the case with other American Swallows, the bluer shade indicating, as we believe, a newly moulted state of plumage.

Young. Sooty brown, lighter on the rump and upper tail-coverts; below ashy white, the throat dark brown.

Hab. The Andes of Bolivia, Peru, Ecuador, and Colombia.

This species appears to have been first described by Père Feuillet, in a book which we have not seen, entitled 'Journal des Observations physiques' (p. 33), published in 1725. From this work Brisson took his description of the "Hirondelle du Pérou," which was subsequently the origin of Latham's "Ash-coloured Swallow" and Gmelin's *Hirundo cinerea*.

Fifty years after, the species was described by D'Orbigny and Lafresnaye as *Hirundo andecola*, from a specimen procured by the former at La Paz in Bolivia. Tschudi next met with it in Peru, where he says that it inhabits all the hot valleys of the Sierra. Messrs. Sclater and Salvin have also recorded specimens obtained by Mr. Henry Whitely in Western Peru, viz. at Arequipa in May, and again at Tinta in the same month. Mr. Jelski obtained it in Central Peru between Cucas and Paleamayo, and Mr. Stolzmann at Tamiapampa.

In Ecuador Mr. L. Fraser met with the species near Quito, where it was very common in and about the city. In May he observed that this Swallow was building under the caves of houses, and the nest forwarded by him was, according to Dr. Sclater, "a shallow structure, composed of moss and lined with a little wool. The egg is of a spotless white, 0·72 inch in length by about 0·51 inch in breadth, and has the usual character of birds of this group." The late Mr. Clarence Buckley procured specimens at Sical, and these are now in the Salvin-Godman collection. Messrs. Stolzmann and Siemiradski have also met with the species in Western Ecuador at Tiesan, at an altitude of from 7000 to 9000 feet. Count von Berlepsch and Dr. Taczanowski, in recording the above specimen, state their belief that the description of *Hirundo cinerea* of Gmelin is not sufficiently definite to distinguish the species. In this opinion we are unable to follow them, while the series in the British Museum shows that there is no specific difference between birds from Peru and Ecuador.

The species also inhabits Colombia, as there are specimens in the Sclater and Salvin-Godman collections from the vicinity of Bogotá.

The descriptions are copied from the British Museum 'Catalogue,' and the figure of the old bird is drawn from a specimen in the Salvin-Godman collection, while that of the young one is taken from a specimen in Mr. Wyatt's collection.

ATTICORA TIBIALIS

ATTICORA TIBIALIS (Cassin).

WHITE-THIGHED SWALLOW.

Petrochelidon? tibialis, Cass. Proc. Philad. Acad. 1853, p. 370; id. Cat. Hirund. Mus. Philad. Acad. p. 6 (1853).
Microchelidon tibialis, Sclater, Cat. Amer. B. p. 39 (1862).
Neochelidon tibialis, Sclater. t. c. p. xvi, errata (1862); Scl. & Salv. P. Z. S. 1864, p. 317; iid. P. Z. S. 1869, p. 598.
Atticora tibialis, Baird, Review Amer. B. p. 307 (1865); Gray, Hand-l. B. i. p. 72, no. 859 (1869); Scl. & Salv. Nomencl. Av. Neotr. p. 14 (1873); iid. P. Z. S. 1879, p. 495; Salv. & Godm. Biol. Centr.-Amer., Aves, i. p. 231 (1883); Taez. Orn. Pérou, i. p. 212 (1884); Sharpe, Cat. Birds in Brit. Mus. x. p. 185 (1885).

A. subtùs brunnea ; tibiis albis.

Hab. in Americâ centrali et in provinciâ Colombianâ Americæ meridionalis usque ad Peruviam.

Adult. General colour above sooty brown, with an oily green gloss on the head and back, the rump and upper tail-coverts rather paler brown; wing-coverts and quills glossy brown; tail slightly forked, the feathers glossy brown; lores velvety black; ear-coverts and sides of neck dark brown, the latter with a slight greenish gloss like the head; cheeks and entire under surface of body dark earthy brown, a little darker on the under wing- and tail-coverts; thighs white; quills dusky brown below. Total length 4·4 inches, culmen 0·25, wing 3·3, tail 1·8, tarsus 0·4.

A male from Antioquia (*Salmon*), in the Salvin-Godman collection, is moulting, and shows that the new feathers on the head and mantle and wings are distinctly greenish black; the under surface is also deeper and more sooty brown; and it is evident that the pale coloration in some specimens is caused by the age and abrasion of the feathers.

Hab. From Panama to Colombia, extending as far south as Peru.

THIS species is easily distinguished by its white thighs, which contrast strongly with its brown under surface. It was first described by the late Mr. Cassin as from Brazil, a locality which has not been confirmed by any subsequent observer, although Messrs. Salvin and Godman mention that in the Cambridge Museum there is a Swainsonian specimen said to be from Brazil. The Sclater collection also had a skin supposed to be Brazilian, but all these records are probably erroneous.

The late Mr. J. McLeannan procured this Swallow on the line of railway in Panama, and subsequently it was met with by Mr. Salmon in Antioquia, breeding near Remedios. A Colombian specimen also exists in the Bremen Museum. Mr. Wyatt has the following note:—"I undoubtedly met with *A. tibialis* when descending the Cordillera from Bucaramanga, at an elevation of about 1000 feet, and shot three or four specimens; but the vegetation was so dense that it was impossible to get them, unless they had chanced to fall on the path. There was a large flock of them, and some of them allowed me to approach within three or four yards, as they sat on a tree-fern. This was opposite to the locality where Salmon obtained the species, but on the other side of the Magdalena." A single specimen was obtained near Cosnipata in Peru, by Mr. Henry Whitely, but it has not yet been found in any of the intervening localities.

Mr. Salmon states that the nest was made of dry grass and was placed in the hole of a bank.

The descriptions and figure are taken from specimens in the Salvin-Godman collection, and now in the British Museum.

ATTICORA MELANOLEUCA

ATTICORA MELANOLEUCA (Temm.).

BLACK-COLLARED SWALLOW.

Hirundo melanoleuca, Temm. Pl. Col. iv. pl. 209. fig. 2 (1823, ex Neuwied, MSS.);
Neuwied, Beitr. Naturg. Bras. iii. p. 371 (1831); Gray, Gen. B. i. p. 58 (1845);
Cab. in Schomb. Reis. Guian. iii. p. 672 (1848); Gray, Hand-l. B. i. p. 72, no. 854
(1869).
Cecropis melanoleuca, Less. Compl. Buff. viii. p. 499 (1837).
Herse melanoleuca, Bp. Consp. i. p. 341 (1850).
Atticora melanoleuca, Burm. Syst. Uebers. iii. p. 146 (1856); Baird, Review Amer.
B. p. 310 (1865); Pelz. Orn. Bras. pp. 18, 102 (1871); Scl. & Salv. Nomencl. Av.
Neotr. p. 14 (1873); Salv. & Godm. Biol. Centr.-Amer., Aves, i. p. 229 (1883);
Sharpe, Cat. Birds in Brit. Mus. x. p. 185 (1885); Salvin, Ibis, 1885, p. 206.

A. subtùs alba; fasciâ præpectorali indigotico-nigrâ.

Hab. in Brasiliâ.

Adult. General colour above dull blue-black, the feathers with ash-coloured bases; lesser and median wing-coverts like the back; greater coverts, bastard-wing, primary-coverts, and quills brown, glossed slightly with blue on the outer web; tail-feathers brown, also faintly glossed with blue; lores velvety black; ear-coverts and feathers below the eye blue-black; cheeks and throat white, separated from the breast by a broad band of blue-black; remainder of under surface white, washed with brown on the sides of the body and thighs; in the centre of the chest a longitudinal spot of blue-black feathers below the breast-band; sides of upper breast blackish washed with blue; under tail-coverts blackish, slightly washed with blue; axillaries and under wing-coverts blackish brown, the coverts near the edge of the wing edged with white; quills dusky below: " bill black; legs blackish ashy brown; iris dark" (*Neuwied*). Total length 5·5 inches, culmen 0·3, wing 4·8, tail 2·9, tarsus 0·45.

Hab. Brazil.

This species is extremely rare in collections, and we only know of one specimen in this country. It was discovered more than fifty years ago by the late Prince Maximilian of Neuwied, and since that time no one but the celebrated traveller Natterer appears to have met with it in that country.

Although Temminck, in the 'Planches Coloriées,' states that the species figured by him was the *Hirundo melanoleuca* of Prince Max., the latter does not appear to have actually published the name until 1831, and therefore Temminck's becomes the first real description of the species, the date of the 'livraison' in which it appeared being 1823.

Prince Max. gives the following note on the species:—"This graceful Swallow lives on the banks of the rivers in the interior of Brazil, and I met with it on the Rio Grande de Belmonte, where it was flying over the water and the large rocks on the shore, in company with the Red-throated and White-winged Swallows. In the beginning of September I found it mostly in pairs, and it seemed to prefer those places where the water from the rocks caused some movement in the river and formed cascades and whirlpools. Its flight is very rapid, like that of our Chimney-Swallow, which it also much resembles in the form of the tail. In the brilliant noonday sun I have often seen it sitting and sunning itself on the rocks."

Natterer's localities for the species are the following:—Bordo do Matto da Paranaiva: June. Forte do Principe: August. Bananeira: September. Salto Theotonio: November. Rio Negro: December. Maribatanas: January.

According to Prof. Cabanis (*l. c.*) Schomburgk met with the species in British Guiana; but no other collector has procured specimens in that country. Can it be possible that *Atticora cyanoleuca*, which is common near Roraima, was the species intended?

Our description and figure are taken from one of Natterer's specimens from Forte do Principe, in the Sclater Collection, and now in the British Museum.

ATTICORA CYANOLEUCA

ATTICORA CYANOLEUCA (*Vieill.*).

BLUE-AND-WHITE SWALLOW.

Golondrina de los limoncles negros, Azara, Apunt. ii. p. 508 (1802); Hartl. Ind. Azara, p. 19 (1847).
Hirundo cyanoleuca, Vieill. N. Dict. d'Hist. Nat. xiv. p. 509 (1817); Gould in Darw. Voy. 'Beagle,' Birds, p. 41 (1841); Gray, Gen. B. i. p. 58 (1845); id. Cat. Fissir. Brit. Mus. p. 27 (1848); Scl. P. Z. S. 1867, p. 321; Gray, Hand-l. B. i. p. 72, no. 851 (1869).
Hirundo minuta, Temm. Pl. Col. iv. pl. 209. fig. 1 (1823); Neuwied, Beitr. Naturg. Bras. iii. p. 369 (1830).
Hirundo melanopyga, Licht. Verz. Doubl. p. 57 (1823); Tschudi & Cab. Faun. Peruan. p. 133 (1855).
Hirundo patagonica, Lafr. & d'Orb. Syn. Av. 1837, p. 69; Gray, Hand-l. B. i. p. 72, no. 855 (1869).
Hirundo melanoleuca (nec Neuwied), Gray, Cat. Fissir. Brit. Mus. p. 26 (1848).
Herse cyanoleuca, Bp. Consp. i. p. 341 (1850).
Atticora cyanoleuca, Cab. Mus. Hein. Th. i. p. 47 (1850); Burm. Th. Bras. iii. p. 147 (1856); Baird, Review Amer. B. p. 309 (1865); Cab. J. f. O. 1860, p. 401, 1861, p. 92; Burm. Reis. La Plata, ii. p. 479 (1861); Sclater, Cat. Amer. B. p. 40 (1862); id. & Salv. P. Z. S. 1866, p. 178, 1867, pp. 749, 984, 1868, p. 568, 1869, p. 159; Salv. Ibis, 1869, p. 184; id. P. Z. S. 1870, p. 184; Reinh. Vid. Medd. Nat. For. Kjöbenh. 1870, p. 252; Pelz. Orn. Bras. pp. 18, 402 (1871); Wyatt, Ibis, 1871, p. 323; Hudson, P. Z. S. 1872, pp. 544, 545; Scl. & Salv. Nomencl. Av. Neotr. p. 14 (1873); iid. P. Z. S. 1873, p. 258; Tacz. P. Z. S. 1874, p. 510; Scl. & Salv. P. Z. S. 1876, p. 16; Durnford, Ibis, 1876, p. 158, 1877, pp. 32, 170, 1878, p. 392; Tacz. P. Z. S. 1879, p. 224; Scl. & Salv. t. c. pp. 495, 595; Tacz. P. Z. S. 1880, p. 192; W. A. Forbes, Ibis, 1881, p. 320; Salv. Cat. Strickl. Coll. p. 152 (1882); Tacz. P. Z. S. 1882, p. 8; White, t. c. p. 596; Salv. & Godm. Biol. Centr.-Amer., Aves, i. p. 229 (1883); Tacz. Orn. Pérou, i. p. 214 (1884); Sharpe, Cat. Birds in Brit. Mus. x. pp. 186, 634 (1885); Sclater & Hudson, Argentine Orn. i. p. 33 (1888).
Petrochelidon cyanoleuca, Sclater, P. Z. S. 1858, p. 551, 1859, p. 138, 1860, pp. 75, 85; id. Cat. Amer. B. p. 40 (1862).
Atticora hemipyga, Burm. Reis. La Plata, ii. p. 479 (1861).
Atticora patagonica, Baird, Review Amer. B. p. 311, note (1865); Salvin & Godman, Biol. Centr.-Amer., Aves, i. p. 229 (1883).

Atticora cyanoleuca, var. *montana*, Baird, Review Amer. B. p. 310 (1865); Lawr. Ann. Lyc. N. Y. ix. p. 96 (1868); v. Frantzius, J. f. O. 1869, p. 294; Boucard, P. Z. S. 1878, p. 67.

A. subtùs alba: suprà indigotica.

Hab. in regione Neotropicâ ferè totâ.

Adult. General colour above glossy blue, the feathers of the hind neck slightly mottled, with white bases to the feathers; scapulars, lesser and median wing-coverts like the back; bastard-wing, primary-coverts, and quills black, externally glossed with dull blue; tail-feathers blackish; lores, feathers below the eye, and ear-coverts black; cheeks and under surface of body pure white, the sides of the neck glossy blue, descending in a half-crescent on the sides of the chest; sides of body and flanks brown, with a patch of silky white feathers on the sides of the lower back; thighs blackish brown; under tail-coverts black glossed with blue; axillaries and under wing-coverts smoky brown, the coverts near the edge of the wing edged with white: "bill black; legs dark brown; iris dark" (*Neuwied*). Total length 4·7 inches, culmen 0·25, wing 4·05, tail 2·2, tarsus 0·45.

The sexes are alike in colour.

Young. Brown, with pale edges to the feathers, particularly those of the lower back, rump, and upper tail-coverts; quills and tail brown, with white fringes to the ends of the inner secondaries; under surface of body dull white, with a little brown on the fore neck (sometimes forming a collar) and on the flanks; the chin tinged with salmon-colour; the under tail-coverts white, washed with smoky brown towards the ends.

After the first moult the white margins to the inner secondaries disappear, the blue plumage is donned, though never quite so brilliant as in the old birds, and the throat and fore neck are distinctly salmon-coloured. This last character seems to be a sign of immaturity, but only occurs after the first moult.

Professor Baird separated the species from Costa Rica and the Andean subregion as *A. montana*, on account of its longer bill, but we have not found that the distinctive characters amount to much. The race which he separates as *A. patagonica*, and which Burmeister called *A. hemipyga*, is really recognizable and may prove to be a distinct species. It differs in having the vent and the basal under tail-coverts white. All the Chilian specimens in the British Museum show this character, as do also examples from Cosquin, in the province of Cordova. We should feel inclined to recognize *A. patagonica* as a race, but for the fact that specimens from Cosnipata in Peru appear to be intermediate, and we must leave the subject to future inquirers to determine.

The following is a list of some measurements of specimens from various portions of the bird's range :—

	Total length.	Culmen.	Wing.	Tail.	Tarsus.
	in.	in.	in.	in.	in.
a. Ad. Costa Rica (*Arcé*).	4·4	0·3	3·8	2·1	0·45
b. Ad. „ „	4·0	0·3	3·7	2·0	0·45
c. Ad. Irazu district, C. R. (*Rogers*)	..	0·3	3·7	imp.	0·45
d. Imm. Panama (*McLeannan*)	4·3	..	3·8	1·8	0·45
e. Imm. „ „	4·4	0·3	3·7	2·0	0·45

	Total length. in.	Culmen. in.	Wing. in.	Tail. in.	Tarsus. in.
f. Imm. Panama (*McLennan*)	4·5	0·3	3·9	2·0	0·45
g. Juv. Veragua (*Arcé*)	3·9	0·25	3·45	1·6	0·4
h. Juv. „ „	3·7	0·3	3·45	1·8	0·4
i. ♀ ad. Frontino, Colombia (*Salmon*)	4·4	0·3	3·5	1·7	0·4
k. ♂ imm. Roraima, 8,5 82 (*Whitely*)	4·5	0·3	3·8	1·8	0·45
l. Ad. „ 10.12.81 „	4·2	0·25	3·8	1·9	0·4
m. Ad. Ecuador (ex *Gould*)	4·6	0·3	3·85	1·95	0·4
n. Ad. Sical, Ecuador (*Buckley*)	4·5	0·3	3·7	2·1	0·45
o. Ad. Chiguinda, Ecuador (*Buckley*)	4·4	0·3	3·8	1·95	0·45
p. Ad. Ecuador (ex *Gould*)	4·3	0·25	3·7	1·95	0·45
q. ♂ ad. Arequipa (*Whitely*), 6.6.'67	5·1	0·3	3·9	2·2	0·4
r. ♂ ad. Cosnipata „ 2.9.68	5·0	0·25	4·1	2·1	0·4
s. Ad. Cangalli, Bolivia (*Buckley*)	4·5	0·3	4·1	2·15	0·45
t. ♀ ad. Chili (*Philippi & Landbeck*)	5·0	0·3	3·85	2·05	0·45
u. Ad. Chili (*Reed*)	5·3	0·3	4·05	2·2	0·45
v. ♀. Cosquin, Cordova, Argentine Republic (*White*), 17,8.82	4·7	0·3	4·0	2·1	0·45
w. Ad. Bahia (*Wucherer*)	4·4	0·3	3·75	2·2	0·45
x. Ad. Brazil	4·4	0·25	3·8	2·1	0·4
y. ♂ juv. Pelotas, Rio Grande do Sul, Brazil (*Joyner*)	4·0	0·3	3·5	1·75	0·4

Many specimens have some ovate spots of dark brown on the breast, as in *Progne tapera*, and we have not been able to account for this appearance, which is perceptible in both old and young birds. It is present in nearly all Chilian specimens, but is not confined to them, as we find traces of the same markings in others from Arequipa, Cosnipata, Bahia, and they are present in young birds from Cocchupata, Peru, Quito, and Puerto Cabello in Venezuela. This spotting is therefore apparently not a sign of age or seasonal plumage.

Hab. From Costa Rica southwards, throughout the whole of South America to Bolivia and the Argentine Republic. In the interior of the latter country, in Chili and Patagonia, a white-vented race occurs.

THE present species is spread over the greater part of South America and ranges into Central America. Messrs. Salvin and Godman record it from Costa Rica and Panama. Dr. Hoffmann and M. Carmiol met with it at San José in the former country, and the latter collector also found it at Barranca. Specimens in immature plumage are in the Salvin-Godman collection, so that it probably breeds in that country, but no nests have as yet been found. Mr. Rogers met with the species in the Irazu district, and M. Boucard procured two specimens near Cartago; they were on the ground in a small forest. In the Salvin-Godman collection are two individuals obtained by Arcé at Tucurriqui in the summer of 1864; they are both fully adult. The same collection contains several specimens from Panama, procured by the late Mr. McLennan, as well as some from Calovevora, sent by Arcé in 1869. All McLeannan's specimens are young birds just commencing to don their glossy blue plumage, but the date of their capture is not recorded. Two of Arcé's specimens are in a similar plumage, but one is quite adult. Besides these birds we have examined one fully plumaged specimen from the "Valley of Aragua," wherever that may be. Such is the locality attached to the skin by the late Mr. G. R. Gray.

Our records from Colombia are few. An adult from Bogotá is in the Sclater collection; and Mr. Wyatt writes:—"We did not observe this species in the Magdalena valley; and it seems to be a bird of the 'tierra templada;' its upward range, so far as our observations went, terminates at an altitude of about 8000 feet. It was a common bird at Ocaña, in the Cordillera, and might generally be seen with *Progne tapera* on the roof of our house."

A female from Frontino, in Antioquia, obtained by the late T. K. Salmon, is in the Salvin-Godman collection.

Mr. Goering sent a young male in first moult from Puerto Cabello in Venezuela, shot in June, and further to the east Mr. Henry Whitely met with the species in British Guiana. He procured two young birds in brown plumage with a few blue feathers appearing, on the 6th and 8th of May, 1882, and two fully plumaged birds on Roraima on the 23rd of November and the 10th of December, 1881.

From Ecuador we have examined quite a series, both old and young birds, from Mr. Gould's collection, probably all from the neighbourhood of Quito. Fully adult birds from Sical and Chiquinda, obtained by the late C. Buckley, are in the Salvin-Godman collection. Mr. Fraser met with the species at Riobamba, Pallatanga, Quito, in May, "common in and about the city," and at Nanegal and Perucho, where it was "common and building in the roofs."

In Peru, Tschudi states that they are seldom found as high as the Sierra region, and he has noticed their nests in hollow trees. Dr. Taczanowski, who has described the Peruvian collections of Jelski and Stolzmann, has recorded both old and young birds from that country and gives the following localities:—Lima, Aimable Maria, Tambillo, Nov. 22; Pacasmayo, June 14; Callacate, May 22; Huambo, April 5. The following specimens are in the British Museum from Mr. H. Whitely's Peruvian collections:— Cosnipata, adults, February and September; Arequipa, adults in June, and young in February; Cosnipata, adults in February, March, and September; and Chanchamayo, young in first moult, in August and September. He also met with it at Maranura, north of Cuzco. If one may read the history of the species in Peru from the specimens before us, it would seem that two broods at least must be reared, and that some young birds are beginning to moult in August and September, others not till February. The old birds are in very worn plumage in February, and are moulting in March. After completing the moult they are probably breeding by June, to judge by the worn plumage, and do not quit the country at all.

An adult specimen was obtained by Mr. Bridges in Bolivia, with totally black under tail-coverts, and an adult bird from Cangalli, in the province of Yungas, collected by

Mr. C. Buckley, agrees with the latter; but a specimen from "Bolivia" in the Sclater collection is of the *H. patagonica* type, with the basal under tail-coverts white. D'Orbigny met with it in the province of Moxos.

From the Upper Amazons we have not seen many specimens, and young birds were procured by Mr. E. Bartlett on the Ucayali River, as well as at Nauta, Chyavetas, and Yurimaguas. Mr. Bartlett states that it does not breed on the Upper Amazon.

In Brazil it is apparently widely distributed, and the birds all have entirely black under tail-coverts. We have seen both young and old birds from this country, so that the species probably breeds there. Mr. Graham met with it at Para; and in his notes from Pernambuco the late Mr. W. A. Forbes writes:—" I did not bring home any specimens of this Swallow, the only one I shot having been too much damaged to skin; I have, however, little doubt that this is the species I met with, as I continually saw it in numbers, and was able to examine it often through my field-glasses. It was very abundant at Cabo, and might be seen there sitting in numbers, particularly in the morning, on the telegraph-wires of the railway opposite Mr. Hood's house; I also saw it at Parahyba and Garanhuns, perched on the roofs and eaves of the churches, and therefore not to be shot at with impunity. In Recife, on the other hand, I never saw it at all, though *H. leucorrhoa* abounded there."

Natterer met with the species at Rio de Janeiro in August and September, and at Ypanema in June, July, and December. He says that it frequents houses, and nests under the eaves, affecting buildings in towns as well as isolated houses in the country. It stays at Ypanema throughout the year, but was not seen in Cuyaba. Dr. Lund found it in Minas Geraes, and procured a young specimen at Lagoa Santa on the 12th of January, which was beginning to put on its full plumage.

Prince Neuwied writes:—" This dainty Swallow I have only encountered in the southern parts of Brazil. In Rio de Janeiro it is particularly common, and frequently nests in the buildings. It also flies over the meadows, pasturages, and woods, and is found in abundance in the towns and dwellings, where it takes the place of our Martin (*Hirundo urbica*). In the month of August it begins to nest in Rio de Janeiro. The nest is simple, and consists merely of a few straws thrown together on a beam under the roof; two eggs are found in it."

It was originally found by Azara in Paraguay; and in Mr. Barrows' notes from Uruguay he writes as follows:—

"This species was first seen at Concepcion on the 4th of September, 1880, when it was observed in considerable numbers, associated with *H. leucorrhoa*, from which it was easily distinguished by its smaller size and the absence of the white rump. For nearly six weeks it was observed here from time to time, but after October 20th it was not noted, until at Azul it was found in large flocks on the 27th of January, 1881, seemingly ready to migrate northward. It was seen, however, at Bahia Blanca, a few days later, and then almost daily until March 28th at Puan, after which it was not again observed. Of its breeding-habits I know nothing."

Professor Burmeister gives the following note:—

"Of all the Swallows of Brazil this has been the commonest in the countries visited by me; in each town, in each village, they exist in crowds. They nest under the eaves, where they repose on the cornices, like the Sparrows in Europe; it builds a simple nest of dry grass and hair; it lays two white eggs. The species appears to be especially plentiful in the inhabited districts; it is also present throughout the whole of South America; Azara describes it from Paraguay; von Tschudi from Peru; I myself found it in Colombia as well as in Rio de Janeiro, Novo Fribourgo, Congonhas, and Lagoa Santa."

A young specimen obtained by Mr. Joyner at Pelotas in Rio Grande do Sul is in the Salvin-Godman collection.

On the occurrence of the species near Buenos Ayres, excellent notes are given below from the pen of Mr. W. H. Hudson. Mr. Durnford has also written on the subject; he observes:—

"Arrives at the end of September, and generally leaves in March; but this year I observed two, a little north of Buenos Ayres, on the 30th April. This, the smallest species of Hirundinidæ, always reminds me of the Sand-Martin at home. In its habit of flying close to the ground and frequenting the neighbourhood of pools and streams, from which it never wanders far, it is essentially like that bird. It nests in holes in the banks of streams, sandpits, and similar localities.

"On October 3rd I saw two pairs frequenting some holes in a sand-pit near Flores; as they often returned to the pit, and clung to the face of its perpendicular sides, I think they had nests near. I thrust the whole length of my walking-stick into two or three of the holes, without touching the end of any of them. I am told that this Swallow remains the whole year near Buenos Ayres; and a friend assures me that he once shot one when Duck-shooting in the winter." (See, however, Mr. Hudson's notes given below.)

Mr. E. W. White met with it at Catamarca in August. Professor Burmeister, during his journey through the La Plata region, found this the commonest Swallow, but in Mendoza he met with the white-vented race which he named *Atticora hemipyga*. This is also the form from Chili, as is shown by the specimens in the British Museum, which possesses nine examples from that country. Mr. White's specimen from Cosquin in the province of Cordova also belongs to the white-vented form.

Mr. Darwin found the species nesting along with the Purple Martin in holes in banks near Bahia Blanca in Northern Patagonia. His specimen in the British Museum agrees with the Chilian specimens above recorded.

Mr. H. Durnford writes:—

"Common throughout our journey in Central Patagonia about the rivers and lakes. A few are seen at Chupat on warm days in the winter; but the great majority leave at the approach of cold weather." It was pretty common in the Chupat valley, nesting in the banks of some of the upper reaches of the river.

Like many other South-American Swallows the nesting-habits of the present species vary with locality, and the observations recorded above should be compared with the following interesting observations of Mr. W. H. Hudson:—

"I have already spoken in former communications of all but one of the species of Hirundinidæ that visit us in this region; the bird I have yet to describe is the *Atticora cyanoleuca*—the *Golondrina de los limonetes negros* of Azara, and the smallest of our Swallows. I cannot say what are the limits of its range, as my wanderings have not extended far in any direction, and I have never yet been in any region where it is not well known. In Buenos Ayres these Swallows appear early in September, coming before the three species of *Progne* that visit us, but preceded by the *Hirundo leucorrhoa*. They are bank-birds, breeding in forsaken holes and burrows (for they never bore into the earth themselves), and are consequently not much seen about the habitations of man. They sometimes find their breeding-holes in the banks of streams, or in peopled districts in the sides of ditches, and down in wells. But if in such sites alone fit receptacles for their eggs were found, the species, instead of one of the commonest, would be rare indeed; for on the level pampas most of the watercourses have marshy borders, or at the most but low and gently sloping banks. But the burrowing habits of two other animals, the Vizcacha (*Lagostomus trichodactylus*) and the Minera (*Geositta cunicularia*) have everywhere afforded the Swallows abundance of breeding-places on the plains, even where there are no streams or any other irregularities in the smooth surface of earth.

"The *Geositta* bores its holes in the sides of the Vizcacha's burrows; and in this burrow within a burrow the Swallow lays its eggs and rears its young, and is the guest of the Vizcacha and as much dependent on him as the Wren or the Swallow we call domestic is on man; so that in spring when this species returns it is in the village of the Vizcacha we see them. There they live and spend the day, sporting about the burrows, just as the domestic Swallow does about our houses. The nest, constructed of dry grass lined with feathers, is placed at the extreme end of the burrow, and contains five or six white, pointed eggs. After the young have flown, they sit close together on a weed, thistle-top, or low tree; and the parents continue to feed them many days.

"As in size and brightness of plumage, so in language also is this Swallow inferior to his congeners, his only song consisting of a single weak, trilling note, much prolonged, which the bird repeats with great frequency when on the wing. But sometimes he utters two notes; and then the second note, though much the same, is longer and more inflected than the first; yet his voice has ever a mournful monotonous sound. If a rapacious bird or a Fox chances to intrude upon the burrows when they are breeding, these Swallows summon each other with cries indicative of fear and anxiety; but even then these cries are neither loud nor shrill. When flying, these Swallows glide along very close to the earth, and when weary settle down (contrary to the custom of other Swallows) and rest on the level grassy plains. Like other birds of this family they possess the habit of gliding to and fro before a rider's horse to snatch up the little twilight moths startled from the grass. Seldom does a person ride on the pampas in summer without having a number of Swallows gather round him; often I have thought that more than a hundred were before my horse at one time; but, from the rapidity of their motions, it is impossible to count them. I have also noticed individuals of the four most common species of Swallow following me together; but after sunset, and when the other species have long forsaken the grass plains for the shelter of trees and houses, this diminutive Swallow continues to keep the traveller company. At such a time, as they glide about in the dusk of evening conversing together in low tremulous tones, they have a peculiarly sorrowful appearance, seeming like homeless little wanderers over the great level plains.

"When the season of migration approaches, they begin to congregate in parties not very large (though sometimes as many as one or two hundred are seen together); these companies spend much of their time perched close together on weeds, low trees, fences, or other slightly elevated situations, and pay very little attention to a person approaching, but seem preoccupied or preyed upon by some anxiety that has no visible cause.

"This time immediately preceding the departure of the Swallows is indeed a season of deep interest to the observer of nature. The birds seem to forget their songs and aerial recreations; the attachment of the sexes, the remembrance of the spring is obliterated; they already begin to feel the premonitions of that marvellous instinct that urges them hence: not yet an irresistible impulse, it is a vague sense of disquiet; but its influence is manifest in their language and gestures, their wild manner of flight, and listless intervals.

"The little *Atticora cyanoleuca* disappears immediately after the other larger species. Many stragglers continue to be seen after the departure of the main body; but before the middle of March not one remains, the migration of this species being very regular."

The descriptions are taken from the series in the British Museum, and the adult is figured from a Colombian specimen in Mr. Wyatt's possession, the young bird from a Pelotas skin in the Salvin-Godman collection. The Argentine fishing-cart is from a drawing of Mr. Vidal's.

ATTICORA PILEATA.

GUATEMALAN SWALLOW.

Atticora pileata, Gould, P. Z. S. 1858, p. 355; Scl. & Salv. Ibis, 1859, p. 13; Baird, Review Amer. B. p. 307 (1865); Gray, Hand-l. B. i. p. 72. no. 860 (1869); Scl. & Salv. Nomencl. Av. Neotr. p. 11 (1873); Salv. & Godm. Biol. Centr.-Amer., Aves, i. p. 230, tab. xv. fig. 2 (1813); Sharpe, Cat. Birds in Brit. Mus. x. p. 188 (1885).

Notiochelidon pileata, Baird, Review Amer. B. p. 306 (1865).

A. subtùs alba, menti gulæque plumis brunneo basaliter maculatis; interscapalio brunneo; pileo indigotico-nigro; hypochondriis brunneis.

Hab. in provinciâ Guatemalensi Americæ centralis.

Adult male. General colour above chocolate-brown on the hind neck, mantle, and back; the scapulars, lower back, rump, and upper tail-coverts darker and more sooty brown; lesser and median wing-coverts blue-black; greater coverts, bastard-wing, and primary-coverts dark brown, the quills and tail-feathers blackish brown; crown of head and nape blue-black; lores and feathers round the eye velvety black; ear-coverts blackish with a slight blue gloss; cheeks and chin blackish brown, edged with white; throat, breast, and abdomen white, the feathers on the throat and chest more or less mottled with dark brown bases to the feathers; sides of breast and flanks dark brown; thighs white; vent and under tail-coverts blackish brown; axillaries and under wing-coverts dark brown; quills dark brown below. Total length 4·8 inches, culmen 0·25, wing 3·7, tail 2·05, tarsus 0·4.

Adult female. Similar to the male in colour. Total length 4·8 inches, culmen 0·3, wing 3·65, tail 2·2, tarsus 0·45.

The only difference which we can detect between specimens of this species is a greater or less amount of mottling on the throat, owing to the way in which the brown bases of the feathers show through. This may be caused, it appears to us, by the abrasion or wearing away of the white edges to the feathers.

The males vary in length of wing from 3·6 to 3·75 inches, and the females from 3·65 to 3·8.

Young. Differs from the adult in being lighter brown, the feathers of the back being tipped with rufous-brown, particularly distinct on the lower back and rump; wings and tail as in the adult; crown of head dull sooty black, with scarcely any blue gloss; under surface of body silky white, with a tawny tinge on the throat and chest, the sides of the body being rufous-brown. Wing 3·45 inches.

Hab. Highlands of Guatemala, Central America.

The present species of Swallow was discovered by the late Mr. G. N. Skinner, the pioneer of ornithological discovery in Guatemala. He sent home specimens to Mr. Gould, who described them in 1858, and afterwards handed them over to the British Museum. Messrs. Salvin and Godman afterwards found it themselves and have given the following note in the 'Biologia':—"Our first intimate acquaintance with this Swallow was in February 1862, when staying at Coban, where it was a common species, frequenting the great church of the town; and our specimens were secured as they flew round over the courtyard of the house where we were staying, and which was close to the church. Having thus become familiar with the bird, we frequently observed it subsequently in the higher lands of the main Cordillera. Thus it was common at several points on the road from the city of Guatemala to Antigua, and we also observed it in several parts of the Altos, at an elevation of at least 8000 feet above the sea. In its habits and mode of flight we noticed nothing to distinguish it from other Hirundines." The localities mentioned by Messrs. Salvin and Godman are Coban, Quiché, Totonicapam, Quezaltenango, Barranco de Los Chocoyos, Calderas, the ridge above Barsinas, Villa Lobos, and Aceytuno.

The descriptions are taken from birds collected by Messrs. Salvin and Godman, in the British Museum, and the figure is drawn from one of this same series.

ATTICORA FUCATA (Temm.).

TAWNY-HEADED SWALLOW.

Hirundo fucata, Temm. Pl. Col. iv. pl. 161. fig. 1 (1823); Gray, Gen. B. i. p. 58 (1845).
Cotile fucata, Boie, Isis, 1826, p. 971; White, P. Z. S. 1882, p. 596.
Herse fucata, Less. Compl. Buff. viii. p. 498 (1837).
Cotyle fucata, Gray, Cat. Fissir. Brit. Mus. p. 30 (1848); Bp. Consp. i. p. 342 (1850); Cass. Cat. Hirund. Mus. Philad. Acad. p. 10 (1853); Burm. Th. Bras. iii. p. 145 (1856); id. Reis. La-Plata St. ii. p. 478 (1861); Reinh. Vid. Medd. Nat. For. Kjöbenh. 1870, p. 251; Pelz. Orn. Bras. pp. 18, 402 (1871); Scl. & Salv. Nomencl. Av. Neotr. p. 14 (1873).
Atticora fucata, Baird, Review Amer. B. p. 308 (1865); Gray, Hand-l. B. ii. p. 72. no. 858 (1869); Sharpe, Cat. Birds in Brit. Mus. x. p. 188 (1885); Salvin, Ibis, 1885, p. 206; Berl. & Ihering, Zeitsch. ges. Orn. ii. p. 117 (1885); Scl. & Hudson, Argent. Orn. i. p. 35 (1888).

A. subtùs alba : gutture et præpectore cervinis ; pileo cervino-rufo.

Hab. in Americâ meridionali.

Adult. General colour above brown, the rump and upper tail-coverts obscurely edged with dull whity brown; wing-coverts like the back, the inner greater coverts edged with whity brown near their ends; bastard-wing, primary-coverts, and quills blackish brown, the innermost secondaries with whity-brown edges; tail-feathers dark brown; crown of head deep tawny rufous, becoming clearer on the hinder crown and nape; the ear-coverts and sides of neck tawny rufous, extending round the hind neck; cheeks, throat, and breast pale tawny; sides of body brown, slightly washed with rufous; centre of breast, abdomen, and under tail-coverts white; thighs brown; under wing-coverts and axillaries smoky brown, slightly washed with rufous; quills ashy brown below. Total length 4·6 inches, culmen 0·25, wing 4·15, tail 2, tarsus 0·45.

The sexes are alike in colour and there is not much seasonal variation in plumage. The following are the measurements of the series of specimens in the British Museum:—

				Total length. in.	Wing. in.	Tail. in.	Tarsus. in.
a. ♂ ad.	Roraima (*Whitely*)			4·0	3·9	1·7	0·35
b. ♀ ad.	,,	,,		4·2	3·7	1·6	0·4
c. ♂ ad.	,,	,,		4·3	3·8	1·65	0·4
d. ♀ ad.	,,	,,		4·2	3·9	1·7	0·4
e. ♂ ad.	Ypanema (*Natterer*)			4·3	4·1	1·7	0·4
f. ♀ ad.	,,	,,		4·3	4·0	1·75	0·4
g. Ad.	Pampas Argentinas (*Leybold*)			4·5	3·95	2·0	0·45
h. ♂ ad.	Mendoza (*Weisshaupt*)			4·7	3·75	1·6	0·45
i. ♂ ad.	Cosquin (*White*)			4·6	4·0	1·8	0·4

Hab. Venezuela and British Guiana (Roraima), Southern Brazil and the Central Argentine Republic to Mendoza.

This pretty little Swallow has all the outward appearance of a Sand-Martin (*Cotile*), but its structure proves that it is a member of the genus *Atticora*, though it differs considerably in its style of plumage from all the other species of the genus.

Very little is known respecting its distribution and habits. Its occurrence in Venezuela rests on a specimen said by Professor Reinhardt to exist in the museum at Copenhagen; but none of the well-known collectors in that country, Goering, Spence, &c., appear to have met with it, and the locality needs some confirmation. Mr. Henry Whitely obtained several specimens on Roraima in January, and it is possible that the species winters in this quarter, as the birds collected by him are all in more perfect plumage than others from more southern localities, and have distinct whitish edgings to the greater coverts and secondaries.

Throughout the whole of the Amazon valley and the greater part of Brazil we have absolutely no record of the species, and we do not know even whether it passes over these countries on migration. That the species is migratory to a certain extent we gather from a remark of the late Mr. E. W. White, who speaks of it as increasing in numbers near Cosquin in the province of Cordova in August. A specimen shot by him on the 29th of September shows traces of having bred in the neighbourhood, as the rufous edges to the feathers of the crown are abraded, so that the bird appears to have a cap of sooty brown. The same may be said of a specimen collected by Mr. Leybold on the Pampas of the Argentine Republic, and Mr. Weisshaupt in Mendoza in February. Not only is the rufous colour entirely gone from the crown, but the throat and breast are also much less rufous than in others from more northern localities.

A summary of the dates when the species has been observed in Southern Brazil and the adjoining countries gives the following result:—

Mendoza (*Weisshaupt*), February. Cosquin in Cordova (*White*), July to September. Taquara (*Ihering*), November. Campos of San Paulo and Minas Geraes: Byen Franca and Paracatú (*Lund*), September; Lagoa Santa (*Lund*), March. Casa Pintada (*Natterer*), January; Ytararé (*Natterer*), February; Ypanema (*Natterer*), July.

It would appear, therefore, that the species occurs in the south in every month from July to March, and the only months in which it is absent are April, May, and June. Swallows are, however, so uncertain in their times of migration that it is quite possible that many of the present species reach their winter home in Southern Guiana by January, while some may not migrate at all. If, however, later investigations prove that no migration takes place northward across the Amazon valley, it may turn out that the Roraima bird is specifically distinct.

So far as we can discover, nothing has been published regarding the habits of this species.

The description has been taken from a specimen in the British Museum, and the figure has been drawn from one in the same collection, formerly in that of Messrs. Salvin and Godman.

APPENDIX

TO THE

GENUS ATTICORA.

ATTICORA FASCIATA [antea, p. 195].

Add:—

Atticora fasciata, Sharpe & Wyatt, Monogr. Hirund. pt. xii. (1889).

For the geographical distribution of this species, *vide suprà*, Plate 83 [Map].

ATTICORA CINEREA [antea, p. 199].

Add:—

Atticora cinerea, Sharpe & Wyatt, Monogr. Hirund. pt. xv. (1892).

For the geographical distribution of this species, *vide suprà*, Plate 82 [Map].

ATTICORA TIBIALIS [antea, p. 501].

Add:—

Atticora tibialis, Sharpe & Wyatt, Monogr. Hirund. pt. x. (1889).

For the geographical distribution of this species, *vide suprà*, Plate 81 [Map].

ATTICORA MELANOLEUCA [antea, p. 503].

Add:—

Atticora melanoleuca, Sharpe & Wyatt, Monogr. Hirund. pt. viii. (1888).

For the geographical distribution of this species, *vide suprà*, Plate 84 [Map].

ATTICORA CYANOLEUCA [anteà, p. 505].

Add :—

Atticora cyanoleuca, Berlepsch & Ihering, Zeitschr. ges. Orn. ii. p. 21 (1885); Sharpe & Wyatt, Monogr. Hirund. pt. xii. (1889).
Atticora cyanoleuca montana, Cherrie, Auk, ix. p. 22 (1892).

Dr. Ihering procured this species at Taquara, in Rio Grande do Sul, on the 28th of November, and again on the 6th of January.

Mr. Cherrie gives the following note from Costa Rica :—"A common resident. Breeds in the roofs of the houses. The young birds begin appearing about the 1st of July. They differ from the adult in being washed with pinkish buff below, including the under tail-coverts, while above the metallic lustre of the feathers is not so bright. In some examples the throat and belly are white, and the breast is crossed by a buffy band. The male of a pair that had their nest in the roof of the Museum was accidentally killed before the eggs hatched. The female did not desert her post, and when the young were hatched attended to the wants of the young alone."

For the geographical distribution of this species, *vide suprà*, Plate 85 [Map].

ATTICORA PILEATA [anteà, p. 513].

Add :—

Atticora pileata, Sharpe & Wyatt, Monogr. Hirund. pt. vi. (1887).

For the geographical distribution of this species, *vide suprà*, Plate 83 [Map].

ATTICORA FUCATA [anteà, p. 515].

Add :—

Atticora fucata, Sharpe & Wyatt, Monogr. Hirund. pt. viii. (1888); Berl. & Ihering, Zeitschr. ges. Orn. ii. p. 21 (1885).

Procured at Taquara, in Rio Grande do Sul, on the 19th of November by Dr. Ihering.

For the geographical distribution of this species, *vide infrà*, Plate 102 [Map].

	Migratory.
← · ←	Bird of passage.
← ⊖ ←	Remains locally during the winter.
← ⋏ ←	Transplanted.
← · ←	Winter resident.

	Nearctic Region.										Neotropical Region.					
	Arctic Sub-Region		Cold Temperate Sub-Region.				Warm Temperate Sub-Region				Central American Sub-Region.					
							Humid Province		Arid Province							
	Arctic Province.	Alaskan Arctic Province.	Hudsonian Province.	Canadian Province.	Sitkan Province.	Aleutian Province.	Appalachian Sub-Province	Austroriparian Sub-Province	Campestrian Sub-Province	Sonoran Sub-Province	Antillean Sub-Region.	Mexican Province.	Isthmian Province.	Sub-Andean Sub-Region.	Amazonian Sub-Region.	Brazilian Sub-Region.	Patagonian Sub-Region.	Arctic Sub-Region.
1. A. fusciata	..	..												○	○	○	
2. A. cinerea		..			..						..			..	..		○
3. A. tibialis	..	..											○				
4. A.	..	..												○	○		
5. A. custoditus	..	..							..		○	○		○	○	○	○
6. A. pileata	..	..										○					
7. A. fusca	..	..			..	..								..	○	○	

V   Guest.
†   Wanderer.

☐ Rarely ⎫
▨ Generally ⎬ nesting.
▨ In colonies ⎭

Ethiopian Region.									Indian Region.					Australian Region.					
Malagasy Sub-Region.	Nyanza Sub-Region.	West African Sub-Region.	Mozambian Sub-Region.	East African Sub-Region.	South African Sub-Region. – Cape Province.	South African Sub-Region. – Native or Proper.	Ethiopian Sub-Region.	Leonitian Sub-Region.	Indian Peninsular Sub-Region.	Indo-Malayan Sub-Region.	Himalo-Malayan Sub-Region.	Himal. et Ind. – Sub-Region.	Celebes Sub-Region.	Moluccan Sub-Region.	Papuan Sub-Region.	Australian Sub-Region.	New Zealand Sub-Region.	Fijian Sub-Region.	Hawaiian Sub-Region.

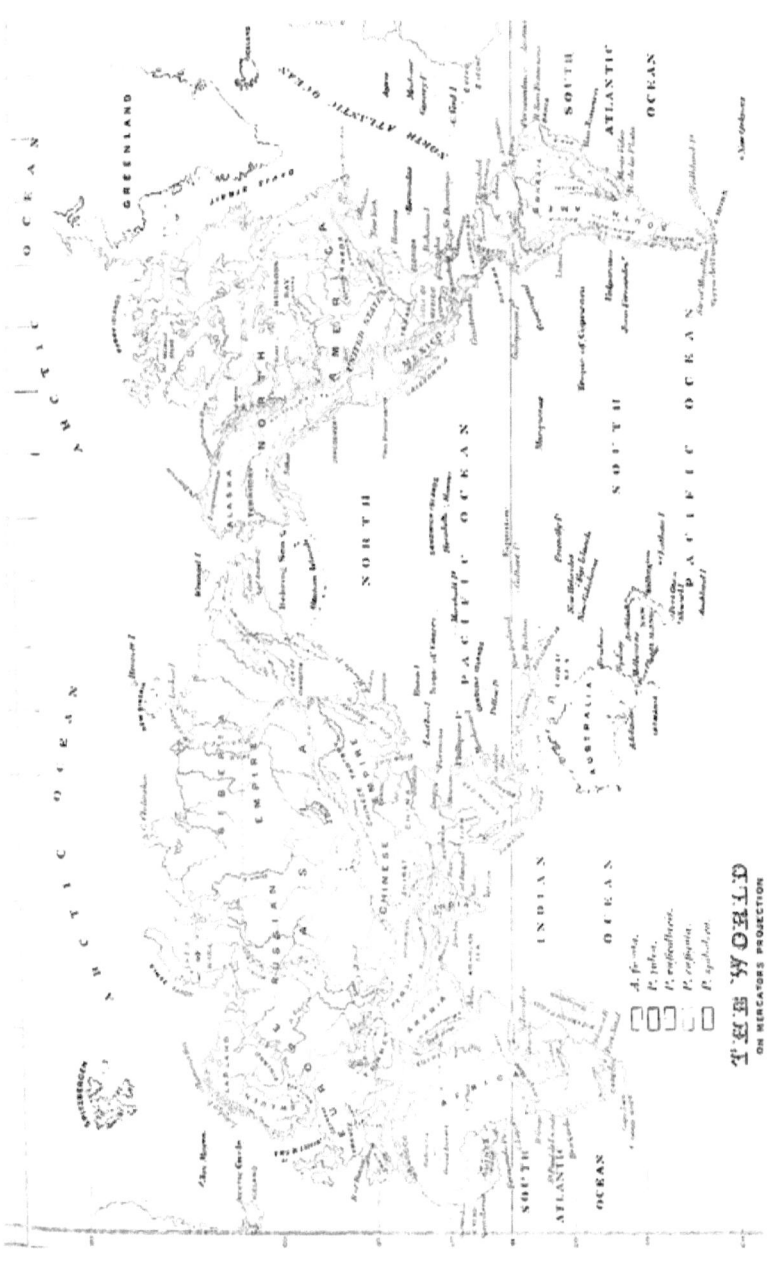

Genus X. PETROCHELIDON.

	Type.
Petrochelidon, Cab. Mus. Hein. i. p. 47 (1850) . . .	*P. swainsoni*.
Hylochelidon, Gould, Handb. B. Austr. i. p. 111 (1865). .	*P. nigricans*.
Lagenoplastes, Gould, tom. cit. p. 113 (1865)	*P. ariel*.
Atticochelidon, Bald. J. f. O. 1869, p. 106	*P. nigricans*.

Range. North America; Central America; South America to Brazil and Peru; Antilles; South and South-west Africa; Central India; Australia and the Papuan Islands.

Clavis specierum.

a. Frons fulvescens aut rufa.
    a'. Uropygium albicans aut fumoso-albicans; guttur albicans, minuté nigro striolatum.
        a''. Major: uropygium albicans . . . . 1. *nigricans*, p. 525.
        b''. Minor: uropygium fumoso-albicans; gastræum fumoso-brunneo adumbratum . . . . 2. *timoriensis*, p. 529.
    b'. Uropygium rufum: guttur rufum.
        c''. Frons albicans aut fulvescens; torques nuchalis minimé obvia; mentum ad basin nigrum; jugulum imum fascia cærulescenti-nigra ornatum; hypochondriis cinerascenti-brunneis . . . . 3. *pyrrhonota*, p. 531.
        d''. Frons castanea; torques nuchalis rufa obvia, regioni parotical conjuncta.
            a'''. Mentum ad basin nigrum; fascia jugularis cærulescenti-nigra; hypochondriis cinerascenti-brunneæ . . . . 4. *swainsoni*, p. 555.
            b'''. Mentum minimé nigrum; fascia jugularis nulla; guttur rufum; hypochondriis rufæ . . . . 5. *fulva*, p. 561.
    c'. Uropygium rufum; guttur album; fascia præpectoralis rufa . . . . 6. *ruficollaris*, p. 567.
b. Frons angusté rufo transfasciata; pileum cærulescenti-nigrum, dorso concolor; uropygium rufum; gastræum rufum; guttur et crissum castanea . . . . 7. *rufigula*, p. 571.
c. Fascia frontalis rufa nulla; tectrices subalares et axillares pallidé rufæ; tectrices supracaudales et subcaudales nigræ, rufo apicatæ . . . 8. *spilodera*, p. 573.
d. Pileum rufum.
    d'. Uropygium fumoso-brunneum, fusco marmoratum; guttur et præpectus late nigro striolata . . . . 9. *fluvicola*, p. 577.
    e'. Uropygium albicans; guttur angusté fusco striolatum . . . . 10. *ariel*, p. 583.

PETROCHELIDON NIGRICANS.

PETROCHELIDON NIGRICANS (*Vieill.*).
WHITE-RUMPED CLIFF-SWALLOW.

Hirundo nigricans, Vieill. N. Dict. d'Hist. Nat. xiv. p. 523 (1817); Quoy et Gaim. Voy. Astrol., Zool. i. p. 205, pl. 12. fig. 2 (1830); Gray, Gen. B. i. p. 58 (1845); id. Cat. Fissir. Brit. Mus. p. 24 (1818); id. P. Z. S. 1858, pp. 171, 189; id. Cat. B. New Guinea, pp. 18, 54 (1859); id. P. Z. S. 1861, p. 433; Finsch, Neu-Guinea, p. 162 (1865); Gray, Hand-l. B. i. p. 70, no. 817 (1869); Buller, B. N. Zeal. p. 141 (1873); Finsch, Ibis, 1881, p. 536; Buller, Man. B. N. Zeal. p. 6 (1882).

Dun-rumped Swallow, Lath. Gen. Hist. vii. p. 309 (1823).

Hirundo pyrrhonota, Vig. & Horsf. Trans. Linn. Soc. xv. p. 190 (1826, ex Lath. MSS., nec V.).

Herse nigricans, Less. Compl. Buff. viii. p. 497 (1837); Gray, Gen. B. i. p. 58 (1845); Bp. Consp. i. p. 340 (1850); Rosenb. J. f. O. 1864, p. 120.

Herse pyrrhonota, Less. Compl. Buff. Ois. viii. p. 497 (1837).

Cecropis nigricans, Boie, Isis, 1844, p. 175.

Cecropis pyrrhonota, Boie, t. c.

Collocalia arborea, Gould, B. Austr. ii. pl. 14 (c. 1848).

Chelidon arborea, Gould, t. c., Intr. p. xxix (1848).

Hirundo pyrrhonota australis, Temm. & Schl. Faun. Jap., Aves, p. 35 (1850).

Petrochelidon nigricans, Cab. Mus. Hein. Th. i. p. 47 (1850); Cass. Cat. Hirund. Mus. Philad. Acad. p. 7 (1853); Sharpe, Cat. Birds in Brit. Mus. x. p. 190 (1885).

Chelidon nigricans, Licht. Nomencl. Av. p. 61 (1854).

Hylochelidon nigricana, Gould, Handb. B. Austr. i. p. 111 (1865); Masters, Proc. Linn. Soc. N. S. W. i. p. 47 (1875); Ramsay, t. c. p. 389 (1876); id. & Casteln. t. c. p. 389 (1876); Ramsay, op. cit. ii. p. 179 (1878); id. op. cit. iv. p. 98 (1879); Salvad. Ann. Mus. Civic. Genov. x. p. 131 (1877); id. P. Z. S. 1878, p. 95; id. Ann. Mus. Civic. Genov. xiv. pp. 491, 648 (1879); Buller, Trans. N. Zeal. Inst. xi. p. 360 (1878); Salvad. Orn. Papuasia, &c. ii. p. 6 (1881); id. Report Voy. 'Challenger,' ii. Birds, p. 78 (1884).

Hirundo (Herse) arborea, Pelz. Reis. 'Novara,' Vög. p. 41 (1875).

Hydrochelidon (lapsu) *nigricans*, Ramsay, Proc. Linn. Soc. N. S. W. iii. p. 275 (1879).

P. fasciâ frontali rufâ; uropygio albicante; gutture albicante angustissimè nigro striolato.

Hab. in Australiâ et in insulis Australianis, in Novâ Zealandiâ, Novâ Guineâ, et in insulis 'Aru' et 'Ké' dictis.

Adult male. General colour above deep steel-blue, slightly streaked with dusky white where the light bases of the feathers show through; lesser wing-coverts like the back, the remainder dusky brown as well as the quills, the innermost secondaries with a narrow edging of dull white at the tip; lower back and rump whity brown, slightly washed with sandy rufous, the feathers edged with creamy white and having blackish shafts; upper tail-coverts dusky brown, rather broadly edged with creamy white; tail-feathers dusky brown; a frontal band of pale brick-red extending backwards to the corner of the eye; the base of the forehead near the culmen minutely spotted with dull steel-blue; lores, feathers round the eye, and ear-coverts sooty blackish; sides of the neck sandy buff, streaked with dull black; cheeks and throat dull whitish, with a tinge of buff, the feathers minutely streaked with dusky blackish shaft-lines; fore neck, chest, and sides of body pale sandy rufous, with narrow shaft-lines of dusky, less distinct on the flanks; breast and abdomen paler, being whitish with a sandy-rufous tinge; the under tail-coverts similarly coloured, and having dusky shaft-lines; sides of upper breast with a patch of blackish or dull blue; under wing-coverts and axillaries deeper sandy rufous, with dusky shaft-lines; quills dusky below, rather paler along the inner web: "bill blackish brown; legs and feet olive-brown; iris blackish brown" (*Gould*). Total length 5·2 inches, culmen 0·3, wing 4·2, tail 2·1, tarsus 0·5.

Young. Distinguished from the adult by the absence of the rufous band on the forehead, which is replaced by a few sandy-buff feathers. The whole tone of coloration is duller in the young than in the old birds, the upper surface being dusky brown with more or less of a blue gloss, the inner secondaries edged with pale rufous at the tips. The under surface is paler than in the adult.

Some specimens are remarkable for the rufous glow which pervades their lower surface; these are probably old birds killed in spring. It seems certain that, after breeding, this tinge is lost and the plumage becomes more or less abraded, the chest fades to smoky brown in colour, and the throat, breast, and under tail-coverts are purer white. The rump, which in breeding birds is strongly suffused with rufous, also becomes gradually bleached, and fades to a dull whitish or pale smoky brown.

The size of the present species appears to vary to an unusual extent for a Swallow—the wing in adults ranging from 4 to 4·35 inches, a remarkable difference for so small a bird.

Mr. Gould seems to consider that these differences of size are coincident with locality; but we have not remarked this particularly, and it is hardly likely to be the case with such a strictly migratory species.

Hab. Australia generally and Tasmania. Accidental in New Zealand. New Britain, New Guinea, Aru Islands, Ké Islands.

THE broad whitish band across the lower back and rump easily distinguishes this species of Cliff-Swallow, which is essentially an Australian bird. It is very widely distributed over the Australian continent, and, according to Mr. Ramsay, it is found everywhere with the exception of Port Darling and Port Essington; it doubtless occurs in these places also, but has not yet been observed by a competent naturalist.

Mr. Gould has given the following account of the species as observed by him in Australia:—

"The Tree-Swallow is a very common summer visitant to the southern portions of

Australia and Tasmania, arriving in August and retiring northwards as autumn approaches. It is a very familiar species, and frequents the towns in company with the Swallow. I observed it to be particularly numerous in the streets of Hobart Town, where it arrives early in September; the more southern and colder situation of the island rendering all migratory birds later in their arrival there.

"It breeds during the month of October in the holes of trees, making no nest, but laying its eggs on the soft dust generally found in such places: the eggs are from three to five in number, of a pinky white faintly freckled at the larger end with fine spots of light reddish brown; they are eight lines long by six lines broad.

"Considerable difference exists both in size and in the depth of colouring of specimens killed in New South Wales, Swan River, and Tasmania; but as there exists no distinctive character of marking, I regard them as local varieties rather than as distinct species. Tasmanian specimens are larger in all their admeasurements, and have the fulvous tint of the under surface and the band across the forehead much deeper than in those killed in New South Wales; individuals from the latter locality again exceed in size those from Western Australia."

Sir Walter Buller has recorded several instances of the occurrence of this Swallow in New Zealand, where it is only of rare and occasional occurrence. Mr. Lea shot a specimen at Taupata, near Cape Farewell, on the 14th of March, and the specimen is in the Otago Museum. Mr. F. Jollie observed a flight at Wakapuaka, in the vicinity of Nelson, in the summer of 1851, and shot one specimen. According to Sir David Monro, it has occurred several times near Nelson (Trans. N. Z. Inst. vii. p. 510). Lastly, Mr. J. R. W. Cook, writing to Sir W. Buller, states that he noticed a Swallow on the 9th of June about two miles from Blenheim, on the bank of the Opawa River, and from the description given it was evidently the Australian species.

In South-eastern New Guinea Mr. Goldie has procured this Swallow about 15 miles inland from Port Moresby, but it was not common. Dr. Finsch mentions it in 'The Ibis' (*l. c.*) as occurring in New Britain, but he does not allude to the species in his 'Vögel der Südsee.' D'Albertis met with it at Sorong, in North-western New Guinea, and a specimen from Dourga, in the same island, is in the Leyden Museum. Mr. Wallace procured it in the Aru Islands, where it was also collected by the naturalists of the 'Challenger' expedition. Dr. Beccari has also shot the species in the Ké Islands. On Timor it appears to be replaced by a slightly modified race.

The descriptions are taken from the British-Museum 'Catalogue of Birds,' and the figure in the Plate is drawn from a specimen in the possession of Captain Wardlaw Ramsay.

PETROCHELIDON TIMORIENSIS.

TIMOR CLIFF-SWALLOW.

Hirundo nigricans (nec Vieill.), Wallace, P. Z. S. 1863, p. 485.
Petrochelidon timoriensis, Sharpe, Cat. Birds in Brit. Mus. x. p. 192 (1884).

P. similis P. nigricanti, sed minor, uropygio et corpore subtùs fumoso lavatis.

Hab. in insulis Moluccanis 'Timor' et ' Flores ' dictis.

Adult male. Similar to *P. nigricans*, but very much smaller in size, and distinguished by the dark smoky-brown colour of the rump, the smoky colour of the underparts, and the greater extent of the shaft-striping, which is very distinct and continues over the throat, breast, and entire sides of the body. Total length 4·5 inches, culmen 0·3, wing 3·65, tail 1·65, tarsus 0·4.

In the other two examples in the British Museum the wing measures 3·6 and 3·75 inches respectively.

Hab. Island of Timor, and probably Flores.

THE characters above given sufficiently describe the difference between the Timor Cliff-Swallow and its congener from Australia. They scarcely amount to specific distinctions, and are perhaps characteristic of an island race only. Three specimens are in the British Museum, from Mr. Wallace's collection, all having been obtained by that naturalist in the island of Timor. Mr. Wallace likewise records it as occurring in Flores; but we have never seen a specimen from the last-mentioned island, nor was there one in Mr. Wallace's collection when it passed into the hands of the Museum. It is quite possible, however, that he saw this Swallow flying about in the island of Flores, in which case the species would no doubt be the same as that from Timor.

The description is copied from the pages of the British Museum ' Catalogue.'

PETROCHELIDON PYRRHONOTA (*Vieill.*).
NORTH-AMERICAN CLIFF-SWALLOW.

Hirundo no. 35, Forster, Philos. Trans. p. 408 (1772).
? *Hirondelle à croupion roux et queue carrée*, Montb. Hist. Nat. Ois. vi. p. 698 (1779).
? *Rufous-rumped Swallow*, Lath. Gen. Syn. ii. pt. 2, p. 582 (1783).
? *Hirundo americana*, Gm. Syst. Nat. i. p. 1017 (1788, ex Lath.); Gray, Hand-l. B. i. p. 71, no. 810 (1869).
Golondrina rabadilla acanelada, Azara, Apunt. ii. p. 511, no. 305 (1802); Hartl. Ind. Azara, p. 19 (1847).
Hirundo pyrrhonota, Vieill. Nouv. Dict. d'Hist. Nat. xiv. p. 519 (1817); Gray, Gen. B. i. p. 58 (1845).
Hirundo lunifrons, Say in Long's Exped. Rocky Mts. ii. p. 47 (1823); Swains. Faun. Bor.-Amer., Birds, p. 331 (1831); Brewer, Proc. Bost. Soc. N. H. 1852, p. 270; Wood, Report Zuni and Color. R. 1853, p. 64; Cass. Ill. B. Calif. p. 243 (1856); Brewer, N. Amer. Ool. p. 94. pl. 5. figs. 68-73 (1857); Baird, in Baird, Cass., & Lawr. B. N. Amer. p. 309 (1858); Xantus, Proc. Philad. Acad. 1859, p. 191; Blakist. Ibis, 1863, p. 64; Coues, Ibis, 1865, p. 163; Dresser, t. c. p. 479; Baird, Ibis, 1867, p. 274; Brown, Ibis, 1868, p. 427; Gray, Hand-l. B. i. p. 71, no. 826 (1869); Dall & Bann. Trans. Chicago Acad. i. p. 279 (1869); Cooper, B. Calif. p. 104 (1870); Allen, Bull. Mus. Comp. Zool. iii. p. 176 (1872); Harting, Handb. Brit. B. p. 125 (1872).
Hirundo opifex, De Witt Clinton, Ann. Lyc. N. Y. i. p. 161 (1824).
Hirundo respublicana, Audub. Ann. Lyc. N. Y. i. p. 164 (1824).
Hirundo fulva (nec V.), De Witt Clinton, Ann. Lyc. N. Y. i. p. 156 (1824); Bp. Amer. Orn. i. p. 63, pl. 7. fig. 1 (1825); Audub. B. Amer. pl. 68 (c. 1826); id. Orn. Biogr. i. p. 353 (1831); Bp. Comp. List B. Eur. & N. Amer. p. 9 (1838); Audub. B. Amer. 8vo, i. p. 77, pl. 47 (1840); Gray, Gen. B. i. p. 58 (1845, pt.).
Cecropis lunifrons, Boie, Isis, 1828, p. 315, 1844, p. 175.
Cecropis pyrrhonota, Boie, Isis, 1844, p. 173.
Hesse fulva, pt. (nec V.), Bp. Consp. i. p. 341 (1850).
Petrochelidon americana, Cab. Mus. Hein. Th. i. p. 47. note (1850); Pelz. Orn. Bras. pp. 17, 102 (1871).
Petrochelidon fulva (nec V.), Bp. C. R. xxxviii. p. 650 (1854, pt.).
Hirundo fulvus (nec V.), Willis, Smiths. Rep. 1858-59, p. 281.
Petrochelidon lunifrons, Cass. Cat. Hirund. Mus. Philad. Acad. p. 4 (1853), Lawr. Ann.

Lyc. N. Y. vii. p. 317 (1861); Sel. Cat. Amer. B. p. 40 (1862); Coues, Key N. Amer. B. p. 114 (1872); id. B. N.-West, p. 88 (1874); Baird, Brewer, & Ridgw. Hist. N. Amer. B. i. p. 334, pl. 16. fig. 13 (1874); Henshaw, Rep. Expl. 100th Merid., Zool. p. 215 (1875); Ridgw. Rep. Survey 40th Par. iv. p. 440 (1877); Coues, B. Color. Vall. p. 426 (1878); Sennett, Bull. U. S. Geol. Surv. iv. p. 15 (1878); Coues, t. c. p. 371 (1878); Brewst. Bull. Nutt. Orn. Club, ii. p. 63 (1878); Coues, t. c. p. 105; Merrill, Proc. U. S. Nat. Mus. i. p. 125 (1878); Scott, Bull. Nutt. Orn. Club, iv. pp. 93, 142 (1878); Belding, t. c. p. 408 (1879); Ridgw. Proc. U. S. Nat. Mus. iii. p. 175 (1880); Roberts & Benner, Bull. Nutt. Orn. Club, v. p. 14 (1880); Knowlton, op. cit. vi. p. 55 (1881); Merriam, t. c. p. 229 (1881); Hoffm. Bull. U. S. Geol. Surv. vi. p. 220 (1881); Coues, Check-list N. Amer. B. p. 43 (1882); Belding, Proc. U. S. Nat. Mus. v. p. 547 (1882); Nehrling, Bull. Nutt. Orn. Club, vii. p. 11 (1882); Brown, t. c. p. 27; Batch. t. c. p. 110; Brewst. t. c. p. 146; Merriam, t. c. p. 235; Allen & Brewst. op. cit. viii. p. 160 (1883); Lawr. Mem. Bost. Soc. N. H. ii. p. 271 (1884); Coues, Key N. Amer. B. 2nd ed. p. 323 (1884); Drew, Auk, ii. p. 15 (1885); Agersb. t. c. p. 279; Turner, Proc. U. S. Nat. Mus. viii. p. 239 (1885); A. O. U. Check-l. p. 292 (1886); Anthony, Auk, iii. p. 169 (1886); Everm. t. c. p. 183; Fox, t. c. p. 317; Thompson (Seton), t. c. p. 324; Ferrari-Perez, Proc. U. S. Nat. Mus. ix. p. 139 (1886); Ridgw. t. c. p. 139, note; Dwight, Auk, iv. p. 15 (1887); Beckh. t. c. p. 123; Lloyd, t. c. p. 294; Beckh. t. c. p. 304; Nelson, Nat. Hist. Alaska, p. 197 (1887); Ridgw. Man. N. Amer. B. p. 460 (1887); Towns. Proc. U. S. Nat. Mus. x. p. 221 (1887); Ridgw. t. c. pp. 510, 579; Beckh. t. c. p. 682; Richm. Auk, v. p. 23 (1888); Scott. t. c. p. 31; Faxon & Allen. t. c. p. 150; Merrill, t. e. p. 360; Brewst. t. c. p. 389; Warren, B. Pennsylv. p. 205 (1888); Everm. Auk, vi. p. 25 (1889); Faxon, t. c. pp. 45, 102; F. H. Allen, t. c. p. 77; Mearns, Auk, vii. p. 48 (1890).

Herse lunifrons, Coues, Ibis, 1865, p. 159.

Petrochelidon pyrrhonota, Scl. & Salv. Nomencl. Av. Neotr. p. 14 (1873); Duruf. Ibis, 1877, p. 169, 1878, p. 58; White, P. Z. S. 1882, p. 595; Salvin & Godman, Biol. Centr.-Amer., Aves, i. p. 226 (1883); Sharpe, Cat. Birds in Brit. Mus. x. pp. 193, 635 (1885); Gibson, Ibis, 1885, p. 277; Salvin, Ibis, 1885, p. 256; Sclater & Hudson, Argent. Orn. i. p. 30 (1888);

Hirundo fulca, var. *lunifrons*, Cooper, Proc. U. S. Nat. Mus. ii. p. 246 (1880).

P. uropygio rufo: gulâ rufâ: fasciâ frontali pallide arcuariâ: torque collari cinerascenti-brunneâ posticè interruptâ: mento ad basin nigro: maculâ jugulari saturate chalybeo-nigro: hypochondriis cinerascenti-brunneis.

Hab. in Americâ septentrionali, in Americâ centrali occidentali et in Americâ meridionali usque ad terram Argentinam.

Adult male. General colour above glossy dark steel-blue, streaked on the back with more or less concealed ashy-whitish edges to the feathers; lower back and rump cinnamon-rufous, the upper tail-coverts brown with ashy margins; wing-coverts black, slightly glossed with steel-blue, the inner greater coverts slightly edged with ashy whitish; bastard-wing, primary-coverts, and quills blackish, the inner secondaries with narrow ashy margins at the tips of the feathers; tail-feathers blackish with a greenish gloss; crown of head glossy steel-blue, separated from the back by an indistinct collar of ashy brown; forehead pale sandy buff; lores and a narrow frontal band black; ear-coverts, cheeks, and sides of face deep chestnut-rufous, spreading on to the sides of the hind neck; chin also deep chestnut-rufous, glossed with a few steel-blue feathers, the lower throat entirely glossy steel-blue, forming a patch; fore neck and chest light ashy brown washed with rufous; the sides of the body and flanks similarly coloured, with narrow dusky shaft-lines on the flanks; centre of the breast and abdomen whitish with a slight tint of brown; vent pale rufous; under tail-coverts ashy brown, darker towards the ends, the feathers distinctly margined with white; under wing-coverts and axillaries ashy brown, distinctly tinged with rufous, especially near the edge of the wing; quills dark ashy brown below. Total length 5·3 inches, culmen 0·3, wing 4·35, tail 2·05, tarsus 0·45.

Adult female. Similar to the male in colour. Total length 5·5 inches, culmen 0·3, wing 4·1, tail 2·15, tarsus 0·5.

The length of wing in the males varies from 4·2 to 4·4 inches, and the bulk of the female birds in the Henshaw collection measure 4·2 or 4·3 inches, but two specimens, both marked females, have a wing of 4·45 inches, so that there is probably very little difference in the size of the two sexes.

Young. Dull blackish, with rufescent margins to the feathers, the head duller than the back, which has a slight shade of blue; the reddish forehead only faintly indicated and having a few white feathers intermixed; a slight indication of a rufescent collar on the hind neck; upper tail-coverts, wings, and tail brown, with ashy rufous margins to the tail-coverts, greater wing-coverts, and inner secondaries; sides of face blackish brown, with a white feather or two on the ear-coverts; cheeks and throat chestnut, the lower throat black, all these parts irregularly spotted with white; remainder of the under surface of body as in the adults, but the rufous on the chest and sides very strongly marked, and the under tail-coverts broadly edged with rufous.

The amount of white markings on the throat and forehead in the young birds varies greatly. Some of them have abundance of white on the throat and none on the forehead, while others have the forehead thickly spotted, but show no white at all on the throat. By the end of July the original colour of the bird becomes much obliterated, the upper surface is dusky blackish without any blue, the cinnamon rump and the rufous of the under surface almost disappear by abrasion, and it is perfectly comprehensible that the body-feathers must be renewed before the bird migrates to summer climates.

The series in the Henshaw collection is very complete, and shows all the stages of plumage excepting the absolute nestling. Both sexes are equally bright in colour when they arrive in May, and the rufous on the forehead is strongly pronounced. During June the frontal band bleaches to whity brown, but by the end of July the whole of the feathers are very much worn and discoloured, and the whitish edgings to the under tail-coverts become completely abraded, while most of the white streaks on the back disappear. The plumage of the hen bird appears to suffer more than that of the male, and the black spot on the throat is all but obliterated.

That the moult of the old birds commences before they leave their northern home is proved by a female bird procured at Washington on the 11th of August which is beginning to renew its body-feathers. In the case of the young birds the moult is often much advanced, and in a series procured by Dr. Fisher at Sing Sing, N.Y., in August, several of the specimens are in active moult. These may be the earlier hatched individuals, as some specimens have not commenced to moult.

Hab. North America at large, migrating down Central America to Brazil and the Argentine Republic.

The Cliff-Swallow of North America is distinguished by its sandy-buff frontal band and rufous rump and throat.

Its range in summer is very extensive, but the line of its winter migrations is still somewhat difficult to indicate, as it has occurred in various parts of Central America, but principally on the Eastern or Atlantic side, so that it is probably by this route that the species finds its way to its winter home in South America, where it visits Brazil and the Argentine Republic. The earliest assured name of the species is undoubtedly *Hirundo pyrrhonota* of Vieillot, founded on Azara's "*Golondrina rabadillo acanelada*"; and although Professor Ridgway challenges this identification, there can scarcely be any doubt that it is correct.

The best account of the species in North America is that published by Professor Elliott Coues in his 'Birds of the Colorado Valley,' and this is such a perfect Monograph of the Cliff-Swallow that we cannot resist quoting it in its entirety:—

"Discovery of this notable Swallow, commonly attributed to Say, was made long before Long's expedition to the Rocky Mountains, though the species was first named in the book which treats of that interesting journey. The bird may have been discovered by the celebrated John Reinhold Forster; at any rate, the earliest note I have in hand respecting the Cliff-Swallow is Forster's, dating 1772, when this naturalist published in the Philosophical Transactions 'An Account of the Birds sent from Hudson's Bay; with observations relative to their Natural History, and Latin Descriptions of some of the most Uncommon,'—a rather noted paper, in which seven new species, viz. *Falco spadiceus, Strix nebulosa, Emberiza* [i. e. *Zonotrichia*] *leucophrys, Fringilla* [i. e. *Junco*] *hudsonius, Muscicapa* [i. e. *Dendroeca*] *striata, Parus hudsonicus,* and *Scolopax* [i. e. *Numenius*] *borealis,* are described, with references to various other new birds by number, such as '*Turdus* No. 22,' which is *Scolecophagus ferrugineus,* and '*Hirundo* No. 35,' which is *Petrochelidon lunifrons.* The next observer—in fact, a rediscoverer—was, perhaps, Audubon, who says that he saw Republican or Cliff Swallows for the first time in 1815, at Henderson, on the Ohio; that he drew up a description at the time, naming the species *Hirundo republicana* [*sic*]; and that he again saw the same bird in 1819 at Newport, Ky., where they usually appeared about the 10th of April, and had that year finished about fifty nests by the 20th of the same month. The next year, namely 1820, Major Long and Sir John Franklin found these birds again, in widely remote regions, the first-named during his expedition to the Rocky Mountains, and the latter on the journey from Cumberland House to Fort Enterprise, and on the banks of Point Lake, in latitude 65°, where its earliest arrival was noted the following year on the 12th of June. Dr. Richardson says that their clustered nests are of frequent occurrence on the faces of cliffs of the

Barren Grounds, and not uncommon throughout the course of the Slave and Mackenzie Rivers, and that their first appearance at Fort Chipewyan was on the 25th of June, 1825. Major Long's discovery was named *Hirundo lunifrons* by Say in 1823; and the following year Audubon published his hitherto MS. name *republicana* in the 'Annals of the New York Lyceum of Natural History,' with some remarks on the species, in connection with some observations of Governor de Witt Clinton, who called the bird *Hirundo opifex*. Meanwhile, Vieillot had described the West Indian conspecies as *Hirundo fulva*; and the future Prince Bonaparte adopted this name for our species in 1825. Thus in the short space of two years, 1823-25, the interesting Anonyma, 'No. 35,' before known only by number, like the striped inmates of some of our penal establishments, suddenly became quite a lion, with titles galore in the binomial *haut ton*. But it was not till 1850 that it was actually raised to the sublime degree of *Petrochelidon*, though it had long been taken and held to be a master mason.

"The Cliff-Swallow has been supposed by some to be an immigrant of comparatively recent date in the Eastern United States; but it does not appear that any broad theory of a general progressive eastward extension is fairly deducible from the evidence we possess. On the contrary, much of the testimony is merely indicative of the dates when, in various parts of the country, the birds began to build under eaves, and so establish colonies where none existed before; and some of the evidence opposes the view just mentioned. The Swallows, as a rule, are birds of local distribution in the breeding-season notwithstanding their pre-eminent migratory abilities; they tend to settle in particular places, and return year after year; and nothing is better known than that one town may be full of Swallows of several kinds unknown in another town hard by. I suppose the real meaning of the record is 'only this and nothing more.' Nevertheless, these accounts are interesting, and all have their bearing on the natural history of this remarkable bird. It was unknown to Wilson. In 1817, between Audubon's times of observation in Kentucky, Clinton says he first saw Eave-Swallows at Whitehall, New York, at the southern end of Lake Champlain. Zadock Thompson found them at Randolph, Vt., about the same time. Mr. G. A. Boardman tells me that they were no novelty at St. Stephen's, New Brunswick, in 1828. Dr. Brewer received their eggs from Coventry, Vt., in 1837, when they were new to him; but the date of their appearance there was not determined. They are said by the same writer to have appeared at Jaffrey, N.H., in 1838; at Carlisle, P., in 1841; and the appearance of a large colony which he observed at Attleborough, Mass., in 1842, indicated that they had been there for several years. During the last-mentioned year they were present, apparently for the first time, in Boston and neighbouring metastatic foci of the globe. The record also teaches that these birds do not necessarily change from 'Cliff' to 'Eave' Swallows in the east, for in 1861 Professor Verrill discovered a large colony breeding on limestone cliffs of Anticosti, remote from man, and in their primitive fashion. That the settlement of the country has conduced to the general dispersion of the birds during the breeding-season in places that knew them not before is undoubted; but that any general eastward migration ever occurred, or that there has been in recent times a progressive spread of the birds across successive meridians, is less than doubtful—is almost disproven. Birds that fly like Swallows, and go from South America to the Arctic Ocean, are not likely to cut around *via* Mississippi or the Rocky Mountains, houses or no houses. Moreover, the scarcity or apparent absence of these birds in the Southern States, or most portions thereof, may be simply due to the ineligibility of the country, and only true for a part of the year. It cannot be that the breeding-birds of Pennsylvania, New York, and New England come and go by other than a direct route, and if not detected in the Southern States, it must be because they fly over the country in their migrations and do not stop to breed. It is authenticated that they nest at least as far south as Washington, D.C., where Dr. Coues and Dr. Prentiss found them some twenty years ago to be summer residents, arriving late in April and remaining until the middle of September, though they were not so abundant as some of the other Swallows."

The American Cliff-Swallow is a very widely distributed species in North America, and its winter range extends to Southern Brazil, Paraguay, and the Argentine Republic.

We have received from Mr. Ernest Thompson the following details of its range in Canada:—

"*Distribution in Ontario.*

"*London and vicinity.* Ten years ago abundant, breeding on fully half the farms. Now I do not see very many except in fall, when they are abundant in localities. Think possibly they are drawing into larger communities, though I have no evidence of real value to support this idea (*W. E. Saunders*).

"*Hyde Park.* Summer resident (*John A. Morden*).

"*Listowel, Co. of Perth.* Very numerous in some country places. Have seen 56 nests on one out-building (*Wm. L. Kells*).

"*Hamilton.* Early in May the Cliff-Swallow crosses the southern borders of Ontario .... in colonies .... all over the country. Two broods are raised in the season, and by the end of August they begin to move off (*T. McIlwraith*, 'Birds of Ontario,' p. 256).

"*Toronto.* A common summer resident about here, breeding under eaves of barns and houses. Dr. Brodie calls my attention to the fact that it is much less common now than formerly. I have it noted as follows: Arrived May 11th in 1885.

"*Springfield, and Credit Valley, southward to Lake Ontario.* Noted this species there in 1888 as rare. First seen June 2nd.

"*Elora.* Summer visitant. Common (*Hon. Chas. Clarke*).

"*Bruce Co., Central region, about Mildmay.* Summer resident. Common (*W. A. Schoenau*).

"*Lindsay.* Ten years ago very abundant about the barns. I have counted as many as seventy nests under the eaves about a single barnyard. It may be so yet, as I have not since visited the locality.

"*Millbrook.* Summer resident, abundant. Noted first 11th April (1885) (*Geo. Southeran*).

"*Peterborough.* Common (*Rev. Vincent Clementi*).

"*Yarker, Addington Co.* Summer resident, abundant. April 27th to May 11th (*John J. Ewart*).

"*Kingston.* Abundant (*Dr. C. K. Clarke*).

" *Distribution in the Province of Quebec.*

"*Montreal.* Summer resident, abundant (*W. W. Dunlop*).

"*Point de Monts.* A small colony nested in the deserted Hudson's Bay Trading Post at Godbout this year (1882) (*Dr. C. Hart Merriam*).

"*County of Quebec and north to Lake St. John.* Summer resident, abundant (*John Neilson*).

"*Distribution in Labrador.*

"Verrill reports it breeding in large numbers, July 15th, 1861, on Anticosti (*L. M. Turner, Proc. U.S. Nat. Mus.*, 1885, p. 239).

"*Distribution in Manitoba and the North-west.*

"*Carberry.* About Carberry and on the Big Plain I noted it only as a migrant: apparently there were no suitable building sites. Aug. 26th, 1882: Swarm of Cliff-Swallows migrating to-day, flying east.

"*Turtle Mountain, in Southern Manitoba.* Here in 1882, on 20th May, I saw several apparently just arrived from the south.

"*Brandon.* At this place on 25th May, 1882, I saw a number of the birds and 54 nests under one high cave, 50 feet long, facing the south.

"*Portage la Prairie.* Common summer resident (*C. W. Nash*).

"*Winnipeg.* Abundant summer resident (*W. L. Hine*). Common (*R. H. Hunter*).

"*Shoal Lake, in Western Manitoba.* I have noted, June 4th, 1884, Cliff-Swallows nesting; one had in gizzard water-beetles and flies.

"*Assessippi, or Shell River, Western Manitoba.* Cliff-Swallows nesting in abundance.

"*Fort Ellice.* Abundant, breeding.

"*Qu'Appelle.* Summer visitant; arrives about 10th May; breeds (*Geo. F. Guernsey*).

"*North-west.* Abundant (*Prof. John Macoun*).

"This is the most abundant of the Swallows that are found in the North-west, although its distribution there is somewhat erratic, and evidently governed by the presence of suitable places for nesting. Apparently, a high cave or overhanging wall, in a sheltered valley, near water, and with a southerly aspect, are the favourite surroundings of this bird, and when all these circumstances are combined, the place is usually encrusted with the long bottle-shaped nests, and the welkin resounds with the twittering of the birds during the breeding-season. As already noted, I saw 54 of the completed nests, and many in various stages of advancement, under a 50-foot eave, down in the river valley by Brandon. Similarly, the sheltered buildings by the river near Fort Ellice were colonized. At Shoal Lake I saw a somewhat low building with about thirty nests under the eaves. This was not in a sheltered place, but it overlooked the water. About our own building at Carberry there never were any Cliff-Swallows, for the reason, I believe, that they were out on the open prairie, remote from shelter and water. On the other hand, the new mill at Assessippi, deep down in the sheltered valley, by the millpond, offered every inducement, and, as I myself saw in June 1884, over 300 pairs of Cliff-Swallows had commenced to build before the carpenters were out of the building. The air around was filled with the birds, like bees about a hive, and their continual twittering made in the aggregate such a volume of sound as to be an annoyance to the inhabitants of the village.

"In estimating their number I have assumed that each nest represented a pair.

"The accompanying photograph will illustrate the manner of their nesting in the North-west of Canada."

Capt. Blakiston writes:—"The Cliff-Swallow is also given in the 'Fauna Boreali-Americana' and by Mr. Ross on the Mackenzie; and I observed it in considerable numbers under the eaves of the buildings at Fort Pitt, on the north branch of the Saskatchewan, in June. While travelling over the prairie in the neighbourhood of Bow River, our party came upon an immense granite-boulder, about 25 feet high, standing alone on the plain. This had been taken advantage of by the Cliff-Swallow, the mud-formed nests of which were clustered together in a mass. The steep cliffy banks of some parts of the Saskatchawan River are also used by this bird for nesting-places." To the northward, in Alaska, Mr. Dall found the Cliff-Swallow, and he observes:—"This is the most common species at Nulato, where the eaves of the fort, inside and out, are lined with their clay-domes. It is also found at Fort Yukon, and the Redoubt, St. Michael's. The Indians say that before the forts were built this bird made its nest on the face of some sandstone cliff under some projecting fragment. *H. horreorum* frequently builds on the Indian *caches*, but I have never known this species to do so."

Mr. E. W. Nelson writes:—"The lack of proper surroundings on the coast of Alaska and the Arctic Ocean appears to limit the range of this bird to the interior, and although I kept a continual look-out for it during my residence in the north, I did not see a single individual. At Nulato, Dall records its arrival from May 10th to 16th, and from these dates up to the 24th. At the same place he found it nesting commonly about the trading stations, and was told by the natives that it nested on the faces of the sandstone cliffs along the Yukon, before the advent of the white man placed at its disposal the convenient shelter of the trading posts. The birds were quick to take advantage of the hospitality offered them, and to change from their primitive nesting-sites to civilized domiciles.

"It is also found breeding at Fort Yukon. Mr. Dall records the presence of this bird at St. Michael's, but not one was seen during the four years passed by me at that place, and the evidence seems to point to a mistaken identification, whereby the common Barn-Swallow (which is very common there) was mistaken for the present bird. These Swallows are recorded from Point Lake, latitude 65°, in British North America, and in Alaska they are known to extend north of the Arctic Circle. Its extension north to the Arctic Ocean is doubtful—at least in our territory—owing to the low and unsuitable nature of the country, in addition to the harsh and repelling climate. There is a single specimen in the National Museum Collection, obtained by Kennicott at Fort Resolution, June 23, and this and the points previously given constitute the northernmost limits of its range. There is no evidence of its presence in the south-eastern part of the Territory."

Mr. Agersborg states that it is common in South-eastern Dakota, and breeds; and the following note is given by Dr. Coues in his paper on the Birds of Dakota and Montana:—

"This is the most abundant, generally distributed, and characteristic species of the family throughout the region under consideration. The various streams that cut their devious ways through the prairie afford an endless succession of steep banks exactly suited to its wants during the nesting-season; and at various places great clusters of the curious bottle-nosed mud-nests were found, while the flocks of Swallows which often hung about our camps were mainly composed of this species. At some points, the Bank-Swallows were breeding with them; the same banks being peppered with their little round holes, generally in the soft soil just below the surface, while the projecting nests of the Cliff-Swallows studded the harder or rocky exposures below. At Fort Pembina the Cliff-Swallows were so numerous as to become a nuisance; their incessant twittering was considered a bore, while the litter they brought and their droppings resulted in a sad breach of military decorum. Nevertheless, it was found almost impossible to dislodge them, and one could not but admire the courage and perseverance which they displayed in reconstructing or repairing their nests, though these were repeatedly destroyed. In examining scores of nests, I was rather surprised to find how small a proportion was finished into the complete retort-shape, even among those which had not been disturbed. Some were little more than cups, like those of the Barn-Swallow, partially arched over, and many were simply conical, while in other details they varied greatly according to the position in which they happened to be fixed, or their relations to each other. The laying-season in this latitude is at its height during the second and third weeks in June. Probably only one brood is reared each season. Young birds are on the wing by the middle or latter part of July."

Messrs. Roberts and Benner state that they found the Cliff-Swallow common in Minnesota, and Mr. Evermann says that in Indiana it is an abundant summer resident.

To the eastward it is recorded by Mr. Dwight in his paper on the summer birds of Cape Breton Island. He writes :—"At Whycocomagh, 20 miles south-west of Baddeck, I saw the first flock of Swallows (mostly Bank and Cliff Swallows) ostentatiously ready to migrate. The latter species was still breeding on barns in two localities I visited, but not abundantly. There were not many nests, all told."

Mr. Batchelder states that in New Brunswick he found the species common at Grand Falls on the Upper St. John, and it was also abundant at Fort Fairfield.

"These Swallows," writes Mr. Stearns, "enter and leave New England about the same time that the Barn-Swallows do, and are among our common summer birds. They are more numerous and more equally dispersed in settled districts than formerly; but I think that a good deal that has been written of their supposed irruption from the West is to be taken with salt. Some records have been laboriously collected to show the dates of appearance of these birds in particular localities; such writing has its own interest as a matter of fact, but not as sustaining 'eastward-ho!' theory. The 'Cliff' Swallows, as their name implies, and as every one knows, naturally fix their queer bottle-nosed nests to the perpendicular faces of rocks and hard embankments; and have latterly acquired the name of 'Eave' Swallows, from the circumstance that they have readily availed themselves of the eligible nesting-sites afforded by the walls of houses under shelter of the eaves. Therefore, the settlement of the country affords unlimited breeding resources where formerly there were none; and these Swallows have consequently become common in New England. They were actually known in this part of the country before their discovery by Say in the West; but natural breeding-places, such as these birds require, are not to be found everywhere in the Eastern States."

In the State of New York it has been recorded as breeding in the Adirondack Mountains by Dr. Hart Merriam, and a large series of old and young birds procured by Dr. A. K. Fisher near Sing Sing are in the Henshaw collection. Dr. Merriam also obtained young birds in August near Locust Grove. Mr. Brewster says that the species is common, and breeds near Winchendon in Massachusetts; and Mr. Faxon states that it is common in Berkshire County of the same State. "According to Dr. Emmons, this bird first appeared in Williamstown in 1825" (Amer. Journ. Sci. & Arts, xxvi. p. 208). Messrs. Faxon and Allen have also recorded it as common in New Haven.

The Henshaw collection contains some specimens from the neighbourhood of Washington, procured in May and August, but Mr. Richmond considers the species to be one of the rarer birds breeding in the District of Columbia.

Mr. Warren gives the following account in his 'Birds of Pennsylvania':—

"Common summer resident; generally distributed throughout the State. Breeds mostly in colonies of from twenty to forty individuals; sometimes, however, as many as fifty or seventy-five nests are found together. Although I have known these birds to breed, for three consecutive seasons, under the eaves of long sheds in a cow-yard, I am inclined to think that they usually breed but one season in the same place. The Cliff-Swallow arrives here about the last week in April, and disappears early in September. This bird when flying can easily be distinguished from other Swallows by its almost even tail-feathers and the conspicuous rusty-coloured rump. During migration this species is found in greatest numbers in the vicinity of rivers, ponds, and lakes."

Mr. Rives, in his account of the birds noticed by him at Salt Pond Mountain in Virginia, states that he found a small colony of Cliff-Swallows which had attached their nests to the shed of a stable at Blacksburg. Mr. Fox, writing about the birds of Roane County, Tennessee, says that the Cliff-Swallow was only once seen by him, on the 23rd of April, 1884, and was not observed at all by him in 1885.

In his paper on the birds observed at Bayou Sara, in Louisiana, Mr. Beckham states that he observed the Cliff-Swallow only once, on the 23rd of April.

Dr. Merrill writes of the species in Texas:—"Very common in Southern Texas from early in April until the latter part of August. It is one of the most abundant of the summer visitors, and is the only Swallow that breeds here." Mr. Dresser's note is as follows:—"Common at San Antonio and Matamoras during the summer. At Eagle Pass I noticed a couple on the 7th March, and on the 10th they were very numerous. In July, on the way from Nuevo Laredo to Matamoras, when seeking after water, I saw a long cliff overhanging a ravine, which was literally covered with the nests of these birds."

In his paper on the birds of Southern Texas, Mr. Beckham writes:—

"I did not see this bird at San Antonio, but, according to Dresser, it is common there during the summer. Brown records it as a common summer resident at Boerne, arriving there on March 20th." Mr. Nehrling states that he noticed it in great numbers in South-eastern Texas during September, but it does not breed in this region. According to Mr. Lloyd, it is a common summer visitant in Western Texas, arriving early in April. The species sometimes breeds in barns, and Mr. Lloyd believes that two broods are raised, as he found his first nest under a bluff on May 4th, with three eggs, while another, taken on the 20th of July, had four fresh eggs. Mr. N. C. Brown, in his 'Reconnaissance in South-western Texas,' says that he found the present species to be a common summer resident there, arriving about the 20th of March.

Mr. G. B. Sennett has given the following interesting account of the species in his paper on the birds of the Rio Grande:—

"None were seen lower down the river than Hidalgo, much to our wonder, for the conditions seem quite as favourable for them at Brownsville or Matamoras as at points above. In the absence of cliffs in the vicinity of Hidalgo, they adapt themselves to the eaves of the buildings in the town. Through the kindness of Sheriff Leo, we occupied the court-house, and these Swallows were incessantly working and chattering about us from daylight to dark, and even in the night we could hear them in their nests. We had ample opportunity to observe their habits. They are gregarious in all their occupations. In collecting mud for their houses, the choice spots of their selection on the margin of the river were so thickly covered with them that often more than a hundred huddled on and over a space of two feet in diameter. The curious bottle-shaped nests were crowded so closely together that little could be seen of them but their mouths. We endeavoured to obtain a sample of the nests entire, but there was so much quicksand in the mud of which they were made that we found it impracticable to do so. None of the nests were lined. In some we found stones and bits of broken crockery, which had been thrown in by the boys before the nests were completed; and yet the birds had laid their eggs among this rubbish. In making the nest, the first choice is a corner formed by wall, eaves, and rafter, very little labour, therefore, being necessary to make the remaining side. This side of the nest is made spherical, with the mouth and the neck standing out some two inches from it. The next ones lap on to it, others lap on to them, and so on. As soon as a shelf is formed large enough to hold the bird, it stands on it and works from within. The pair work in turn. To gather the eggs it is necessary to demolish a part of the nest, unless, as we sometimes found, eggs were laid before the nest was finished. In the completed nests, the clutch varied from four to seven; but in one extra large nest, which from its size and shape looked as if two birds occupied it in common, we took ten eggs. From the window of our sleeping-room we could watch the birds at their work without disturbing them, although but four feet distant from some of them. When we took the eggs, on May 7th, some were nearly ready to hatch, but most of them were fresh, and many birds were just beginning their nests.

"The ground-colour of the eggs is a dull white. The markings are brown and very variable. Some are speckled, others blotched; some regularly over the whole egg, and others with far the greater number of spots on the larger end. The longest egg was 0·90, the shortest 0·70; the broadest 0·60, and the narrowest 0·53. The average of fifty eggs is 0·80 by 0·56."

Turning once more northward, we find that Mr. Scott records this Swallow as common in Western Missouri, arriving about the 10th of April and breeding. The same gentleman says that in Arizona he observed the species in numbers at Riverside in

April, and Mr. Brewster states that he found the birds breeding abundantly at Yuma, along a bluff above the town. Dr. Elliott Coues also says, in his paper on birds observed from Arizona to the Pacific, that immense numbers made their nests on the precipitous and rocky sides of the rivers.

The vertical range of the species in Colorado is given as follows by Mr. Drew:— "Spring 6000 feet; summer 11,000 feet; autumn 9500 feet. Breeds from the plains up to 10,000 feet."

Mr. Scott says that at Twin Lakes he found it very abundant. On the 20th of June the birds began to build under the eaves of a barn. Many breed on the faces of the cliffs of the Arkansas River. Messrs. Allen and Brewster, in their paper on Colorado birds, state that it was first observed about the 18th of May, but doubtless arrived somewhat earlier.

Mr. Henshaw gives the following account:—"Observed in Snake Valley, Nevada, and in many localities in Middle and Southern Utah, living in colonies, and building their nests at times in inaccessible spots, in lofty cliffs, and again in places at a few feet above the plain. A widespread species, both in Arizona and New Mexico, as their mud-nests, attached to the cliffs everywhere, attest.

"Seen near Fort Garland, Colorado, in large numbers, building under the eaves of the post quarters. I noticed here a very curious departure from the usual method of constructing the nest. Under the projecting eaves of one of the store-houses, a large colony had established themselves, there being in the neighbourhood fifty nests, most of which were built in the usual fashion. But a few pairs, taking advantage of circumstances, had established themselves in certain small passages which opened directly under the eaves, and had served as ventilators. The mouth of each one of these had been built up with mud, a small hole being left as an entrance. Some twelve inches beyond was the proper nest, consisting of a small pile of straws and feathers, on which the eggs were deposited. The wisdom of the birds in thus availing themselves of these holes was very clearly demonstrated, since nearly the entire labour of nest-making was obviated and a much safer domicile secured."

"This species," writes Mr. Hoffman in his paper on the Birds of Nevada, "is usually abundant in the vicinity of rivers, streams, and even large springs in fertile valleys, as at one locality near the divide between Deep Spring and Smoky Valleys. In many places against the face of the limestone cliffs the nests of these birds were built, and apparently heaped upon one another in the greatest confusion. Immediately beneath the ledges, which were vertically about 80 feet high, and extended horizontally for about 100 yards, there was continuation of the piñon woods visible in every direction, except about an eighth of a mile below, where the timber ended and the grassy valley stretched away towards the east. The springs and a small rivulet rising in the hills on the south were fringed with an abundance of willows and small cotton woods, where we first noticed these birds during the afternoon of our going into camp. The next day, however, we found their habitations, and even saw the birds flying in all directions over the hills above the cliff in pursuit of insects, as various localities, though presenting an absence of timber, were amply covered with various flowering plants, upon and about which there appeared sufficient numbers of lepidoptera and orthoptera, furnishing, perhaps, the principal food of these birds in this portion of the State."

Dr. Cooper writes:—

" An abundant species throughout California, and as far north as Columbia River on the coast. I saw the first of them at San Diego on March 15th, 1862, and at San Francisco they arrive about March 25th, being a week earlier than the Barn-Swallow, and also remaining later in autumn. I have seen them as late as October 5th, and they probably remain longer towards the south. They live almost everywhere during summer, except on the high and wooded mountains, building on the cliffs of the sea-coast, where the cold wind blows, as well as in the hottest valleys, under eaves of houses, and sometimes on the sides of large branches or trunks of trees. Their bottle-shaped nests of mud, lined with straw, are conspicuous objects wherever they are allowed to build them, some even being visible in the noisy city of San Francisco, which only this species visits, sweeping through the crowded streets with entire fearlessness. The eggs are usually four, white, spotted with dusky brown, and they hatch two broods in the season in most parts of the State. When about the nest, they make a creaking noise very different from the twitter of the Barn-Swallow. In June I saw a flock of these birds busily catching young grasshoppers on the dry hill-side, where these insects were swarming. As I have never heard of other Swallows eating grasshoppers, I suppose that this species is specially adapted for such food, other insects being very scarce during the dry season, and in the dry regions it inhabits so frequently, where other species of Swallows are unknown. This Swallow leaves Santa Cruz about September 1st, but probably only goes to the large rivers and lakes of the interior. To determine the question as to bed-bugs being brought to houses by these Swallows, I allowed about twelve pairs to raise broods under the eaves of the house I lived in at Santa Cruz in 1866. They built between April 12th and 26th, and the young were fledged July 1st; some also had laid new broods of two and three eggs by the 5th. On tearing down the nests I found bugs (*Cimex*) in every one, whatever part of the roof it occupied, showing that they were *brought* by the birds, none having been observed in the house. But these bugs were evidently a distinct species from the *Cimex lectularius*, being different in form, narrower, and pale yellowish, instead of the characteristic colour from which the name 'Puce' is derived, through the French name of this insect. Moreover, although many crawled into the cracks of the weather-boards, and could easily have entered the low bedroom windows, none were seen afterwards. So I think we may relieve the Swallows of the charge of bringing in these pests, and encourage their building in suitable places, on account of the immense numbers of insects they destroy. As usual, their parasites are peculiar to them, and may be called *Cimex lunifrontis*."

According to Mr. C. H. Townsend, the species is " common in Northern California in certain localities. A moderate number of Cliff-Swallows inhabited some buildings at the west base of Mount Shasta in midsummer, and they were abundant in the cultivated region about Susanville, Lassen County. They were very rarely seen in the Sacramento Valley, and were never found breeding in cliffs or other natural situations."

Mr. Evermann, in his paper on the birds of Ventura County, California, writes:—
"An abundant summer resident. In 1881, a colony of more than a hundred pairs nested in a shed in Santa Paula. The nests were fastened to the rafters, much after the manner of the Barn-Swallow. Many horse-hairs were plastered into the nests, and these often caused the death of the builders. I took from this shed some six or eight dead birds which I found hanging about the nests, they having got entangled in the hairs."

Mr. Belding's Californian notes are as follows:—
"A few of these birds were occasionally seen at Big Trees in July. It was rare at Murphy's about September 1st, and I did not find it at Stockton on or after September 6th. It is abundant at both the latter places during the breeding-season. At Stockton it builds under the eaves of buildings; at Murphy's, in the limestone boulders exposed by mining. It arrived at Murphy's on March 15th, 1877; at Stockton on March 17th, 1878; and at North-American Hotel on March 12th, 1878." The same gentleman observes that he saw the first individual of this species at San José del Cabo, in Lower California, on the 29th of April.

Dr. Merrill writes that the bird was common at Fort Klamath in Oregon, nesting abundantly in the buildings about the Fort; and Mr. Anthony, in his paper on the birds of Washington County, Oregon, observes:—"Abundant summer resident. A colony of about two hundred built at Beaverton this spring, for the first time in the memory of its inhabitants."

The late Mr. J. K. Lord's collections from British Columbia contained several specimens of the Cliff-Swallow, but up to the present time the species has not been recorded from Vancouver Island, although, as Dr. Robert Brown says, it ought to occur there.

Of the range of this *Petrochelidon* in Central America we are still without knowledge on many points. Colonel Grayson found the species "breeding in the banks of the Mazatlan River in May." We would remark, however, that the breeding of this Swallow *in* banks of rivers is nowhere else recorded. Either it has been a misprint for 'on' the banks, or the note refers to *Stelgidopteryx* and has got misplaced. He says that it was apparently only a summer visitant, and he did not observe it during the winter months. As Messrs. Salvin and Godman remark:—"Mazatlan, therefore, may be considered the extreme southern limit of its breeding-quarters." Since the above-named gentlemen wrote in their 'Biologia Centrali-Americana,' the species has been obtained by Mr. Ferrari-Perez at Acatlan, in the State of Puebla; by Mr. W. Lloyd at Santana, near Guadalajara; and by Trujillo, one of Mr. Godman's collectors, at Juachengo, in Oaxaca, in April.

Mr. Gaumer procured a single specimen in the island of Cozumel, and Mr. C. H. Townsend obtained one at Truxillo, in Honduras, on the 21st of September. Mr. Ridgway records the species from Costa Rica, an adult male having been obtained at San José on the 3rd of September by Señor Alfaro, the Director of the Museum at that place. A second Costa-Rican specimen is stated by Mr. Ridgway to be in the U.S. National Museum.

Professor Baird has recorded the capture of a specimen by Capt. Dow off the west coast of Central America; and Mr. G. N. Lawrence identified one of McLeannan's specimens from Panama as belonging to the present species.

This completes the known Central-American record, and we hear nothing of *P. pyrrhonota* till we get to Brazil. Here Natterer observed it between September and March, his localities being as follows:—Ytararé, February and March; Parnapitanga, December; Irisanga, December; Engenho do Cap. Gama, September. Its occurrence in Paraguay is recorded by Azara; and Mr. Durnford's notes on the species near Buenos Ayres are as follows:—

"The only occasion on which I have seen this bird was on the 25th of March of the present year, when I observed about half a dozen at different times during the day, all flying steadily in a north-easterly direction. This was about thirty miles to the west of Buenos Ayres. From their manner of flight, always keeping in the same general course, though occasionally turning aside to chase some insect, I have no doubt they were migrating; they kept about ten feet from the ground. At a distance they are not easy to distinguish from *Hirundo leucorrhoa*; but on a nearer approach their greater size and chocolate throat, but more especially their reddish-brown rumps, are clearly discernible. The museum possesses one specimen, killed in this neighbourhood." Writing again in 1878, he says:—"This Swallow was observed on its migration on the 4th March, 1877, at Moreno, and on the 15th April, 1877, at Lujan bridge. On both occasions they were flying steadily N.N.E., and in considerable numbers. I shot some on each occasion, to be sure of the identification."

Mr. Gibson even says that the species breeds in its winter-quarters, for in his paper on the birds of Paysandu in Uruguay he gives a note:—" Found a nest in the wall of outbuildings 18th November, containing young and an addled egg."

This statement requires confirmation, as will be seen by Mr. Hudson's note in the 'Argentine Ornithology' written by Dr. Sclater and himself, where the habitat of the species is given as "South" America, surely a misprint for "North" America.

Mr. Hudson observes:—" This species does not breed in Buenos Ayres, and is only seen there in spring, flying south or south-west, and again in much larger numbers on its return journey in autumn. On the Rio Negro, in Patagonia, I did not meet with it, and suppose that its summer resort must be south of that locality; and, judging from the immense numbers visible in some seasons, I should think that they must, in their breeding-place in Patagonia, occupy a very extensive area. They do not seem to be as regular in their movements as other Swallows here; some years I have observed them passing singly or in small parties during the entire hot season: usually they begin to appear, flying north, in February; but in some years not until after the middle of March. They are not seen passing with a rapid flight in close flocks, but straggle about, hawking after flies; first one bird passing, then two or three, and a minute or two later half a dozen, and so on for the greater part of the day. So long as the weather continues warm they journey in this leisurely manner; but I have known them to continue passing till April, after all the summer migrants had left us, and these late birds flew by with great speed in small close flocks, directly north, as if their flight had been guided by the magnetic needle. While flying, this species continually utters sharp twitterings and grinding and squealing notes of various lengths."

Whether misled by Dr. Sclater's statement as to the habitat of the species, or not, it is well to observe Mr. Hudson's belief in the breeding of the species in Patagonia. He apparently does not seem to know of its nesting in North America. Our own belief is that it only visits South America as a winter home, and we should require some very definite evidence to make us credit that it breeds there.

We quote herewith the admirable account of the nesting of the present species, written by Dr. Elliott Coues, in the 'Birds of the Colorado Valley':—

"It may be remembered in this connection that a happy conjunction of circumstances is required to satisfy these birds. Not only are cliffs or their substitutes necessary, but these must be situated where clayey mud, possessing some degree of adhesiveness and plasticity, can be procured. This conjunction is met at large in the west, along unnumbered streams, where the birds most do congregate; and their very general dispersion in the West, as compared with their rather sporadic distribution in the East, is thus readily explained. The great veins of the West—the Missouri, the Columbia, the Colorado, and most of their venous tributaries, returning the humours from the clouds to their home in the sea—are supplied in profusion with animated congregations of the Swallows, often vastly more extensive than those gatherings of the feathered Sons of Temperance beneath our eaves, where the sign of the order—a bottle, neck downward—is set for our edification.

"All are familiar, doubtless, with the architecture of these masons; if any be not, the books will remove their ignorance. But there are many interesting details, perhaps insufficiently elucidated in our standard treatises. It is generally understood that the most perfect nest, that is, a nest fully finished and furnished with a neck, resembling a decanter tilted over,—that such a 'bottle-nosed' or 'retort-shaped' nest is the typical one, indicating the primitive fashion of building. But I am by no means satisfied of this. Remembering that the Swallows are all natural hole-breeders, we may infer that their early order of architecture was a wall, rampart, or breastwork, which defended and, perhaps, enlarged a natural cavity on the face of a cliff. Traces of such work are still evident enough in those frequent instances in which they take a hole in the wall, such as one left by a missing brick, and cover it in, either with a regular domed vestibule, or a mere cup-like rim of mud. It was probably not until they had served a long apprenticeship that they acquired the sufficient skill to stick a nest against a perfectly smooth, vertical support. Some kind of domed nest was still requisite, to carry out the idea of hole-breeding, a trait so thoroughly ingrained in Hirundine nature, and implying perfect covering for the eggs; and the indication is fully met in one of the very commonest forms of nest, namely a hemispherical affair, quite a 'breastwork' in fact, with a hole at the most protuberant part, or just below it. The running on of a neck to the nest, as seen in those nests we consider the most elaborate, seems to merely represent a surplusage of building energy, like that which induces a House-Wren, for example, to accumulate a preposterous quantity of trash in its cubby-holes. Such architecture reminds me of the Irishman's notion of how cannon are made—by taking a hole and pouring the melted metal around it. It is the rule, when the nest is built in any exposed situation. But since the Swallows have taken to building under eaves, or other projections affording a degree of shelter, the bottle-necked, even the simply globular nests seem to be going out of fashion; and thousands of nests are now built as open as those of the Barn-Swallow, being simply half cups attached to the wall, and in fact chiefly distinguished from those of Barn-Swallows by containing little or no hay. I suppose this to be a piece of atavism,—a reversion to primitive ways. The Barn- and Eave Swallows are our only kinds that do not *go into a hole* or its equivalent; and the indication of shelter or covering, in all cases indispensable, being secured by the roof itself beneath which they nestle, the special roofing of each nest becomes superfluous. Hence the open cups these Swallows now construct.

"Considering how sedulously most birds strive to hide their nests, and screen themselves during incubation, it becomes a matter of curious speculation why these Swallows should ever build beneath our eaves, in the most conspicuous manner, and literally fly in the face of danger. Richardson comments on this singular and excessive confidence in man, too often betrayed, and which cannot, on the whole, be conducive to the best interests of their tribe. He speaks of a colony that persisted in nesting just over a frequented promenade, where they had actually to graze people's heads in passing to and from their nests, and were exposed to the curiosity and depredations of the children; yet they stuck to their first choice, even though there were equally eligible and far safer locations just at hand. Sir John wonders what cause could have thus suddenly called into action such confidence in the human race, and queries what peculiarity of œconomy leads some birds to put their offspring in the most exposed situation they can find. We have all seen the same thing, and noted the pertinacity with which these and other Swallows will cling to their caprices, though subjected to every annoyance, and repeatedly ejected from the premises by destruction of their nests. I have two notable cases in mind. At Fort Pembina, Dakota, a colony insisted on building beneath the low portico of the soldiers' barracks, almost within arm's reach. Being noisy and untidy, they were voted a nuisance, to be abated; but it was 'no use'; they stuck, and so did their nests. In the adjoining British province of Manitoba, at one of their trading-posts I visited, it was the same thing over again; their nests were repeatedly demolished, on account of the racket and clatter they made, till the irate lord of the manor found it cheaper in the end to let the birds alone, and take his chances of the morning nap. I think such obstinacy is due to the birds' reluctance to give up the much-needed shelter which the eaves provide against the weather—indeed, this may have something to do with the change of habit in the beginning. The Cliff-Swallow's nest is built entirely of mud, which, when sun-baked into 'adobe,' is secure enough in dry weather, but liable to be loosened or washed away during a storm. In fact, this accident is of continual occurrence, just as it is in the case of the *Chimney-Swifts*. The birds' instinct—whatever that may mean : I despise the word as a label of our ignorance and conceit ; say rather, their reason—teaches them to come in out of the rain. This may also have something to do with the clustering of the nests, commonly observed when the birds build on the face of cliffs ; for obviously such a mass would withstand the weather better than a single edifice.

"It is pleasant to watch the establishment and progress of a colony of these birds. Suddenly they appear, quite animated and enthusiastic, but undecided as yet, an impromptu debating society on the fly, with a good deal of sawing the air to accomplish before final resolutions are passed. The plot thickens ; some Swallows are seen clinging to the slightest inequalities beneath the eaves, others are couriers to and from the nearest mud-puddle, others again alight like feathers by the water's side, and all are in a twitter of excitement. Watching closely these curious sons and daughters of Israel at their ingenious trade of making bricks, we may chance to see a circle of them gathered around the margin of the pool, insecurely balanced on their tiny feet, tilting their tails and ducking their heads to pick up little gobs of mud. These are rolled round in their mouths till tempered, and made like a quid into globular form, with a curious working of their jaws ; then off go the birds, and stick the pellet against the wall, as carefully as ever a sailor, about to spin a yarn, deposited his chew on the mantelpiece. The birds work indefatigably ; they are busy as bees, and a steady stream flows back and forth for several hours a day, with intervals for rest and refreshment, when the Swallows swarm about promiscuously a-fly-catching. In an incredibly short time the basement of the nest is laid, and the whole form becomes clearly outlined ; the mud dries quickly, and there is a standing-place. This is soon occupied by one of the pair, probably the female, who now stays at home to welcome her mate with redoubled cries of joy and ecstatic quivering of the wings, as he brings fresh pellets, which the pair, in the closest consultation, dispose to their entire satisfaction. In three or four days, perhaps, the deed is done ; the house is built, and nothing remains but to furnish it. The poultry-yard is visited, and laid under contribution of feathers ; hay, leaves, rag, paper, string—Swallows are not very particular—may be added ; and then the female does the rest of the 'furnishing' by her own particular self. Not impossibly, just at this period, a man comes with a pole, and demolishes the whole affair ; or the *enfant terrible* of the premises appears, and removes the eggs to enrich his sandy tray of like treasures ; or a tom-cat searches for his supper. But more probably matters are so propitious that in due season the nest decants a full brood of Swallows, and I wish nothing more harmful ever came out of the bottle.

"Seeing how these birds work the mud in their mouths, some have supposed that the nests are agglutinated, to some extent at least, by the saliva of the birds. It is far from an unreasonable idea—the Chimney-Swift sticks her bits of twigs together, and glues the frail cup to the wall with viscid saliva; and some of the Old World Swifts build nests of gummy spittle, which cakes on drying, not unlike gelatine. Undoubtedly some saliva is mingled with the natural moisture of the mud; but the readiness with which these Swallows' nests crumble on drying shows that saliva enters slightly into their composition, practically not at all, and that this fluid possesses no special viscosity. Much more probably, the moisture of the birds' mouths helps to soften and temper the pellets, rather than to agglutinate the dried edifice itself.

"In various parts of the West, especially along the Missouri and the Colorado, where I have never failed to find clustering nests of the Cliff-Swallow, I have occasionally witnessed some curious associates of these birds. In some of the navigable cañons of the Colorado I have seen the bulky nests of the Great Blue Heron on flat ledges of rock, the faces of which were stuccoed with Swallow-nests. How these frolicsome creatures must have swarmed around the sedate and imperturbable *Herodius*, when she folded up her legs and closed her eyes, and went off into the dreamland of incubation, undisturbed in a very Babel! Again, I have found a colony of Swallows in what would seem to be a very dangerous neighbourhood, all about the nest of a Falcon, no other than the valiant and merciless *Falco polyagrus*, on the very minarets and buttresses of whose awe-inspiring castle, on the scowling face of a precipice, a colony of Swallows was established in apparent security. The big birds seemed to be very comfortable ogres, with whom the multitude of hop-o'-my-thumbs had evidently some sort of understanding, perhaps like that which the Purple Grackles may be supposed to have with the Fish Hawks when they set up housekeeping in the cellar of King Pandion's palace. If it had only been a Fish Hawk in this case instead of *Falco polyagrus*, we could understand such amicable relations better, for Cliff-Swallows are cousins of Purple Martins, and, if half we hear be true, *Progne* was Pandion's daughter."

The following account of the habits of the species appeared in the 'Field' for 1880, from the pen of Mr. Ernest Ingersoll:—

"In its primitive method of nesting we now see it only in the far west, where, throughout all the mountain-ranges, and elsewhere in suitable localities, hundreds of colonies are found associated in a happy and prosperous home-life. I have seen their compact villages clinging to the steep faces of rock by which the mountains are walled in, from one end to the other of Colorado and Wyoming; have been within reach of their nests among the crumbling earth-bluffs along the eastern base of the Snowy Range, and in the interior parks; have enjoyed their chatter and graceful entanglement of flight as they were roused from their extensive colonies among the towering headlands of the Upper Missouri—the scene and the birds simulating in miniature the beetling crags and hosts of seafowl that front the coast of Labrador or the Hebrides. No altitude below timber-line seems too great for them—no region too bleak or desolate. Here, a mere little ledge of tough gravel, where a bit of a brook has made a cut-bank, will be the home of a dozen pairs; there some lofty vertical wall becomes completely covered with their cloisters. Nothing suits them better than the perpendicular columns and faces of basalt so common in the northern Rockies, against whose black and shining surfaces their villages and the bright inhabitants make a busy and beautiful picture. The eastern half of the country being covered with dense forests, and exposing few places naturally fitted for a Cliff-Swallow's residence, it appears not to have been generally inhabited by this species previous to the advent of Europeans, and the subsequent preparation of the way for the Swallows by the clearing of the forests and the erection of buildings. At the same time some points widely remote were doubtless occupied by them every summer—for instance, the lofty and cavernous cliffs on the north-eastern shore of Maine and about the Bay of Fundy, and the limestone precipices at Anticosti. It is only *known*, nevertheless, that they bred in early times among the bluffs on Lake Champlain, and that they went each summer to Hudson's Bay. The fact, however, that these Swallows were reported as breeding at these two points among the very earliest of Eastern records, and within a very few years of their discovery by Say in the Rocky Mountains, supports the idea that they had always lived there, but only showed themselves commonly when settlements brought them into view. It was not until 1842 that the species appeared in the neighbourhood of New York city.

"In their wild state, as I have mentioned, these Swallows build their nests against cliffs in companies, constructing them of mud, which is often gathered from a considerable distance by the industrious birds, all going to the same spot for supplies. While still wet, it is moulded in the bill into pellets as large as peas, which one by one are plastered into a firmly compacted wall, that is made to assume a shape so symmetrical as to cause us to wonder at the skill of the tiny architect. Normally, this form is that of a chemist's flask or retort—a bulb adhering by its base to the cliff, and terminating outwardly in a contracted horizontal neck, which serves as entrance to the nest, and ordinarily slopes slightly downward, shedding the rain—a disastrous contingency further guarded against in most cases by the choice of a cliff which overhangs at the top.

"But many circumstances arise to vary the exact design of these mud retorts. In the first place, the character of the foundation must be regarded, an earthen bank not being able to support so long a neck as a roughly rocky wall, to which mud will cling tenaciously. Then, so very social are the birds that they crowd their homes together until every inch of the surface of the cliff for many feet, and often for many yards, square is entirely hidden; and the structures are so compact that, like the cells in a honeycomb, a single wall answers for two adjoining nests, and little more remains visible of each than the round mouth, which is likely to be misshapen, to adapt it to the irregular room behind.

"Like other birds, the young Swallows return year after year to the old homestead. But, instead of building on an adjoining section of the cliff, they will found their new nests on the remains of the old, late comers in many cases even building upon and closing over the finished homes and fresh-laid eggs of their precursors. Finally, this accumulation of hundreds of nests becomes too heavy for the foundations to uphold, when the whole mass, perhaps twenty feet wide and four feet deep, will break off and be dashed to pieces at the foot of the crag. Such a catastrophe is a frequent result of the passion the birds have for huddling their homes together; and there is a possible moral in it, looking towards a necessary check upon the enormous increase of a species otherwise almost wholly safe from enemies or accident.

"How each Swallow knows which of all those round holes, looking (to our eyes) so exactly alike, is his own, is a marvel; yet no greater one, perhaps, than the wonderment of the country boy at the readiness with which his city friend finds his own door among the long blocks of uniform brown stone or marble fronts covering Murray Hill and the region about Central Park. The Swallows seem to dwell at peace in their city, and to be neighbourly, for it often happens that other species of Swallows will nestle close by; and in Dakota Dr. Coues saw them living in close proximity to Buzzards and Falcons, yet apparently on good terms with their powerful neighbours. Dr. Cooper mentions, however, that in Montana the blue birds often 'jumped' Swallows' nests and held possession successfully. The most remarkable instance of fraternity is related by Mr. J. A. Allen, who saw them at Topeka, Kansas (where also they nested about dwellings), 'frequenting the holes in the banks of the Kaw River made by the Sand-Martin, keeping in the company of those birds, entering their holes, and presenting the same appearance of breeding in them as the Sand-Martins themselves.' Afterwards Mr. Allen discovered them occupying niches of rock in Dakota.

"So much for the manners of the Cliff or Republican Swallows, in their uncivilised life. When white men invaded their wilderness, erecting houses and barns, these birds were quick to perceive their availability, and the more knowing ones instantly abandoned the always insecure rocks for the greater stability and protection of eaves and rafters; for which, indeed, they already had a sort of precedent in the practice of some Californian colonies, which occupied now and then the trunks and branches of large trees (*vide* Cooper) as building sites. This adoption of the new custom happened at once in all parts of the country. There was no hesitation or experiment or doubt about the matter at all. The first squatter was welcomed as an old friend by the Swallows, who instantly made themselves at home on his premises; the most venturesome pioneer in the Indian country, and the remotest fur-trader among the lakes of British America, were each cheered by the companionship of those affectionate feathered settlers.

"The facility with which the Hirundinidæ adapt themselves to new circumstances is proverbial. Changes in the architecture might therefore have been looked for here, and are really to be found, all tending toward greater convenience and dispensing with useless labour. In building and repairing their nests they work with great diligence and marvellous celerity. 'Where they exist in a large colony,' to quote the late Dr. Brewer, 'it is not an uncommon thing to see several birds at work upon the same nest—one bird, apparently the female owner, always assisting and directing the whole.' When a pair are at labour, they work in turn, first making a shelf upon which the workman stands and builds out the nest from within, making the inside smooth, but leaving the outside as rough as cobble-work. If, as frequently happens, eggs are laid before the whole structure is completed, the female drops her labour, and the male finishes the dwelling. This business is said to occupy them six days; no doubt the time required varies, depending on the weather, and is often much less. They show extreme persistence. You may pull down their nests many times before they will abandon a chosen site, and they love to return to the same spot year after year.

"That the mud out of which the shells are composed owes its adhesiveness to a sticky saliva with which it is mixed, I do not believe to be true to any noteworthy extent. Although in their globular shape and position they will resist a winter's storm, if once lowered from their fastenings, or cracked, they crumble very easily. Lining, properly speaking, there is none; but the eggs repose on a more or less scanty pallet of straw and feathers, with wool, fur, &c., in proportion to the coldness of the climate.

"Where the nests are simply plastered on the outside of a barn, underneath the projecting eaves, as is common, the aboriginal shape is well preserved, and you cannot reach the eggs without breaking away the bottle-neck entrance; but if the Swallows have learned enough to go inside, or wherever they find some snug corner, their labour is lessened, and a structure results that owes its shape to its position, and hence may be widely abnormal, lacking perhaps the narrow neck, or, if adequately sheltered, the whole dome, and assuming simply a hemispherical bowl form, like the lower half of the original retort. This is very likely to be almost wholly the shape seen in long-settled districts.

"The Cliff-Swallows appear to be irregular in their laying. Many records show that large embryos will be found in some nests of a colony where other birds were just completing their houses or had laid the first egg. The Swallow villages are thus populous and busy from the first return of their denizens until the September migration, when many helpless fledglings and useless eggs are always left behind. Two broods are generally safely raised, nevertheless.

"The ordinary clutch is from four to six eggs. When a larger number occurs, it is attributed to the laying of two females in the same nest—a thing very likely to occur now and then among birds so communistic in their notions; but I have no proof of it. The colour of the egg is dull white, peppered with infinitesimal points of red, and (on the big end) marked with blotches of dead clay-brown, others of a deep wine colour and fainter suffusions of purple. But the patterns are very variable, and often closely approach those of their neighbours, the Barn-Swallows (*Hirundo horreorum*).

"In sitting, the female is said to be occasionally relieved by the male. But for the most part he busies himself in getting food, and in bravely and vengefully guarding his home, the whole fighting strength of the community mustering at his alarm to repel some real or fancied enemy with a courage which, if its power equalled its fury, would be irresistible."

Mr. F. H. Knowlton, writing in 1881 from Brandon, Vermont, gives some interesting information respecting the habits of the present species:—

"Within my collecting-grounds is a locality where numbers of these birds have nested for many years. This is a shed, open only on one side, where the birds have attached their nests to the sleepers of the loft. In the spring of 1878, they returned about the usual time, and soon began repairing old nests or constructing new ones. One day while watching them, I noticed one bird remained in her half-finished nest, and did not appear to be much engaged. Soon a neighbour, owning a nest a few feet away, arrived with a fresh pellet of clay, and adjusting it in a satisfactory manner, flew away for more. No sooner was she out of sight than the quiet bird repaired to the neighbour's nest, appropriated the fresh clay and moulded it to her own nest! When the plundered bird returned, no notice was taken of the theft, which was repeated as soon as she was again out of sight. I saw these movements repeated numerous times, but was called away, and when I again returned both nests were completed.

"In the same place a nest remained undisturbed, and was occupied by probably the same pair of birds for several seasons. This spring they returned to the old nest, and all appeared prosperous, until one day I noticed a number of Swallows engaged in walling up the entrance of this old nest. This, and the outline of a new nest over the old, was soon completed. I then broke open the closed nest and found within the dead body of a Swallow. This bird had probably died a natural death, and the friends, being unable to remove the body, and knowing it would soon become offensive, adopted this method of sealing it up."

The descriptions are taken from the British Museum 'Catalogue;' and the figures are drawn from specimens sent to us by Dr. A. K. Fisher, of Sing Sing, N. Y.

PETOCHELIDON SWAINSONI.

PETROCHELIDON SWAINSONI, Sclater.

SWAINSON'S CLIFF-SWALLOW.

Hirundo melanogaster, Swains. Philos. Mag. new series, i. p. 366 (1827); Gray, Gen. B. i. p. 58 (1845).

Petrochelidon melanogaster, Cab. Mus. Hein. Th. i. p. 47 (1850).

Petrochelidon swainsoni, Sclater, P. Z. S. 1858, p. 296, 1859, p. 376; id. Cat. Amer. B. p. 40 (1862); Baird, Review Amer. B. p. 290 (1865); Salvin, Ibis, 1866, p. 192; Samiehr. Mem. Bost. Soc. N. H. i. p. 547 (1869); Scl. & Salv. Nomencl. Av. Neotr. p. 14 (1873); Lawr. Bull. U. S. Nat. Mus. no. 4, p. 17 (1876); Dugès, La Nat. i. p. 144 (1878); Salvin & Godman, Biol. Centr. Amer., Aves, i. p. 227 (1883); Sharpe, Cat. Birds in Brit. Mus. x. p. 194 (1885).

Hirundo coronata, Licht. Preis-Verz. Mex. Vög. p. 2 (1830); Cab. J. f. O. 1863, p. 58.

Petrochelidon lunifrons (pt.), Coues, B. Color. Vall. p. 426 (1878).

P. fronte rufâ; uropygio rufo: gutture rufo: mento basali nigro: gutture imo nigro notato: hypochondriis cinerascenti-brunneis.

Hab. in Americâ centrali.

Adult male. General colour above glossy steel-blue, varied on the mantle and back with ashy-whitish streaks, with which the feathers are edged; wing-coverts blackish, slightly glossed with steel-blue; bastard-wing, primary-coverts, and quills also blackish, with scarcely any gloss except on the secondaries, the innermost of which have narrow ashy-whitish margins near the end of the outer webs; lower back and rump pale cinnamon-rufous; upper tail-coverts brown, with narrow blackish shaft-streaks, and edged with ashy-whitish; crown of head glossy steel-blue, separated from the mantle by a narrow collar of deep chestnut, extending from the ear-coverts and followed by a less distinct collar of ashy brown like the sides of the neck; a broad frontal band of deep chestnut; lores velvety black, with reddish-buff bases; cheeks, sides of face, and ear-coverts deep chestnut, as also the throat; a line along the base of the chin black; in the centre of the throat a patch of blue-black feathers, not very distinct; sides of neck, breast, and sides of body pale ashy brown, with a slight rufous tinge, the flanks with indistinct dusky shaft-lines; centre of body and abdomen white; thighs ashy brown, slightly washed with rufous; vent pale rufous; under tail-coverts ashy brown tinged with rufous; the feathers subterminally dark brown and broadly edged with whitish; under wing-coverts and axillaries ashy brown washed with rufous, especially near the edge of the wing; quills dull ashy brown below. Total length 5·1 inches, culmen 0·3, wing 4·15, tail 1·75, tarsus 0·45.

Adult female. Similar to the male in colour, but a trifle smaller. Total length 4·5 inches, wing 4·1, tail 1·8, tarsus 0·45.

y

In the series in the British Museum there is very little variation in plumage. The measurements are as follows:—

	Total length.	Wing.	Tail.	Tarsus.
	in.	in.	in.	in.
a. ♀ ad. Mexico (coll. Jard.)	4·8	4·05	1·8	0·4
b. ♂ ad. ,, (De Saussure)	5·1	4·15	1·75	0·45
c. Ad. ,, ,,	4·9	4·2	1·7	0·45
d. Ad. ,, (Boucard)	4·8	4·0	1·7	0·4
e. Ad. ,, (Sallé)	5·0	4·1	1·8	0·45
f. ♀ ad. Oaxaca (Boucard)	4·5	4·1	1·8	0·45
g. Juv. Dueñas (Salvin)	4·7	4·0	1·75	0·4
h. Juv. Costa Rica	4·0	4·15	1·7	0·45

The young bird differs from the adult in being altogether browner, with no purple gloss, and scarcely any appearance of dorsal streaks; the rump has a pale rufous band; the wings and tail are both brown; crown of head dusky blackish, with a slight blue gloss, the feathers round the hind neck dingy brown; a slight shade of rufous on the forehead and over the eye; ear-coverts, sides of face, cheeks, throat, and chest dusky brown, with a slight wash of rufous on the throat; breast and abdomen white, the flanks and vent washed with pale fulvous brown, the under tail-coverts dusky brown, margined with buffy white. Total length 4·2 inches, wing 4·2, tarsus 0·45.

Another young bird in the Salvin-Godman Collection has the rufous portion of the plumage more strongly marked than the one described, and has the brown feathers of the upper surface fringed with reddish brown or whity brown at the ends.

Hab. Central America, from Mexico to Guatemala.

In 1827 Swainson described specimens of this Cliff-Swallow, which had been obtained by Bullock on the Tableland of Mexico and at Real del Monte, by the singularly inappropriate name of *Hirundo melanogaster*, but in his description he does not mention the black colour of the belly as a character. Messrs. Salvin and Godman suggest that the black spot on the throat may have been intended to be referred to by Swainson, but in any case the wrong impression conveyed by the name fully justified Dr. Sclater in altering it to the more appropriate one of *swainsoni*. The name of *coronata*, published by Lichtenstein in a price-list of Mexican birds in 1830, is unaccompanied by any description, and cannot therefore be used.

Swainson's Cliff-Swallow is nearly allied to the North-American species, *P. pyrrhonota*, but is easily distinguished by its chestnut forehead. In this latter character it resembles *P. fulva*, but the last-named bird has no black patch on the lower throat.

The range of the species has been well summed up by Messrs. Salvin and Godman, whose words we quote from the 'Biologia':—"Though *P. swainsoni* has been met with by many travellers in Mexico, we have nothing recorded of it beyond certain localities where it occurs. Prof. Sumichrast says it is peculiar to the plateau of Mexico, and that it rarely occurs elsewhere; still it has been found in the State of Oaxaca, and, even by Sumichrast himself, subsequently near the city of Tehuantepec, which is situated at but a slight elevation above the Pacific Ocean. In Guatemala it only twice came under our observation—once when we found it flying over the open land near Dueñas, at an elevation of nearly 5000 feet above the sea, and again near Godines, above the mountain-lake of Atitlan, as high as 7000 feet. On both occasions the birds were flying low, hawking for insects after the manner of their kindred."

The specimen from Costa Rica in the British Museum rests upon the authority of a dealer, and the locality requires confirmation.

The figures in the Plates are taken from Mexican specimens in the Salvin-Godman Collection, and the descriptions from the series in the British Museum.

PETROCHELIDON SWAINSONI ERYTHROGASTRA

PETROCHELIDON SWAINSONI
ERYTHROGASTRA.

Hirundo erythrogaster × *swainsoni*, Salvin, Ibis, 1888, p. 256.

The figure of the hybrid Swallow is taken from the Cozumel specimen in the Salvin-Godman collection. Mr. Salvin has given the following account of it:—

"A single specimen, shot in May 1885 by Mr. Gaumer on Cozumel Island, we have little doubt is a hybrid between *Hirundo erythrogaster* and *Petrochelidon swainsoni*, as it curiously combines the characters of both birds. The forehead is the same in both species, but the ear-coverts and the collar are steel-blue, as in *H. erythrogaster*; the tail is also furcate, though to a less extent, and the lateral feathers have the characteristic white spots; the wings, too, are as long as those of *H. erythrogaster*, and the under tail-coverts are tinged with rufous. The characters it has with *P. swainsoni* are the colouring of the under surface, including the black gular patch; it also has the rump rufous grey. Instances of hybrids between *H. erythrogaster* and *P. pyrrhonota* have been recorded, but this is the first we have met with in which *P. swainsoni* appears to have been one of the parents."

It will be seen that the colour of the plumage partakes of the characteristics of both species, the general features of the *Petrochelidon* being preserved, while the slightly forked tail, and, above all, the white spots on the latter, are the characters of a true *Hirundo*. We have considered that the strain of the *Petrochelidon* is stronger in this curious hybrid than that of the *Hirundo*, and have named it accordingly.

That the American Swallow (*Hirundo erythrogastra*) does occasionally cross with the Cliff-Swallow (*Petrochelidon pyrrhonota*) is also known, and a full description of a hybrid between these two species is given by Mr. Spencer Trotter in the 'Bulletin of the Nuttall Ornithological Club' for 1878. This specimen was procured at Linwood, Delaware County, in Pennsylvania, on the 22nd of May, 1878, by Mr. C. D. Wood.

PETROCHELIDON FULVA (*Vieill.*).

CARIBBEAN CLIFF-SWALLOW.

Hirundo fulva, Vieill. Ois. Amér. Sept. p. 62, pl. 32 (1807); Gray, Cat. Fissir. Brit. Mus. p. 24 (1847); Thien. J. f. O. 1857, p. 149; March, Proc. Philad. Acad. 1863, p. 295; Bryant, Proc. Bost. Soc. N. H. x. p. 222 (1866).
Cecropis fulva, Boie, Isis, 1828, p. 315, 1844, p. 173; Less. Compl. Buff. viii. p. 498 (1837).
Hirundo melanogaster (nec Swains.), Denny, P. Z. S. 1847, p. 38.
Hirundo pœciloma, Gosse, B. Jamaica, p. 64 (1847); Osburn, P. Z. S. 1865, p. 63; Gray, Hand-l. B. i. p. 71, no. 837 (1869).
Herse fulva, pt., Bp. Consp. i. p. 341 (1850).
Hirundo coronata, Lembeye, Av. Cuba, p. 45 (1850).
Petrochelidon fulva, Cab. Mus. Hein. Th. i. p. 47 (1850); Cass. Cat. Hirund. Mus. Philad. Acad. p. 4 (1853); Gundl. J. f. O. 1856, p. 3, & 1861, p. 328; Sclater, P. Z. S. 1861, p. 72; id. Cat. Amer. B. p. 40 (1862); Baird, Review Amer. B. p. 291 (1865); Scl. & Salv. Nomencl. Av. Neotr. p. 14 (1873); Gundl. Orn. Cuba, p. 82 (1876); A. & E. Newt. Handb. Jamaica, 1881, p. 107; Salv. & Godm. Biol. Centr.-Amer., Aves, i. p. 228 (1883); Cory, B. Haiti & S. Domingo, p. 47 (1884); Sharpe, Cat. Birds in Brit. Mus. x. p. 195 (1885); Cory, List B. West Indies, p. 10 (1886); id. Auk, iii. p. 57 (1886).
Petrochelidon pœciloma, Baird, Review Amer. B. p. 292 (1865).

P. uropygio rufo; gulâ rufâ; fasciâ frontali castaneâ; torque nuchali angustâ rufâ regioni auriculari concolore; mento minime nigro; maculâ jugulari nigrâ nullâ; pectore rufo, hypochondriis concolore.

Hab. in provinciâ Yucatanicâ Americæ centralis et in Panamâ, præcipue tamen in insulis Antillensibus, 'Cuba,' 'Jamaica,' 'Porto Rico,' et 'San Domingo' dictis.

Adult male. General colour above glossy steel-blue, the feathers of the mantle and back edged with ashy white, giving a strongly streaked appearance; wing-coverts and quills blackish, with a slight greenish gloss, the inner secondaries edged with ashy whitish at the ends; lower back and rump rich chestnut; upper tail-coverts brown with a slight greenish gloss and narrowly edged with ashy whitish; tail-feathers blackish brown, slightly glossed with greenish; crown of head glossy steel-blue, separated from the mantle by a narrow collar of pale rufous, followed by a second collar of ashy brown like the sides of the neck; a broad frontal band of deep chestnut; lores velvety black, with pale rufous bases; cheeks, sides of face, and ear-coverts pale ferruginous, joining the collar round the nape; throat and chest, as well as the sides of the body and flanks, ferruginous, slightly mixed with ashy brown on the sides of the breast and flanks; vent ferruginous; centre of breast and abdomen white; under tail-coverts ashy brown washed with rufous, darker brown before the tips, which are whitish, all the feathers being broadly edged with the latter colour; under wing-coverts and axillaries smoky brown, edged with rufous, more distinct near the edge of the wing; quills dusky brown below, more ashy along the inner web: "bill black; feet dark grey; iris dark brown" (*Gosse*). Total length 4·8 inches, culmen 0·35, wing 4·5, tail 1·75, tarsus 0·45.

There appears to be no difference in the colours of the sexes, and the wing only varies from 4·0 inches to 4·1 inches in length.

The *young bird* is altogether duller in colour than the adult, and is browner on the head, with a whity-brown forehead, with some chestnut plumes intermixed. The inner secondaries are edged with rufous at the tips, and the chestnut feathers of the lower back and rump have ashy whitish margins. The under surface of the body is like that of the adults, but the rufous of the throat is rather paler. Wing 4·0 inches.

Hab. Antilles, Cuba, Jamaica, Porto Rico, and San Domingo. Yucatan and Panama in Central America.

VIEILLOT met with this species himself in San Domingo about the middle of May, and states that Maugé also brought the same bird from Porto Rico, where it was observed in spring. Vieillot came to the conclusion that it was only a bird of passage in the above-mentioned islands from the fact of his observing it only at the same season for two successive years, and he imagined that the species went to the north for breeding, as a similar Swallow settled on the ship in which he was travelling about the latitude of Halifax, in Nova Scotia. This would be of course *P. pyrrhonota*, as we know now that *P. fulva* is strictly confined to a more southern habitat. Vieillot describes this Swallow as congregating at night and roosting in the house in which he was staying.

Mr. Cory states that the species "does not appear to be very abundant in San Domingo; only a few flocks were seen and but two specimens taken. At Gonaives, on the day of our arrival, several flocks were observed flying about the houses, but the next day none were to be seen."

Maugé, as above recorded by Vieillot, was the first naturalist to observe it in Porto Rico, and Messrs. Swift and Latimer sent specimens from that island to the Smithsonian Institution.

Professor Baird separated the Jamaican specimens from those of Cuba on account of the smaller size and darker chestnut coloration. We have not found these differences pronounced in the specimens in the British Museum, and regard the birds from both islands as belonging to one and the same species. Mr. Gosse, who described the Jamaican bird as *Hirundo poeciloma*, has given the following account of its habits:—

"The Cave-Swallow does not appear to be in any degree migratory in Jamaica, being abundantly common at all seasons. It delights in the neighbourhood of caverns and overhanging rocks, in the hollows of which it builds its ingenious nest. About a mile from Bluefields, the sea washes a precipitous rock of no great height, on the summit of which is an old fort, with some great guns, which tradition ascribes to the old Spanish settlers, but now dismantled, and within and without overrun with spiny pinguins and logwood bushes, and tangled with creepers. I have no doubt that this was the site of the Spanish town Oristana, some remains of the houses of which may yet be seen in the provision-ground of a negro peasant adjoining. The foot of the cliff is girt with irregular masses of honey-combed rock, between which the incoming tide rolls, and frets, and boils, in foaming confusion; and the front is hollowed into caves, some of which are long passages with an opening at each end, and others are merely wide-mouthed, but shallow hollows. In one of these I counted forty nests of this species of Swallow, each consisting of a half-cup, built with little pellets of mud, retaining, in so damp a situation, and where the rock itself is covered, a slimy mouldiness—their original humidity. Each was thickly lined with silk-cotton. If we imagine a pint basin divided perpendicularly through the middle, and the one half stuck against a wall, we shall perceive the form of these nests; some, however, were both larger and deeper than this. In many instances advantage was taken of a slight hollow in the rock, which increased the capacity. In one (it was about the middle of July) I found three eggs; in some others the callow young, and in one two full-fledged birds, which lay quietly in the nest, side by side, while their black eyes watched my motions. The parent birds flew about in affright, occasionally coming close up to the nests, and hovering as if about to alight, but scarcely one ventured in. The eggs measure about $\tfrac{8}{10}$ inch long, and $\tfrac{11}{20}$ wide; they are white, studded with dots and spots of dull red; but in many eggs which I have examined there is much variation in size, form, and colour. The young birds scarcely differed from the adult.

"In May, my kind friend Mr. Delcon took me into a curious cavern, situated on the estate called Amity, some few miles from Savannah le Mar, but inland. Through its dark recesses a subterranean river flows, so still and so perfectly transparent, that although two or three feet deep, I did not perceive there was a drop of water there, but took the atoms floating on its surface to be lodged in invisible spiders' webs, stretched across. Numerous Swallows were flying in and out, and the roof was studded with nests similar to those above described.

"Though this little Swallow manifests a decided predilection for cavernous recesses, it does not confine itself to situations so recluse. In that part of the ' King's House,' at Spanish Town, which is called the Arcade, where clerks are writing, and public business is transacted every day, great numbers of these nests are affixed to the beams and joists, and the birds are continually flying to and fro. Before the year 1838 they had built in the Secretary's office from time immemorial; but it was not in consequence of any molestation there, that in the Year of Freedom they chose the viceregal abode. Did they then recognise the administrator of England's power as the friend of Jamaica? In December, January, and February, the birds, though they fly in and out of the august abode without reserve, as if to maintain their right of way, do not make use of the nests; but all the rest of the year, these mud habitations are occupied. In March the old birds begin to repair and tenant their former nests; but the young, having no home ready made, are compelled to wait until the May rains have moistened the earth in the roads, to afford them mud for their structures.

"But as soon as these seasonal changes have taken place, these birds may be seen congregated on the roads, in groups of fifty together, huddled at the edges of the pools formed by the daily rains, and in these places, where the power of the morning sun has already evaporated the water, the mud has begun to acquire a stiffness of consistence which probably is more suitable for moulding to their nests. As they alight to pick up the pellets, their wings are nearly perpendicularly over the back, and they are incessantly fluttering about, apparently hindering one another by their crowding. Many may be seen engaged, where the pools are a little wider, or where the streams that cross the road dilate into a broad surface, in sweeping backward and forward over the water, which at every turn they just kiss with their beaks. I know not whether they are drinking, or capturing minute surface-insects."

Mr. March's account of the species in Jamaica is as follows:—"These Swallows are found in all the caves in the limestone ranges, generally domiciled with large colonies of bats; formerly they occupied parts of all the public buildings and many dilapidated houses about Spanish Town. The *Progne* has, however, driven them from the Secretary's office, and another building now occupied by the Executive Committee; and lately the Palm Swifts have forced them to abandon the House of Assembly; from other public buildings they are also excluded by the vigilance of the keepers, though they often attempt a lodgment. They are now congregated in large colonies at the railway stations. Small parties or solitary pairs still, however, hover about their old haunts in the town, during the breeding-season. One pair built in the Bishop's Registrar's office, and although the office was closed from 3 o'clock on Saturday until 7 o'clock on Monday morning, they built their nest and laid three eggs, which I took from them before they left. They have often attempted to return every season to the House of Assembly, and commence building, but their little neighbours, the Palm Swifts, allow them no rest until they have driven them away. This year, 1863, a few pairs have succeeded in making a lodgment. The nest is a half of an oblong mass of mud and grass well worked together, with a flat top or platform, and a small cup filled with down. The flat side of the section is stuck against the wall or beam; the eggs are three, varying considerably in form, size, and markings, the type, $\frac{7}{8}$ by $\frac{9}{16}$ths long, oval, white, splashed with dots of burnt ochre, thicker at the larger end. In some the marking is almost obsolete."

Dr. Gundlach furnishes a similar account of the species in Cuba to that of Mr. Gosse above recorded. He states that these Swallows quit the northern part of the island in autumn, but merely retire to the southern portions, and in spring he noticed several in the eastern departments. Their nesting-season is from March to June, and their song is agreeable and varied. The nest is variously placed in houses, sheds, and caves.

The occurrence of this species on the mainland of Central America rests at present upon two specimens in the collection of Messrs. Salvin and Godman, and now in the British Museum. One specimen was procured by Mr. G. F. Gaumer in Yucatan, where, says that gentleman, it is resident, frequenting the cave-like holes called "senotes." Another specimen, not fully adult, was obtained in Panama by the late Mr. M'Leannan, and there can be no doubt that it is referable to the present species. Messrs. Salvin and Godman suggest that there is a possibility of an error in the locality attributed to this specimen, as M'Leannan once had some Cuban birds in his possession; but it is quite possible that on the continent of America the species is local and only to be found in colonies, like its congeners, and thus it may be distributed over a wider area than is generally supposed.

Dr. Thienemann has described eggs of this Swallow sent from Cuba by Dr. Gundlach as being similar to those of its North-American relative, the ground-colour being milky white without much gloss, and thickly covered with reddish grey, or else with light or dark spots of a brownish-red colour.

The descriptions are taken from the British Museum 'Catalogue,' and the figure is drawn from the Yucatan specimen in the Salvin-Godman collection.

PETROCHELIDON RUFICOLLARIS

PETROCHELIDON RUFICOLLARIS (Peale).

PERUVIAN CLIFF-SWALLOW.

Hirundo ruficollaris, Peale, U.S. Explor. Exped., Birds, p. 175 (1848); Gray, Hand-l. B. i. p. 71, no. 839 (1869).
Petrochelidon fulva, juv., Cass. U.S. Expl. Exped., Birds, p. 181 (1858).
Petrochelidon ruficollaris, Baird, Review Amer. B. p. 292 (1866); Salvin and Godman, Biol. Centr.-Amer., Aves, i. p. 225 (1883); Sharpe, Cat. Birds in Brit. Mus. x. pp. 196, 636, pl. iii. (1885); Tacz. Orn. du Pérou, iii. App. p. 503 (1886).
Petrochelidon ruficollis, Nation, P. Z. S. 1885, p. 277.

P. uropygio rufo; gulâ albidâ; torque præpectorali rufâ, auricularibus concolore.

Hab. in Peruviâ.

Adult male. General colour above dull purplish blue, streaked on the mantle and back with greyish-white edges to the feathers; lower back and rump pale chestnut; scapulars like the back; wing-coverts and quills brown, with ashy margins to the secondaries; upper tail-coverts pale brown, with ashy-whitish edges to the outer ones; tail-feathers dusky brown, paler brown towards the ends of the inner webs; crown of head purplish blue, separated from the back by a collar of smoky brown, base of forehead dull chestnut; ear-coverts and cheeks ashy white, the former posteriorly marked with light chestnut, which extends backwards and forms a patch on the sides of the hinder crown; throat ashy white; fore neck and chest pale chestnut, with a patch of smoky brown on the sides of the upper breast; centre of breast and abdomen white, the flanks and vent washed with pale chestnut; under tail-coverts pale brown, broadly edged with white, producing a mottled appearance; axillaries and under wing-coverts uniform smoky brown; quills dusky brown below, more ashy along the edge of the inner web. Total length 4·8 inches, culmen 0·35, wing 3·8, tail 1·9, tarsus 0·45.

Young. Much duller in colour than the adult; and distinguished by the narrow ashy margins to the feathers of the upper surface, the wing-coverts, secondaries, and tail-feathers being edged with pale chestnut; lower back and rump paler chestnut than in the adult; upper tail-coverts edged with rufous; throat washed with rufous; chestnut band on breast less pronounced; flanks smoky brown washed with pale rufous. Total length 4·6 inches, culmen 0·3, wing 3·45, tail 1·9, tarsus 0·4.

Hab. Peru.

THE original specimen of this species was discovered by Mr Peale near Callao, in Peru, during the voyage of the United States Exploring Expedition. Mr. Cassin afterwards united Peale's species to the Central-American *P. fulva*, of which he considered it to be the immature bird. Professor Baird, however, in 1865, reinstated the Peruvian bird as a distinct species, and his decision has been amply confirmed by the recent researches of Professor Nation, to whom the rediscovery of Peale's neglected species is due.

After remaining for nearly forty years in comparative obscurity, and being represented by the single type specimen in America, Prof. Nation forwarded specimens to Dr. Sclater and to the British Museum, from the vicinity of Lima, and communicated the interesting notice of the bird's habits which we transcribe below. As far as is known at present, this Swallow does not appear to occur anywhere but in Peru, and even there its range appears to be limited, as will be seen by the following notes of Prof. Nation:—

"Some twenty years ago an American engineer, engaged by the Peruvian Government to survey the Andean valleys and coasts of Peru for railway routes, showed me a letter from his friend the late Mr. John Cassin, requesting him to examine carefully the rocks and cliffs for a Swallow's nest. He informed me that he had searched for it for two or three years without success. Many years after, when the subject of Mr. Cassin's letter had almost escaped my memory, being in the National Library of Lima, looking over some books which had just arrived, I found the two volumes of Birds of the U.S. Exploring Expedition, and saw the description of the Swallows obtained by Peale, near Callao, in, I think, 1835, and named by him *Hirundo reficollis*. With this information I recommenced my search for it.

"One would naturally suppose that if a Crag-Martin had been found in Western Peru, its breeding-place would be found in one of the Andean valleys, where everything necessary for its economy abounds. Such at least was my impression, and from this error I lost many years in searching for it in places which it rarely or perhaps never visits. At length, in 1877, tired and fatigued by a long ramble over the hot sandy hills of the neighbourhood of Lima, I came to some old ruins of a brick- or lime-works, so old that the ditches that had once supplied it with water had in many places disappeared; it must have been abandoned for a quarter of a century at least. Here, while sitting down inside the old kiln, I observed a bit of earth adhering to the wall; on removing it, and blowing away carefully the loose particles of dust, I saw that it was composed of pellets, and that these pellets could not have been formed by any insect. I felt convinced that I had discovered the object of so many fatiguing journeys. Every rock, wall, and building near the ruins was carefully examined by me, and in the course of the day, about twelve miles from the city, I fell in with a large colony of Cliff-Swallows.

"On the following day I returned with a man and a ladder. The house which this bird had selected for its breeding-place was a little Gothic building, used for a telegraph- and railway-station, so near the line that I observed that the nests were surrounded by the smoke of the engine. The man in charge of the station informed me that the building had been scarcely finished before it was taken possession of by the colony. In the neighbourhood there was a large sugar-plantation, with many buildings, of which the roofs and walls had been taken possession of by *Atticora cyanoleuca*, but not a nest of the Cliff-Swallow could be seen on them. On examining the nests, I found them in every stage of construction, from the first circular row of wet pellets to the perfect nest inhabited by a family of young birds nearly fledged. On the outside (for the roofs inside had been taken possession of also) I counted 123 nests. The rafters under the eaves were covered by the nests in many places. The nests were placed one upon another. The sill of one window had a row of nests upon it; and I observed one or two nests affixed to the sides of the walls of the house. The nest is very large for so small a bird. The one I removed weighs two pounds; it stands 7 inches high, and is 6½ inches wide at the base. The neck is about 2½ inches long and 2 wide. The lining is very scanty, scarcely sufficient to cover the bottom of the nest, and is composed of a few bits of fine grasses with one or two feathers. The eggs which I found in this nest, in which incubation had many days commenced, were three in number, white, thickly speckled with reddish brown; they are ten twelfths of an inch long by seven broad.

"I never saw anything more beautiful than the appearance of a colony of these birds in their curious-shaped nests, out of which project the heads of the owners at the slightest alarm. It is by no means a shy bird; while I was examining the nests they flew around me like bees, almost touching my face, uttering piteous cries. I felt sorry to see the distress of the parent birds whose nest I removed.

"Of the nest I brought away I made a drawing, and sent copies of it to almost every part of Peru, and in a short time I was in possession of many important facts respecting its range in Peru. Unfortunately, about this time difficulties between Chili and Peru commenced, and soon after broke out the terrible war of the Pacific. Personal observations and postal inquiries became impossible. Since the departure of the Chilian army and the return of the Peruvian authorities, I have done all I could to add to my knowledge of its range and habits, but I regret to say with little success. The colony I first discovered was swept away, the bones of many of my friends are laid under the battle-field, and the state of the country renders it unsafe to stray far from the city gates.

"According to my present knowledge of this species, it seems to be confined to the cultivated lands in the river districts of the narrow strips of arid country situated between the Pacific and the mouths of the Andean valleys, from the southern border of the great desert of Sechura to the desert of Ica, from about 7° to 13° S. latitude. It is remarkable that I have never been able to obtain any evidence that it builds its nest on a rock or cliff, or that it is seen inside the mouth of the Andean valleys. The nest is always found on human habitations. In the vicinity of Lima and within twelve miles of the walls there are at present fourteen colonies."

The description and the figures in the accompanying Plates have been taken from the specimens presented to the British Museum by Professor Nation.

PETROCHELIDON RUFIGULA.

PETROCHELIDON RUFIGULA (Bocage).

BENGUELA CLIFF-SWALLOW.

Hirundo rufigula, Bocage, Jorn. Lisb. 1878, pp. 256, 269; id. Orn. Angola, p. 545 (1881); Sharpe, ed. Layard's B. S. Afr. p. 840 (1884); id. Cat. Birds in Brit. Mus. x. p. 197 (1885).

P. fasciâ angustissimâ frontali rufâ; pileo chalybeo-nigro dorso concolore; uropygio rufo; corpore subtus rufo, gulâ et subcaudalibus saturatioribus et feré castaneis.

Hab. in provinciâ Angolensi 'Benguela' dictâ.

Adult male. General colour above glossy blue-black, the feathers of the hind neck and mantle edged with isabelline buff or reddish white, producing a streaked appearance; rump and upper tail-coverts chestnut, contrasting with the back; lesser and median wing-coverts dull blue-black; greater coverts, bastard-wing, primary-coverts, and quills dusky, slightly glossed with blue on the outer web; tail-feathers dusky, with a greenish gloss, all but the two centre ones with a large white spot on the inner web; head uniform glossy blue-black; lores pale rufous; in front of the eye a velvety black spot; ear-coverts dull blue-black, slightly varied with rufous margins to the feathers; cheeks and throat deep chestnut; remainder of under surface paler chestnut or rufous, deepening into rich chestnut on the under tail-coverts, the long ones of which have a large sub-terminal spot of blue-black; under wing-coverts and axillaries like the breast; quills dusky below, more ashy along the inner web. Total length 5·2 inches, culmen 0·3, wing 3·75, tail 2·1, tarsus 0·45.

Hab. Benguela.

This Cliff-Swallow was discovered by Senhor Anchieta at Caconda in Benguela. It is a very distinct species, and cannot well be confounded with any of the other members of the genus.

The description is copied from the British Museum 'Catalogue of Birds'; it is there taken from the original specimen lent us by Professor Barboza du Bocage. The figure is drawn from the same bird.

PETROCHELIDON SPILODERA (Sundev.).

SOUTH-AFRICAN CLIFF-SWALLOW.

Hirundo spilodera, Sundev. (Œfv. K. Vet.-Akad. Förh. Stockh. 1850, p. 108; Gray, Hand-l. B. i. p. 79, no. 828 (1869).
Phedina spilodera, Bp. Rivist. Contemp., Torino, 1857, p. 4.
Hirundo lunifrons, Layard, B. S. Afr. p. 56 (1867, nec Say).
Hirundo alfredi, Hartl. Ibis, 1868, p. 153, pl. 4; Layard, t. c. p. 243; Gray, Hand-l. B. i. p. 71, no. 838 (1869).
Petrochelidon spilodera, Sharpe, P. Z. S. 1870, p. 293; Gurney, Ibis, 1874, p. 101; Butler, Feilden, & Reid, Zool. 1882, p. 249; Sharpe, ed. Layard's B. S. Afr. pp. 357, 839 (1884); id. Cat. Birds in Brit. Mus. x. p. 198 (1885).

P. fasciâ frontali nullâ, loris et fronte basali tantum rufescentibus: subalaribus et axillaribus pallidè rufis concoloribus: tectricibus longioribus supracaudalibus et subcaudalibus chalybeo-nigris, angustè rufo apicatis.

Hab. in Africâ meridionali.

Adult male. Head dark brown, obscurely glossed with greenish blue, lighter brown towards the nape; back and scapulars deep blue, the feathers edged latitudinally with ashy white, giving a striped appearance to the whole back, the scapulars and wing-coverts just faintly edged with rusty white; the lower part of the back blue, not marked with whitish stripes: rump and upper tail-coverts pale rufous; wing-coverts and quills brownish black, with a slight blue gloss on the latter and on the extremities of the quills; longer upper tail-coverts blue-black, all but the centre ones rufous at their ends; tail brownish black, also slightly glossed with blue; a patch of feathers in front of the eye pale sienna; cheeks, ear-coverts, and sides of the neck dark blue; throat sienna and covered with little black spots, increasing in size on the lower throat; under surface of the body white, washed on the upper part of the breast and on the flanks with sienna; a few scattered black spots on the chest; under tail-coverts and vent deep sienna, some of the former entirely black, and the others rufous with a blackish spot. Total length 5·9 inches; of bill from front 0·4, from gape 0·6, wing 1·5, tail 2·1, tarsus 0·5, middle toe 0·45, hind toe 0·2.

Adult female. Similar in plumage to the male. Total length 5·6 inches, wing 1·4.

Young. Differs from the adult in being sooty blackish with scarcely any blue gloss; the wing-coverts like the back and narrowly edged with pale sienna, more broadly on the greater coverts and inner secondaries; rump pale sienna, with which also the upper tail-coverts are broadly tipped; quills and tail-feathers blackish; head sooty black, only slightly paler than the back; a narrow line of rufous at base of forehead and over the eye; cheeks, ear-coverts, sides of face, and throat black, the chin mottled with rufous white, the fore neck and chest also largely spotted with black;

remainder of under surface pale fawn-colour, paler in the centre of the breast; under tail coverts fawn-colour, the long ones black, edged and tipped with fawn-colour.

The sexes, when adult, appear to be absolutely alike in colour, nor is there any difference in size. The amount of spotting on the throat, however, varies considerably, even in specimens apparently quite adult and shot at the same time of year. Thus, a male procured by Colonel Butler near Newcastle in October has scarcely any black spots on the throat, while another pair procured in the same month in the same locality have the throat profusely spotted. We imagine that the birds which show the greatest amount of spotting are older individuals, and that the black band across the lower throat is a sign of immaturity, as it is present in a marked degree in the nestling.

Hab. South-eastern Africa from the vicinity of Grahamstown to the interior of Natal, the Orange Free State, and the Transvaal.

The occurrence of a species of *Petrochelidon* in South Africa is especially interesting, particularly when it is discovered that its nearest ally is the Cliff-Swallow of North America (*Petrochelidon pyrrhonota*); and this fact is the more important when taken in conjunction with the fact of the Rough-Winged Swallows being confined to the continents of Africa and America, showing a curious affinity in the relations of the Swallows of these two distant regions.

The present species was first made known to science by the late Professor Wahlberg, who discovered it in Caffraria in 1849. The "Caffraria" of that day was the Transvaal of the present, and this Swallow has been re-discovered in that country by Mr. Ayres. It was first described by the late Professor Sundevall as *Hirundo spilodera*, the specific name indicating the white streaks on the back, which are a prominent feature in this and so many other species of Swallow. It was afterwards found within the precincts of the Cape Colony, and was identified by Mr. E. L. Layard in 1867 as the North-American *P. lunifrons* (i. e. *P. pyrrhonota*). In the following year Mr. Ayres sent home specimens from the Transvaal, and these were described by Dr. Hartlaub as *Hirundo alfredi*, being named after H.R.H. The Duke of Edinburgh. In 1870 we were enabled, by the examination of a typical specimen of *H. spilodera* in the Leiden Museum, to identify with it the more recently described *H. alfredi*.

Mr. Layard writes:—"The circumstances of its re-discovery in Southern Africa were very curious. The author was first led to a knowledge of this species by observing an unusual appearance on an overhanging rock photographed near Middleburg during the journey of H.R.H. Prince Alfred through South Africa in 1860. On applying a strong magnifying-power to the picture, he distinctly made out that the appearance consisted of a cluster of birds' nests. He at once concluded that they were constructed by some kind of Swallow unknown to us, and requested our zealous contributor, Mr. Jackson, to look well after them, if ever he found himself in the neighbourhood. This he did, and tells us he counted about twenty nests, under a rock, clustered together."

Mr. Ortlepp wrote to Mr. Layard from Colesberg:—"The nests are composed of pellets of mud closely packed together. I counted no less than sixty in a square yard against an overhanging bank. Each nest is a half-sphere, with a small hole for entrance. The Boers tell me that formerly these birds were unknown to them, and when first seen they appeared in small numbers, which is not the case now, as I saw hundreds hawking about near Sandport. I calculate that at least two thousand will be hatched at this place this season."

According to Mr. Layard these Swallows also bred near Sidbury, about twenty-eight miles from Grahamstown, in 1870; and about the same time Mr. T. C. Atmore forwarded to him several specimens from the neighbourhood of Eland's Post. According to Colonels Butler and Feilden and Captain Reid, the species was very numerous in the Newcastle district of Natal, breeding in October.

Dr. H. Exton has sent specimens of adults and young birds from the neighbourhood of Bloemfontein in the Orange Free State, and, as already mentioned, Mr. Ayres has found the species breeding in the Transvaal near Potchefstroom.

Colonels Butler and Feilden and Captain Reid give the following account of the nesting of this species:—"The nests are large globular mud structures, very similar to those of *Chelidon urbica*, with a hole near the top, and warmly lined with feathers matted together. As a rule they are built under cliffs and rocks overhanging small streams from one to nine feet above the surface of the water, and are packed closely together. In some instances the entrance-hole slightly projects, but never so much as to form a passage, as in the nests of *Hirundo cucullata*. In a colony at the Ingagane River, visited by Reid, there were as many as 200 nests together in one clump, and several smaller ones close by, quite four hundred nests in all, while in others there were not more than fifteen or twenty. Three eggs appear to be the regular number, for in one nest only did we meet with four. The eggs, which vary much in size, are white. rather finely spotted and blotched with reddish brown and chestnut, or inky purple, the markings being rather more numerous towards the obtuse end. We took them in October and November. The birds were first noticed about their nesting-places at the end of August. They appear to resort to the same place to breed every year. It would appear that they make use of the 'daaga,' or cement-like mixture of which the ants form their hills, in the construction and repair of their nests; one was shot by Reid, sitting on the top of a broken ant-hill, with its mouth full of this material, which, from its binding properties, is collected and used as mortar throughout the upper districts of the colony."

Of the eggs sent by Mr. Ortlepp, Mr. Layard observes as follows:—"The eggs sent are very beautiful, being a delicate white, tinged with the faintest blush of pink, spotted, chiefly in a ring near the larger end, with different sized spots of various shades of brown, verditer, and even yellow."

The descriptions are taken from specimens in the British Museum, and the figures have been drawn from an adult bird procured by Colonel Butler near Newcastle, the young one from a specimen shot near Bloemfontein by Dr. Exton.

PETROCHELIDON FLUVICOLA (*Blyth*).

INDIAN CLIFF-SWALLOW.

? *Red-headed Swallow*, Lath. Gen. Syn. ii. pt. 2, p. 57, pl. lvi. (1783).
? *Hirundo erythrocephala*, Gm. Syst. Nat. i. p. 1024 (1788, ex Lath.); Gray, Cat. Fissir. Brit. Mus. p. 25 (1848).
Herse erythrocephala, Bp. Consp. i. p. 340 (1850).
Hirundo fluvicola, Blyth, J. A. S. B. xxiv. p. 471 (1855, ex Jerd. MSS.); Jerd. B. Ind. i. p. 161 (1862); Blyth, Ibis, 1866, p. 337; Blanf. Ibis, 1867, p. 462; Gray. Hand-l. B. i. p. 70, no. 819 (1869); Jerd. Ibis, 1871, p. 352; Hayes Lloyd, Ibis, 1873, p. 406; Adam, Str. F. 1873, p. 370; Aitken, Str. F. 1875, p. 213; Butler, t. c. p. 439; Davidson & Wenden, Str. F. 1878, vol. ii. p. 76; Hume, t. c. p. 97; Ball, t. c. p. 202; Hume, Str. F. 1879, p. 84; Butler, Cat. B. Sind &c. p. 13 (1879); id. Cat. B. S. Bomb. Pres. p. 14 (1880); Vidal, Str. F. 1880, p. 43; Butler, t. c. p. 378; Davidson & Wenden, Str. F. 1882, p. 293.
Lagenoplastes empusa, Blyth, Ibis, 1866, p. 337 (ex Gould, MSS.).
Hirundo fluminicola, Sclater, P. Z. S. 1867, p. 832.
Lagenoplastes flucicola, Gould, B. Asia, i. pl. 33 (1868); Hume, Nests and Eggs of Indian Birds, p. 80 (1873); id. Str. F. 1875, p. 452; Fairb. Str. F. 1876, p. 254; Butler, Str. F. 1877, p. 217.
Petrochelidon fluvicola, Sharpe, Cat. Birds in Brit. Mus. x. p. 200 (1885).

P. pileo rufo; uropygio fumoso-brunneo, plumis basaliter fusco-centibus; gutture et praepectore distincte nigro striolatis.

Hab. in peninsulâ Indicâ.

Adult male. General colour above glossy blue-black, mottled with white streaks where the bases to the feathers show through; lesser wing-coverts like the back, the remainder dusky blackish, glossed with steel-green externally; rump and upper tail-coverts dark smoky brown, mottled with blackish bases to the feathers, many of which are glossed with blue; upper tail-coverts smoky brown; tail-feathers blackish with a slight steel-green gloss; crown of head dull brick-red with blackish shaft-lines; lores white, separated from the forehead by a line of black; ear-coverts dusky brown, with narrow streaks of fulvous brown; cheeks, throat, and breast white, broadly streaked with blackish shafts; abdomen and under tail-coverts pure white, with narrow dusky shaft-lines; sides of body smoky brown, streaked with blackish shaft-lines; under wing-coverts and axillaries also dark smoky brown, with narrow shaft-lines of darker brown; quills dusky below, paler along the inner web. Total length 4·5 inches, culmen 0·25, wing 4·6, tail 1·75, tarsus 0·4.

There is scarcely any difference in the colour of the sexes when adult. The female is a little duller in colour, and has some distinct blackish stripes on the head; these are seen, however, occasionally in males. The following are some measurements of birds in the Hume Collection, from Bhurtpur and Ajmere:—

	Total length. in.	Wing. in.	Tail. in.	Tarsus. in.
a. ♂ ad. Bhurtpur, Jan. 1868	4·0	3·55	1·55	0·4
b. ♀ ad. ,, ,,	4·3	3·5	1·6	0·4
c. ♀ ad. ,, ,,	4·2	3·6	1·6	0·35
d. ♂ ad. Ajmere, Nov. 1869	4·2	3·55	1·65	0·4
e. ♀ juv. ,, Dec. 1869	4·4	3·65	1·6	0·35
f. ♀ ad. ,, ,,	4·3	3·5	1·6	0·4
g. ♀ juv. ,, ,,	4·2	3·55	1·55	0·4
h. ♀ ad. ,, ,,	4·3	3·6	1·6	0·4

The old birds have whitish edgings to the ends of the inner webs of the outer tail-feathers, which are wanting in the young birds. Some stress has been laid on this point by various writers, and Mr. Gould separated a species as *Lagenoplastes empusa*, which Mr. Blyth and Mr. Jerdon were at one time inclined to recognize, the latter author mainly upon the absence of any mention of these white markings in Gould's description. Jerdon considered that these markings were absent in the females and young birds, but the adult females have them, and they are only absent in the young birds. The type of Gould's *L. empusa* is in the British Museum, and it is nothing but the young of *P. fluvicola*, with which it was apparently never compared.

Young birds are distinguished by being dusky brown with scarcely any blue, the wing-coverts and inner secondaries being edged at the end with pale rufous or isabelline buff; the feathers of the rump and upper tail-coverts also have rufescent edges; the head is browner, with distinct streaks of blackish; the throat and chest are dusky brown, with blackish streaks; the underparts are washed with rufous, and the under wing-coverts and axillaries are dusky brown, with a rufous tinge.

The labels of Mr. Hume's Ajmere specimens give the soft parts as follows:—"Bill horny black; feet purplish brown, the soles and edges of scales greyish white." A male had the "iris reddish brown, the bill dusky, the feet brown, with the soles grey." An immature bird, collected by Colonel Butler at Belgaum, had "the irides dark brown, the feet and bill blackish."

Immature birds, although blue above, may be distinguished from the adults by their reddish-brown crowns, and the whitish fringes to the feathers of the back and secondaries.

Hab. The peninsula of India, ranging from Cashmere to Ferozepur, the Sambhur Lake, Kathiawar, and Kutch, its eastern boundary being Behar and the neighbourhood of Mirzapur, whence it extends through the Central Provinces and the Deccan as far south as Coimbatore.

The present species and *P. ariel* of Australia constitute a section of the genus *Petrochelidon* wherein the head is rufous. The Indian bird differs from its Australian ally in having the rump smoky brown, and the throat and fore neck broadly and distinctly streaked with black.

The Indian Cliff-Swallow is everywhere a more or less local bird. Its northward range appears to be bounded by the Ganges, and its western one by the Indus, as there is at present no evidence of its crossing the limits of these rivers. It is not known in Sind, and cannot be plentiful in the Northern Punjab. The late Professor Leith Adams procured a specimen of a Swallow which he described in the 'Proceedings' of the Zoological Society for 1859 (p. 176), and which has always been identified as the present species. He says it was "common on the lakes and streams in the Vale of Cashmere during the summer months, and likewise in the Punjab at certain seasons." Dr. Jerdon comments on this passage, and states that he never saw the species at all in Cashmere. It certainly does occur there; for a specimen obtained by Mr. W. E. Brooks at Chungus, in June 1871, is in the Hume Collection. A skin collected by Captain Stackhouse Pinwill at Kangra, in the Punjab, is also in the British Museum.

Mr. Hume gives the following summary of its range in the north:—

"The Indian Cliff-Swallow is one of the commonest of our Swallows in Upper India, at any rate. From the Tonse River, near Mirzapúr to the Sutledge, near Ferozopúr, it abounds wherever there is water and cliffs or ruined buildings, against which it can plaster its huge mud honeycomb-like congeries of nests. In the Dhoon, under the Solanee Aqueduct, in Ajmere, at Ahmedabád in Guzerat, in Saugor, in the Central Provinces, and in twenty other places, I have noticed numerous colonies in and on buildings; and as for breeding in cliffs, to give one single instance (and I could give fifty), visiting the river Chambal where the Etawah and Gwalior Road crosses it, and following its course downwards to its junction at Bhurrey with the Jumna, one will meet with at least one hundred colonies of this species, all with their clustered nests plastered against the faces of the high clay cliffs which overhang the river."

When in Kathiawar, Colonel Hayes Lloyd states:—

"I shot two out of a small party of these Swallows flying about the rocky bed of a river near the town of Dhrole; and on another occasion, when lying out on the shores of the Gulf of Kuchh waiting for Waders, a single bird of this species flew round close to me. I have not noticed it on any other occasion."

Colonel E. A. Butler records the species from Kutch, Kathiawar, and Gujarat. He says it is rare in the former districts, and only locally distributed in the other. He met with it about ten miles north of Ahmedabad, on the Deesa Road. Mr. Hume also writes:—

"I shot several Indian Cliff-Swallows a few miles from Mount Aboo. It does not, I fancy, ascend the hills, and must even in the plains be there a rare straggler, as neither Dr. King nor Capt. Butler appear to have observed it. I have seen a single specimen from Cutch. From Sindh it has not yet been sent. Eastward from Mt. Aboo it becomes more common, and at Ajmere there are large colonies, and again southward in the environs of Ahmedabad."

Mr. R. M. Adam found this Swallow very common to the west of Samblur, and a number of specimens from Ajmere are in the Hume Collection. Mr. Hume also found it plentiful on the lakes in Oodeypore. There are also specimens in the Hume Collection from Bhurtpur, Futtehpur Sikri, and Etawah. Mr. Wyatt has the following note made during his travels in India :—" I met with a colony nesting in March on the cliffs of the Jumna, about a mile from Etawah. The nests were inaccessible, but I obtained the specimens of the birds from which the figures in the plate are drawn. I also found the species nesting on the Nerbudda, ten miles from Jubbulpur. One colony had their nests only about two feet above the water. I tried to cut away a nest from the rock, but it went to pieces like sand. It contained one white egg. The birds hovered around all the time with a Bat-like flight."

Dr. Jerdon gives the following note on the species :—

"I found it first on rivers in Bundelkund, the Sonar, and the Ken, breeding in company on the rocky cliffs overhanging the rivers. I afterwards found it in one or two localities, not very far from Saugor, on the Nerbudda, near Jubbulpore, and also on the Wurdah river, not far from Chanda. It has hitherto, I believe, not been found by any other observer, and is doubtless both rare and local in its haunts, and occurs only in small numbers. Probably fifty or sixty nests, all crowded closely together, were seen by me in several of their breeding-spots, the nests being retort-shaped like the last. The birds were busy breeding at the time I first discovered them, towards the end of April and May, but I could not get at the nests to procure the eggs."

Mr. Blanford observed this Swallow on the Godavery, and makes the following observations :—

"I thrice saw colonies of *Hirundo fluvicola*, Jerdon ; but it is a rare bird. Their nests were in every case massed together, as described by Dr. Jerdon (B. Ind. i. p. 162), beneath an overhanging bank, below which was deep water. My friend Mr. Fedden, who was with me in the same district, told me that he met with a colony beneath a waterfall on the Pem Gunga river, and the birds flew in and out of their nests through the water. In every case the nests were in places which would be covered by the river during the wet season. I was told by the natives that the birds keep about the same spot, and return again to their former nesting-place after the rains. This is highly probable ; for one, at least, of the localities I hit upon was mentioned by Dr. Jerdon—that on the Wurdu river, west of Chanda. The birds appear never to go very far from their nests, and generally keep close to the river, beating for about half a mile or so up and down, not, however, keeping to the river-bed itself, as *H. ruficeps*, Licht., does when breeding. I obtained the eggs, which are very similar in shape and colour to those of *H. ruficeps*, being white, sparingly spotted with claret-colour, or nearly pure white. I suspect the birds have two broods in the year—one in February, the other in April. I found many young birds in the nests at the beginning of March ; while in the middle of April there were eggs in the nests, and the young of the first brood, differing very little from their parents, were flying about."

Commenting on the above notes, Dr. Jerdon writes :—

"Mr. Blanford has recently found it in the same localities as the first procured by myself. He also observed apparently some of the very colonies of nests I had noted, and fortunately procured the eggs. He notices that they 'invariably' build beneath an overhanging rock or bank over deep water, returning to the same spot every year. I observed one colony of nests near Nagpore, however, where the nests, which were in a sort of cavern, were easily reached by the hand from the shallow water at the bottom of the cave, and a greater deviation from this will be noticed further on. I found this Swallow exceedingly abundant in parts of the North-west Provinces of India, less so perhaps in the Punjab. I found it breeding on bridges over the Ganges canal, and on the great Solance aqueduct close to Roorkee; I also, to my surprise, found it breeding under an archway in the town of Dehra Dhoon."

Mr. Aitken writes of the species in Berar:—

"The smallest of our Swallows, and much less familiarly known than the other species, as it lives in colonies and is strictly confined to certain localities. At Akola there is one of these colonies, which build there under a broken portion of a wall which stretches out into the Moorna; the nests are retort-shaped; a few stand apart, but the majority are attached together, the tubular necks all standing out from the wall, and presenting a very peculiar appearance. With the first heavy showers of the monsoon the river comes down in a flood, and washes the whole place clean; as soon as the rains abate, rebuilding commences, and the bustle in the early morning is prodigious, the birds hurrying from all quarters with their bills full of mud. They are much persecuted by Sparrows, who take possession of the eggcup of the nest before the neck is added, and a single pair will cause several nests to be deserted before they suit themselves. As soon as the nests are finished the eggs are laid, and when hatched they simply throw the eggshells into the water instead of carrying them to a distance, as is done by most birds, aware, apparently, that the stream will carry them away. I have noticed this also in the case of the Weaver-bird. The second brood is in February, during which month they swarm about the nests like bees about a hive, while every now and then splash goes some too fragile neck, breaking even under the light weight of the little owner. These breakages do not, however, interfere in the least with the process of incubation, but appear to be repaired even while the mother-bird is sitting. The eggs are two, sometimes three, in number, of a white colour, spotted with faint red; I have seen some, however, pure white; they vary greatly both in colour and size. After the young quit the nest they associate in a large flock, playing about over the surface of the water, and drinking frequently as they fly. The old birds do not by any means confine themselves to the water, but spread freely over the country, and sing much on the wing. Their flight is comparatively feeble."

In the Deccan, according to Messrs. Davidson and Wenden, it is resident from August to March, and probably all the year. It is very local, and they have only found it in two or three places along the Panjra River. It breeds in October and again in January, in immense colonies. Another locality is "under the railway-arch over the standing water of the Sholapoor tank." Colonel Butler never met with it near Belgaum, but considers it to be a permanent resident in the southern Bombay Presidency, locally common, but in many districts unknown. The Rev. S. B. Fairbank met with it near Satara. Mr. Vidal killed a specimen at Dhamapur in the South Konkan on the 12th of February, 1880, and in the Hume collection is a single bird from Coimbatore, shot by Mr. R. H. P. Carter in August.

Mr. Hume has the following account of the nesting of the species in his ' Nests and Eggs of Indian Birds ' :—

"They breed, according to my experience, from February to April and again in July and August; they build a small, more or less retort-shaped mud nest, in clusters of from 20 to 200, packed as closely as possible, so that a section parallel to the wall or cliff face against which a colony has established itself, and about four inches away from the wall, would present an appearance much like that of a honeycomb, though the cells would be less regular. The tubular mouths, from two to five inches long, all point outwards, but those of the exterior nests of the cluster are generally turned somewhat. The chambers vary a good deal in size, but average from four inches in diameter. Their nests are to be found equally in the wildest and most desolate, and again, as at the Kotwalee in Dehra and the city gate at Ajmere, in the most thronged and frequented localities.

"The nests are well lined with feathers, and I remember more than once that when robbing these nests, numbers of feathers were carried away with the wind, all of which the little Swallows industriously captured in their mouths, but at last not knowing what to do with them, the men being still at work at the nests, apparently reluctantly let them fly."

"Mr. R. Thompson says:—'I found large numbers of this Swallow breeding in the Central Provinces, especially about the fine arched bridges on the Great Northern and Deccan road.'

"Mr. F. R. Blewitt enquires :—

"'Does this bird breed twice in the year? I ask the question for the following reason. Though I have occasionally seen this Swallow in other localities, yet only at Talbehut have I found the nest. On the side wall of a Hindoo place of worship facing the main road of the city there are clustered closely together above one hundred of these retort-shaped nests. When I passed there in the latter end of April, the birds, a perfect colony of them, were breeding. Owing to the strong prejudice of the people, who would not permit the nests to be robbed, I with difficulty secured four eggs. Again in the same nests, the birds were found breeding in August, and some twenty eggs obtained. Four appears to be the regular number of eggs.'" "So far as I can judge," adds Mr. Hume, "*three* is the normal number; I have opened a very large number of nests, and only twice or thrice found more than three eggs."

"The eggs of this species vary much in size, shape, and colour. Typically, they are a long oval, a good deal pointed towards one end, but some are fairly perfect ovals, while others are pyriform, and here and there a nearly cylindrical variety is observable. They are smaller, as a rule, than those of *L. erythropygia*, and more glossy, resembling in these respects those of *H. filifera*. The ground-colour in all is white, a good deal tinged, when fresh and unblown, with pale salmon-colour, due to the partial transparency of the delicate shell. About half are pure and spotless white, the rest are more or less streaked, mottled, speckled, or clouded with pale yellowish, or somewhat reddish brown. The markings are never bold or sharply defined as those of *H. filifera* so commonly are; and though the difference may not be very apparent by the description, in practice the two eggs could not well be confounded. As a rule, the markings are more numerous towards the large end, where they have a tendency to form an ill-defined mottled cap, and in many eggs they are almost entirely confined to it.

"In length the eggs vary from 0·65 to 0·8 inch, in breadth from 0·48 to 0·58 inch; but the average struck from fifty eggs is 0·76 by 0·53 inch."

The descriptions are taken from the series of skins in the British Museum, and the figures from birds shot by Mr. Wyatt near Etawah.

PETROCHELIDON ARIEL

PETROCHELIDON ARIEL (*Gould*).

FAIRY CLIFF-SWALLOW.

Collocalia ariel, Gould, P. Z. S. 1842, p. 132; id. B. Austral. ii. pl. 15 (1848).
Hirundo ariel, Gray, Gen. B. i. p. 58 (1845); id. Cat. Fissir. Brit. Mus. p. 25 (1848); id. Hand-l. B. i. p. 70, no. 818 (1869).
Chelidon ariel, Gould, B. Austr. Intr. p. xxx (1848); Ramsay, Ibis, 1865, pp. 299, 300.
Herse ariel, Bp. Consp. i. p. 340 (1850).
Petrochelidon ariel, Cass. Cat. Hirund. Mus. Philad. Acad. p. 6 (1853); Sharpe, Cat. Birds in Brit. Mus. x. p. 199 (1885).
Lillia ariel, Boie, J. f. O. 1858, p. 364.
Lagenoplastes ariel, Gould, Handb. B. Austr. i. p. 113 (1865); Ramsay, Ibis, 1868, p. 275; id. Proc. Linn. Soc. N. S. W. ii. p. 179 (1878); Salvad. Orn. Papuasia e delle Molucche, ii. p. 7 (1881).
Chelidon arborea (nec Gould), Ramsay, Ibis, 1865, p. 299 (lapsu cal.); id. Ibis, 1866, p. 127.

P. capite rufo; uropygio conspicuè albo; gulâ striis nigricantibus angustissimis notatâ.

Hab. in Australiâ.

Adult. General colour above deep blue, the lesser wing-coverts like the back; remainder of the wing-coverts and quills dusky, with a slight gloss externally; lower back and rump creamy white, slightly mottled with pale smoky brown where the bases to the feathers show through; upper tail-coverts dull smoky brown; tail-feathers dusky brown, glossed on the outer web with blue; crown of head bright rufous, with very minute blackish shaft-lines; nape mottled, the feathers being spotted with dark blue and edged with rufous; lores and a line above the eye black; sides of face and ear-coverts dull smoky brown; cheeks and throat white, very minutely spotted with dusky shaft-streaks, these streaks continued on to the fore neck, which is sandy brown like the sides of the body and flanks; breast and abdomen pure white; under tail-coverts white, with a slight smoky tinge; under wing-coverts and axillaries dull sandy brown, the outer coverts mottled with blackish bases; quills dusky below, lighter brown along the inner webs: "bill blackish grey; legs and feet olive-grey; iris blackish brown" (*J. Gould*). Total length 4·6 inches, culmen 0·3, wing 3·7, tail 1·9, tarsus 0·4.

The sexes are alike in plumage, according to Mr. Gould.

Hab. Confined to the continent of Australia.

In the year 1865, the late Mr. Gould instituted the genus *Lagenoplastes* for the Cliff-

Swallow of Australia; but on comparing the latter species with the Cliff-Swallow of America, which belongs to the genus *Petrochelidon*, we were unable to perceive any generic difference, and we have therefore united them. The Australian species has but one near ally, the *P. fluvicola* of India, and these two species form a section of the genus *Petrochelidon*, distinguished by their red heads.

Mr. E. P. Ramsay gives the range of the species as follows—from South Australia and Victoria to New South Wales, and thence northwards along the east coast to the neighbourhood of Port Denison. As will be seen below, Mr. Gould records it from Western Australia, and the late Mr. G. R. Gray, in the 'Hand-list of Birds,' has given the Aru Islands as a habitat of the species. This latter record is justly discredited by Count Salvadori in his work on the avifauna of New Guinea.

Mr. Gould gives the following account of the species in his 'Handbook':—"The Fairy Martin is dispersed over all the southern portions of Australia, and, like every other member of the genus, it is strictly migratory. It usually arrives in the month of August, and departs again in February or March; during this interval it rears two or three broods. The Fairy Martin, unlike the favourite Swallow of the Australians, although enjoying a most extensive range, appears to have an antipathy to the country near the sea, for neither in New South Wales nor at Swan River have I ever heard of its approaching the coast-line nearer than twenty miles; hence, while I never observed it at Sydney, the town of Maitland on the Hunter is annually visited by it in great numbers. In Western Australia it is common between Northam and York, while the towns of Perth and Fremantle on the coast are, like Sydney, unfavoured by its presence. I observed it throughout the district of the Upper Hunter, as well as in every part of the interior, breeding in various localities, wherever suitable situations presented themselves. Sometimes their nests are constructed in the cavities of decayed trees; while not unfrequently clusters of them are attached to the perpendicular banks of rivers, the sides of rocks, &c., generally in the vicinity of water. The long bottle-shaped nest is composed of mud or clay, and, like that of our Common Martin, is only worked at in the morning and evening, unless the day be wet or lowery. In the construction of the nest these birds appear to work in small companies, six or seven assisting in the formation of each nest, one remaining within and receiving the mud brought by the others in their mouths. In shape these nests are nearly round, but vary in size from four to six or seven inches in diameter, the spouts of some being eight or nine inches in length. When built on the sides of rocks or in the hollows of trees, they are placed without any regular order, in clusters of thirty or forty together, some with their spouts inclining downwards, others at right angles, &c.; they are lined with feathers and fine grasses. The eggs, which are four or five in number, are sometimes white, at others spotted and blotched with red; $1\frac{1}{4}$ in. long by $\frac{1}{2}$ in. broad."

Mr. E. P. Ramsay, in his "Notes on Birds Breeding in the Neighbourhood of Sydney," alludes to this species under the heading of *Chelidon arborea* (Ibis, 1865, p. 299). This slip of the pen he corrects in the next volume of the 'Ibis' (1866, p. 127).

He says:—"About the end of November in the year 1860, I discovered a large batch of nests of this species fastened under an overhanging rock upon the banks of the Bell River. I counted upwards of one hundred nests, all built up together so closely that of many the entrances were alone visible, the nest itself being built round by others.

"No Pardalotes were here to disturb them, and the Martins were flying to and from the nests in great numbers, some carrying in grass for the linings, others busily employed in repairing the old and building new nests with the mud from the river's bank. Many also I found were brooding their eggs, and this gave me a good opportunity of procuring some specimens, which I did not fail to seize. There were usually from three to five eggs, but some nests contained seven. Many of the eggs were altogether white, others were spotted with light brownish yellow, occasionally all over, in other instances only at the larger end. They vary in length from 7 to $8\frac{1}{2}$ lines, and from 6 to $6\frac{1}{2}$ lines in breadth."

It is evident from the above note that Mr. Gould was mistaken in supposing that the present bird did not breed near Sydney, unless its emigration to the neighbourhood of the town has taken place since Mr. Gould visited Australia. Mr. Ramsay states that he has known the Fairy Cliff-Swallow to take possession of the upper story of some deserted house, along with *Hirundo frontalis*, the *Petrochelidon* building its long flask-shaped nests in clusters under the eaves, while the Swallow enters at the windows and takes possession of the cross-beams and rafters. He has seen both species breeding under the same roof at the Glebe, Sydney.

We are indebted to Mr. E. P. Ramsay for photographs of a nesting colony of the present bird, from which Mr. Wyatt has drawn the accompanying Plate. The cluster of nests was fixed under a ledge of a bank on the Bell River, Wellington valley, and the photographs were taken at the end of September 1884. The bird figured is in the British Museum, and is the one described in the 'Catalogue of Birds.'

APPENDIX

TO THE

GENUS PETROCHELIDON.

PETROCHELIDON NIGRICANS (antea, p. 525).

Add :—
Ammochelidon nigricans, Bald. J. f. O. 1869, p. 406.
Petrochelidon nigricans, Sharpe, Voy. 'Alert.' p. 21 (1884); Sharpe & Wyatt. Monogr. Hirund. pt. v. (1887); Ramsay, Tab. List Austr. B. p. 3 (1888); Buller. B. New Zeal. 2nd ed. i. p. 74 (1888); North, Cat. Nests & Eggs Austr. B. p. 32 (1889); Salvad. Agg. Orn. Papuasia, ii. p. 69 (1889), iii. p. 225 (1891).
Hirundo nigricans, Finsch, Vög. der Südsee, p. 5 (1884).

Mr. A. J. North has the following note:—" This species is to be found throughout the whole of Australia, Tasmania, and the southern portion of New Guinea. It arrives in New South Wales and Victoria in August, and leaves again at the latter end of February. It deposits its eggs, three in number, on the decayed wood of a hollow branch, or hole, of a tree. The ground-colour is of a pinky white, covered with minute freckles of light rusty brown, particularly towards the larger end, where, in some instances, interrupted with lilac spots, they form a zone. Others, again, are pure white with a few fine dots of light red. A set taken by Mr. K. H. Bennett at Mossgiel on the 16th of September, 1883, measure as follows:—(A) 0·73×0·53 inch; (B) 0·72× 0·54 inch; (c) 0·68×0·54 inch.

For the geographical distribution of this species, *vide supra*, Plate 83 [Map].

PETROCHELIDON TIMORIENSIS [*antea*, p. 529].

Add :—

Petrochelidon timoriensis, Sharpe & Wyatt, Monogr. Hirund. pt. v. (1887).

For the geographical distribution of this species, *vide suprà*, Plate 83 [Map].

PETROCHELIDON PYRRHONOTA [*antea*, p. 531].

Add :—

Petrochelidon pyrrhonota, Sharpe & Wyatt, Monogr. Hirund. pt. xiii. (1890).
Petrochelidon lunifrons, Belding, Occ. Papers Calif. Acad. Sci. ii. p. 184; C. Hart Merriam, N.-Amer. Fauna, no. 3, p. 98 (1890), no. 5, p. 104 (1891); Macf. Pr. U. S. Nat. Mus. xiv. p. 143 (1891); Dwight, Auk, ix. p. 138 (1892); Attwater, t. c. p. 340; Lawrence, t. c. p. 356; Anthony, t. c. p. 366; Hatch, B. Minnesota, p. 351 (1892); Fisher, N.-Amer. Fauna, no. 7, pt. 2, p. 110 (1893); Dwight, Auk, x. p. 12 (1893); Todd, t. c. p. 40; White, t. c. p. 226; Brimley, t. c. p. 213.

Mr. Macfarlane found the present species breeding at Fort Good Hope on the Mackenzie River, and numerously along the Lockhart and Anderson Rivers.

Mr. Dwight says that it is a common bird in Prince Edward's Island during summer, but locally distributed, and nesting under the eaves of houses and barns. On Mackinac Island Mr. White records it as an abundant species. Mr. Dwight, in his paper on the summer birds of the Pennsylvania Alleghanies, observes that a colony of perhaps fifty nests was noticed under the eaves of a barn at Cresson, and another, smaller one, a few miles away.

Mr. Brimley states that the species was tolerably common at Raleigh, in North Carolina, during the spring migration in 1889 and 1891. Mr. Attwater records it as an abundant summer resident at San Antonio, Texas. Mr. Anthony states that a few were seen in South-western New Mexico on the 30th of September.

Mr. Belding gives the following notes in his paper on the birds of the Pacific District :—

"One of the most abundant species in California. Arrives at San Diego in March and April. They built under the eaves of buildings here as they usually do in California, though many still nest in cliffs in different parts of the State.

"Stockton, March; Murphy's, March (*L. B.*).

"Poway. Common summer resident, April (April 12, nesting) to September (*F. E. Blaisdell*).

"Volcan Mountains, Santa Maria, April (*W. O. Emerson*).

"Julian, April (*N. S. Goss*).

"San Bernardino. Abundant summer resident of valley and foothills. When I left Tucson I saw no Cliff-Swallows, Barn-Swallows, or Purple Martins. They are later migrants than the White-bellied and Violet-green Swallows, which had been going and coming for weeks (*F. Stephens*).

"Agua Caliente, San Diego, April (*F. Stephens*).

"Santa Cruz. Arrive March and April; common summer resident (*J. Skirm*).

"San José, April to September (*A. L. Parkhurst*).

"Alameda and Contra Costa counties. Abundant summer resident (*W. L. Bryant*).

"Haywards, April; common (*W. O. Emerson*).

"Stockton, April; common (*J. J. Snyder*).

"Berkeley. Common summer resident, April to August (*T. S. Palmer*).

"Nicasio. First seen April 20, 1884 (*C. A. Allen*).

"Sebastopol, April; common (*F. H. Holmes*).

"Marysville. Arrive March and April (*W. F. Peacock*).

"Murphy's, March (*J. J. Snyder*).

"Beaverton (*A. W. Anthony*).

"Willamette Valley. Abundant in summer, breeding chiefly under caves (*O. B. Johnson*).

"At Olympia a few flying about the streets in July; rather scarce north of the Columbia River, 1860 (*Cooper*).

"Fort Dalles. Moderately abundant; makes its appearance in spring simultaneously with *Tachycineta bicolor* and *T. thalassina*, but not so numerous, 1860 (*Suckley*).

"British Columbia, east of Cascades. Summer resident (*John Fannin*).

"Camp Harney, Bendire. One of the most abundant summer residents.

"Hoffman. Usually abundant in the vicinity of rivers and streams, and even large springs.

"Ridgway. Noticed along every portion of our route across the Great Basin, especially in the vicinity of rivers or lakes, or at settlements either large or small.

"Cooper, 1870. In June I saw a flock of these birds busily catching young grasshoppers on the dry hill-side, where these insects were swarming."

Dr. A. K. Fisher, writing on the Death Valley Expedition, says:—"This widely distributed species was found breeding in various localities visited by the Expedition. In Nevada Dr. Merriam found a colony breeding in the cañon at the lower end of Vegas Wash, May 3, and saw several at the head of the Colorado, May 4; he found it common in Pahranagat Valley, May 22-26, and in Oasis Valley, June 1. In Utah he saw a colony which was breeding near St. George, in the Lower Santa Clara Valley, where many nests were found on the red sandstone cliffs a mile or two from the settlement.

"The Cliff-Swallow was common in Owen's Valley, California. It was seen along the edge of the Lake at Keeler, May 30 to June 4; at the mouth of the cañon above Lone Pine, June 12; and Mr. Stephens found it common at Haway Meadows, May 12-14; abundant at Olancha, May 16-23; at Ash Creek, May 30 to June 3; breeding in the cañon at Benton, July 9-10; and not common at the Queen Mine, Nevada, July 11-16. Mr. Nelson saw it on Willow Creek, in the Panamint Mountains, the last of May, and found it at the head of Owen's River, in the Sierra Nevada, up to 2100 metres (7000 feet) altitude. It was common in Kern Valley, July 3–13, and in Walker Basin, July 13–16. At the latter place a number of nests were found fastened against the ceilings and walls of the rooms in several of the deserted buildings. Dr. Merriam found it breeding commonly at Kernville, under the caves and piazzas of houses, June 23, and in the Cañada de las Uvas, under the caves of Old Fort Tejon, June 28–29.

"At Twin Oaks, in Western San Diego County, he was shown a large sycamore, on the outside of which these Swallows used to fasten their nests, and was told that after heavy rains the nests were frequently washed down in great numbers. This species was common at Bakersfield, in the San Joaquin Valley, July 17–20; and Mr. Stephens found it not uncommon at Reche Cañon, near San Bernardino, September 22–24."

In his paper on the birds of Gray's Harbour, Washington Territory, Mr. Lawrence says that he found the species nesting at the mouth of Lewis River, Clarke County, but never on the coast or Sound.

For the geographical distribution of the present species, *vide infrà*, Plate 113 [Map].

PETROCHELIDON SWAINSONI [*anteà*, p. 555].

Add:—

Petrochelidon swainsoni, Sharpe & Wyatt, Monogr. Hirund. pt. viii. (1888).

For the geographical distribution of this species, *vide suprà*, Plate 84 [Map].

PETROCHELIDON FULVA [*anteà*, p. 561].

Add:—

Petrochelidon fulva, Sharpe & Wyatt, Monogr. Hirund. pt. v. (1887); Cory, B. West Ind. p. 71 (1889); Scott, Auk, vii. pp. 264, 311 (1890); A. O. U. Check-l. Suppl. Auk, viii. p. 86 (1891); Cory, Cat. West Ind. B. p. 115 (1892); Scott, Auk, x. p. 181 (1893).

Mr. W. E. D. Scott met with this species at Garden Key on the Dry Tortugas, off the coast of Florida, on the 22nd and 25th of March. From Jamaica the same naturalist writes as follows:—" An abundant resident species, especially near the coast, and not so common in the interior of the island. The caves in the faces of the cliffs along the shore were favourite roosting- and resting-places for this species, and probably the birds bred here later in the year. Hundreds could be seen about sunset retiring to these caves at Priestman's River."

For the geographical distribution of this species, *vide suprà*, Plate 102 [Map].

PETROCHELIDON RUFICOLLARIS [antea, p. 567].

Add :—

Petrochelidon ruficollaris, Sharpe & Wyatt, Monogr. Hirund. pt. v. (1887).

For the geographical distribution of this species, *vide suprà*, Plate 102 [Map].

PETROCHELIDON RUFIGULA [antea, p. 571].

Add :—

Petrochelidon rufigula, Sharpe & Wyatt, Monogr. Hirund. pt. v. (1887); Bocage, Jorn. Sc. Lisb. (2) viii. pp. 257, 258 (1892).

For the geographical distribution of this species, *vide suprà*, Plate 102 [Map].

PETROCHELIDON SPILODERA [antea, p. 573].

Add :—

Petrochelidon spilodera, Sharpe & Wyatt, Monogr. Hirund. pt. xiii. (1890).

For the geographical distribution of this species, *vide suprà*, Plate 102 [Map].

PETROCHELIDON FLUVICOLA [antea, p. 577].

Add :—

Hirundo fluvicola, W. L. Sclater. Ibis, 1892, p. 73; Barnes, J. Bomb. N. H. Soc. iii. p. 205, iv. pp. 2, 83, 237, v. pp. 1. 97. 315, vi. pp. 1. 129; Oates, ed. Hume's Nests & Eggs Ind. B. ii. p. 191 (1890); id. Faun. Brit. Ind., Birds, ii. p. 280 (1890).

Petrochelidon fluvicola, Sharpe & Wyatt, Monogr. Hirund. pt. viii. (1888).

THIS species was originally described by Blyth from Bundelkund, but the type specimen is no longer to be found in the Calcutta Museum, as we are informed by Mr. W. L. Sclater.

The following additional notes on the nesting of the species appear in Mr. Oates's edition of Mr. Hume's 'Nest and Eggs of Indian Birds':—" Mr. Benjamin Aitken, relating his experiences of this Swallow, says: 'You remark that the Indian Cliff-Swallow builds its nests in clusters of from 20 to 200. It may therefore interest you to know that the only group of their nests I have observed consisted of about 600 nests. It was on the river at Akola, Berar, below the bund. There was a pool at the place, so that unless heavy rain had flooded the river the water was, in wet and dry season alike, breast-high. The nests were therefore much more difficult of access than one would have supposed, looking at the almost dry condition of the channel below the bund. The lowest rows of nests were only a foot or so above the surface of the water, but on wading up I could not see into a single nest, and could not reach more than a few with my hand. The nests were placed under the wreck of an old bridge, and were quite inaccessible from above. The birds were occupied about their breeding twice a year, but either they had two broods each time or some of them delayed much longer than others to lay their eggs. At any rate, the period between the time the flock returned to their breeding-place and the time when the old and young birds were scattered over the country was about two months. I regret that I was very negligent in making exact notes of their nidification; the following are all I have:

"'7th Jan., 1870. Young birds just fledged.

"'17th Jan., 1870. Scores more have left the nest.

"'22nd June, 1870. Swallows have come back to their nests in great numbers.

"'5th Jan., 1871. Swallows breeding.

"'9th Feb., 1871. This morning I waded into the water and examined a number of the nests. I first put my fingers into those with short necks, and found them all empty. I then broke open five nests that had necks 6 inches long. Of these two were empty, but lined with straw, feathers, and rags; two more contained young birds; the fifth had three white eggs. It is worth recording that for some weeks past young birds have been leaving the nest, the old ones feeding them on the wing. The nests are made entirely of pellets of clay, all exactly alike and as large as dry peas. I lately watched about twenty of these Swallows building; they took the mud from the edge of the water about ten yards from the nests, and were in a tremendous hustle. They took several pecks at the mud to make each pellet, and stayed five seconds on the ground each time.'

"Colonel Butler says:—'I have eggs of the Cliff-Swallow taken at Sattara in 1875. Some are pure white, the others are marked all over with pale yellowish brown.'

"Capt. E. R. Shopland, I.M., found this Swallow breeding at Akyab. He says:— 'I found about ten nests in April under a bridge; some contained young birds, others fresh eggs. The nests were composed of mud and lined with grass, casuarina-leaves, and feathers. The greatest number of eggs in any one nest was four, and they were white speckled with two shades of brown, chiefly round the larger end.'"

For the geographical distribution of this species, *vide supra*, Plate 85 [Map].

PETROCHELIDON ARIEL (*antea*, p. 585).

Add:—

Petrochelidon ariel, Sharpe & Wyatt, Monogr. Hirund. pt. iv. (1886).
Lagenoplastes ariel, North, Cat. Nests & Eggs Austr. B. p. 32 (1889).

Mr. North gives the following note:—"On September 29th, 1886, in company with Mr. Geo. Masters, we took a number of nests of this species at Chatsworth, on the Eastern Creek; the eggs varied both in size, shape, and colour, some being white without markings of any kind, others being elongated and heavily marked with yellowish-brown spots; they measure as follows:—(A) 0.67×0.17 inch; (B) 0.69×0.18 inch; (C) 0.75×0.19 inch; (D) 0.73×0.18 inch; (E) 0.68×0.17 inch.

"During a visit to Dubbo, in August 1887, these birds arrived in great numbers, commencing to build on the 17th, and covering the eaves of the schools, churches, and public buildings with their curiously retort-shaped nests."

For the geographical distribution of this species, *vide supra*, Plate 85 [Map].

GEOGRAPHICAL DISTR[IBUTION]

	Migratory.
→/→	Bird of passage.
→⊝→	Remains locally during the winter.
→△→	Transplanted.
→←→	Winter resident.

	Nearctic Region.						Neotropical Region.			
	Arctic Sub-Region	Cold Temperate Sub-Region.			Warm Temperate Sub-Region.			Central American Sub-Region.			
	Arctic Province. / Alaskan Arctic Province.	Hudsonian Province. / Canadian Province.	Nelson Province.	Alentian Province.	Humid Province / Appalachian Province.	Arid Province. / Austro-Riparian Sub-Province. / Campestrian Sub-Province. / Sonoran Sub-Province.	Antillean Sub-Region.	Mexican Province.	Isthmian Province.	Sub-Andean Sub-Region.	Amazonian Sub-Region.
1. P. cericinus ...		..	..								
2. P. transversus ...		..									
3. P. pyrrhonotus .	▦	▦	..		▦	▦		→	→		
4. P. rasiinewsi ...		..						○	○		
5. P. fulvus		..					○	○			
6. P. caspicollaris ..						..			..		
7. P. caspigula		..			..						..
8. P. spilodera		..						..			
9. P. flavicoda		..									..
10. P. arcd		..						..			..

∨ Guest.
† Wanderer.
☐ Rarely
☐ Generally } nesting.
☐ In colonies

			Ethiopian Region.						Indian Region.			Australian Region.					
Mediterranean Province.	Mediterranean-European Province.	Mongolian Province.	Himalo-Tungusian Sub-Region.	Saharan Sub-Region.	Soudanese Sub-Region.	West-African Sub-Region.	Abyssinian Sub-Region.	East African Sub-Region.	South-African Sub-Region.	Comorean Sub-Region.	Persian Sub-Region.	Indian Peninsular Sub-Region.	Indo-Malayan Sub-Region.	Himalo-Malayan Sub-Region.	Himal-Chinese Sub-Region.	Celebes Sub-Region.	Moluccan Sub-Region.	Papuan Sub-Region.	Austrian Sub-Region.	New-Zealand Sub-Region.	Fijian Sub-Region.	Hawaiian Sub-Region.

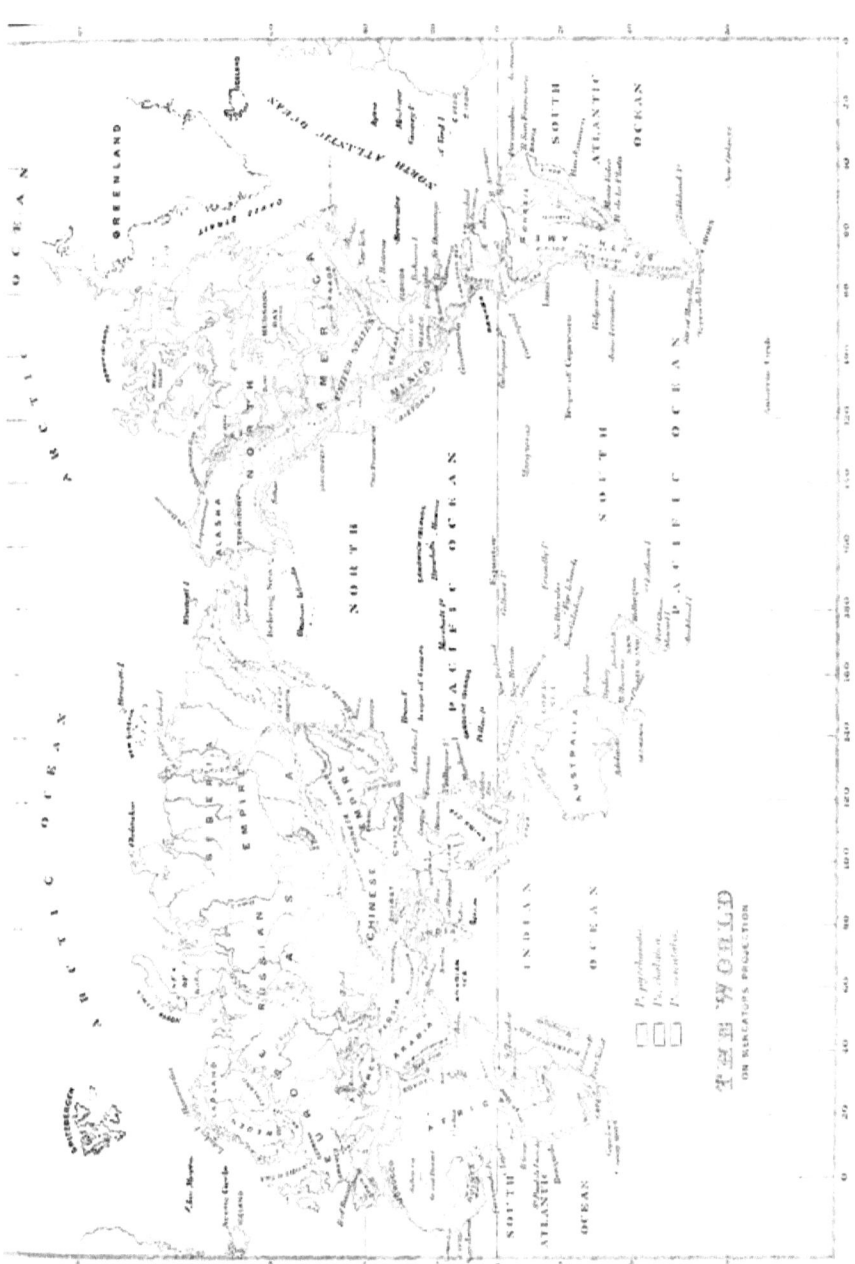

Subfam. II. **PSALIDOPROCNINÆ.**

Clavis generum Psalidoprocninarum.

A. Nigræ; nares longitudinales, operculo obtectæ . . . . . . 11. PSALIDOPROCNE
B. Brunneæ; nares rotundatæ, obviæ, operculo nullo . . . . 12. STELGIDOPTERYX

Genus XI. PSALIDOPROCNE.

Type.
Psalidoprocne, Cab. Mus. Hein. Th. i. p. 48 (1850) . . *P. holomelæna.*
Pristoptera, Bp. Rivist. Contemp. Torino, 1857, p. 4 . . *P. pristoptera.*

Range. Confined to Africa.

Clavis specierum.

a. Pileum dorso concolor.
  a'. Subalares pectori concolores vel viridi-lavatæ.
    a''. Cauda furcata.
      a'''. Virescenti-nigra: interscapulium velutino-nigrum; cauda
        brevior . . . . 1. *holomelæna*, p. 603.
      b'''. Omnino nitide virescenti-nigra: interscapulium dorso
        reliquo concolor . . . . 2. *obscura*, p. 607.
      c'''. Similis præcedenti, sed chalybeo-olivascens . 3. *chalybea*, p. 609.
    b''. Cauda quadrata . . . . 4. *nitens*, p. 611.
  b'. Subalares albæ vel fumosæ, vel chocolatino-brunneæ.
    c''. Viridi-nigræ, aut nigrescentes, viridi-lavatæ; gastræum dorso
      concolor.
      d'''. Subalares fumoso-brunneæ . . . . 5. *orientalis*, p. 613.
      e'''. Subalares albæ . . . . 6. *antinorii*, p. 615.
    d''. Supra chocolatino-brunneæ; gastræum dorso concolor.
      f'''. Subalares pallide fumosæ, interdum vix albicantes . 7. *petiti*, p. 617.
      g'''. Subalares chocolatino-brunneæ, pectori concolores . . 8. *fuliginosa*, p. 619.
    e''. Supra chalybeo-cyanea; subalares albæ . . . . 9. *pristoptera*, p. 621.
b. Pileum album . . . . 10. *albiceps*, p. 624.

PSALIDOPROCNE HOLOMELÆNA

PSALIDOPROCNE HOLOMELÆNA (Sundev.).

BLACK ROUGH-WINGED SWALLOW.

Hirundo holomelas, Sundev. Œfv. K. Vet.-Akad. Förh. Stockh. 1850, p. 108; Hartl. J. f. O. 1856, p. 360; Grill, Zool. Antecku. p. 36 (1858); Layard, Ibis, 1864, p. 134; Gray, Hand-l. B. i. p. 70, no. 823 (1869).

Atticora hamigera, Cass. Proc. Philad. Acad. 1850, p. 57, pl. 12.

Psalidoprocne cypselina, Cab. Mus. Hein. Th. i. p. 48 (1850).

Atticora holomelas, Cass. Cat. Hirund. Mus. Philad. Acad. p. 6 (1882); Gurney, Ibis, 1863, p. 322; Layard, B. S. Afr. p. 57 (1867); id. Ibis, 1869, p. 72; Ayres, Ibis, 1876, p. 424.

Psalidoprocne holomela, Bp. Rivist. Contemp., Torino, 1857, p. 4.

Psalidoprocne holomelæna, Sclater, P.Z.S. 1864, p. 108; Sharpe, P.Z.S. 1870, p. 288 (pt.); id. Cat. Afr. B. p. 45 (1871, pt.); Shelley, Ibis, 1875, p. 67; Barratt, Ibis, 1876, p. 204; Salvin, Cat. Strickl. Coll. p. 152 (1882); Shelley, P.Z.S. 1882, p. 306; Sharpe, ed. Layard's B. S. Afr. p. 356 (1883); id. Cat. Birds in Brit. Mus. x. p. 202 (1885).

Atticora holomelæna, Fischer, Zeitschr. ges. Orn. i. p. 358 (1884).

Ps. nitenti-viridis, dorso quasi velutino vel fuscescenti-viridi, oleagino lavato; pileo dorso concolori; subalaribus pectori concoloribus; caudâ furcatâ.

Hab. in Africâ meridionali et orientali.

Adult male. Above dark greenish black, with scarcely any gloss, the centre of the back velvety greenish black; quills deep black with a slight greenish gloss, the outer web of the first primary distinctly serrated; tail dark greenish black, long, and deeply forked: "bill black; nostrils large and oval; tarsi and feet dusky pale; iris very dark brown" (*T. Ayres*); "legs purplish brown, shading off into flesh-colour on the back of the tarsus and soles of the feet" (*G. E. Shelley*). Total length 5·4 inches, culmen 0·3, wing 4·1, tail 3·0, tarsus 0·3.

Adult female. Similar to the male, but smaller and somewhat more dusky, the outer edge of the first primary smooth and not serrated, and the tail less forked.

Young. Much more dusky than the adults and not so plainly glossed with green.

Hab. From the Knysna districts in the Cape Colony eastwards to Natal, and thence northwards as far as the Zanzibar region in Eastern Africa.

ALTHOUGH of a stouter build than the Rough-winged Swallow of Western Africa, the present species has a considerably shorter tail, and looks at first sight to be the lesser bird of the two. It may be recognized by the velvety black of the back, this being glossy green in *P. obscura* of West Africa.

This is probably the "Martinet vélocifère" of Levaillant's 'Oiseaux d'Afrique' (v. p. 147, pl. 244. fig. 2), named by Vieillot *Hirundo velox* (N. Dict. xiv. p. 533). As Professor Sundevall has already pointed out in his critique on Levaillant's work (Krit. Framst. Levaill. p. 51) there is no known Swift which answers to the description given by the French traveller, and it is probable that he saw this Swallow in South Africa and drew the figure from memory.

In the Cape Colony it appears to be resident at least for the greater part of the year. The late Mr. C. J. Andersson met with it at the Knysna in January; Victorin procured it there in March and April, and again from July to November. In other parts of the Colony it may be more or less migratory, as Mr. L. C. Layard notices its arrival at Grootevadersbosch, in the Swellendam district, on the 5th of September. This seems to be the most easterly range recorded for the species.

Mr. E. L. Layard writes:—"This little Swallow first fell under our notice on the Keurboom's River, Knysna district, where we saw it apparently breeding in holes in the banks, but were unable to investigate its doings more closely. We found it abundantly in the forest, hawking after flies over pools, frequently dipping into the water, and perching on the overhanging boughs in clusters of six or eight, to dry themselves. Their habit of perching is noted by Mr. Cairncross, who writes:—'This bird flies about very much like a bat (this resemblance also occurred to us when we saw it), amongst thick forests, and is generally more visible in rainy, heavy weather; but I have never seen or heard of their breeding here (Swellendam). They remain here after the winter has set in. Sometimes I have seen them roost on trees at the bottom of my garden, where I shot the specimen sent.'"

Mr. Layard also states that it is found throughout the wooded districts of the Eastern province. He saw it near Grahamstown, the Kowie, Fish River bush, &c. In the British Museum is a nestling obtained by Mr. F. C. Rickard at Bat's Cove, near East London, in December, showing that the species breeds in that neighbourhood during the latter month. Captain Trevelyan has also procured it in the Peri bush near Kingwilliamstown.

Mr. Thomas Ayres says that in Natal this species is common all the year round, but he thinks not immediately on the coast. "They are generally to be seen two or three together, searching for insects about the bushy valleys, and occasionally, though not often, alighting to rest on some dead bough. Their food consists of minute beetles and other insects."

Captain Shelley, during his three months' trip to South Africa, found the present species very plentiful about Pinetown, and occasionally to be met with at Durban. It is a woodland bird, usually seen in small flocks, often perching on boughs on the shady side of large trees. They appear to avoid the glare of the midday sun, feeding mostly in the evening, often long after sunset. Mr. T. Ayres noticed the species in the Lydenburg district of the Eastern Transvaal; and Mr. F. A. Barratt procured specimens at Rustenburg and Macamac, where he says the species was rather scarce, and the ones obtained were shot by him as they flew up and down in the open spaces in the forest.

Nothing further is known of the range of the species in South Africa, but it appears in the Zanzibar district in Eastern Africa, as Sir John Kirk sent a specimen from Mambolo to Captain Shelley, who has kindly allowed us to examine it, and there can be no doubt that it is identical with the South-African species. Dr. Fischer has likewise procured a specimen at Maurui in Masai-land, in January, and it is possible that the "black Swallow" noticed by Colonel Grant in his 'Walk across Africa,' along with *Psalidoprocne albiceps* in Usinza, may have been of the present species, though at the same time it may have been the young of *P. albiceps*.

The descriptions are taken from specimens in the British Museum, the figure in the Plate being drawn from a Natal skin in the latter collection.

PSALIDOPROCNE OBSCURA.

PSALIDOPROCNE OBSCURA (*Hartl.*).

(FANTEE ROUGH-WINGED SWALLOW.)

Atticora obscura, Temm. MSS. in Mus. Lugd., undè
Atticora obscura, Hartl. J. f. O. 1855, p. 35; id. Orn. Westafr. p. 26 (1857); id. J. f. O. 1861, p. 103.
Hirundo obscura, Hartl. J. f. O. 1855, p. 360; Gray, Hand-l. B. i. p. 71, no. 831 (1869).
Atticora holomelas, Hartl. Orn. Westafr. p. 25 (1857, nec Sundev.).
Psalidoprocne holomelaena, Sharpe, P. Z. S. 1870, p. 288 (pt.); id. Ibis, 1870, p. 479; id. Cat. Afr. B. p. 43 (1871, pt.); Shelley & Buckley, Ibis, 1872, p. 288; Ussher, Ibis, 1874, p. 61; Reichen. J. f. O. 1875, p. 67.
Psalidoprocne obscura, Sharpe, Cat. Birds in Brit. Mus. x. p. 203 (1885).

Ps. suprà nitenti-viridis; pileo dorso concolore; subalaribus pectori concoloribus; caudâ furcatâ.

Hab. in Africâ occidentali cis-equatoriali.

Adult male. General colour above glossy bottle-green; the head like the back; the rump and upper tail-coverts with somewhat of a steel-blue appearance; lesser and median wing-coverts like the back; greater coverts, bastard-wing, primary-coverts, and quills blackish, washed externally with glossy green like the back; tail-feathers blackish, slightly washed with green; lores velvety black; cheeks, ear-coverts, and entire under surface of body glossy bottle-green like the upper surface; axillaries and under wing-coverts smoky brown with a slight greenish wash; quills dusky brown below. Total length 6·9 inches, culmen 0·25, wing 3·85, tail 4·1, tarsus 0·35.

Adult female. Similar in colour to the male, but smaller, and having the outer edge of the first primary smooth, not serrated. Total length 5·4 inches, culmen 0·25, wing 3·45, tail 3, tarsus 0·35.

Young. Sooty brown with a greenish wash on the back; below dull sooty brown; gape yellow.

Hab. Gold Coast, West Africa.

This is the West-African representative of *Psalidoprocne holomelaena*, with which species we at one time united it. Subsequent study, however, with a larger series of specimens, has induced us to alter our previous opinion, and we now believe that the West-African Bottle-green Swallow is distinct from its South-African representative. It is glossy green, instead of being dull bottle-green with a greenish-black mantle, this last character being very marked in *P's. holomelaena*.

The range of this species appears to be limited to the Gold Coast, where, according to Messrs. Shelley and Buckley (Ibis, 1872, p. 288), it "is very plentiful throughout the country, especially in the more wooded districts, where during the heat of the day flocks may be seen sitting together on the more shaded dead boughs of the large trees, and may frequently be met with after the sun has set, still in pursuit of insects." Governor Ussher gives similar information, but adds:—" I have observed them also in considerable numbers in the morning, collecting in bare gravelly places, and lying on the ground enjoying the morning sun." Mr. Blissett forwarded us examples from the Province of Wasa.

The figure in the Plate has been drawn from a specimen in Capt. Shelley's collection, the description being taken from the 'Catalogue of Birds in the British Museum.'

PSALIDOPROCNE CHALYBEA, *Reichenow*.

CAMEROONS ROUGH-WINGED SWALLOW.

Psalidoprocne chalybea, Reichen. Ber. Allg. deutsch. orn. Ges., Sept. 1892, p. 6.

P. similis P. obscurae, sed nitore chalybeo olivascente distinguenda.

Hab. in montibus Cameronensibus Africae occidentalis.

Adult. Similar to *P. obscura*, but distinguished by its steely-olive colour. Black, with a greenish-teal gloss, the back shining olive-green; the under surface of the body duller; under wing-coverts ashy brown; tail forked.

Hab. Mount Victoria, Cameroons, West Africa.

This Swallow we have not seen, and the above descriptions are copied from Dr. Reichenow's original paper.

The species was discovered in the Cameroon Mountains on Mount Victoria by Dr. Preuss, and the type is in the Berlin Museum.

For the geographical distribution of this species, *vide supra*, Plate 113 (Map).

PSALIDOPROCNE NITENS (Cass.).

SQUARE-TAILED ROUGH-WINGED SWALLOW.

Atticora nitens, Cass. Proc. Acad. Philad. 1857, p. 38; Hartl. Orn. Westafr. p. 262 (1857); Cass. Proc. Philad. Acad. 1859, p. 33; Du Chaillu, Equat. Afr. p. 172 (1861).
Hirundo nitens, Gray, Hand-l. B. i. p. 71, no. 831 (1869).
Psalidoprocne nitens, Sharpe, P. Z. S. 1870, p. 291; id. P. Z. S. 1871, p. 610; id. Ibis, 1872, p. 90; Ussher, Ibis, 1874, p. 61; Sharpe, Cat. Birds in Brit. Mus. x. p. 204 (1885).

P. viridi-nigra: gulâ fuscescenti-griseâ: dorso pileo concolore: subalaribus pectori concoloribus; caudâ haud furcatâ.

Hab. in Africâ occidentali.

Adult male. General colour above glossy bottle-green or greenish black; lesser wing-coverts like the back; remainder of wing-coverts, quills, and tail-feathers black, edged with bottle-green; lores velvety black; sides of face, ear-coverts, cheeks, and under surface of body glossy bottle-green, the under wing-coverts black glossed with green; quills blackish below; throat sooty grey. Total length 4·3 inches, culmen 0·25, wing 3·85, tail 1·95, tarsus 0·3.

Adult female. Similar to the male in colour, but wanting the saw-like edge to the first primary.

Hab. West Africa, from the Gold Coast to the Congo.

WE know so little of this species from the Gold Coast that a larger series of specimens will have to be examined before it can be ascertained for certain whether the square-tailed *Psalidoprocne* from that region is really of the same species as the typical *P. nitens* of Gaboon. At first sight it would appear that the individuals from the Cameroons, Gaboon, and the Congo region differed in having the throat smoky brown instead of greenish black, like the breast; but the British Museum has a specimen from the Muni River in Gaboon which appears to agree precisely with others from the Gold Coast, and on that account we have not separated the two forms specifically.

From the other species of *Psalidoprocne* the present one is easily recognized by its square tail. It was first discovered by M. DuChaillu on the Muni and Ogowé rivers in Gaboon, and it extends to the Congo region, as specimens collected at Landana by M. Petit are in the British Museum. It is likewise known from the Cameroons, where the late Mr. Crossley met with it in January, and our late friend Governor Ussher found it on the Gold Coast. He writes:—"Not uncommon in the morning on the gravelly slopes of Fort Victoria and the other eminences round Cape-Coast Castle, where it appears to bask in the sun, taking short flights among the surrounding bushes. It is gregarious."

The descriptions and figures are taken from specimens in the British Museum. Both forms of variation in plumage are shown in the Plate.

PSALIDOPROCNE ORIENTALIS, Reichenow.

EASTERN ROUGH-WINGED SWALLOW.

? *Atticora holomelaena*, Fischer, J. f. O. 1889, p. 277.
Psalidoprocne petiti orientalis, Reichen. J. f. O. 1889, p. 277.
Psalidoprocne petiti (nec Sh. & B.), Shelley, P. Z. S. 1889, p. 359.
Psalidoprocne orientalis, Sharpe, Ibis, 1892, p. 306; Reichen. Jahrb. Hamb. Wiss. Anst. x. p. 16 (1893).

P. similis P. petiti et subalaribus fumosis, sed nitore viridescente nec chocolatino distinguenda.

Hab. in Africâ orientali.

Adult male. General colour above and below dull black with a steel-green gloss; median and greater wing-coverts, quills, and tail-feathers black, externally glossed with steel-green; under wing-coverts smoky brown: "bill black; feet brown; iris brown" (F. J. Jackson). Total length 6·5 inches, culmen 0·25, wing 4·5, tail 1·9, longest feathers 3·8, tarsus 0·35.

Adult female. Similar to the male, but without any serrations on the outer web of the first primary. Total length 6 inches, wing 4·1, tail 1·55, longest feathers 4·1.

Dr. Reichenow originally described the present species from Lewa, in the Usambara Hills, where it was discovered by Dr. Stuhlmann on the 25th of September. A young bird was subsequently procured by Mr. Hunter, in Taveta, and was identified by Captain Shelley as *Psalidoprocne petiti*, to which species the browner shade of the immature plumage of *P. orientalis* bears some resemblance. Specimens were procured by Mr. F. J. Jackson in the Sotik Country at the end of August 1889, and again on Mount Elgon, at a height of from 7000 to 8000 feet, in February 1890. Mr. Jackson has the following note:—"Found a colony of these birds breeding inside a large cave. The nest was made entirely of *Orchella*-weed, placed inside small recesses in the sides of the cave. The eggs were two, pure white."

In our paper on Mr. Jackson's East-African collection, we stated our opinion that the present species was quite distinct from *P. petiti*, and was fully entitled to specific rank. In this opinion we are glad to see that Dr. Reichenow now concurs.

The late Colonel Grant in his journal had the following note, which he communicated to us in 1870:—"Usui, Central Africa, October 16, 1861. Black Swallow with

white forehead and throat under the jaw, with forked tail. Black Swallow, smaller."
The first of these species was *P. albiceps*, Sclater, but the second has never been identified; it may have been only the young of *P. albiceps*, or, again, it may have been *P. orientalis*. Colonel Grant says that they were both seen together about scarped rocks, which certainly favours the first proposition.

The descriptions, as well as the figures on the Plate, have been taken from the pair of birds procured by Mr. Jackson on Mount Elgon.

The specimen from Maurui, recorded by Dr. Fischer as *Atticora holomelaena*, was probably of the present species. We have, unfortunately, not been able to trace the bird in question, as Dr. Reichenow informs us that it is not in Berlin. He thought that it might be in the Hamburg Museum, but Dr. Kraeppelin tells us that it is not in that collection.

For the geographical distribution of this species, *vide suprà*, Plate 113 [Map].

PSALIDOPROCNE ANTINORII, Salvad.

ANTINORI'S ROUGH-WINGED SWALLOW.

Psalidoprocne antinorii, Salvad. Ann. Mus. Civic. Genov. (2) i. p. 123 (1884); Sharpe, Cat. Birds in Brit. Mus. x. p. 205 (1885).

P. pileo dorso concolore: subalaribus albis.

Hab. in Africa septentrionali-orientali usque ad provinciam Zambesianam.

Adult. General colour above sooty brown with a greenish gloss; wing-coverts like the back; quills and tail-feathers brown, externally glossed with greenish; crown of head, sides of face, and under surface of body sooty brown, excepting the under wing-coverts and axillaries, which are pure white; quills ashy below: "bill black, feet dusky, iris dusky" (*Antinori*). Total length 5 inches, culmen 0·25, wing 3·9, tail 2·1, tarsus 0·35.

The typical specimen from Shoa measured as follows:—Total length 5·5 inches, culmen 0·25, wing 4·15, tail 2·95, tarsus 0·35.

Hab. Eastern Africa, from Shoa to the Zambesi.

Antinori's Swallow is closely allied to *P. petiti* and *P. fuliginosa*, but is easily distinguishable by its white under wing-coverts and axillaries. In this respect it resembles *P. pristoptera*, but is sooty brown instead of blue.

It was discovered in Shoa by the late Marquis Antinori, at a place called Denz, on the 27th of May, 1880; and in a small parcel of birds presented to the British Museum by Sir John Kirk in 1884 (a remnant of his collections made during the Livingstone Expedition on the Zambesi and Shiré rivers) there was a damaged skin of this Swallow. It is probable, therefore, that it inhabits the whole of the interior of Eastern Africa from Shoa to the northern shores of the Zambesi.

The description is taken from Sir John Kirk's specimen, and the figure has been drawn by Mr. Wyatt from the type specimen, which was sent to England by our friend Count Salvadori.

PSALIDOPROCNE PETITI.

PSALIDOPROCNE PETITI, Sharpe & Bouvier.

PETIT'S ROUGH-WINGED SWALLOW.

Psalidoprocne petiti, Sharpe & Bouvier, Bull. Soc. Zool. France, i. p. 38, pl. ii. (1876); Oustalet, Bull. Soc. Philom. (7) i. p. 106 (1877); Bocage, Orn. Angola, p. 188 (1881); Oustalet, Nouv. Arch. Mus. (2) ii. p. 96 (1879); Sharpe, Cat. Birds in Brit. Mus. x. p. 204 (1885).

Ps. suprà fumoso-nigra; capite dorso concolore; subalaribus et axillaribus fumoso-albis.

Hab. in Africâ occidentali trans-equatoriali.

Adult male (type of species). General colour above sooty black; lesser and median wing-coverts like the back; greater coverts, bastard-wing, primary-coverts, and quills black; tail-feathers black; lores velvety black; cheeks, ear-coverts, and under surface of body sooty black like the upper surface; under wing-coverts and axillaries pale smoky brown; quills dusky below, browner along the inner web: "eyes black" (*Petit*). Total length 5·8 inches, culmen 0·25, wing 4·05, tail 2·9, tarsus 0·35.

Adult female. Similar to the male in colour, but wanting the serrated edge to the outer web of the first primary. Total length 5·2 inches, culmen 0·25, wing 3·55, tail 2·5, tarsus 0·4.

Young. Similar to the adult, but not so glossy; below much paler and more earthy brown.

Hab. West Africa; from the Congo to Gaboon.

This species was discovered by Mr. Louis Petit at Landana on the Congo, and was also met with by Dr. Lucan at Chinchonxo in the same district and about the same time. We have recently seen several specimens also collected by Mr. Petit in the Congo region. Dr. Oustalet records a specimen from Sam-Quita in Gaboon, where it was obtained by the well-known traveller Marche on the 18th of December 1875.

Of all the rough-winged Swallows of Africa this is one of the most distinct, being distinguished by the pale smoky-brown axillaries and under wing-coverts. The nearest ally is *Ps. antinorii*, which, however, has the under wing-coverts pure white.

The figure in the Plate is drawn from a specimen in the British Museum, and the descriptions are taken from the 'Catalogue of Birds.'

PSALIDOPROCNE FULIGINOSA.

PSALIDOPROCNE FULIGINOSA, Shelley.

JOHNSTON'S ROUGH-WINGED SWALLOW.

Psalidoprocne fuliginosa, Shelley, P. Z. S. 1887, p. 123.

P. suprà saturatè chocolatina : pileo dorso concolore ; subalaribus chocolatino-brunneis.

Hab. in Africâ occidentali.

Adult male. General colour above dark chocolate-brown, the head being like the back, the lores velvety black ; bastard-wing, primary-coverts, quills, and tail rather blacker ; entire under surface of body also chocolate-brown, the under wing-coverts somewhat lighter and more smoky brown. Total length 5·2 inches, culmen 0·25, wing 4·2, tail 2·5, tarsus 0·35.

Hab. Mountains of the Cameroons district, West Africa.

This species was discovered by the well-known African traveller, Mr. H. H. Johnston in the Cameroons Mountains, at a height of 9000 feet. Captain Shelley mentions a female bird as having been procured by Mr. Johnston; but in our opinion both specimens are males, the rough edge of the wing being a little less pronounced in one than in the other.

The description and figure are both taken from the typical specimen in the British Museum.

PSALIDOPROCNE PRISTOPTERA

PSALIDOPROCNE PRISTOPTERA (*Rüpp.*).

BLUE ROUGH-WINGED SWALLOW.

Hirundo pristoptera, Rüpp. Neue Wirb. Taf. 39. fig. 2 (1835).
Hirundo (*Chelidon*) *pristoptera*, Rüpp. t. c. p. 105 (1835).
Atticora albiscapulata, Boie, Isis, 1844, p. 172 (ex Rüpp. MSS.); Gray, Hand-l. B. i. p. 75, no. 861 (1869).
Chelidon pristoptera, Rüpp. Syst. Uebers. p. 22 (1845).
Atticora pristoptera, Gray, Gen. B. i. p. 58 (1845); id. Cat. Fissir. Brit. Mus. p. 21 (1848); Bp. Consp. i. p. 337 (1850); Heugl. J. f. O. 1861, p. 420, 1863, p. 4; Brehm, Reis. Habesch, p. 208 (1863); Finsch, Trans. Zool. Soc. vii. p. 217 (1870).
Chelidon (?) *pristoptera*, Heugl. Syst. Uebers. p. 17 (1856).
Pristoptera typica, Bp. Rivist. Contemp., Torino, 1857, p. 4.
Psalidoprocne pristoptera, Sclater, P. Z. S. 1864, p. 109; Heugl. Orn. N.O.-Afr. i. p. 118 (1869); Pfauf. Geol. & Zool. Abyss. p. 349 (1870); Sharpe, P. Z. S. 1870. p. 290; Antin. & Salvad, Viagg. Bogos, p. 71 (1873); Salvad. Ann. Mus. Civic. Genov. (2) i. p. 123 (1884); Sharpe, Cat. Birds in Brit. Mus. x. p. 205 (1885).

Ps. omnino chalybeo-niger ; subalaribus et axillaribus albis.

Hab. in Africa septentrionali-occidentali.

Adult. Above glossy blue-black, with a greenish tinge on the wings and tail; quills greenish black, the inner web dusky; tail much forked, greenish black above, dusky underneath; under surface of the body glossy blue-black; under wing-coverts and axillaries white: " bill black ; feet and iris dusky " (*Von Heuglin*). Total length 5·5 inches ; of bill from front 0·6, from gape 0·4 ; wing 0·4. tail 3 ; tarsus 0·35, middle toe 0·4, hind toe 0·2, lateral toes 0·25.

The *adult female*, according to Von Heuglin and Salvadori, does not differ from the male.

Hab. Confined to the mountains of North-eastern Africa, from Bogos Land through Abyssinia to Shoa and Galla Land.

This very distinct species of Rough-winged Swallow was discovered by the late Dr. Rüppell during his travels in Abyssinia in the early part of the present century. It is easily recognized from all other species of the genus *Psalidoprocne* by its white under wing-coverts and blue coloration.

Rüppell found it in the province of Sémien, in Abyssinia, where he says that it was building its nest in the crevices of rocks in the valleys, a statement at variance with the experience of Dr. Von Heuglin (*vide infrà*). Mr. Blanford states that he shot but one specimen of the bird in Abyssinia, at Dongolo in Tigrè, at a height of 6500 feet above the sea. He saw it occasionally both on the highlands and in the Anseba valley, but never below 4000 feet elevation. Mr. Jesse, during the British expedition to Abyssinia, procured a specimen at Rayray-guddy in the last-named country, and met with the species again at Bejook in Bogos Land. The late Marquis Antinori likewise procured specimens at Keren in Bogos Land, in May. He states that a little flock of eight individuals appeared about the middle of May, and stayed for some days in the mountains near Keren, but they disappeared soon afterwards, and he did not see any during the succeeding months: he believes the species to be rare to the north of Abyssinia.

The late Baron Von Heuglin gives the following account of the species as observed by him:—" It is migratory in Abyssinia, and appears in Galla Land, in Central and Northern Abyssinia (as far north as 17° N. lat.), at the end of April and the beginning of May. It then lives in pairs in the mountain valleys at a height of from 4000 to 10,000 feet. It sings during flight and when perched on the dead tops of trees, after the manner of the Chimney-Swallow; and about the beginning of July it makes its nest in horizontal holes, from about one to three feet in depth, these being apparently excavated by the birds themselves. These holes are found in steep banks of wild rivulets and gorges, generally singly, never more than two or three together, each nest being in a separate hole. The alluvium in which they are placed is often so hard that it is with the greatest difficulty that the nest can be drawn out entire into the daylight. The nest is large, flat, and tolerably artistically woven together with blades of grass, and lined with finer substances. I found two eggs, very thin-shelled and pure white in colour; the length was $8\frac{1}{2}'''$, and the diameter $5'''\cdot 8$. The birds undoubtedly have two broods in the season.

" I never saw this species on the White or Blue Niles, nor in any part of the east Soudan province. It is seen along mountain torrents and pasture-lands, and on rocks, and occasionally rests on the dead branches of the lower trees. Its flight is generally high and swift.

" Rüppell says that this Swallow places its nest in crevices of rocks, whereas I myself, as mentioned above, only knew them as building in holes, and I had a good many opportunities of observing their nesting-places." The late Marquis Antinori obtained two specimens in Shoa at Sciotalit in March, and in the forests of Fecherié-Ghem in June.

The description and figure of this bird are both taken from Mr. Blanford's Dongolo specimen in the British Museum.

PSALIDOPROCNE ALBICEPS, Sclater.

WHITE-HEADED ROUGH-WINGED SWALLOW.

Psalidoprocne albiceps, Sclater, P. Z. S. 1864, p. 108, pl. xiv.; Heugl. Orn. N.O.-Afr. p. 147 (1869); Sharpe, P. Z. S. 1870, p. 291; id. Cat. Birds in Brit. Mus. x. p. 206 (1885); Shelley, P. Z. S. 1888, p. 40.
Psalidoprocne obscura? (nec Temm.), Heugl. Orn. N.O.-Afr. i. p. 118 (1869).
Atticora albiceps, Gray, Hand-l. B. i. p. 73, no. 862 (1879); Finsch & Hartl. Vög. Ostafr. p. 133 (1869).

P. viridi-nigricans : pileo gulâque albis.

Hab. in Africâ æquatoriali.

Adult male. General colour above sooty black glossed with olive-green; wing-coverts like the back; quills and tail blackish, externally glossed with olive-green; crown of head white as far as the nape; lores, eyelid, feathers behind the eye, and ear-coverts sooty black; cheeks and feathers below the eye white, extending over the fore part of the ear-coverts; entire throat white; remainder of under surface of body sooty black with an olive-green gloss; under wing-coverts and axillaries light smoky brown; quills below dusky brown, somewhat lighter along the inner edge. Total length 6 inches, culmen 0·25, wing 4·2, tail 2·9, tarsus 0·35.

Adult female. Similar to the male in colour, but wanting the saw-like edge to the first primary. Total length 5·4 inches, culmen 0·25, wing 3·85, tail 2·4, tarsus 0·35.

Young male. Like the adults, but has the head and throat sooty black, slightly mixed with a few white feathers.

Hab. Equatorial Africa, from Usui to Wadelai.

COLONEL GRANT discovered the present species during his celebrated expedition with Captain Speke through Equatorial Africa. In his journal he has the following note, with which he has favoured us:—" Usui, Central Africa, Oct. 16, 1861. Black Swallow with white forehead and throat under the jaw, with forked tail. Black Swallow, smaller. Seen together about scarped rocks; at least it was here that I first observed them." One specimen was brought home in spirits, and was described by Dr. Sclater, and figured in the 'Proceedings' of the Zoological Society; it was afterwards presented to the British Museum, and it is much to be regretted that it was not immediately preserved as a skin. In 1870, when we were writing on African Swallows, the specimen could not be found; but on the removal and re-arrangement of the national collections at South Kensington, we discovered the specimen in its original bottle of spirits, but too much deteriorated to admit of its being made into a skin for scientific purposes. It will be noticed that Colonel Grant mentions a second kind of Swallow as observed by him along with *P. albiceps* at Usui. This bird has given rise to all kinds of conjectures as to the species observed by the travellers. Drs. Finsch and Hartlaub suggested that Grant's smaller black Swallow might possibly be *Psalidoprocne obscura*, and the late Baron von Heuglin appears to have had scarcely any doubt on the subject; but we were careful to suggest in 1870 that it was just as likely to have been the female of *P. albiceps*.

Nearly thirty years elapsed since Colonel Grant shot the first specimen of the White-headed Swallow before examples of the species were again obtained. It is to Emin Pasha that we owe its rediscovery, for he forwarded in 1887 to the British Museum three specimens procured by him in the neighbourhood of Wadelai. An adult male, killed on the 28th of June, is in worn plumage and is moulting, as is also a female obtained on the 5th of July. The white feathers on the crown in the latter specimen are so much abraded that the dusky bases of the feathers show through on the sinciput and hinder crown, and give the head a spotted appearance.

The young bird, obtained by Emin Pasha in December, is uniformly smoky black, but has a good many white feathers on the crown and throat. Before the white feathers appear, it is evident that the young birds must be perfectly uniform, and it is most likely that the smaller black Swallow observed by Colonel Grant was the young of *P. albiceps*, which would probably be flying about with the parent birds in October, as Emin Pasha's specimen is only beginning to assume the adult plumage early in December. The young bird in its uniform plumage bears some resemblance to the adult of *P. holomelaena*; but it is altogether a browner bird, and has not the bottle-green gloss which distinguishes the last-named bird at all seasons.

The figures in the Plate represent an adult and a young bird. They have been drawn from the specimens sent by Emin Pasha, and the descriptions have been taken from the same individuals.

APPENDIX

TO THE

GENUS PSALIDOPROCNE.

PSALIDOPROCNE HOLOMELÆNA [antea, p. 603].

Add:—

Psalidoprocne holomelaena, Sharpe & Wyatt, Monogr. Hirund. pt. iii. (1886).

For the geographical distribution of this species, *vide infra*, Plate 123 [Map].

PSALIDOPROCNE OBSCURA [antea, p. 607].

Add:—

Psalidoprocne obscura, Sharpe & Wyatt, Monogr. Hirund. pt. i. (1885); Reichen. J. f. O. 1891. p. 381.

RECORDED from Togo Land by Dr. Reichenow.

For the geographical distribution of this species, *vide infra*, Plate 124 [Map].

PSALIDOPROCNE NITENS [antea, p. 611].

Add:—

Psalidoprocne nitens, Sharpe & Wyatt, Monogr. Hirund. pt. vii. (1888); Reichen. J. f. O. 1890. p. 117.

For the geographical distribution of this species, *vide infra*, Plate 125 [Map].

PSALIDOPROCNE ANTINORII [anteà, p. 615].

Add :—
Psalidoprocne antinorii, Sharpe & Wyatt, Monogr. Hirund. pt. vi. (1887).

Mr. Alexander Whyte procured an adult female of this species at Zomba in Nyassa Land in January.

For the geographical distribution of this species, *vide infrà*, Plate 123 [Map].

PSALIDOPROCNE PETITI [anteà, p. 617].

Add :—
Psalidoprocne petiti, Sharpe & Wyatt, Monogr. Hirund. pt. vii. (1888); Reichen. J. f. O. 1887, p. 300; Bocage, Jorn. Sc. Lisb. (2) viii. p. 258 (1892).

It is the young birds which have the smoky-brown under wing-coverts most pronounced. Some of the old males in the British Museum collection have them nearly white, resembling those of *P. antinorii*. The latter species, however, is green not brown in general shade.

Professor Barboza du Bocage states that the present species has been obtained at Quindumbo in Angola by Senhor Anchieta.

Mr. Bohndorff met with it at Manyanga on the Lower Congo between Vivi and Stanley Pool.

For the geographical distribution of this species, *vide infrà*, Plate 124 [Map].

PSALIDOPROCNE FULIGINOSA [anteà, p. 619].

Add :—
Psalidoprocne fuliginosa, Sharpe & Wyatt, Monogr. Hirund. pt. vii. (1888); Reichen. J. f. O. 1890, p. 118.

For the geographical distribution of this species, *vide infrà*, Plate 124 [Map].

PSALIDOPROCNE PRISTOPTERA [antea, p. 621].

Add:—

Psalidoprocne pristoptera, Sharpe & Wyatt, Monogr. Hirund. pt. iii. (1886).

For the geographical distribution of this species, *vide infrà*, Plate 123 [Map].

PSALIDOPROCNE ALBICEPS [antea, p. 624].

Add:—

Psalidoprocne albiceps, Reichen. J. f. O. 1887, p. 62; Sharpe & Wyatt, Monogr. Hirund. pt. vii. (1888); Jackson, Ibis, 1889, p. 584; Emin, J. f. O. 1891, pp. 313, 345; Hartl. Abhandl. nat. Ver. Bremen, p. 31 (1891); Sharpe, Ibis, 1892, p. 306.

Found by Dr. Fischer at Ugaia, east of the Victoria Nyanza, and at Kawanga, to the N.E. of the Lake. Emin Pasha met with it at Bukoba in November and December, and on the island of Kassarasi in October. Dr. Stuhlmann procured specimens at Mjonjo in Uganda in January. Mr. F. J. Jackson brought examples of this pretty Swallow from Makarungu, where he met with them in January and February. He says that it was plentiful in Ukambani.

For the geographical distribution of the present species, *vide infrà*, Plate 124 [Map].

		→	Migratory.
		–/→	Bird of passage.
		‥→	Remains locally during the winter.
		‥△→	Transplanted.
		‥●→	Winter resident.

	Nearctic Region.									Neotropical Region.					
	Arctic Sub-Region		Cold Temperate Sub-Region.			Warm Temperate Sub-Region.					Central American Sub-Region.				
	Arctic Province.	Alaskan Arctic Province.	Hudsonian Province.	Canadian Province.	Sitkan Province.	Alleghan Province.	Humid Province; Appalachian Sub-Province	Arid Province; American-Riparian Sub-Province.	Georgeean Sub-Province.	Sonoran Sub-Province.	Antillean Sub-Region.	Mexican Province.	Isthmian Province.	Sub-Andean Sub-Region.	Amazonian Sub-Region.	Brazilian Sub-Region.	Patagonian Sub-Region.
1. P. ludovicianus				..		..								..	..	..
2. P. obscurus		..	..		..						..			..	..	..
3. P. chilybea			..		..					..				..	..	..
4. P. nitens			..		..	..								..		..
5. P. orientalis					..									..	..	..
6. P. nativocii		..	..		..				..		..			..	..	..
7. P. petiti		..			..									..	..	..
8. P. fuliginosa		..			..						..			..	..	..
9. P. pristoptera		..		..	..						..			..	..	..
10. P. albiceps		..	..		..						..			..	..	..

V   Guest.
†   Wanderer.
☐   Rarely
▦   Generally nesting.
▦   In colonies

		Ethiopian Region.							Indian Region.						Australian Region.				

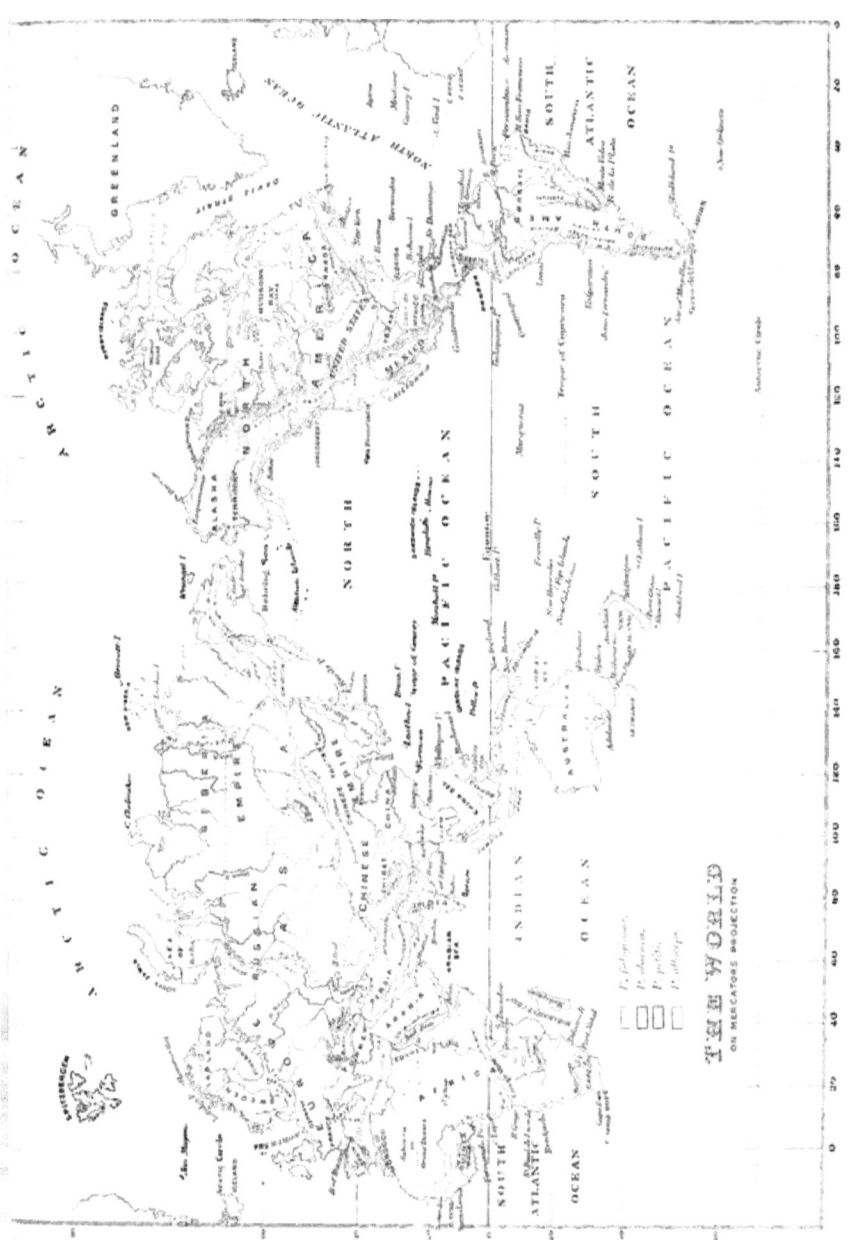

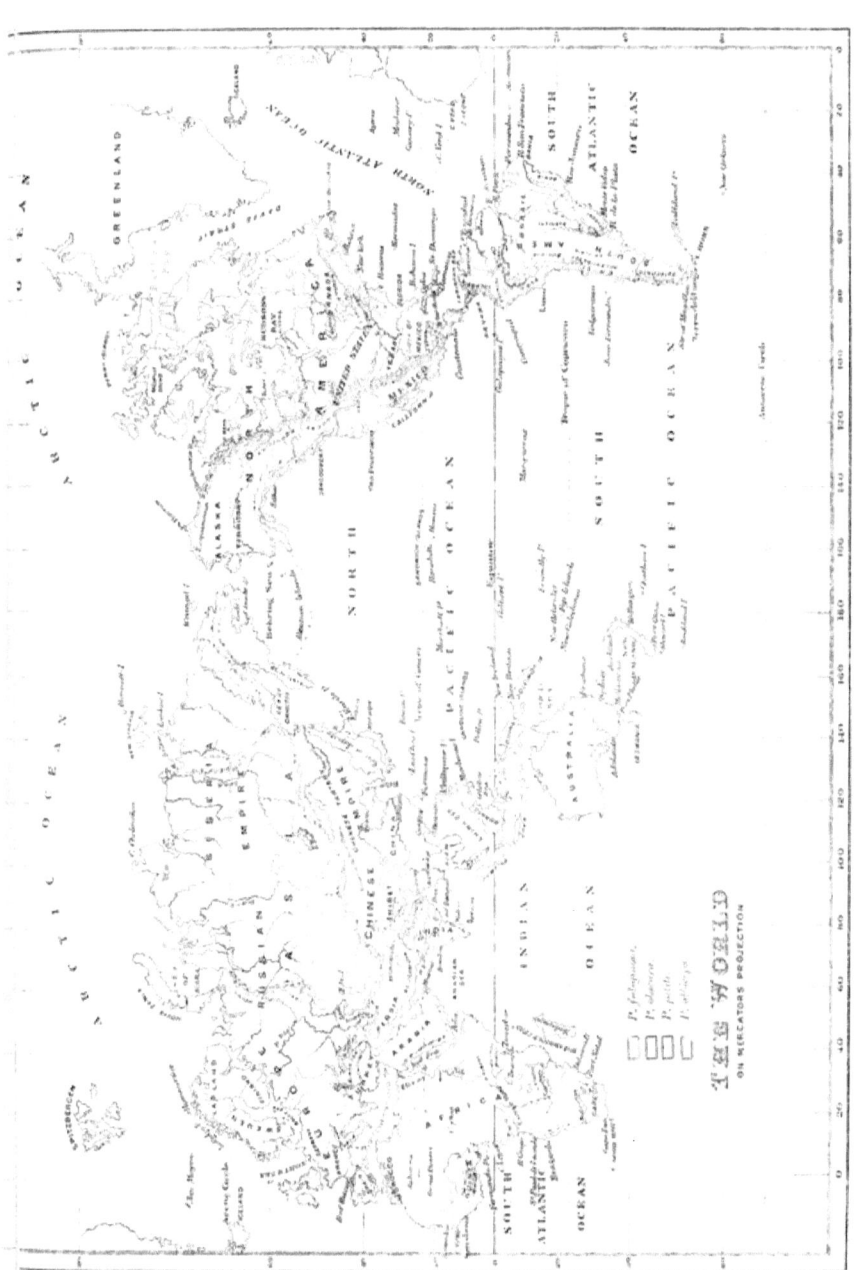

Genus XII. STELGIDOPTERYX.

Stelgidopteryx, Baird, B. N. Amer. p. 312 (1858). . Type. *S. serripennis*.

Range. North America, not extending into the high north. The whole of Central America, and South America to Bolivia and Southern Brazil.

Clavis specierum.

a. Jugulum cinerascenti-brunneum, forsan rufo tinctum : gastræum imum parè
album . . . . 1. *serripennis*, p. 645.
b. Jugulum rufescens : abdomen sulphurascens : subcaudales albæ vel pallidè
 flavæ, brunneo subterminaliter notatæ.
  a'. Uropygium pallidè brunneum . . . . . . 2. *ruficollis*, p. 647.
  b'. Uropygium cinerascens .   . . . 3. *uropygialis*, p. 651.

STELGIDOPTERYX SERRIPENNIS

STELGIDOPTERYX SERRIPENNIS (Audub.).

NORTH-AMERICAN ROUGH-WINGED SWALLOW.

Hirundo serripennis, Audub. Orn. Biogr. iv. p. 593 (1838); id. B. N. Amer. 8vo, i.
p. 193, pl. 51 (1840); Maynard, B. East. N. Amer. p. 76 (1881).
Cotyle serripennis, Boie, Isis, 1844, p. 170; Bp. Consp. i. p. 342 (1850); Cass. Cat.
Hirund. Mus. Philad. Acad. p. 11 (1856); id. Ill. B. Calif. & Texas, p. 247
(1856); Scl. & Salv. Ibis, 1859, p. 13; G. C. Taylor, Ibis, 1860, p. 111; Baird,
Cass., & Lawr. B. N. Amer. p. 313 (1860); Owen, Ibis, 1861, p. 61; Scl. Cat.
Amer. B. p. 41 (1862); Coues, Ibis, 1865, p. 163; Dresser, t. c. p. 479; Brown,
Ibis, 1868, p. 121; Cooper, Orn. Calif. p. 110 (1870).
Cotyle fulcipennis, Scl. P. Z. S. 1859, p. 364; id. & Salv. Ibis, 1860, p. 31; Scl. Cat.
Amer. B. p. 41 (1862).
Stelgidopteryx serripennis, Baird, B. N. Amer. p. 312 (1858); id. Review Amer. B.
p. 311 (1865); Coues, Key N. Amer. B. p. 114 (1872); Scl. & Salv. Nomencl.
Av. Neotr. p. 15 (1873); Coues, B. N.-West, p. 90 (1874); Baird, Brewer, &
Ridgw. Hist. N. Amer. B. i. p. 350, pl. 16, fig. 12 (1874); Ridgw. Rep. Surv.
40th Par. iv. p. 446 (1877); Coues, B. Color. Vall. p. 438 (1878); Belding, Proc.
U.S. Nat. Mus. i. p. 400 (1878); Ridgw. op. cit. iii. p. 175; Purdie, Bull. Nutt.
Orn. Club, ii. p. 21 (1877); Mearns, op. cit. iii. p. 46 (1878); Brown, op. cit. iv.
p. 7 (1879); Stannis, t. c. p. 119; Scott, t. c. p. 213; Loomis, t. c. p. 213;
Berier, op. cit. vi. p. 126 (1881); Hoffman, Bull. U. S. Geol. Surv. vi. p. 221
(1881); Coues, Check-l. N. Amer. B. p. 43 (1882); Brown, Bull. Nutt. Orn. Club,
vii. p. 37 (1882); Nehrling, t. c. p. 12 (1882); Brewster, t. c. p. 146; Beckh. t. c.
p. 162; Salvin & Godman, Biol. Centr.-Amer., Aves, i. p. 237 (1883); Bailey,
Bull. Nutt. Orn. Club, viii. p. 39 (1883); Allen & Brewster, t. c. p. 160; Coues,
Key N. Amer. B. 2nd ed. p. 121 (1884); Brown, Auk, p. 121 (1884); Sharpe, Cat.
Birds in Brit. Mus. x. pp. 206, 636 (1885); Drew, Auk, ii. p. 15; Beckh. t. c.
p. 141; Agersb. t. c. p. 279; A. O. U. Check-l. N. Amer. B. p. 294 (1886); Brewster,
Auk, iii. p. 111 (1886); Everm. t. c. p. 183; Fox, t. c. p. 317; Ferrari-Perez,
Proc. U. S. Nat. Mus. ix. p. 139 (1886); Saunders, Auk, iv. p. 248 (1887); Beckh.
t. c. p. 302; Towns. Pr. U. S. Nat. Mus. x. p. 222 (1887); Beckh. t. c. p. 682;
Richm. Auk, v. p. 23 (1888); Scott, t. c. p. 31; Merrill, t. c. p. 360; Everm.
Auk, vi. p. 26 (1889); Langdon, t. c. p. 201; Jeffries, t. c. p. 223; Pindar,
t. c. p. 315; Scott, t. c. p. 326.
Cotile serripennis, Gray, Hand-l. B. i. p. 73, no. 867 (1869).
Cotile fulcipennis, Gray, t. c. p. 73, no. 869 (1869).

Stelgidopteryx fulvipennis, Salv. P. Z. S. 1870, p. 184; Scl. & Salv. Nomencl. Av. Neotr. p. 15 (1873); Boucard, P. Z. S. 1878, p. 67.
Stelgidopteryx fulvigula, Lawr. Ann. Lyc. N. Y. ix. p. 96 (1870).

S. gutture cinerascenti-brunneo, vix rufescente lavato: abdomine et subcaudalibus albis, nec flavicantibus.

Hab. in Americâ septentrionali et in Americâ Centrali usque ad terram Panamensem.

Adult male. General colour above brown, the lesser and median wing-coverts like the back; median and greater coverts blackish brown, washed externally with the same colour as the back; bastard-wing, primary-coverts, and quills blackish brown, the inner secondaries edged with lighter brown; tail-feathers dark brown, paler towards the base of the inner web; head a trifle darker brown than the back; a narrow line of whity brown from the base of the forehead above the eye; lores blackish; ear-coverts dark brown; cheeks, throat, and breast, as well as the flanks and sides of the body, light brown, shaded with hoary whitish on the throat and fore neck, the chin and throat slightly washed with rufous; abdomen and under tail-coverts pure white; the breast-feathers with a few dusky shaft-lines; thighs white, with brown bases; axillaries brown; under wing-coverts brown, with hoary-white edges to those near the edge of the wing: "tail black; legs brownish black; iris dark brown" (*H. E. Dresser*). Total length 1·8 inches, culmen 0·35, wing 1·45, tail 2·25, tarsus 0·4.

The *adult female* resembles the male in colour, but is rather smaller. Total length 1·4 inches, culmen 0·3, wing 4·1, tail 1·9, tarsus 0·45.

It has generally been supposed, and in the British Museum 'Catalogue of Birds' it is authoritatively stated, that the female lacked the serrations on the first primary. This we now find to be a mistake, as a large series of female specimens in the Henshaw collection shows that the hooklets on the first primary-quill are present in the old female, though not to the same extent as in the adult male.

Young birds (*S. fulvipennis*, Sclater) are easily distinguished from the adults by the rufous edgings to the wing-coverts and secondaries. The back is also washed with rufous. The throat and breast are light rufous, and the flanks are washed with the same colour; the under wing-coverts are broadly edged with rufous, and the gape is yellow.

Before leaving their birthplace in the United States, a good deal of the rufous colour becomes obliterated in the young birds, and many of them are almost as brown as the adults. The moult takes place in their winter-quarters and is completed by December, as is shown by specimens in the Salvin-Godman collection.

This species has a distinct winter plumage, the edgings to the secondaries being white, while a rufous tinge is evident on the throat. On the approach of the breeding-season, the white edges to the secondaries quickly become abraded, but the rufous on the throat lasts for some time. Occasionally the longer upper tail-coverts show a blackish-brown spot at the end; this is apparently a sign of a very old bird, as it is not confined to specimens from any one locality; it is most strongly developed in a specimen obtained by Mr. Henshaw near Washington, on the 22nd of July, 1883.

Hab. North America generally, but somewhat local in its distribution; breeding also in parts of Central America, where it extends as far as Costa Rica and Panama.

This species is widely spread throughout North America, and extends into Central America as far south as Panama; and, as far as is known, it breeds wherever it is found in summer. It is only a migrant to the United States and Southern Canada, and the birds which nest there doubtless visit Central America in winter, but the species also breeds in certain countries of the Central-American subregion.

To commence a history of the Rough-winged Swallow, it is only necessary to quote the writings of that admirable field-naturalist, Professor Elliott Coues, who has given us a full account of its distribution in his 'Birds of the Colorado Valley,' published in 1878. Some further instances of its occurrence in previously unrecorded localities have been published since the above date, but the account given by Professor Coues seems to us to embody all the information respecting its known range in North America up to the above-mentioned year.

Writing, therefore, in 1878, Professor Coues observes :—

"Its distribution is now known to include the entire breadth of the United States, excepting some portions of New England, whence we have no record as yet. But the bird certainly enters New England. This fact was first announced, as far as I know, by Mr. H. A. Purdie, who states that an individual was shot at Sheffield, Conn., by Mr. Shores, June 6th, 1874; and Mr. Merriam states that Mr. E. P. Bicknell found the bird in numbers at Riverdale, New York, within a few miles of the Connecticut line. I had written in 1868 that it was singular there should be no New England instances on record, 'as the species *certainly* ought to be there'; and some of the New England ornithologists may learn in the course of time that every bird known in a certain portion of the Middle States will also be found in the Connecticut Valley. Determining thus the north-easternmost point at which the Rough-winged Swallow has been found, we may turn in another direction along its supposed northern boundary. Its name appears in Gregg's Elmira list, but not in McIlwraith's Canada West, nor in Trippe's Minnesota. I never saw the bird in Dakota or Montana; but west of the Rocky Mountains, Mr. J. K. Lord seems to have met with it along the same parallel of 49°; and we also have Brown's Vancouver record. This exhibits a northern limit coincident with that of *Tachycineta thalassinus*, and we may suppose that the northern border of the United States is nearly the terminus of the species, excepting in New England, where the bird is not known to go so far.

"In the Middle, Southern, and Western States the dispersion of the species is general, calling for no comment; but the various records from the West may be profitably analyzed. Dr. A. L. Heerman early found the bird in California, as recorded by himself and by Cassin in 1855, as well as at other places in Texas, New Mexico, and Arizona. Audubon's original surmise respecting its extension to the Columbia was verified by Dr. Newberry, and also by Drs. Cooper and Suckley, who found the bird common in

Oregon and Washington Territories, especially coastwise, about the cliffs of the bays and inlets. Dr. Cooper noted its arrival near the Columbia in May and its departure in August. In his later work on Californian Birds, the latter records his first observation of the bird at Fort Mojave, on the 27th of February, but adds that he has seen them at San Diego on the 9th of November and 27th of January, 'so that if they do not winter within the State, they do not go far beyond it.' . . . . In higher portions of Arizona, I found it to be a common summer resident, arriving at Fort Whipple late in April, and remaining through the greater part of September. Henshaw saw it in numbers in Southern Colorado during May, and also about the pueblo of Zuñi in New Mexico; it was still more abundant at Provo, Utah, and other points in the same general area, where also Mr. Ridgway attests its presence in great numbers. In some places, says the last-named, it was the most numerous representative of the family next after the Cliff and White-bellied Swallows; it is generally distributed over the United States, excepting most of New England, but not much further northward; agreeing in this respect with the Violet-green Swallow, and being, next after this species, more restricted in its habitat than any other Swallow of North America."

Our account of the Rough-winged Swallow, therefore, aims at supplementing the excellent summary quoted above, and we trust that it will be found a tolerably exact record of the observations of North-American naturalists since Professor Elliott Coues wrote his 'Birds of the Colorado Valley.'

We are first of all indebted to our friend Mr. Ernest E. Thompson, for some Canadian notes as to the distribution of the species in Ontario:—

"*London.* Regularly distributed and uniformly common all over this section. Also noted at Hamilton. (For 'full details' this is very slight on this species, but it amply covers the ground.) They breed in any bank suitable, railway-cuttings, gravel-pits, river-banks, it makes no difference, generally one, seldom two, never three pairs breeding close together (*W. E. Saunders*).

"*Hyde Park.* Summer resident (*John A. Morden*).

"*Toronto.* As yet not observed here by anyone."

The accompanying sketch is also sent by Mr. Thompson, who writes :—

"The shaded portion would fall within the region of the Alleghanian Fauna. This appears to trend along the north shore of Lake Ontario, and ultimately to run as far northward as Ottawa. This is a region well defined by relative altitude, as well as by its geology, botany, &c. Throughout this area I expect we shall ultimately find the Rough-winged Swallow."

In the 'Auk' for 1887, Mr. Saunders writes :—

"Mr. McIlwraith refers to me as the sole evidence of the occurrence of the Rough-winged Swallow, and makes the statement that I have found it breeding for the past year or two; while in 1882, in the Morden-Saunders list of the birds of Western Ontario, we stated that it 'breeds in the same localities as the last (Bank-Swallow),' and I have found it common within a radius of twenty-five miles round London in all suitable places. He follows the reference to me by stating, 'nests having been found in crevices of rocks and on beams under bridges,' &c., from which one might infer that such are its habits in Ontario. This, however, is not the case, as in the large number of nests I have examined all were in holes in banks, and I have never seen these Swallows frequenting bridges at all, but always near sand-banks; and we have no rocks."

Mr. Edgar Mearns, in a paper on several rare birds observed near West Point, New York, observes :—

"I have found this Swallow on but one occasion, in May, 1872, when a single pair nested in this neighbourhood, in a bank close to a stable, beside a pond. I watched this pair while they constructed their nest, during which time they were often seen to alight, close together, on a board-fence, from which they descended after the rough materials of which the nest was composed,—hay and feathers. Late in May I captured the female sitting upon four fresh eggs. I had no difficulty in doing this, for the hole was quite large, and not very deep, so that, by baring my arm, I could easily introduce it to the back of the hole."

In the Henshaw collection are several birds, both old and young, obtained by Dr. A. K. Fisher near Sing Sing, N.Y. Dr. Berier also states that he shot a specimen near Utrecht on the 29th of April, 1878.

Mr. J. A. Stannis, writing on the "Rough-winged Swallow in Connecticut," says :— "Although not given by Samuels as a bird of New England, and classed as 'a rare summer visitant' by C. H. Merriam in his 'Birds of Connecticut,' the Rough-winged Swallow breeds regularly in this State. It has nested for the past three seasons in the old stone abutments at a road crossing over the New York, New Haven, and Hartford Railroad, within eight or ten rods of the depôt at Green's Farms, twenty miles west of New Haven. Half a dozen pairs nested there last season, and perhaps more; but, judging from the number seen, I should say there were fewer than during the season of 1877. I have been unable to account for the fact that more than thirty trains could pass within six or eight feet of their nests each day, and not drive them away or apparently disturb them in the least."

Quite a large series, consisting of old and young birds from the District of Columbia, is contained in the Henshaw collection, the specimens having been obtained there in April and May. Mr. Richmond speaks of it as abundant here, and adds :—

"Numbers of these birds nest along the river in crevices among the rocks. I know of a small colony that frequents a stone culvert, over which is a railroad track, and through which a small stream passes. This culvert is built of rough uncut stones, and presents innumerable fine nesting-sites for the Swallows. One nest found here was placed in a crevice about one foot above running water, and contained young. Six or seven eggs are laid, and first clutches are completed by May 17. A set of seven eggs was found during June, 1887, which contained six of this species and one of the Barn-Swallow."

Dr. F. W. Langdon, writing in 1889, mentioned the present species as having occurred in large numbers in Ohio; and Mr. Evermann states that in Carroll County, Indiana, it is a summer resident, but is not so common as *Cotile riparia*. Specimens have been procured by Mr. H. K. Coale near Riverdale, Illinois, in April; and in the southern part of the same State Mr. Robert Ridgway says that the Rough-winged Swallows nest in communities in company with *C. riparia*, occupying adjoining holes and having entirely the same habits, but they are much more numerous there than the common Bank-Swallow.

Mr. Pindar also records it as a common summer resident in Fulton County, Kentucky, and according to Mr. Fox it was the most plentiful of all the Swallows in Roane County, Tennessee, arriving there early in April. Mr. Loomis says that it is rather common in summer in South Carolina, and is also common during its migrations; it is generally distributed, but is most abundant in the vicinity of water. Mr. Bailey found the eggs in Georgia on the 18th of April.

Mr. Maynard writes of the species in Florida:—"The quaint and ancient city of St. Augustine is situated on an arm of the ocean; consequently it is necessary to protect the lower section by a sea-wall, which extends the entire length of the town. This wall, being broad upon the top, is used as a promenade by the inhabitants. While sauntering along this walk one day in April, I observed some Swallows alighting in front of me. I saw at once that they were a species I had never seen before, but a closer view proved them to be Rough-winged Swallows. At first there were only four or five to be seen, but in a few days there were quite a number flying about the place. This is the only time I ever met with the species living, and I have never found it breeding in the State; but having met Mr. Allen, in Jacksonville, a few weeks later the same season, he informed me that he found a small colony evidently about to breed on some bluffs along the St. John's river, not far from the mouth. This species is said to breed in holes in buildings, under bridges, etc."

Mr. W. E. D. Scott, in his paper on the Birds of the Gulf Coast of Florida, states that this species was not very common in April 1877, in the vicinity of Tarpon Springs, which is the only point where he observed it.

Mr. N. C. Brown states that it was a rather common summer resident near Coosada, in Central Alabama, where it arrived on the 22nd of March, but was not generally distributed until the first week in April. Mr. Scott states that it was tolerably abundant in Western Missouri, arriving about the 15th of April, and breeding. Mr. Beckham, in his essay on the Birds of Bayou Sara in Louisiana, says:—"The Rough-winged Swallows, which arrived in March, were present in force, and were breeding in holes in the banks along Alexander's Creek, where the Kingfishers were also nesting."

Mr. Dresser, in his account of the Birds of Texas, writes:—"At Eagle Pass, the first of these birds I noticed arriving from the South I saw on the 21st of February. Both there and near San Antonio they are very common during the summer, breeding in the towns, making their nests under the eaves and in holes in the old walls, and laying pure white eggs; the first of which, that I got, were taken at San Antonio on the 25th April."

Mr. Nehrling says that it is a very abundant summer resident in Texas. It often nests under the roofs of walks, and on old buildings in Houston, but is more a companion of the Bank-Swallow (*Cotile riparia*) on the high banks on Buffalo-Bayou and Galveston Bay. In South-western Texas Mr. N. C. Brown states that he only observed two specimens on the 3rd and 4th of March.

Mr. Brewster, in a paper on the Birds of Western North California, says that it was "the characteristic Swallow of the valley region, common almost everywhere throughout the settled country up to about 2500 feet, and nesting in ledges and clay banks formed by railroad-cuttings or the erosion of streams."

Mr. Belding writes:—"This bird arrived at Murphy's on March 15th, 1877, and remained till May 3rd, or probably later. They constituted only a fraction of the multitude of Swallows of the place, and were, perhaps, altogether not more than two dozen in number. I have not seen it elsewhere."

Mr. Hoffman, in his paper on the Birds of Nevada, observes:—

"Dr. Cooper found this species as early as February 27th, and Mr. Ridgway observed it in April at Carson City, where it was the most abundant species of the family. I noticed these birds also along the banks of the Humboldt River, north of Battle Mountain, during the last days of May, where they are probably summer residents. They build in burrows in the sandy banks, the openings leading to the nests being from one to two feet below the upper edge of the bank, similar in this respect to those of *C. riparia*."

In Arizona Mr. Brewster observed it commonly and breeding; but about Tucson Mr. Herbert Brown found it rather rare, arriving about the middle of March. Messrs. Allen and Brewster state that they first observed the Rough-winged Swallow about the 10th of May in Colorado, and that it was not uncommon later. At Pueblo it was plentiful along the streams, according to Mr. Beckham. Mr. Drew states that it breeds in the plains of Colorado up to 7000 feet.

Dr. Merrill, writing from Fort Klamath, Oregon, says:—"A few pairs breed in the banks of the streams near the Fort, but there are few suitable places, as the edges of the streams are usually low and grassy. Nests, examined June 18, contained half-fledged young; the burrows were about two feet in length, and were much larger than those dug by the Bank-Swallow." Finally, Mr. Agersborg states that, although rarer than *C. riparia*, it breeds in South-western Dakota in common with that species, along the Vermilion and Big Sioux rivers.

Beyond the borders of the United States it becomes more difficult to trace the range of the Rough-winged Swallow. As Messrs. Salvin and Godman state, it is doubtless resident in Mexico, but the evidence on this point is not satisfactory. Professor Ferrari-Perez records a specimen from Jalapa in August, and from this district came the type of *Cotile fulcipennis* of Sclater, obtained by de Oca; this is nothing but the immature bird of *S. serripennis*. The other localities given by Messrs. Salvin and Godman in the 'Biologia' are Nuevo Leon (*Couch*), valley of Mexico (*Le Strange*), Cordova (*Sallé*). The bird obtained by Botteri near Orizaba is in full nesting-plumage, and the bird probably breeds in that district, but that the Rough-winged Swallow breeds within Mexican limits is proved by two nestling specimens obtained by Mr. A. Forrer near Presidio in June. Nor is the nesting of the species in Mexico to be wondered at, for we have undoubted evidence that it breeds in Guatemala. Messrs. Salvin and Godman have received specimens from Mr. Ferrari-Perez, collected in the Valley of Mexico in November and May, at Jalapa in June (one specimen being a nestling), and at Huatusco in August. Mr. W. B. Richardson has sent examples from Bolaños in Jalisco (March), and Mr. W. Lloyd procured one at Beltran and Zapotlan in the same province (April). Trujillo has also procured the species at Sola, in Oaxaca, in April, and at Juchatengo in April. Messrs. Salvin and Godman give many localities where they observed it in Guatemala, and Mr. Salvin states that it was common in July on the open lands, and flying about the lake of Dueñas. Mr. Robert Owen, who found one nest and five eggs near San Gerónimo, writes:—

"The nest is composed of grass and fine roots, the inside being strewn with pieces of dead flag. The eggs are white, and measure, axis ·7, diam. ·5 inch. The nest was dug out of the white sandy soil of a barranco in the Convent garden. The cave ran horizontally, and was about two feet in length, terminating in a chamber of just sufficient dimensions to allow the bird to turn round."

Dr. Schott procured the present species at Merida, in Yucatan, and Mr. George Cavendish Taylor believed that he saw it in Honduras, but that the evidence is not considered convincing by Messrs. Salvin and Godman is proved by their having omitted it from the 'Biologia.' Carmiol procured specimens at Attiro, in Costa Rica, and Mr. Boucard records "several specimens from San José, March to May." He adds: "They are principally seen flying near the streams, sometimes in large numbers. The first time I had a shot at them I killed six; there were about fifty on a small tree. Although I have killed a good many, I never found a female amongst them. I suppose the females must have been in their nests somewhere, but where I was never able to find out." Two specimens are recorded by Mr. Salvin from Calovevora, in the State of Panama, collected by Arcé, and this is the most southern limit of the range of the Rough-winged Swallow yet recorded.

The late Dr. Brewer gives the following account of the nesting of this Swallow:—
"This species was first found breeding in Carlisle, Penn., by Professor Baird, in the summer of 1843. The following year I visited this locality early in June, and had an opportunity to study its habits during its breeding-season. We found the birds rather common, and examined a number of their nests. None that we met with were in places that had been excavated by the birds, although the previous season several had been found that had been apparently excavated in banks in the same manner as the Bank-Swallow. All the nests (seven in number) that we then met with were in situations accidentally adapted to their need, and all were directly over running water. Some were constructed in crevices between the stones in the walls and arches of bridges. In several instances the nests were but little above the surface of the stream. In one, the first laying had been flooded, and the eggs chilled. The birds had constructed another nest above the first one, in which were six fresh eggs, as many as in the other. One nest had been built between the stones of the wall that formed one of the sides of the flume of a mill. Two feet above it was a frequented foot-path, and, at the same distance below, the water of the mill-stream. Another nest was between the boards of a small building in which revolved a water-wheel. The entrance to it was through a knot-hole in the outer partition, and the nest rested on a small rafter between the outer and the inner boardings. The nests were similar in their construction to those of the Bank-Swallow, composed of dry grasses, straws, and leaves, lined with a few feathers; but a much greater amount of material was made use of, owing, perhaps, to the exposed position in which they were built. The eggs, six in number, in every instance that we noticed, were pure white, about the size of those of *C. riparia*, but a little more uniformly oblong in shape, and pointed at one end. Their length varies from ·78 to ·69 of an inch, the average being ·75. Their average breadth is ·53 of an inch."

Concerning the above notice of Dr. Brewer's, Professor Coues remarks:—

"In this picture of the bird at home we see it already modified in habits by contact with civilization, and require another portraiture, which fortunately Mr. Walter Van Fleet has furnished. In an interesting article entitled 'Notes on the Rough-winged Swallow (*Hirundo serripennis*) in Pennsylvania,' published in the Bulletin Nuttall Club, i. p. 9 (1876) he gives the results of two years' careful observation of the economy of the bird, especially in comparison with *Cotile*. I condense most of his article in the following paragraph:—

"The Rough-wing, unlike the Bank-Swallow, is not gregarious while nesting, the pairing being their only association. The nests are not crowded together, but scattered at irregular intervals along the banks of streams, wherever favourable sites occur. The birds seldom excavate holes for themselves, preferring to take some suitable cavity and refit it to their taste; thus, they are often found in deserted Kingfishers' holes, where the nest is placed a foot or so from the entrance. They will also, on finding a decayed root of sufficient size leading in from their favourite sand banks, remove the soft punky wood, following the winding of the root to a depth of about two feet, where they place the nest in an enlarged cavity. Besides this, they like to build in holes in masonry, near water. In the few observed instances of their digging a hole for themselves, they worked in rather a slovenly way, making holes larger than appeared necessary, and invariably *circular* at the entrance—the Bank-Swallows' holes, on the contrary, being quite symmetrically elliptical, with the longer axis horizontal, and no larger than required for the free passage of the birds—too small to admit the hand, while the Rough-wings' nests may usually be reached without difficulty, except when built in masonry, in which latter case the birds may pass through a crevice barely wide enough to admit them, providing the cavity within be suitable for a nest. The nests of *S. serripennis* are more carelessly constructed, as a rule, than those of *C. riparia* are; the birds do not seem to search at any distance for particular materials, being satisfied with anything that may be at hand. One nest, built in a Kingfisher's hole in a sand bank about fifteen rods from a poultry-yard, was composed entirely of the feathers of domestic fowl. In another instance, three fresh eggs were found on the bare sand, in a mere pocket barely six inches deep, indicating that the mother bird was so pressed to lay that she had no time to complete her nest. Not infrequently fresh eggs are found in the same nest with others far advanced in incubation, and occasionally fresh eggs, others newly hatched, and young birds may be found together.

"Other writers witness a still wider range of variation in the nidification of the Rough-wings. Cooper speaks of their nesting in California in burrows in sandy banks, two or three feet deep, closely crowded together, and near the upper edge of the embankment; as well as of their resorting sometimes to natural clefts in banks, in adobe buildings, and even in knot-holes. Their breeding in the last-named places is probably exceptional, but it is known that even the Bank-Swallow, the most inveterate and conservative of the family, will sometimes take to a tree, and Henshaw furnishes probable confirmation of Cooper's statement. He noticed Rough-wings several times in suspicious proximity to some dead stubs; and though he never saw one entering the cavities, he thought it probable that the birds sometimes availed themselves of such retreats in the absence of banks suitable for excavation.

"The general presence and behaviour of our Swallows is so little varied, as well as so familiar, that nothing need be said on this score; the Rough-wing resembles the Bank-Swallow in these respects as closely as it does in coloration and physique. The eggs, as in all our species excepting the Barn and the Cliff, are immaculate white, and about as large as the Barn-Swallow's, measuring about 0·75 in length by a trifle over 0·50 in breadth; they are said to be rather more uniformly oblong and pointed than those of the species just named, and commonly five or six in number.

"I may conclude by referring to a note which I published not long since, on a supposed change of habit of the Bank-Swallow, but which proves to have really been based on the present species instead. As recorded in Am. Nat. x. June 1876, p. 372, under head of 'Notable Change of Habit of the Bank-Swallow,' I was informed by Dr. Rufus Haymond that a Bank-Swallow had nested in a building in Brookville, Indiana.

Mr. Ridgway fairly questioned, in the August number of the same periodical, p. 193, whether the species was not the Rough-wing, which breeds exactly as Dr. Haymond described, and as the two species are so similar as to be confounded sometimes, even by good observers. Dr. Haymond shortly sent me a second communication to the same effect, which I published in the 'Bulletin' of the Nuttall Club, vol. i. n. 4, Nov. 1876, p. 96. In this other instance, 'a weather-board had become detached from the building, leaving a small opening, in which I watched for two days a Bank-Swallow building a nest.' Since then, however, he informed me by letter, in answer to my further inquiries, that Mr. Ridgway was right in supposing that the birds were really Rough-wings, and not Bank-Swallows."

The birds described and figured in the accompanying Plates are in the British Museum. An adult and a young bird are represented.

STELGIDOPTERYX RUFICOLLIS (*Vieill.*)
RED-THROATED ROUGH-WINGED SWALLOW.

Golondrina de la vientre amarillazo, Azara, Apunt. ii. p. 512 (1802); Hartl. Ind. Azara, p. 19 (1847).
Hirundo ruficollis, Vieill. N. Dict. d'Hist. Nat. xiv. p. 523 (1817).
Hirundo flavigastra, Vieill. N. Dict. d'Hist. Nat. xiv. p. 534 (1817).
Hirundo jugularis, Neuwied, Beitr. Naturg. Bras. iii. p. 365 (1830); Temm. Pl. Col. iv. pl. 161. fig. 2.
Hirundo hortensis, Licht. Verz. Doubl. p 57 (1823).
Cotyle jugularis, Gray, Gen. B. i. p. 60 (1845).
Cecropsis ruficollis, Boie, Isis, 1844, p. 175.
Cotyle flavigastra, Gray, Cat. Fissir. Brit. Mus. p. 30 (1848); Bp. Consp. i. p. 342 (1850); Cab. Mus. Hein. Th. i. p. 49 (1850); Cass. Cat. Hirund. Mus. Philad. Acad. p. 11 (1853); Burm. Th. Bras. iii. p. 144 (1856); Sclater, P. Z. S. 1860, p. 274; Pelz. Orn. Bras. pp. 17, 402 (1871).
Cotyle ruficollis, Gray, Gen. B. i. p. 60 (1845); Cass. Cat. Hirund. Mus. Philad. Acad. p. 11 (1853); Sclater, P. Z. S. 1860, p. 292; id. Cat. Amer. B. p. 41 (1862); Reinh. Vid. Medd. Nat. Forh. Kjöbenh. 1870, p. 249.
Stelgidopteryx ruficollis, Baird, Review Amer. B. p. 315 (1865); Scl. & Salv. P. Z. S. 1866, p. 178, 1867, p. 749, 1873, pp. 185, 259; iid. Nomencl. Av. Neotr. p. 15 (1873); Layard, Ibis, 1873, p. 377; Tacz. P. Z. S. 1874, p. 510; Scl. & Salv. P. Z. S. 1879, p. 596; Salv. & Godm. Biol. Centr.-Amer., Aves, i. p. 237 (1883); Tacz. Orn. Pérou, i. p. 246 (1884); Sharpe, Cat. Birds in Brit. Mus. x. p. 208 (1885); Salvin, Ibis, 1885, p. 206; Sclater & Hudson, Argent. Orn. i. p. 36 (1888).
Cotile ruficollis, Gray, Hand-l. B. i. p. 73, no. 868 (1869); Barrows, Bull. Nutt. Orn. Club, viii. p. 90 (1883).

S. gutture rufo: abdomine sulphureo: subcaudalibus albis vel pallidè flavis, longioribus subterminaliter brunneo notatis.

Hab. in Americâ meridionali.

Adult male. General colour above brown, the head decidedly darker than the back, the rump and upper tail-coverts paler brown; wing-coverts blackish brown, the inner median and greater coverts edged with paler brown; bastard-wing, primary-coverts, and quills blackish, the secondaries rather browner, the inner ones edged with white towards the tip and round the latter; upper tail-coverts and tail-feathers blackish brown, the latter paler towards the base of the inner web; lores and ear-coverts dark brown, the latter a little paler than the crown; cheeks and throat brick-red; sides of neck, breast, and sides of body brown; centre of breast and abdomen sulphur-yellow, extending on to the thighs and vent; under tail-coverts white, the basal ones with a tinge of yellow, the long ones with a broad subterminal bar of blackish brown; axillaries brown; under wing-coverts brown, with rufous edges to the feathers; quills dusky blackish below: "bill and legs brownish black, the latter sometimes paler brown or flesh-colour; iris greyish brown" (*Neuwied*). Total length 4·9 inches, culmen 0·35, wing 4·3, tail 2·2, tarsus 0·4.

Adult female. Similar to the male in colour, but without the serrations on the outer edge of the outer web. Total length 4·5 inches, culmen 0·35, wing 3·7, tail 1·9, tarsus 0·4.

The series from different parts of South America in the British Museum shows that very little variation takes place in individuals from the various countries inhabited by the species. The brown colour of the upper surface is deeper in some birds than it is in others, but this may be due to age. On the whole, however, southern birds are darker than northern ones, and the palest of all are the specimens from Roraima, which have a decidedly lighter brown shade on the lower back and rump, showing an approach to *S. uropygialis*.

The following are the measurements of some specimens from different localities:—

	Total length. in.	Wing. in.	Tail. in.
a. Ad. Roraima, Nov. 29 (*H. Whitely*)	5·2	4·2	1·9
b. ♀. „ Nov. 23 „	5·0	4·0	1·9
c. ♂. „ Jan. 5 „	4·7	4·3	1·85
d. Ad. Cayenne (*Mus. P. L. S.*)	5·0	4·3	1·9
e. Ad. Bahia (*Wucherer*)	4·9	4·3	1·95
f. Ad. „ „	4·9	3·9	1·95
g. ♀ ad. Para (*Layard*)	4·9	3·9	1·9
h. ♂ ad. Rio (*Mus. P. L. S.*)	4·9	4·25	1·95
i. ♂ ad. Yquitos (*H. Whitely*)	4·9	4·3	2·1
k. ♀ ad. „ „	4·5	3·7	1·9
l. ♂ ad. „ „	5·0	4·35	2·05
m. ♂ ad. Upper Ucayali (*E. Bartlett*)	4·8	4·35	2·15
n. ♀ ad. Yurimaguas „	4·1	3·9	1·95
o. [♀] ad. Copataza River (*C. Buckley*)	4·7	4·0	2·15
p. [♂] ad. Rio Napo	5·2	4·4	2·05
q. [♂] ad. Yuyo, Bolivia (*C. Buckley*)	4·7	4·3	1·9
r. [♂] ad. „ „	5·0	4·45	2·2

Young. Darker than the adults, and having the feathers of the upper surface edged with rusty edges, especially distinct on the quills; the throat and breast as well as the sides of the body are ferruginous, the lower breast and abdomen washed with sulphur-yellow.

Many specimens have rather broad white edgings to the secondaries, and as we have not been able to find other traces of youth on these individuals, we believe that these margins may be merely indicative of freshly moulted plumage, and that they become abraded as the plumage gets worn.

Hab. South America.

This species enjoys a wide range in South America and extends from Rio to Bolivia and Peru, throughout Brazil and Amazonia, to Guiana. The specimens from Roraima have a slightly paler rump, but cannot be confounded with *S. uropygialis*, which, moreover, is the Rough-winged Swallow of Colombia. In Ecuador both forms occur.

There has been some mistake in the enumeration of the specimens in the British Museum 'Catalogue of Birds' (vol. x. App. p. 636), where certain of the Roraima specimens have been included under the heading of *S. uropygialis*.

Azara considered the present species to be rare in Paraguay. Mr. Barrows, however, writing on the Birds of the Lower Uruguay, found it abundant at Concepcion through the summer, arriving from the north early in August. He writes:—

"It is said to nest in holes in banks, and I once dug out several deserted Swallows' nests supposed to belong to this bird, though none were seen in the neighbourhood. The nests were of straw and feathers at the end of holes about two feet in depth, and in pretty hard earth, which formed a bank eight or ten feet high, beside a small stream. A bird of this species frequently visited an open and deep well, just in front of my door. I repeatedly saw it descend into the well, but could never see it come out, or find it within. Probably it hid itself between the stones of the wall, where it was prospecting for a home which it failed to find."

The Sclater Collection has a specimen from the neighbourhood of Rio de Janeiro, and Dr. Burmeister considers it to be a common and widely spread species throughout the Campos of the interior of Brazil; and Lund gives the same testimony regarding the Campos of Lagoa Santa. Burmeister found it nesting at Congonhas. The following localities for the species are given by Natterer:—Rio de Janeiro: July, December; Casa Pintada: January; Ypanema: December; Cuyaba, Caiçara: January. He says also that it is found near Cuyaba throughout the year.

Specimens collected by Dr. Wucherer at Bahia, and by Mr. W. A. Forbes at Pernambuco, are in the Salvin-Godman Collection; and Mr. E. L. Layard, writing from Para, observes:—

"This Swallow is not uncommon, but except in a few favoured localities in the town, I never saw it in any number together. It feeds on minute flies, and perches readily on trees. It is certainly resident in Para all the year round, though it is very scarce from September to December, on the 27th of which month I procured a pair, after noting their absence in September."

It probably extends throughout the Amazon Valley, as it has been found by Mr. Henry Whitely at Yquitos in March and April, and Mr. Edward Bartlett met with it at Yurimaguas and also on the Upper and Lower Ucayali Rivers. Mr. Henry Whitely also procured specimens at Cosnipata, in Peru, and Mr. Jelski at Monterico. Mr. C. Buckley likewise sent examples from Yuyo in Bolivia.

The latter traveller also procured this species on the Copataza River in Ecuador, and the Salvin-Godman Collection has other specimens from this country. At Esmeraldas and Babahoyo Fraser met with *S. uropygialis*. A large series was forwarded by Mr. Whitely from Roraima, and a Cayenne specimen, obtained by Jelski, is in the Salvin-Godman Collection.

Dr. Burmeister states that this Swallow lays two white eggs, which it deposits in holes in the ground, like our Sand-Martin. Mr. Edward Bartlett writes:—

"The nest, like that of *Atticora fasciata*, is composed of leaves, stems of a prickly climber, fine bents, and fibres of bark very loosely put together, and is placed in holes in banks. Four or five white eggs are laid in September; but I also took nests on the Huallaga in July."

The descriptions of the birds are taken from the series in the British Museum, and the figures in the Plate are drawn from specimens in the Salvin-Godman Collection. Both light and dark forms are represented.

STELGIDOPTERYX UROPYGIALIS

STELGIDOPTERYX UROPYGIALIS (*Lawr.*).

ASHY-RUMPED ROUGH-WINGED SWALLOW.

Cotyle flavigastra (nec V.), Cass. Proc. Philad. Acad. 1860, p. 133; Scl. P. Z. S. 1860, p. 292; Lawr. Ann. Lyc. N. Y. vii. p. 317 (1861).
Cotyle ruficollis (nec Vieill.), Sclater, P. Z. S. 1860, p. 292; id. Cat. Amer. B. p. 41 (1862, pt.).
Cotyle uropygialis, Lawr. Ibis, 1863, p. 181; id. Ann. Lyc. N. Y. viii. p. 3 (1863); Scl. & Salv. P. Z. S. 1864, p. 348; Gray, Hand-l. B. i. p. 73, no. 870 (1859).
Stelgidopteryx uropygialis, Baird, Review Amer. B. p. 317 (1865); Salv. P. Z. S. 1870, p. 184; Wyatt, Ibis, 1870, p. 109; Scl. & Salv. Nomencl. Av. Neotr. p. 15 (1873); iid. P. Z. S. 1879, p. 496; Tacz. P. Z. S. 1877, p. 744; Salvin & Godman, Biol. Centr.-Amer., Aves, i. p. 238 (1883); Sharpe, Cat. Birds in Brit. Mus. x. pp. 209, 637 (1885); Tacz. Orn. Pérou, i. p. 247 (1884).
Stelgidopteryx fulvigula, Baird, Review Amer. B. p. 318 (1865); v. Frantz. J. f. O. 1869, p. 295; Salv. Ibis, 1869, p. 313, 1870, p. 108, 1874, p. 307.
Cotyle fulvigula, Gray, Hand-l. B. i. p. 73, no. 871 (1869).

S. similis *S. ruficolli*, sed saturatior et uropygio magis cinerascente.

Hab. in Costa Rica usque ad Panamam, Venezuelam, Colombiam et regionem Andensiensem usque ad Ecuadorium et Peruviam occidentalem.

Adult male. Similar to *S. ruficollis*, from which it differs only in having the upper surface much darker and the rump more ashy and in rather more pronounced contrast to the back. The brown on the under surface is darker on the breast and flanks, and the yellow on the abdomen somewhat more restricted. Total length 5 inches, culmen 0·4, wing 4·2, tail 1·9, tarsus 0·35.

Adult female. Similar to the male in colour. Total length 4·5 inches, culmen 0·4, wing 3·9, tail 1·8, tarsus 0·4.

Young. Differs from the adult in having the rump creamy buff, and in having distinct rufous margins to the feathers of the upper surface, especially the wing-coverts and inner secondaries; the throat is bright rufous, as well as the fore neck; the sides of the body brown washed with rufous, and the rest of the underparts white with a slight tinge of yellow.

Hab. Central America, from Costa Rica to Panama. In South America, from Venezuela to Colombia, Western Ecuador and Western Peru.

This is a northern race of the ordinary *Stelgidopteryx ruficollis* of South America, from which it differs in the ashy colour of the rump. This character is always well marked in specimens from the localities recorded below, but a slight approach to it is seen in examples from various parts of South America, though never to the same extent as in the birds of Central America and Ecuador.

The present species was first named by Mr. G. N. Lawrence, from specimens procured by McLeannan in Panama, and several individuals collected by him on the line of railway in this State are in the Salvin-Godman collection.

Mr. Salvin himself noticed the species in abundance at Obispo in May 1873, its favourite resting-place being the telegraph-wires placed along the line of railway. Schott found it on the Truando River, and specimens obtained at Chitra near Chiriqui in the State of Panama by Arcé are in the Salvin-Godman collection. It extends northwards to Costa Rica (*con Frantzius, Zeledon*), and Carmiol procured examples at Angostura in that country, in June and August.

In South America it has not a very extended range, but it occurs not unfrequently in "Bogota" collections. Mr. Wyatt met with it at Ocaña and Bucarramanga in the Magdalena Valley. Salmon also found it at Santa Elena and Remedios in the Cauca Valley; at the latter place it was breeding. A Venezuelan specimen is in the British Museum.

In Ecuador Fraser procured specimens of the present species at Esmeraldas and Babahoyo, and an example obtained by Stolzmann at Lechugal in Western Peru, on the 5th of October, is recorded by Dr. Taczanowski; and a specimen from Paucal is in the Raimondi collection.

A skin said to be from Bahia is in the British Museum, but there must be some mistake as to the locality of this specimen.

No further notes on the habits of this species have been published, but they will doubtless be found to be identical with those of its congener, *S. ruficollis*. The eggs procured by Salmon at Remedios are white.

The adult bird figured in the Plate is drawn from a specimen in Mr. Wyatt's collection from Ocaña, and the young bird from a Costa Rican example in the Salvin-Godman collection. The descriptions are from birds in the British Museum.

APPENDIX
TO THE
GENUS STELGIDOPTERYX.

STELGIDOPTERYX SERRIPENNIS (*antea*, p. 635).
Add:—

Stelgidopteryx serripennis, Sharpe & Wyatt, Monogr. Hirund. pt. xiii. (1890); Belding, Occ. Papers Calif. Acad. ii. p. 193 (1890); Mearns, Auk, vii. p. 48 (1890); Loomis, t. c. p. 125; Cherrie, t. c. p. 335; id. Auk, ix. p. 22 (1892); Scott, t. c. p. 213; Ridgw. t. c. p. 307; Attwater, t. c. p. 310; Lawr. t. c. p. 356; Hatch, B. Minnesota, p. 356 (1892); Fisher, N. Amer. Faun. no. 7, pt. 2, p. 112 (1893); Thompson, Auk, x. p. 50 (1893); White, t. c. p. 227; Brimley, t. c. p. 243; Sargent, t. c. p. 369.

The following additional notes on this species have appeared since our article was published.

Mr. Thompson records the species from the vicinity of Lake Winnipeg, on the authority of Mr. Hine. Mr. S. E. White found one of these Swallows dead on Mackinac Island in July, but he never succeeded in procuring another example. Professor Ridgway noticed its arrival near Washington, D.C., on the 8th of April, 1893. In Minnesota Dr. Hatch states that it arrives about the same time as *Cotile riparia*, and it is "no less common in some sections. Dr. Hvoslef reports it as one of the very common Swallows, arriving at Lanesboro' on the 19th of April in 1884."

Mr. H. B. Sargent records the meeting of the species at Shelter Island, N.Y., as follows:—"While collecting with Mr. W. W. Worthington of Shelter Island, June 3, 1893, I found a nest of the Rough-winged Swallow containing four much incubated eggs. The nest was placed in a bank about forty feet high, on the shore; it looked like an old Bank-Swallow's burrow. It was two feet from the top of the bank and twenty-seven inches deep. The chamber the nest was in was twelve inches in diameter, and was completely filled with dried sea-grasses on which the eggs were laid.

"I shot the female, and as it fell in the water the male came up and tried to help its disabled mate, at the same time uttering a most plaintive cry."

Mr. Brimley says that in North Carolina the species has "apparently been getting rarer near Raleigh, or else has found nesting-places more suited to its needs than the old ones, for it has deserted its old haunts almost entirely, and, instead of being our commonest Swallow, it is much more nearly our rarest one." Mr. Loomis, in his paper on the summer birds of Pickens' County, S. Carolina, states that it was tolerably common, and was seen daily "hawking for insects over the bottom lands along the Oolenay."

Mr. Attwater says that the Rough-winged Swallow is a "common migrant" at San Antonio in Texas. Mr. Scott also records it as a migrant in the Caloosahatchie Region of Florida.

In Arizona, Mr. Mearns states that it breeds on the lower edge of the pine belt. Near Gray's Harbour, in Washington County, Mr. Lawrence records it as a summer resident, but not very common.

In the memoir on the Death Valley Expedition occurs the following note by Dr. A. K. Fisher:—"The Rough-winged Swallow was tolerably common in a number of the desert valleys, where it was a summer resident. It was first seen at Ash Meadows, Nevada, March 10, and in Vegas Wash, near the bend of the Colorado River, March 10-13. A specimen was secured at Hot Springs, in Panamint Valley, April 22, and Mr. Nelson observed a few migrants along Willow Creek, in the Panamint Mountains, the last of May. Dr. Merriam saw this Swallow at Saratoga Springs, in Death Valley, April 26; at the bend of the Colorado River, May 4; in the Valley of the Virgin, near Bunkerville, Nevada, May 8; and in Pahranagat Valley, Nevada, where it was tolerably common and doubtless breeding, May 22-26. He found it common where Beaverdam Creek joins the Virgin in north-western Arizona, May 9-10, and the commonest Swallow in the Santa Clara Valley, Utah, May 11-15. In Owen's Valley a pair was seen about a pond at Lone Pine, June 8, and others were observed at Big Pine, June 10. At Furnace Creek, Death Valley, several were secured about the reservoir June 19-21, and a number were seen in Kern River Valley, June 22-23."

Mr. Belding, in his synopsis of the birds of the Pacific coast of North America, gives the records as follows:—

"Poway. Usually common in spring (*F. G. Blaisdell*).

"San José. Common summer resident, arriving in March (*Parkhurst*).

"San Bernardino. Rare migrant through the valley (*F. Stephens*).

"Agna Caliente. Seen in March (*F. Stephens*).

"Southern California. Occurs commonly (*Henshaw*).

"Santa Cruz. Common summer resident (*Skirm*); breeds (*Ingersoll*).

"Contra Costa County. Summer resident (*W. G. Bryant*).

"Calaveras County (*L. B.*).

"Sacramento. Common, June and July (*Ridgway*).

"Found in California as far north as Columbia river (*Newberry*).

"Common about the sandy cliffs and islets of this coast. It arrived near the Columbia river in May and remained until the middle of August, 1860 (*Cooper*).

"Rather abundant both in Oregon and Washington Territory (*Suckley*).
"British Columbia. Common summer resident (*J. Fannin*).
"Present along much of the Eastern slope (*Henshaw*).
"Nevada. I noticed these birds along the banks of the Humboldt River, north of Battle Mountain, during the last days of May (*Hoffman*).
"Next to the Cliff and White-bellied Swallows this was the most abundant species of the family. Arrived at Carson, April 15.
"I saw them at Fort Mojave on the 22nd of February, but I have seen them at San Diego November 9 and January 27, so that if they do not winter in the State they do not go far beyond it (*Cooper*, 1870).
"Whidby Island, W.T., April 2 (*Lawrence Wessel*).
"Walla Walla, W.T., May and August (*Williams*)."

Mr. G. K. Cherrie, writing in 1890, states that the Rough-winged Swallow is very common in Costa Rica "during the rainy season, but is seldom seen in the dry season, from early in December until the latter part of April." Again, in 1892, he speaks of it as "a common resident and breeding abundantly."

This statement has rather taken us by surprise, as we should have expected that *S. uropygialis* was more likely to have been the species which nested in Costa Rica.

For the geographical distribution of the present species *vide infrà*, Plate 128 [Map].

STELGIDOPTERYX RUFICOLLIS [*anteà*, p. 647].

Add:—

Stelgidopteryx ruficollis, Sharpe & Wyatt, Monogr. Hirund. pt. viii. (1888); Berl. & Ihering, Zeitschr. ges. Orn. ii. p. 21 (1885).

OBTAINED by Dr. Ihering at Linha-parajá, Rio Grande do Sul, on the 6th of June.

For the geographical distribution of this species, *vide infrà*, Plate 129 [Map].

STELGIDOPTERYX UROPYGIALIS [*anteà*, p. 651].

Add:—

Stelgidopteryx uropygialis, Sharpe & Wyatt, Monogr. Hirund. pt. xii. (1889).

For the geographical distribution of this species, *vide infrà*, Plate 129 [Map].

GEOGRAPHICAL DISTRIBUTION

⟶ Migratory.	△
⟵⟶ Bird of passage.	○
⊖ Remains locally during the winter.	⊂⊃
⟵△⟶ Transplanted.	∼
⟵⟶ Winter resident.	⁓

Nearctic Region.								Neotropical Region.						Euras Sub-Reg
Arctic Sub-Region.	Cold Temperate Sub-Region.			Warm Temperate Sub-Region.				Central American Sub-Region.					Arctic Sub-Region.	
				Humid Province		Arid Province								
Arctic Province.	Aleutian Arctic Province.	Hudsonian Province.	Canadian Province.	Sitkan Province.	Alleghanian Province.	Appalachian Sub-Province.	Austro-Riparian Sub-Province.	Campestrian Sub-Province.	Sonoran Sub-Province.	Antillean Sub-Region.	Mexican Province.	Isthmian Province.	Sub-Andean Sub-Region.	Amazonian Sub-Region.	Brazilian Sub-Region.	Patagonian Sub-Region.	Arctic Sub-Region.	European Province.	Central Siberian Province.

∨ Guest.
† Wanderer.
☐ Rarely
☐ Generally } nesting.
☐ In colonies

Ethiopian Region.
- Mediterraneo-Asiatic Sub-Region.
- Mediterranean Province.
- Mongolian Province.
- Himalo-Caucasian Sub-Region.
- Saharan Sub-Region.
- Nubian Sub-Region.
- West African Sub-Region.
- Mascaren Sub-Region.
- East African Sub-Region.
- South-African Sub-Region.
- Cape Province.
- Natalese Province.

Indian Region.
- Caucasian Sub-Region.
- Iranian Sub-Region.
- Indian Peninsular Sub-Region.
- Indo-Malayan Sub-Region.
- Himalo-Malayan Sub-Region.
- Himalo-Chinese Sub-Region.

Australian Region.
- Celebean Sub-Region.
- Moluccan Sub-Region.
- Papuan Sub-Region.
- Australian Sub-Region.
- New-Zealand Sub-Region.
- Fijian Sub-Region.
- Hawaiian Sub-Region.

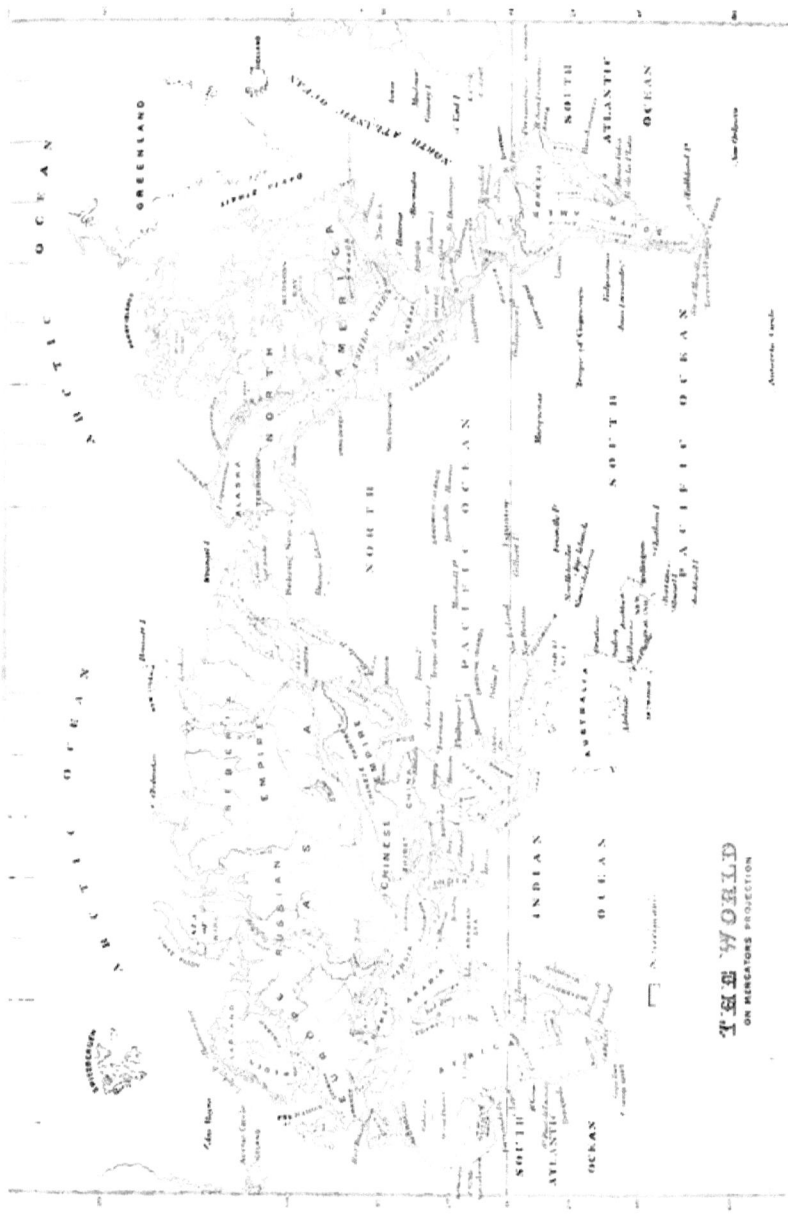

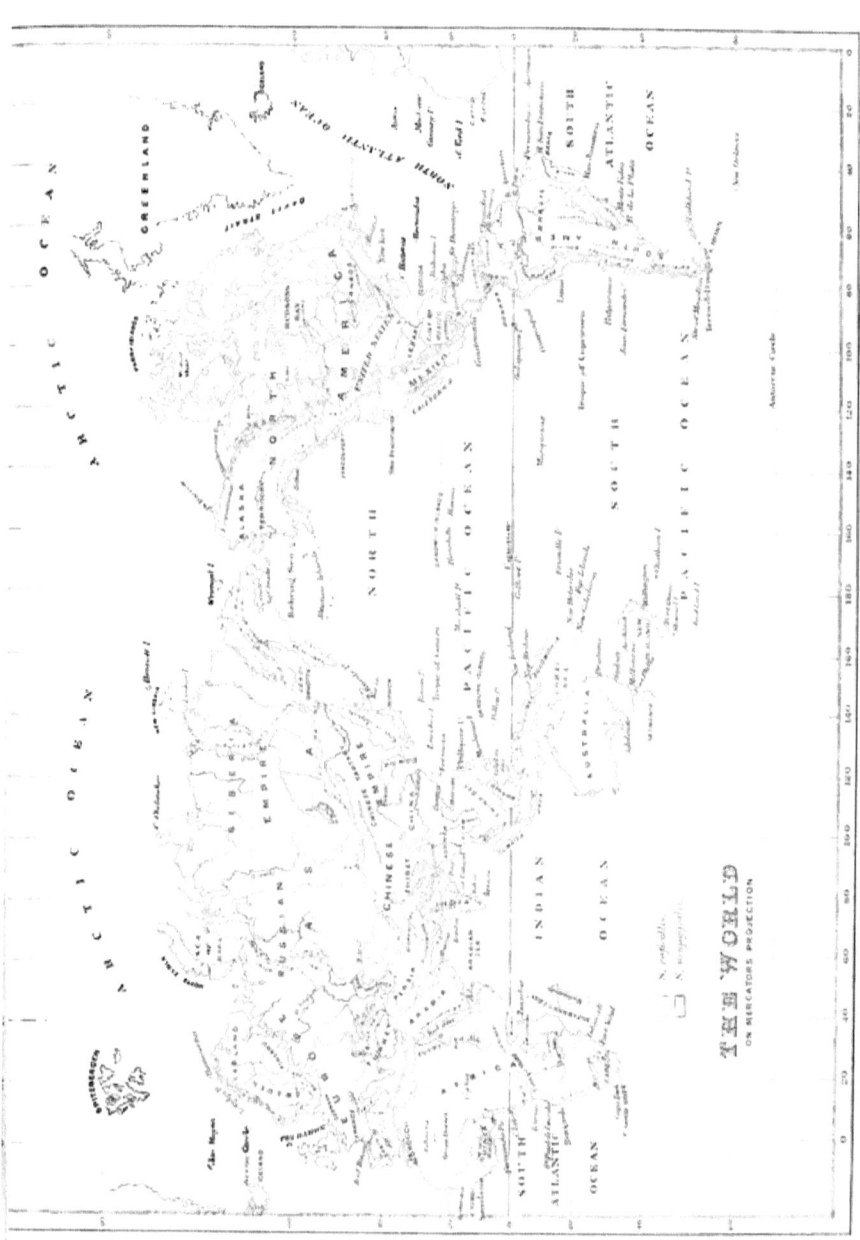

INDEX.

abyssinica, Cecropis, 341.
——, Hirundo, lii, 341.
Acanthylis, xlvii.
acuta, Chætura, xxxiii, xxxvi.
——, Hirundo, xl.
æthiopica, Hirundo, xliv, 210, 307, 322, 413.
africanus, Cypselus, xliv, xlv.
——, Micropus, xli.
agrestis, Hirundo, xliii.
alba, Hirundo, xxxix.
albiceps, Atticora, 623.
——, Psalidoprocne, lix, 604, 623, 624, 625, 630.
albicollis, Hirundo, xliv.
albigena, Chelidon, lviii, 6, 29, 38.
——, Chelidonaria, 5.
albigula, Hirundo, 393.
albigularis, Hirundo, xli, liv, lvi, 210, 303, 307, 322, 413.
albilinea, Hirundo, 149.
——, Petrochelidon, lviii, 149.
——, Tachycineta, lx, lxii, 149, 187, 190.
albilineata, Hirundo, 149.
Albino Swallows, lxvii.
albiscapulata, Atticora, liii.
albiventer, Hirundo, xxxvi, xxxvii, xxxvii, 139.
——, Petrochelidon, 139.
albiventris, Cotyle, lvi, 73.
——, Hirundo, xliv, 139, 465.
——, Petrochelidon, 139.
——, Tachycineta, xxxiii, lxvi, 39, 187, 190.
alfredi, Hirundo, lx, lxii, 573.
——, Petrochelidon, lx.
alpestris, Cecropis, 347, 357.
——, Hirundo, xxxiv, 347, 357, 366.

alpestris japonica, Hirundo, lii.
——, Lillia, lvii, 357.
Ambergris Swallow xxxvii, xl.
ambiguus, Hirundo, lxii, 303.
ambrosiaca, Hirundo, xxxvi, xxxvii, xl, xliii.
American Chimney-Swallow, 253.
americana, Cecropis, 254.
——, Hirundo, xxxvi, xxxix, xlii, xliii, 249, 253, 531.
——, Petrochelidon, 531.
Amnochelidon, 523.
anchieta, Hirundo, lx, 320.
andamanensis, Hirundo, lx, 242.
Andean Swallow, 499.
andecola, Hirundo, l, 499.
andersoni, 894bis, 97, 119, 130, 134.
——, Cotile, 119.
——, Ptyonoprogne, l.
Anderson's Rock-Martin, 119.
Angola Swallow, 293.
angolensis, Hirundo, lx, lxiv, 210, 293, 300, 412.
antinorii, Psalidoprocne, lxiii, 604, 615, 625, 630.
Antinori's Rough-winged Swallow, 615.
Antochelidon, lx.
—— nigricans, lx.
Ascenblachka Swallow, xxxvii, xl.
apus, Cypselus, xxxii, xxxiii, xxxiv, xxxvi, xl.
——, Hirundo, xxxii, xxxiii, xxxiv, xxxviii, xl, xliii.
——, Micropus, xxxii.
arborea, Chelidon, 525, 585.
——, Collocalia, liii, 525.
——, Herse, 525.
archetes, Cecropis, lxii, 393.

archetes, Hirundo, 393.
arctincincta, Hirundo, lxvi, lxvii.
arcticincta, Cecropis, lxi, 305.
——, Hirundo, 210, 295, 300, 305.
——, Lillia, 306.
arenaria, Hirundo, xliii.
ariel, Chelidon, 585.
——, Collocalia, li, 525.
——, Herse, 585.
——, Hirundo, 585.
——, Lagenoplastes, lix, 585.
——, Lillia, 585.
——, Petrochelidon, li, 523, 585, 585, 586.
Ash-bellied Swallow, xxxvii, xl, 499.
Ashy-rumped Rough-winged Swallow, 651.
astigma, Hirundo, lxvii, 383.
atra, Hirundo, xliv.
atrocœrulea, Hirundo, liv, 210, 319, 322, 413.
Atticora, lii, lvi, 403, 517.
—— albiceps, 623.
—— albiscapulata, liii.
—— cinerea, xxxii, xl, l, lii, lv, lxvi, 403, 499, 517, 520.
—— cyanoleuca, xliv, xlv, xlvi, xlvii, l, lviii, lix, 403, 505, 518, 520.
—— cypseloides, lviii, 355.
—— fasciata, liii, 317, 493, 495, 517, 520.
—— fucata, 493, 515, 518, 520.
—— griseopyga, lx, 335.
—— hemigera, lv, 603.
—— hemiprocne, lviii, 505.
—— holomelaena, 603, 613.
—— holomelas, 603, 607.

4 P

INDEX.

Atticora melanoleuca, xlvii, 493, 503, 517, 520.
—— melläna, lv, 335.
—— montana, lix, 506.
—— murina, 499.
—— nigrita, 317.
—— nitens, lvi, 601.
—— obscura, lvi, 607.
—— pileata, lvii, lix, 493, 513, 518, 520.
—— pristoptera, 621.
—— tibialis, lv, 493, 501, 517, 520.
Australian Swallow, 289.
australis, Hirundo, 525.
——, Hirundo pyrrhonota, lii.
Azara's Purple Martin, 469.

badia, Cecropis, lv, 393.
——, Hirundo, lxii, 211, 393, 422, 428.
Bahama Swallow, 185.
balcalensis, Hirundo, lxiii, 249.
Barn-Swallow, xlvi.
beaussoneauti, Hirundo, li.
Benguela Cliff-Swallow, 571.
Biblis, l, li, 97, 129.
—— anderssoni, 97, 119, 130, 134.
—— concolor, xlix, 97, 123, 131, 134.
—— fuligula, lii, 97, 115, 130, 134.
—— obsoleta, lv, lxi, 97, 111, 129, 134.
—— rufigula, 97, 121, 130, 134.
—— rupestris, xxxix, l, li, lii, 97, 100, 129, 134.
bicolor, Chelidon, 155.
——, Herse, 155.
——, Hirundo, xlii, lxii, 155.
——, Iridoprocne, lxii, 156.
——, Petrochelidon, 156.
——, Tachycineta, xxxvii, xlii, xlvi, xlvii, xlviii, 155, 156, 189, 190.
Black-collared Swallow, 503.
Black Rough-winged Swallow, 603.
—— Swallow, xxxvii, xl.
blakistoni, Chelidon, lviii, 23.
Blakiston's Martin, 23.
Blanford's Swallow, 397.
Blue-and-white Swallow, 505.
Blue Rough-winged Swallow, 621.
—— Swallow, xlvi, 319.
boissoneauti, Cecropis, 237.
——, Hirundo, li, 215, 237.
borbonica, Cotyle, 201.

borbonica, Hirundo, xxxiv, xxxvi, xxxviii, xxxix, xliv, 201, 205.
——, Phedina, lvii, 201, 208.
——, Progne, 205.
borealis, Hirundo, lxiii, 242.
Bourbon Striped Swallow, 201.
Brazilian Swallow, xxxvii.
brazzæ, Phedina, lxiv, lxvi, 207.
brevicaudata, Cotyle, 81.
——, Hirundo, li, 81.
brevirostris, Colloealia, li.
——, Hirundo, li.
Brown-collared Sand-Martin, 67.
—— Swallow, xxxvii, xl, 67.
Brunette, La, xli, 73.
—— Swallow, xlvi.

cachirica, Cotyle, 111.
cærulea, Hirundo, xli, xliii, 439.
caffer, Cypselus, xli, xliv, xlv.
cahirica, Cecropis, 237.
——, Cotyle, lv, 111.
——, Hirundo, xlvi, 215, 237, 238.
Callichelidon, lix.
—— cyaneoviridis, lix, 185.
—— euchrysea, 407.
Cameroons Rough-winged Swallow, 609.
caminicola, Hirundo, xliii.
Canada Swallow, xxxvii, 439.
candida, Hirundo, 8.
Cape Swallow, xxxvii, xxxix.
capensis, Cecropis, 337.
——, Hirundo, xxxix, xli, xlv, xlviii, xlix, 337, 341, 347.
——, Lillia, 337.
Caribbean Cliff-Swallow, 561.
—— Purple Martin, 465.
Cashmere Martin, 19.
cashmiriensis, Chelidon, lvii, lxiv, 6, 9, 19, 35, 38.
——, Chelidonaria, 5.
——, Hirundo, 19.
castanea, Hirundo, xlix, 237.
cayennensis, Hirundo, xl.
——, Panyptila, xxxiii, xxxvi, xl.
Cecropis, xlviii, xlix, 209.
—— abyssinica, 341.
—— alpestris, 347, 357.
—— americana, 254.
—— archæta, lxii, 393.
—— arctivitta, lxi, 395.
—— badius, lv, 393.

Cecropis boissoneauti, 237.
—— cahirica, 237.
—— capensis, 337.
—— chalybea, 473.
—— cucullata, 337.
—— cyanopyrrha, 254.
—— daurica, 371.
—— erythropygia, 366.
—— fasciata, 495.
—— filicauda, 330.
—— filicaudata, 330.
—— filifera, 329.
—— frontalis, 280.
—— fulva, 561.
—— hyperythra, 389.
—— javanica, 242.
—— jowan, 242.
—— lunifrons, 531.
—— melanocrissa, liii, 379, 309.
—— melanoleuca, 503.
—— nigricans, 525.
—— nipalensis, 395.
—— pagorum, xlix, 215.
—— panayana, 242.
—— pyrrhonota, 525, 531.
—— riocouri, 237.
—— rufa, 254.
—— ruficollis, 647.
—— rufifrons, 307.
—— rustica, xlix, 215.
—— rusticoides, 242.
—— savignii, 237.
—— senegalensis, 399.
—— smithii, 329.
—— striolata, liii, 341, 361.
—— subis, 440.
—— tahitensis, 275.
—— violacea, 440.
cerdo, Hirundo, xl.
Ceylonese Chestnut Mosque-Swallow, 389.
Chætura, xlviii.
—— acuta, xxxiii, xxxvi.
—— pelasgia, xxxiv, xl.
—— poliura, xxxiv, xxxvi, xxxix.
—— spinicauda, xxxiv, xxxix.
—— zonaris, xliv, xlvi.
chalybea, Cecropis, 473.
——, Hirundo, xxxii, xxxvi, xl, 473.
——, Progne, xxxiii, xl, 437, 473, 488, 490.
——, Psalidoprocne, lxvi, 601, 609, 625, 630.

INDEX.

Chalybeate Swallow, xxxvii, xl, 473.
Chelidon, xliv, xlvii, lxi, lxiii, lxv, 209.
—— albigena, lviii, 6, 29, 38.
—— arborea, 505, 525.
—— ariel, 585.
—— bicolor, 155.
—— blakistoni, lviii, 23.
—— cashmiriensis, lvii, lxiv, 6, 9, 19, 35, 38.
—— dasypus, lviii, lxiv, 6, 19, 23, 35, 38.
—— erythrogastra, 249, 254.
—— fenestrarum, xlix.
—— gutturalis, 242, 411.
—— lagopus, lviii, 6, 25, 36, 38.
—— leucogastra, 155.
—— leucopyga, lvi.
—— leucosoma, 311.
—— microrhynchos, xliv.
—— namiyei, lxiv, 287.
—— nigricans, 325.
—— nipalensis, lxvi, 6, 31, 36, 38.
—— pristoptera, l, 621.
—— progne, xliii, 215.
—— rupestris, xlvi, xlix, 99.
—— savignii, 238.
—— thalassina, 175.
—— tytleri, 249.
—— urbica, xxxiii, xlvi, xlix, lxiv, lxvi, 5, 7, 19, 38.
—— whitelyi, lviii, 25.
Chelidonaria, lxv, 5.
—— albigena, 5.
—— cashmiriensis, 5.
—— dasypus, 5.
—— lagopus, 5.
—— nipalensis, 5.
—— urbica, 5.
Cheramœca, liv, 3, 131, 437.
—— leucosternum, li, liv, 433.
Chilian Swallow, 153.
Chimney-Swallow, xxxvii, xliii, 213, 215, 233.
——, American, 253.
——, Eastern, lxvii, 241.
——, Senegambian, 297.
——, White-bodied, 311.
chinensis, Hirundo, xlix, 81.
Chinese Swift, xl.
cincta, Clivicola, 41, 89.
——, Cotyle, xxxiii, lx, lxvi, 41, 67, 89, 94.
——, Cotyle, 41, 67.

cincta, Hirundo, xxxvi, xxxvii, xxxviii, xl, 67.
cinerascens, Hirundo, xliii.
cinerea, Atticora, xxxii, xl, l, lii, lv, lvi, 493, 499.
——, Clivicola, 46.
——, Hirundo, xxxvi, xxxvii, xl, xliv, 43, 499.
Cliff-Swallow, Benguela, 574.
——, Caribbean, 561.
——, Fairy, 585.
——, Indian, 577.
——, North-American, 531.
——, Peruvian, 507.
——, South-African, 573.
——, Swainson's, 555.
——, Timor, 529.
——, White-rumped, 525.
Clivicola, xliv, xlvi, lxiii, 41.
—— cincta, 41.
—— cinerea, 46.
—— congica, 41.
—— cowani, 41.
—— diluta, 41.
—— europæa, xliii, 43.
—— minor, 41, 89.
—— paludicola, 41.
—— riparia, 41, 45.
—— rupestris, 100.
—— shelleyi, 41.
—— sinensis, 41.
Collared Swallow, xlvi.
Cotyloecha arborea, liii, 525.
—— ariel, li, 585.
—— brevirostris, li.
—— esculenta, xxxii, xxxiv.
—— francica, xxxviii.
—— linchi, xlvi, xlix.
Common Martlet, xliii.
concolor, Biblis, 97, 123, 131, 134.
——, Cotile, lxv, 123.
——, Cotyle, 123.
——, Hirundo, xlix, l, 123.
——, Krimnochelidon, lxii, 123.
——, Progne, l, li, 457, 463, 487, 489.
——, Ptyonoprogne, l, 123.
congica, Clivicola, 41.
——, Cotile, 41, 71, 94.
Congo Sand-Martin, 71.
Coromandel Swallow, xlvi.
coronata, Hirundo, xlviii, 555, 561.
Cotile, xlv, xlvi, lxiii, 3, 41.
—— andersoni, 119.

Cotile cincta, xxxiii, lx, lxvi, 41, 67, 89, 94.
—— concolor, 123.
—— congica, 41, 71, 94.
—— cowani, lxi, 41, 79, 90, 94.
—— diluta, lxvi, 41, 53, 63, 94.
—— eques, lx, 67.
—— fucata, 515.
—— fuligula, xli, lxiv, 115, 119.
—— fulvipennis, lvii, 635, 642.
—— minor, liv, 41, 53, 77, 89, 94.
—— obscurior, lxi, 81.
—— obsoleta, liv, lxiv, 111.
—— paludicola, lxvi, 41, 73, 94.
—— riparia, xxxiii, xliv, xlvi, li, lxvi, 41, 94, 610, 641, 642, 643, 644, 653.
—— ruficollis, 647.
—— rufigula, lxiii, 121.
—— rupestris, lxvi, 100.
—— shelleyi, lxiv, 41, 53, 65, 94.
—— sinensis, xlvi, li, lxi, 41, 46, 81, 90, 94.
—— subsoccata, 81.
Cotyle, xlviii.
—— albiventris, lvi, 73.
—— borbonica, 204.
—— brevicaudata, 81.
—— cachirica, 111.
—— cahirica, lv, 111.
—— concolor, 123.
—— eques, 67.
—— flavigastra, 647, 651.
—— fluviatilis, xlix, 44.
—— fucata, 515.
—— fuligula, lvii, 115, 121, 651.
—— jugularis, 647.
—— leucoptera, 139.
—— littoralis, lvi, 65, 77.
—— microrhynchos, xlix, 45.
—— minor, 77.
—— obsoleta, 81, 111.
—— pallida, 111.
—— paludibula, l, 73.
—— paludicola, l, lvii, 111.
—— palustris, 73, 77.
—— riparia, xlviii, xlix, 44, 65.
—— ruficollis, 647, 651.
—— rupestris, xlviii, xlix, 99, 111.
—— serratirostris, lvi.
—— sinensis, l, 81.
—— subsoccata, 81.

4 P 2

Cotyle tapera, 479.
—— torquata, 67.
—— uropygialis, 651.
cowani, Clivicola, 41.
——, Cotile, 41, 79, 90, 94.
Crag-Martin, Pale, 111.
Crag-Swallow, xxxviii, xxxix, 99.
Crested Swallow, xlvi.
cristata, Hirundo, xlv, lvii.
cryptoleuca, Progne, lxx, 440.
cucullata, Cecropis, 337.
——, Hirundo, xxxv, xxxvii, xxxviii, xxxix, lvi, 210, 337, 354, 418.
cyanoeoviridis, Callichelidon, lix, 185.
——, Hirundo, lvii, 185.
——, Tachycineta, 185, 193, 196.
cyanoleuca, Atticora, xliv, xlvi, l, lviii, lix, 483, 505, 518, 520.
——, Herse, 505.
——, Hirundo, xli, xliv, xlvii, liii, 505.
——, Petrochelidon, 505.
——, Pygochelidon, lix.
cyanopyrrha, Cecropis, 254.
——, Hirundo, xli, xliv, 254.
cypselina, Psalidoprocne, liv, 603.
cypseloides, Atticora, lviii, 335.
——, Hirundo, 335.
Cypseloides niger, xxxii, xxxiii, xxxvi, xxxvii, al.
—— rutilus, xlv, xlix.
Cypselus africanus, xliv, xlv.
—— apus, xxxii, xxxiii, xxxiv, xxxvi, xl, xliii.
—— caffer, xli, xliv, xlv.
—— gutturalis, xli.
—— melba, xxxiv, xxxvi.
—— major, xliii.
—— niger, xliii.

Darwin's Purple Martin, 463.
dasypus, Chelidon, lviii, lxiv, 6, 19, 23, 35, 38.
——, Chelidonaria, 5.
——, Delichon, 23.
——, Hirundo, 23.
Daurian Mosque-Swallow, 357.
—— Swallow, xxxvi.
daurica, Cecropis, 365, 371.
——, Hirundo, xxxiv, xl, lxii, lxvi, 210, 257, 347, 361, 365, 371, 376, 419.
——, Lillia, 365.

Dean Cowan's Sand-Martin, 79.
Delichon, lvi, 5.
—— nipalensis, lvi, 31.
dichroa, Hirundo, lvi.
——, Clivicola, 41.
diluta, Cotile, lxvi, 41, 63, 94.
dimidiata, Hemicecrops, 313.
——, Hirundo, liv, lv, lvi, 210, 313, 322, 414.
domestica, Hirundo, xli, xlii, xliii, xliv, 7, 213, 437, 469.
——, Progne, 437, 469, 473, 488, 490.
domicella, Hirundo, lxi, lxiv, 211, 381, 386.
——, Lillia, 381.
domicola, Hirundo, lii, 280.
——, Hypurolepis, lv, 280.
dominicensis, Hirundo, xxxii, xxxiii, xxxvi, xl, xlii, lx, 465.
——, Progne, xlii, 437, 465, 469, 473, 487, 490.
——, Hirundo euchrysea, var., 469.
Dun-rumped Swallow, xlvi, 825.
Dusky Rock-Martin, 123.
—— Swallow, xlvi.

Eastern Chimney-Swallow, lxvii, 241.
—— Rough-winged Swallow, 913.
Egyptian Sand-Martin, 65.
—— Swallow, 237.
elegans, Progne, lix, 440, 459, 469.
Elgon Swallow, 295.
eoous, Hirundo, lxvi, lxvii, 211, 383, 386.
empusa, Lagenoplastes, lix, 577.
eques, Cotile, lx, 67.
——, Cotyle, 67.
erythrocephala, Herse, 577.
——, Hirundo, xli, 577.
erythrogaster, Chelidon, 249.
——, Hirundo, xxxiii, xxxv, xxxvii, xxxix, xli, xlii, xliv, xlviii, 253, 559.
erythrogastra, Chelidon, 254.
——, Hirundo, xxxiii, lxvi, 209, 217, 218, 249, 253, 254, 272.
erythropygia, Cecropis, 356, 371.
——, Hirundo, xlix, lxvi, 211, 347, 365, 371, 386, 421.
——, Lillia, 371.
Esculent Swallow, xxxviii, xxxix.
esculenta, Collocalia, xxxii, xxxiv.

esculenta, Hirundo, xxxii, xxxiv, xxxviii, xxxix.
euchrysea, Callichelidon, 407.
——, Herse, 407.
——, Hirundo, lii, liv, lx, lxvi, 211, 407, 426, 428.
——, var. dominicensis, Hirundo, 407.
——, Petrochelidon, 407.
——, Tachycineta, 407.
europæa, Clivicola, xliii, 43.
——, Riparia, xliv.

Fairy Cliff-Swallow, 585.
Fantee Rough-winged Swallow, 607.
fasciata, Atticora, liii, 317, 433, 495, 517, 520, 659.
——, Cecropis, 495.
——, Hirundo, xxxiii, xxxvii, xl, xliii, 495.
fenestrata, Hirundo, xliii.
fenestrarum, Chelidon, xlix, 8, 9.
filicauda, Cecropis, 330.
——, Hirundo, 330.
filicaudata, Cecropis, 330.
——, Hirundo, xlix, 329.
filifera, Cecropis, 329.
——, Hirundo, xlviii, 329.
——, Uromitus, 330.
filiferus, Uromitus, 330.
Fischer's Rock-Martin, 121.
flavigastra, Cotyle, 647, 651.
——, Hirundo, xliv, 647.
flavigula, Stelgidopteryx, 636.
flaviventer, Hirundo, xlix.
flavinicola, Hirundo, 577.
fluvialis, Hirundo, xlii.
fluviatilis, Cotyle, xlix, 45.
fluvicola, Hirundo, lvi, 577.
——, Lagenoplastes, 577.
——, Petrochelidon, xxxvii, xl, lix, 577, 593, 598.
franciæ, Collocalia, xxxviii.
——, Hirundo, xxxix.
frenata, Hirundo, 242.
frenensis, Hirundo, liv, 242, 280.
frontalis, Cecropis, 380.
——, Herse, 289.
——, Hirundo, xlviii, l, lvi, 143, 279, 289.
fucata, Atticora, 493, 515, 518, 520.
——, Cotile, 515.
——, Cotyle, 515.

INDEX.

cucuta, Herse, 515.
——, Hirundo, xlvii, xlviii, 515.
fuliginosa, Psalidoprocne, 661, 619, 625, 670.
fuligula, Biblis, lii, 97, 115, 130.
——, Cotile, xli, lxiv, 115.
——, Cotyle, lvii, 115.
——, Hirundo, xli, li, lii, lvi, 115.
——, Ptyonoprogne, l.
fulva, Cecropis, 561.
——, Herse, 531, 561.
——, Hirundo, xlii, xlvii, 531, 561.
——, Petrochelidon, xli, xlvi, liii, 525, 531, 561, 567, 592, 598.
fulvigula, Cotyle, 651.
——, Stelgidopteryx, lix, 651.
fulvipennis, Cotile, lvii, 635, 642.
——, Stelgidopteryx, 636.
Fulvous Swallow, xlvi.
fulvus, Hirundo, 531.
fumaria, Hirundo, xlviii, 254.
furcata, Progne, xxxvii, liii, lix, 437, 450.
fusca, Hirundo, xlv, 479.
——, Phaeoprogne, lix, 479.
——, Progne, 479.
fuscopileata, Hirundo, lxi, 256.

Golondrina domestica, xli, xliv, 469.
—— parda, xli, xliv, 479.
—— rabadilla acanelada, xli, 531.
—————— blanca, xli, xlv, 143.
—— tijuanelos negros, xli, xliv, xlvi, 505.
—— vientre amarallazo, xli, xliv, xlvi, 647.
—————— rosazo, xli.
gordoni, Cecropis, 397.
——, Hirundo, lv, lxiv, 211, 397, 424, 428.
Gordon's Swallow, 397.
gouldii, Hirundo, lv, 143.
Grande Hirondelle brune à ventre tacheté, 201.
—————— à ventre roux du Sénégal, xxv.
Grand Martinet, xxxiii.
—————— de la Chine, xxxix.
Great African Mosque-Swallow, 399.

Great American Martin, xxxiii, 439.
Green Swallow, South-American, 142.
Grey-rumped Swallow, xxxviii, xxxix.
griseocincta, Atticora, lx, 335.
——, Hirundo, liv, lv, lviii, lxiii, 210, 335, 354, 417.
Guatemalan Swallow, 513.
gularis, Hirundo, xlv.
gutturalis, Chelidon, 242.
——, Hirundo, xxxv, xxxix, xli, xlix, liii, lix, lx, lxiii, lxvi, 209, 217, 218, 241, 242, 249, 272, 411.

haitensis, Atticora, lv, 603.
Hemicecropis, lvii, 209.
——, leucosoma, lvii, 311.
Hemipyga, Atticora, lviii, 505.
Herse arborea, 525.
—— ariel, 585.
—— bicolor, 155.
—— cyanoleuca, 505.
—— erythrocephala, 577.
—— euchrysea, 407.
—— montana, 289.
—— fucata, 515.
—— fulva, 531, 561.
—— hyperythra, 589.
—— leucoptera, 139.
—— leucorrhoa, 143.
—— lunifrons, 531, 582.
—— melanoleuca, 593.
—— nigricans, 525.
—— pyrrhonota, 525.
—— tahitica, 275.
—— talitensis, 275.
—— thalassina, 175.
hesperia, Progne, lxvi, 455.
Heuglin's Martin, 29.
Hibernation of Swallows, supposed, lxix.
Himalayan Martin, 31.
Hirondelle à bande blanche sur le ventre, xxxiii, 495.
—— à ceinture blanche, xxxv, 495.
—— à croupion blanc, 7.
—— à croupion gris, Petite, xxxviii.
—— à croupion rouge et queue carrée, xxxvi, 531.
—— à croupion roux, xxxviii.
—— acutipenne, xxxix.
—— à front roux, xli, xlv, xlvi, lvii.

Hirondelle à queue pointue de Cayenne, xxxiv.
—— à queue pointue de la Louisiane, xxxiv.
—— à tête rousse du Cap de Bonne Espérance, xxxiii, 337.
—— à ventre blanc, xlii.
—— à ventre blanc de Cayenne, xxxiii, xxxvi, xxxviii, 139.
—— à ventre roux, xxxix.
—— à ventre roux de Cayenne, xxxiii, xxxv, 253.
—— à ventre roux du Sénégal, xxxv, 399.
—— ambrée, xxxvi.
—— au caparhon roux, xxxv.
—— au croupion blanc, xxxvi.
—— bicolor, xli.
—— blanche, xxxi, xxxvii.
—— bleue, xxxviii, xli.
—— brune à collier du Cap de Bonne Espérance, xxxiii, 67.
—— brune acutipenne de la Louisiane, xxxvi.
—— brune à ventre tacheté, Grande, xxxvi, xxxviii, 201.
—— brune de l'Isle de Bourbon, xxxviii.
—— brune et blanche à ceinture brune, xxxvi, xxxviii.
—— Oumara, xxxix.
—— d'Amérique, xxxi, xxxii, xxxiii, 465.
—— d'Antigue, xxxv, xxxix, 241.
—— d'Antigue à gorge couleur de rouille, 241.
—— de Cayenne, xxxii, xxxiii, xxxvi, xxxviii, 479.
—— de Cheminée, xxxi, xxxv, xxxviii, 213.
—— d'Espagne, Grande, xxxii.
—— de Fenêtre, xxxvi, 7.
—— de l'Amérique, 479.
—— de la Baie de Hudson, xxxiii, xxxvi.
—— de la Caroline, xxxii.
—— de la Louisiane, xxxiii, 439.
—— de la Martinique, xxxii, xxxiii.
—— de l'isle de Bourbon, xxxviii, xxxix, 201.
—— de Marais, xli, xlv, xlvi, lvii.

INDEX.

Hirondelle de Rivage, xxxii, xxxiii, xxxvi, xxxviii, 43.
— de Rivage de la Cochinchine, xxxii.
— de Rivage du Sénégal, xxxii, xxxvi.
— de S. Domingue, xxxii, xxxiii, 465.
— des Blés, xxxvi, xxxviii, 201.
— des Cheminées, xxxiii, xlv.
— des Marais, 73.
— domestique, xxxv.
— du Pérou, xxxii, 499.
— — du Pérou, Grande, xxxii.
— fauve, xli, xlii, xlvi, lvii, 115.
— grise des Rochers, xxxvi, 97.
— huppée, xli, xlv, xlvi, lvii.
— , Petite, 7.
— noire à croupion gris, xxxvi.
— noire acutipenne de la Martinique, xxxvi, xxxviii.
— noire à ventre cendrée, La Petite, xxxvi, 499.
— rousse, xlii.
— rousseline, xli, xlv, xlix, lvi.
— tachetée, xxxiii, xxxviii.
Hirundo, 3, 200, 411.
— abyssinica, lii, 341.
— acuta, xl.
— æthiopica, lxiv, 210, 307, 322.
— agrestis, xliii, 413.
— alba, xxxix.
— albicollis, xlv.
— allágula, 303.
— albigularis, xli, liv, lvi, lxii, 210, 303, 307, 322, 413.
— albilinea, 149.
— albilineata, 149.
— albiventer, xxxvi, xxxvii, xxxviii, xl, 139.
— albiventris, xliv, 139, 465.
— alfredi, lx, 573.
— alpestris, xxxiv, 317, 357, 366.
— alpestris japonica, lii.
— ambigua, lxii, 303.
— ambrosiaca, xxxii, xxxvi, xxxvii, xl, xliii.
— americana, xxxvi, xxxix, xlii, xliii, 249, 253, 331.
— anchietæ, lx, 330.
— andamanensis, lx, 242.
— andecola, l, 499.
— angolensis, lx, lxiv, 210, 293, 300, 412.

Hirundo apus, xxxii, xxxiv, xxxviii, xl, xliii.
— arborea, 525.
— arcticincta, lxvi, lxvii, 210, 295, 300, 412.
— arenaria, xliii.
— ariel, 585.
— astigma, lxvii, 383.
— atra, xliv.
— atrocærulea, liv, 210, 319, 322, 415.
— australis, 525.
— badia, lxii, 211, 393, 422, 428.
— baicalensis, lxii, 249.
— beaussoneauti, li.
— — — latirostris, 237.
— — — microrhynchos, 237.
— — — minor, 238.
— bicolor, xlii, 155.
— boissoneauti, li, 215, 237.
— borbonica, xxxiv, xxxvi, xxxviii, xxxix, 201, 205.
— borealis, lxiii, 242.
— brevicaudata, li, 81.
— brevirostris, li.
— cærulea, xli, xliii, 439.
— cahirica, xlvi, 215, 237, 238.
— caminicola, xliii.
— capensis, xxxix, xli, xlv, xlix, 337, 341, 347.
— castanea, xlix, 237.
— cayennensis, xl.
— cerlo, xl.
— chalybea, xxxii, xxxvi, xl, 473.
— chinensis, xlix, 81.
— cincta, xxxvi, xxxvii, xxxviii, xl, 67.
— cinerascens, xliii.
— cinerea, xxxvi, xxxvii, xl, xliv, xlv, 43.
— concolor, xlix, l, 123.
— coronata, xlviii, 555, 561.
— cristata, xliv, xlv, lvii.
— cucullata, xxxiii, xxxv, xxxvii, xxxviii, xxxix, xli, lvi, 210, 337, 354, 412.
— cyanoviridis, lvii, 185.
— cyanoleuca, xli, xliv, liii, 505.
— cyanopyrrha, xli, xliv, 254.
— cypseloides, 335.
— daurica, xxxiv, xl, lxvi, lxvii, 210, 357, 347, 361, 365, 371, 386, 419.
— dichroa, lvi.

Hirundo dimidiata, liv, lv, lvi, 210, 319, 322, 414.
— domestica, xli, xlii, xliii, xliv, 215.
— domicella, lx, lxi, lxiv, 211, 381, 386, 421.
— domicola, 280.
— dominicensis, xxxii, xxxiii, xxxvi, xxxvii, xl, xlii, lii, 465.
— emini, lxvi, lxvii, 211, 383, 386.
— — · erythrocephala, xl, 577.
— — erythrogaster, xxxiii, xxxv, xxxvii, xxxix, xli, xlii, xliv, xlix, 253, 550.
— — erythrogastra, lxvi, 209, 217, 218, 249, 253, 254, 272.
— — erythropygia, xlix, lxvi, 211, 347, 365, 371, 386, 421.
— — esculenta, xxxii, xxxiv, xxxvi, xxxviii, xxxix.
— — euchrysea, liii, liv, lx, lxvi, 211, 407, 426, 428.
— — , var. dominicensis, 409.
— — fasciata, xxxiii, xxxvii, xl, xliii, 495.
— — fenestrala, xliii.
— — filicauda, 360.
— — filicaudata, xlix, 329.
— — filifera, xlviii, 329.
— — flavigastra, xliv, 647.
— — flaviventer, xliii.
— — fluminicola, 577.
— — fluvicola, lvi, 577.
— — fluvialis, xliii.
— — francica, xxxix.
— — frenata, 242.
— — fretensis, lix, 242, 280.
— — frontalis, xlviii, l, lv, 143, 279, 289.
— — fucata, xlvii, xlviii, 515.
— — fuligula, li, 115.
— — fulva, xlii, xlvii, 531, 561.
— — fulvus, 531.
— — fumaria, xlviii, 254.
— — fusca, xliv.
— — fuscicapilla, lx, 330.
— — gordoni, lv, lxiv, 211, 397, 421, 428.
— — gouldii, lv, 143.
— — griseopyga, liv, lviii, lxiii, 210, 335, 354, 417.
— — gularis, xlv.
— — gutturalis, xxxv, xxxix, xlii,

xlix, liii, lix, lx, lxiii, lxvii, 209,
217, 218, 241, 242, 249, 272, 411.
Hirundo holomelas, liv, 663.
—— horreorum, xli, 253.
—— hortensis, xlvi, 647.
—— hyemalis, hi, 115.
—— hyperythra, liv. 211, 389, 422,
428.
—— indica, xl, xlv.
—— inornata, lii, 100.
—— intermedia, 357.
—— japonica, 361, 365.
—— javanica, xl, xlvi, xlvii, xlviii,
lii, lxvi, 209, 279, 289, 390, 411.
—— jewan, xlix, 242.
—— jugularis, xlv, xlvii, 647.
—— kamtschatica, lxiii, 242.
—— kamtschatika, 242.
—— kleebo, xlvi.
—— korthalsi, lvi, 341.
—— lagopoda, xlii.
—— latirostris, lix.
—— leucogaster, 155.
—— leucoptera, xl, 139.
—— leucopyga, liv, 143, 153.
—— leucopygia, lxii, 149, 153.
—— leucorrhoa, xli, xliv, xlv, xlvii,
139, 143, 153.
—— leucosoma, l, lxiv, 210, 311,
311, 322, 414.
—— leucosternum, li.
—— lucida, lvii, 210, 207, 300, 413.
—— ludoviciana, xlii, 439.
—— lunifrons, xlvii, 331, 373.
—— maculata, xxxviii.
—— marina indigena, xliii.
—— martinicana, xxxii.
—— melanocrissa, 211, 379, 386,
387, 389, 421.
—— melanogaster, xlviii, lvii, 555,
561.
—— melanoleuca, xlv, xlvii. liii,
503, 505.
—— melanopyga, xlvi, 505.
—— mella, xxxiii, xxxiv, xl.
—— melbina, 355.
—— meyeni, 153.
—— microrhynchos, lix.
—— minuta, xlv, xlvii, l, 81, 505.
—— modesta, li, 163.
—— montana, xxxix, 99.
—— monteiri, lviii, 211, 403, 425,
428.
—— moschata, lvi.

Hirundo marina, 499.
—— namiyei, lxvi, 209, 287, 300,
412.
—— neoxena, li, 210, 280, 289, 300.
—— nigra, xxxii, xl, 412.
—— nigricans, xliv, xlviii, lii, lix,
525, 529.
—— nigrita, liii, 210, 317, 322, 414.
—— nigroruta, lxii, 210, 325, 354,
416.
—— nipalensis, l, lxi, lxvi, 210,
347, 365, 386.
—— nitens, 611.
—— obscura, 607.
—— opifex, xlvi, 531.
—— orientalis, lii, 215, 237.
—— pacifica, 280, 289.
—— paludicola, xli, xliv.
—— palustris, xliv, xlv, 73.
—— panayana, xxxix, xliii, 242.
—— pascuum, xlviii, 479.
—— patagonica, l.
—— payana, 242.
—— pelagica, xxxii.
—— pelasgia, xxxii, xxxiv, xxxviii,
xxxix, xl.
—— peruviana, xl, lii.
—— philippenensis, xliii.
—— platensis, xlv.
—— pœcilema, liii, 561.
—— poucheti, lxiii, 355.
—— prasina, xlviii, 155.
—— pratincola, xxxiv.
—— pristoptera, l, 621.
—— puella, lii. liii, lv, 210, 341,
354, 418.
—— purpurea, xxxi, xxxii, xxxiv,
xxxvii, xxxix, 439.
—— pyrrholæma, lii, 275.
—— pyrrhonota, xli, xliv, xlv,
xlvii, lii, 525.
—— republicana, xlvii, 531.
—— riocouri, xlvii, lx, 215, 237,
238.
—— riparia, xxxiii, xxxiv, xxxvi,
xxxvii, xxxviii, xxxix, xlii, xliii,
43.
—— robini, xlix.
—— rufa, xxxix, xlii, 237, 249, 253.
—— ruficeps, xlvi, 329.
—— ruficollaris, liii, 567.
—— ruficollis, xli, xliv, 647.
—— rufifrons, xli, xliv, xlv, li. 363,
507.

Hirundo rufigula, lxii, 571.
—— rufula, xliii, xlix, li, 210, 337,
347, 354, 379, 399, 418.
—— rupestris, xxxiv, xxxvi, xxxix,
xliii, 99.
—— rupicola, xliii, l, 100.
—— rustica, xxxi, xxxiii, xxxiv,
xxxv, xxxvii, xxxviii, xli, xlii,
xliii, xlv, xlvi, xlix, l, li, lxiii,
lxvi, lxvii, 209, 213, 217, 218,
242, 249, 254, 272.
—— rusticoides, liii.
—— rutila, xliv.
—— saturata, lxiii, 249.
—— savignii, xlv, xlvi, xlvii, xlix,
li, 209, 215, 217, 218, 237, 249,
272, 411.
—— scapularis, lv, lxiv, 313.
—— sclateri, lx, lxiii, 211, 409, 426,
428.
—— scullii, lxiii, 347.
—— semirufa, liv, lxiv, 211, 395,
424, 428.
—— senegalensis, xxxii, xxxiv,
xxxv, xxxvii, xxxviii, xl, 211,
399, 425, 428.
—— serripennis, li, 643.
—— sinensis, xl, xlix, 81.
—— smithii, xxxvii, xlv, xlvi, xlix,
lx, lxiv, 210, 327, 354.
—— spilodera, liv, 573, 416.
—— spinicauda, xlvii.
—— striolata, lii, liii, lxiv, lxvi,
210, 341, 361, 386, 419.
—— subfusca, lvi, 275.
—— subis, xxxiv, xxxvii, xxxviii,
xl, 439.
—— subsocenta, l, 81.
—— substriolata, 357, 361.
—— tahitica, xxxvii, xxxix, xlii.
lii, lxvi, 209, 273, 300, 411.
—— taitensis, 275.
—— tapera, xxxii, xxxiv, xxxvi,
xxxvii, xxxviii, xl, xli, xliii,
479.
—— thalassina, xlviii, 175.
—— torquata, xxxvi, xl, 67.
—— tytleri, lix, lxiii, lxiv, 209, 217,
218, 249, 272.
—— unalaschkensis, xl.
—— urbica, xxxi, xxxvi, xxxvii,
xxxvii, xxxix, xliii, li, 5.
—— velocissima, 350.
—— velox, xli, xliv, xlv.

INDEX.

Hirundo versicolor, xliv, 439.
—— vespertina, lxii, 156.
—— violacea, xl, 439.
—— virescens, xliv.
—— viridis, xlii, xlvii, 155.
Hodgson's Mosque-Swallow, 365.
holomelaena, Atticora, 603, 613.
——, Psalidoprocne, xli, li, liv, lv, 603, 625, 630.
holomelas, Atticora, 603, 607.
——, Hirundo, liv, 603.
——, Psalidoprocne, 603.
horreorum, Hirundo, xli, 253.
hortensis, Hirundo, xlvi, 647.
House-Martin, 7.
Hydrochelidon nigricans, 525.
hyemalis, Hirundo, lii, 115.
Hylochelidon, lix, 523.
—— nigricans, lix, 525.
hyperythra, Cecropis, 389.
——, Herse, 389.
——, Hirundo, liv, 211, 389, 422, 428.
Hypurolepis, lx.
—— domicola, lx, 280.

Indian Cliff-Swallow, 577.
—— Martin-Swallow, xlvi.
—— Sand-Martin, 81.
indica, Hirundo, xl, xlv.
inornata, Hirundo, lii, 100.
intermedia, Hirundo, 357.
——, Lillia, lxii, 357.
Iridoprocne, lxii, 137.
—— bicolor, xlii, 156.

Jamaican Swallow, 467.
japonica, Cecropis, 365.
——, Hirundo, li, 361, 365.
——, Lillia, 366.
Javan Mosque-Swallow, 361.
—— Swallow, xlvi, 279.
javanica, Cecropis, 242, 280.
——, Herse, 280.
——, Hirundo, xl, xlii, xlvi, xlvii, lii, lvvi, 260, 279, 280, 300, 411.
——, Hypurolepis, 280.
jewan, Cecropis, 242.
——, Hirundo, xlix, 242.
Johnston's Rough-winged Swallow, 649.
jugularis, Cotyle, 647.
——, Hirundo, xlv, xlvii, 647.

kamtschatica, Hirundo, lxiii, 242.
kamtschatika, Hirundo, 242.
kashmiriensis, Chelidon, 35.
Klecho Swallow, xlvi.
klecho, Hirundo, xlvi.
korthalsi, Hirundo, 341.
Krimtschelidon, lxii, 97.
—— concolor, lxii, 123.

Lagenoplastes, lix, 523.
—— ariel, lix, 585.
—— cinerea, lix, 577.
—— fluviola, 577.
lagopoda, Chelidon, 25.
——, Hirundo, xlii, 25.
lagopus, Chelidon, lviii, 6, 25, 36, 38, ——, Chelidonaria, 5.
Large Rufous-headed Swallow, 397.
latirostris, Chelidon, 9.
——, Hirundo, lix, 237.
leucogaster, Hirundo, 155.
leucogastra, Chelidon, 155.
——, Progne, 473.
leucoptera, Cotyle, 139.
——, Herse, 139.
——, Hirundo, xl, 139.
—— Petrochelidon, 139.
leucopyga, Chelidon, lvi.
——, Hirundo, liv, lxii, 143, 153.
leucopygia, Hirundo, 140, 153.
leucorrhoa, Cotyle, 143.
——, Herse, 143.
——, Hirundo, xli, xliv, xlv, xlvi, 139, 143, 153.
——, Petrochelidon, 143.
——, Tachycineta, lvi, 143, 196.
leucorrhous, Tachycineta, xlvii, l, lv, 143, 187, 196.
leucosoma, Chelidon, 311.
——, Hemicecropis, lvii, 311.
——, Hirundo, l, liv, 210, 311, 313, 322, 414.
leucosterna, Atticora, 433.
——, Cheramoeca, 433.
leucosternon, Cheramoeca, 433.
leucosternum, Atticora, 433.
——, Cheramoeca, li, liv, 433, 435.
——, Hirundo, li, 433.
leucosternus, Hirundo, 433.
Lillia, lvii, lxii, 209.
—— alpestris, lvii, 357.
—— arcivitta, 366.
—— ariel, 585.

Lillia capensis, 357.
—— daurica, 365.
—— intermedia, lxii, 357.
—— japonica, 366.
—— melanocrissa, 379.
—— nipalensis, 366.
—— striolata, 361.
—— substriolata, lxii, 357.
linchi, Collocalia, xlvi.
Liuchi Swallow, xlvi.
littoralis, Cotyle, lvi, 65, 77.
littorea, Petrochelidon, lix, 149.
Liu-Kiu Swallow, 289.
longipennis, Macropteryx, xlvi.
lucida, Hirundo, lvii, 210, 297, 300, 413.
ludoviciana, Hirundo, xlii, 439.
lunifrons, Cecropis, 531.
——, Herse, 532.
——, Hirundo, xlvii, 531, 573.
——, Petrochelidon, 531, 555.

Macropteryx longipennis, xlvi.
maculata, Hirundo, xxxviii.
Madagascar Striped Swallow, 205.
madagascariensis, Phedina, lviii, 205, 207, 208.
major, Cypselus, xlii.
Malayan Chestnut Mosque-Swallow, 385.
Martin, xlviii, 7, 8.
——, Azara's Purple, 469.
——, Blakiston's, 23.
——, Caribbean Purple, 465.
——, Cashmere, 19.
——, Darwin's Purple, 463.
——, Great American, xxxi, xxxiii, 453.
——, Heuglin's, 29.
——, Himalayan, 31.
——, House, 7.
——, Patagonian Purple, 459.
——, Purple, xxxi, 439.
——, Rock, 99.
——, Sand, xliii, 43.
——, Tree, 479.
——, Western Purple, 455.
——, White-bellied Purple, 175.
Martinet à collier blanc, xxxvi, xxxix.
—— à collier de Cayenne, xxxiii.
—— à croupion blanc, xlii, xlv.
—— à cul blanc, xxxi, 7.

Martinet à gorge blanche, xli, xlv.
—— de la Caroline, xxxii, 430.
—— —— de la Louisiane, xxxiii.
—— de St. Domingue, xxxii.
——, Le Grand, xxxiii, 465.
—— noir, xxxvi, xxxix.
—— noir à ventre blanc, xxxvi.
—— noir et blanc à ceinture grise, xxxvi.
——, Petit, xxxiii, xxxvi, 7.
—— velocifere, xli, xlv.
martinicana, Hirundo, xxxii.
Martlet, Common, xliii.
melanocrissa, Cecropis, liii, 379, 399.
——, Hirundo, 214, 379, 383, 386, 397, 399, 421.
——, Lillia, 379.
melanogaster, Hirundo, xlviii, lvii, 555, 561.
——, Petrochelidon, liv, 555.
melanoleuca, Atticora, xlvii, 493, 503, 517, 570.
——, Cecropis, 509.
——, Herse, 503.
——, Hirundo, xlv, xlvii, liii, 503, 505.
melanopyga, Hirundo, xlvi, 505.
melba, Cypselus, xxxiv, xxxvi.
——, Hirundo, xxxiii, xxxiv, xl.
melbina, Atticora, lv, 335.
—— ——, Hirundo, 335.
—— ——, Psalidoprocne, 335.
meyeni, Hirundo, 153.
——, Petrochelidon, liv, 153.
——, Tachycineta, 137, 153, 188, 196.
Microchelidon, lviii, 463.
—— tibialis, lviii, 501.
Micropus atricaeus, xli.
—— —— apus, xxxii.
microrhynchos, Cotyle, xlix, 45.
——, Hirundo, lix, 237.
minor, Clivicola, 41, 89.
——, Cotile, liv, 41, 77, 89, 94.
——, Cotyle, 77.
—— ——, Hirundo, 238.
minuta, Hirundo, xlv, xlvii, l, 81, 505.
modesta, Hirundo, li, 463.
——, Progne, liii, 459, 463.
montana, Atticora, lix, 506.
——, Hirundo, xxxix, 99.
monteiri, Hirundo, lviii, 214, 423, 425, 428.

Monteiro's Swallow, 403.
Mosque-Swallow, Ceylonese Chestnut, 389.
——, Dourian, 357.
——, Great African, 399.
——, Hodgson's, 365.
——, Javan, 361.
——, Malayan Chestnut, 393.
——, Small African, 384.
— — —, Sykes', 371.
murina, Atticora, 499.
——, Hirundo, 499.
——, Petrochelidon, lv, 499.

unanivet, Chelidon, lxiv, 287.
——, Hirundo, lxvi, 200, 287, 300, 412.
Neochelidon, lviii, 493.
—— tibialis, 501.
neoxena, Hirundo, li, 210, 280, 289, 300, 412.
niger, Cypseloides, xxxii, xxxiii, xxxvi, xxxvii, xl.
—— ——, Cypselus, xliii.
nigra, Hirundo, xxxii, xl, 412.
nigricans, Autprochelidon, lx.
——, Cecropis, 525.
——, Chelidon, 525.
——, Herse, 525.
——, Hirundo, xliv, xlviii, liii, lix, 525, 528.
——, Hydrochelidon, 525.
——, Hylochelidon, lix, 525.
——, Petrochelidon, xlv, xlvi, 525, 525, 526, 528.
nigrita, Atticora, 317.
——, Hirundo, liii, 210, 317, 322, 414.
——, Ptyonoprogne, 317.
——, Waldenia, lvi, 317.
nigrorufa, Hirundo, lxii, 210, 325, 354, 416.
nipalensis, Cecropis, 365.
——, Chelidon, lxvi, 9, 31, 36, 58.
——, Chelidomaria, 5.
——, Delichon, lvi, 31.
——, Hirundo, l, lvi, lxvi, 31, 210, 347, 365, 386, 420.
——, Lillia, 366.
nitens, Atticora, lvi, 611.
——, Hirundo, 611.
——, Psalidoprocne, 601, 611, 625, 630.

North-American Cliff-Swallow, 531.
—— Rough-winged Swallow, 635.
Notiochelidon, lix, 493.
—— pileata, lix, 513.

obscura, Atticora, lvi, 607.
——, Hirundo, 607.
——, Psalidoprocne, lvi, lxiv, 601, 607, 623, 625, 630.
obscurior, Cotile, lxi, 81.
obsoleta, Biblis, lv, lxi, 97, 111, 129, 134.
——, Cotile, liv, lxiv, 111.
——, Cotyle, 81, 111.
——, Ptyonoprogne, l, 111.
opifex, Hirundo, xlvii, 531.
orientalis, Hirundo, lii, 215, 237.
——, Psalidoprocne, lxvi, 601, 613, 625, 630.
Otaheite Swallow, xxxvii, xxxix, 275.

Pacific Swallow, 275.
pacifica, Hirundo, 280, 289.
——, Petrochelidon, 275.
pagorum, Cecropis, xlix, 215.
——, Hirundo, 215.
Pale Rock-Martin, 111.
—— Sand-Martin, 63.
pallida, Cotyle, 111.
——, Hirundo, 8.
——, Ptyonoprogne, lxi, 111.
palmhelonia, Cotyle, l, 73.
paludicola, Clivicola, 41.
——, Cotile, lvi, lxi, 41, 73, 79, 94.
—— ——, Cotyle, l, lvi, 73, 111.
——, Hirundo, xli, l, lvi, 73.
palustris, Cotyle, 73, 77, 111.
Panayan Swallow, xxxvii, xxxix, 241.
panayana, Cecropis, 242.
——, Hirundo, xxxix, 242.
Panyptila cayennensis, xxxiii, xxxvi, xl.
pascuana, Hirundo, xlviii.
——, Progne, 479.
Patagonian Purple Martin, 459.
patagonica, Atticora, 505.
——, Hirundo, l, 505.
payana, Hirundo, 242.
pelagica, Hirundo, xxxi.

4 Q

pelasgia, Chætura, xxxiv, xl.
———, Hirundo, xxxii, xxxiv, xxxviii, xxxix, xl.
Peruvian Cliff-Swallow, 567.
—— Swallow, xxxvii, xl.
peruviana, Hirundo, lii.
Petit Martinet, xxxiii.
———— noir, xxxix.
Petite Hirondelle, xxxi.
petiti, Psalidoprocne, lxi, lxvi, 601, 613, 617, 625, 630.
Petit's Rough-winged Swallow, 617.
Petrochelidon, liv, lix, lx, 3, 523, 589.
—— albiventer, lviii, 139.
—— albiventris, 139.
—— alfredi, lx.
—— americana, 531.
—— ariel, li, 523, 585, 595, 598.
—— bicolor, 156.
—— cuchrysea, 407.
—— fluvicola, xxxvii, xl, lix, 523, 577, 583, 598.
—— fulva, xlii, xlvii, 523, 531, 561, 567, 592, 598.
—— leucoptera, 139.
—— leucorrhoa, 143.
—— littorea, lix, 149.
—— lunifrons, 531, 555.
—— melanogaster, liv, 555.
—— meyeni, liv, 153.
—— neurina, lv, 499.
—— nigricans, xliv, xlvi, 523, 525, 589, 598.
—— pacifica, 275.
—— poeciloma, 561.
—— pyrrhonota, xxxviii, xxxix, xliv, xlvii, 523, 531, 532, 590, 598.
—— ruficollaris, 523, 567, 569, 593, 598.
—— rufigula, lxiii, 523, 571, 593, 598.
—— spilodera, liv, lx, lxvi, 523, 573, 593, 598.
—— swainsonii, xlviii, lvii, 523, 555, 559, 592, 593.
—— tahitica, 275.
—— tapera, 479.
—— thalassina, 175.
—— tibialis, 561.
—— timoriensis, xliv, 523, 529, 590, 598.

Phæoprogne, lix, 437.
—— fusca, lix, 479.
—— tapera, 479.
Phedina, lvii, 3, 196, 199.
—— borbonica, xliv, lvii, 196, 199, 201, 208.
—— brazzæ, lxiv, 196, 199, 207.
—— madagascariensis, lviii, 196, 199, 205, 207, 208.
philippenensis, Hirundo, xliii.
Pied Swallow, xlvi.
pileata, Atticora, lviii, lix, 493, 513, 518, 520.
——, Notiochelidon, lix, 513.
platensis, Hirundo, xlv.
poeciloma, Hirundo, liii, 561.
——, Petrochelidon, 561.
poliura, Chætura, xxxiv, xxxvi, xxxix.
pouchoti, Hirundo, lxiii, 335.
prasina, Hirundo, xlviii, 155.
pratincola, Hirundo, xxxiv.
Pristoptera, lvii, 601.
—— typica, 621.
pristoptera, Atticora, 621.
——, Chelidon, l, 621.
——, Hirundo, l, liii, 621.
——, Pristoptera, lvii, 621.
——, Psalidoprocne, liii, 601, 621, 625, 630.
Progne, lxi, 3, 437, 487.
—— borbonica, 205.
—— chalybea, xxxiii, xl, 437, 469, 473, 488, 490.
—— concolor, l, li, 437, 463, 487, 490.
—— cryptoleuca, lix, 440.
—— domestica, 437, 469, 473, 488, 490.
—— dominicensis, xli, xliv, 437, 465, 469, 473, 487, 490.
—— elegans, lix, 440, 459, 469.
—— furcata, liii, lix, 437, 469, 487, 490.
—— hesperia, lxvi, 437, 455, 490.
—— leucogastra, 473.
—— modesta, liii, 459, 463.
—— purpurea, xxxi, xxxiii, xxxiv, xxxvi, xxxvii, xl, xli, xlii, xliv, xlviii, lxvi, 437, 439, 455, 459, 469, 473, 490.
—— subis, lxvi, 440, 455.

Progne tapera, xxxiv, 437, 479, 488, 490.
progne, Chelidon, 215.
Psalidoprocne, liv, lxi, 601.
—— albiceps, lix, 601, 624, 625, 630.
—— antinorii, lxiii, 601, 615, 625, 630.
—— chalybea, lxvi, 601, 609, 625, 630.
—— cypselina, liv, 601.
—— fuliginosa, 601, 619, 625, 630.
—— holomelæna, xli, liv, lv, lvi, 601, 603, 625, 630.
—— holomelas, 603.
—— mellbina, 315.
—— nitens, 601, 611, 625, 630.
—— obscura, lvi, lxiv, 601, 607, 623, 625, 630.
—— orientalis, lxvi, 601, 613, 625, 630.
—— petiti, lxi, lxvi, 601, 613, 617, 625, 630.
—— pristoptera, liii, 601, 621, 625, 630.
Ptyonoprogne, l, liv, 97.
—— anderssoni, l.
—— concolor, l, 123.
—— fuligula, l.
—— nigrita, 317.
—— obsoleta, l, 111.
—— pallida, lxi, 111.
—— rufigula, l.
—— rupestris, l, liv, 100.
puella, Hirundo, lii, liii, lv, 210, 341, 354, 418.
Purple Martin, xxxi, 439.
——, Azara's, 469.
——, Caribbean, 465.
——, Darwin's, 463.
——, Patagonian, 459.
——, Western, 455.
——, White-bellied, 473.
—— Swallow, xxxvii, 439.
—— Swift, 439.
purpurea, Hirundo, 439.
——, Progne, xxxiii, xxxiv, xxxvi, xxxvii, xxxix, xl, xli, xlii, xlviii, lxvi, 437, 439, 455, 459, 473, 490.
Pygochelidon, lix, 463.
—— cyanoleuca, lix.
pyrrholæma, Hirundo, lii, 275.
pyrrhonota, Cecropis, 525, 531.
——, Herse, 525.

INDEX. 671

pyrrhonota, Hirundo, xli, xliv, xlv, xlvii, lii, 525, 531.
———, Petrochelidon, xxxviii, xxxix, xliv, xlvii, lxvi, 525, 531, 532, 590, 598.

Red-breasted Swallow, 395.
Red-headed Swallow, xxxvii, xl, 577.
Red-rumped Swallow, 347.
Red-throated Rough-winged Swallow, 647.
republicana, Hirundo, xlvii, 531.
riocouri, Cecropis, 237.
———, Hirundo, xlvii, 215, 237, 238.
Riparia europæa, xliii.
riparia, Clivicola, 41, 45.
———, Cotile, xxxiii, xliv, xlvi, li, 41, 43, 93, 94, 640, 641, 642, 643, 644, 653.
———, Cotyle, xlix, 41, 44, 60, 65.
———, Hirundo, xxxii, xxxiv, xxxvi, xxxvii, xxxviii, xxxix, xliii, xlix, 41, 43.
———, Riparia, xliv.
robini, Hirundo, xlix.
Rock-Martin, 99.
———, Anderson's, 119.
———, Dusky, 129.
———, Fischer's, 121.
———, Pale, 111.
———, Rufous-throated, 115.
Rock-Swallow, xxxvii, xxxix, 99.
Rough-winged Swallow, Antinori's, 615.
——— ———, Black, 604.
——— ———, Blue, 624.
——— ———, Cameroons, 606.
——— ———, Eastern, 613.
——— ———, Fantee, 607.
——— ———, Johnston's, 619.
——— ———, North-American, 635.
——— ———, Petit's, 617.
——— ———, Square-tailed, 611.
——— ———, White-headed, 623.
rufa, Cecropis, 254.
———, Hirundo, xxxix, 237, 249, 254.
ruficeps, Cecropis, 329.
———, Hirundo, xlvi, 329.
ruficollaris, Hirundo, liii, 567.
———, Petrochelidon, 523, 567, 590, 598.
ruficollis, Cecropis, 647.

ruficollis, Cotile, 647.
———, Cotyle, 647, 651.
———, Hirundo, xli, xliv, xlv, 647.
———, Petrochelidon, 569.
———, Stelgidopteryx, xliv, xlvi, xlvii, xlix, 647, 655.
rufifrons, Cecropis, 307.
———, Hirundo, xli, xliv, xlv, li, 305, 307.
rufigula, Biblis, 97, 121, 130, 134.
———, Cotile, lxiii, 121.
———, Cotyle, 121.
———, Hirundo, l, lxii, 571.
———, Petrochelidon, lxii, 523, 571, 593, 598.
———, Ptyonoprogne, li.
Rufous-and-black Swallow, 325.
Rufous-bellied Swallow, xxxvii, xxxix, 253.
Rufous-headed Swallow, xxxvii, xl, 337.
Rufous-fronted Swallow, xlvi.
Rufous-rumped Swallow, xxxix, xlv, 531.
Rufous-throated Rock-Martin, 115.
rufula, Cecropis, 347.
———, Hirundo, xlix, l, lxiii, 337, 347, 354, 379, 399, 428.
———, Lillia, 347.
rupestris, Biblis, lii, 97, 100, 129, 134.
———, Chelidon, xlvi, xlix, 8, 9, 97.
———, Clivicola, 100.
———, Cotile, lxvi, 97, 100.
———, Cotyle, xlix, 97, 100.
———, Hirundo, xxxiv, xxxix, xliii, 99.
———, Ptyonoprogne, l, liv, 100.
rupicola, Hirundo, xlii, l, 100.
rustica, Cecropis, 315.
———, Chelidon, 215.
———, Hirundo, xxxi, xxxiii, xxxiv, xxxv, xxxvii, xxxviii, xxxix, xli, xlii, xliii, xlv, xlvi, xlix, l, li, lxiii, lxvi, lxvii, 209, 213, 215, 217, 218, 242, 249, 254, 272.
rusticoides, Cecropis, 242.
———, Hirundo, liii.
rutila, Hirundo, xliv.
rutilus, Cypseloides, xliv, xlix.

Salangane, La, xxxvi.
Sand-Martin, xxxvii, xliii, 43.

Sand-Martin, Brown-collared, 67.
——— ———, Congo, 71.
——— ———, Deans Cowan's, 79.
——— ———, Egyptian, 65.
——— ———, Indian, 81.
——— ———, Pale, 64.
——— ———, Soudan, 77.
——— ———, South-African, 73.
saturata, Hirundo, lxiii, 249.
savignii, Cecropis, 237.
———, Chelidon, 238.
———, Hirundo, xlv, xlvi, xlvii, xlix, lii, 209, 215, 217, 218, 237, 249, 272, 411.
scapularis, Hirundo, lv, 343.
sclateri, Hirundo, lx, lxiii, 211, 409, 423, 428.
Sclater's Swallow, 409.
scullii, Hirundo, lxii, 347.
semirufa, Hirundo, liv, lxiv, 211, 395, 424, 428.
Senegal Swallow, xxxvii.
senegalensis, Cecropis, 369.
———, Hirundo, xxxii, xxxiii, xxxiv, xxxv, xxxvii, xl, lxiv, 211, 369, 425, 428.
Senegambian Chimney-Swallow, 297.
——— Swallow, 297.
septentrionalis, Chelidon, 9.
serratipennis, Cotyle, lvi.
serripennis, Cotile, 635.
———, Cotyle, lxi, 635.
———, Hirundo, li, 635, 643.
———, Stelgidopteryx, lvii, lxvi, 635, 642, 644, 653.
Severn Swallow, xlvii.
Sharp-tailed Swallow, xl.
shelleyi, Clivicola, 41.
———, Cotile, lxiv, 41, 65, 94.
sinensis, Clivicola, 41.
———, Cotile, l, li, lxi, 41, 46, 81, 90, 94.
———, Cotyle, xlvi, 41, 81.
———, Hirundo, xl, xlix, 81.
Small African Mosque Swallow, 389.
Smaller Stripe-breasted Swallow, 341.
smithii, Cecropis, 329.
———, Hirundo, xlv, xlvi, xlix, lx, lxiv, 329, 354, 416.
Soudan Sand-Martin, 77.
South-African Cliff-Swallow, 573.
——— Sand-Martin, 73.

South-American Green Swallow, 143.
spilodera, Hirundo, liv, lxvi, 673.
———, Petrochelidon, liv, lv, 523, 573, 593, 598.
———, Phedina, 573.
spinicauda, Clivicola, xxxiv, xxxix.
———, Hirundo, xlvii.
Square-tailed Rough-winged Swallow, 644.
St. Domingo Swallow, xxxvii, xl, 465.
stabulorum, Cecropis, 215.
Stelgidopteryx, lvii, lxi, 633.
——— fulvigula, lix, 636, 651.
——— fulvipennis, 636.
——— ruficollis, xliv, xlv, xlvi, xlvii, xlix, 633, 647, 655.
——— serripennis, lvii, lxvi, 633, 635, 643, 653.
——— uropygialis, lviii, lix, 633, 649, 651, 655.
striolata, Cecropis, liii, 341, 361.
———, Hirundo, lii, lxiv, lxvi, 210, 341, 361, 386, 420.
———, Lillia, 361.
Stripe-breasted Swallow, Smaller, 341.
Striped Swallow, Bourbon, 201.
——— ———, de Brazza's, 207.
——— ———, Madagascar, 205.
subfusca, Hirundo, lii, 275.
———, Phedina, 275.
subis, Cecropis, 440.
———, Hirundo, xxxiv, xxxviii, xl, 439.
———, Progne, lxvi, 440, 455.
subsoccata, Cotile, 81.
———, Cotyle, 81.
———, Hirundo, l, 81.
substriolata, Hirundo, 357, 361.
———, Lillia, lxii, 357.
Superciliosa Swallow, xlvii.
swainsoni, Petrochelidon, xlviii, lvii, lxvi, 523, 555, 559, 592, 598.
Swainson's Cliff-Swallow, 555.
Swallow, 525. See also Cliff-Swallow.
———, Albino, lxvii.
———, Ambergris, xxxvii, xl.
———, American Chimney, 253.
———, Andean, 439.
———, Angola, 293.
———, Antinori's Rough-winged, 615.
———, Aoonalashka, xxxvii, xl.

Swallow, Ash-bellied, xxxvii, xl, 409.
———, Ashy-rumped Rough-winged, 651.
———, Australian, 289.
———, Bahama, 185.
———, Barn, xlvi.
———, Black, xxxvii, xl.
———, Black-collared, 593.
———, Black Rough-winged, 603.
———, Blanford's, 307.
———, Blue, xlvi, 319.
———, Blue-and-white, 505.
———, Blue Rough-winged, 621.
———, Bourbon Striped, 201.
———, Brazilian, xxxvii.
———, Brown-collared, xxxvii, xl, 67.
———, Brunette, xlvi.
———, Cameroons Rough-winged, 669.
———, Canada, xxxvii, 439.
———, Cape, xxxvii, xxxix.
———, Ceylonese Chestnut Mosque, 389.
———, Chalybeate, xxxvii, xl, 473.
———, Chilian, 153.
———, Chimney, xxxvii, xliii, 213, 215, 253.
———, Collared, xlvi.
———, Common, xxxi.
———, Coromandel, xlvi.
———, Crag, xxxvii, xxxix.
———, Crested, xlvi.
———, Daurian, xxxvii.
———, ———, Mosque, 357.
———, Dun-rumped, xlvi, 525.
———, Dusky, xlvi.
———, Eastern Chimney, lxvii, 241.
——— ——— Rough-winged, 613.
———, Egyptian, 237.
———, Elgon, 295.
———, Esculent, xxxviii, xxxix.
———, Fanti Rough-winged, 607.
———, Fulvous, xlvi.
———, Gordon's, 307.
———, Great African Mosque, 309.
———, Grey-rumped, xxxviii, xxxix.
———, Guatemalan, 513.
———, Hodgson's Mosque, 365.
———, Indian Martin, xlvi.
———, Jamaican, 407.
———, Javan, xlvi, 279.
———, ———, Mosque, 361.

Swallow, Johnston's Rough-winged, 610.
———, Klecho, xlvi.
———, Large Rufous-headed, 337.
———, Linchi, xlvi.
———, Liu-Kiu, 289.
———, Madagascar Striped, 205.
———, Malayan Chestnut Mosque, 393.
———, Monteiro's, 403.
———, North-American Rough-winged, 635.
———, Otaheite, xxxvii, xxxix, 275.
———, Pacific, 275.
———, Panayan, xxxvii, xxxix, 241.
———, Peruvian, xxxvii. xl.
———, Petit's Rough-winged, 617.
———, Pied, xlvi.
———, Purple, xxxvii, 439.
———, Quebec, xlvi.
———, Red-breasted, 395.
———, Red-headed, xxxvii, xl, 577.
———, Red-rumped, 347.
———, Red-throated Rough-winged, 647.
———, Rock, xxxvii, xxxix, 99.
———, Rufous-and-black, 325.
———, Rufous-bellied, xxxviii, xxxix, 253.
———, Rufous-fronted, xlvi.
———, Rufous-headed, xxxvii, xl.
———, Rufous-necked, xlvi.
———, Rufous-rumped, xxxvii, xxxix, 531.
———, Sclater's, 409.
———, Senegal, xxxvii.
———, Severn, xlvii.
———, Sharp-tailed, xl.
———, Small African, 381.
———, Smaller Stripe-breasted, 341.
———, South-American Green, 143.
———, Square-tailed Rough-winged, 611.
———, St. Domingo, xxxvii, xl, 465.
———, Supercilious, xlvii.
———, Sykes' Mosque, 371.
———, Tawny-headed, 515.
———, Tropical, 279.
———, Tytler's, 249.
———, Violet, xxxvii, xl, 439.
———, Violet-and-green, 175.
———, Wheat, xxxviii, xxxix, 201.
———, White, xxxvii.
———, White-banded, 495.

INDEX.

Swallow, White-bellied, xxxvii, xl, 155, 495.
——, White-bodied Chimney, 311.
——, White-breasted, 433.
——, White-collared, xl.
——, White-gorgeted, 317.
——, White-headed Rough-winged, 623.
——, White-throated, 363.
——, White-winged, xxxvii, xl, 139.
——, Wire-tailed, xlvi. 327.
Swallows, supposed hibernation of, lxix.
Swift, Chinese, xl.
——, Purple, 439.
Sykes' Mosque-Swallow, 371.

Tachycineta, liv, 137.
—— albilinea, lix, lxii, 137, 188,196.
—— albiventris, xxxvii, lxvi. 137, 139, 181, 196.
—— bicolor, xlii, xlvi, xlvii, xlviii, lxii, 155, 189, 196.
—— cyaneoviridis, 137, 185, 193, 196.
—— euchrysea, 407.
—— leucorrhous, xlvii, l, lv, lvi, 137, 143, 187, 196.
—— meyeni, 137, 153, 188, 196.
—— thalassina, liv, 175.
—— thalassinus, lxvi, 137, 175, 196, 637.
tahitica, Chelidon, 275.
——, Herse, 275.
——, Hirundo, xxxiv, xxxix, xliii, li, lvi, lxvi, 260, 275, 300, 411.
——, Petrochelidon, 275.
tahitensis, Cecropis, 275.
——, Herse, 275.
——, Hirundo, 275.
tapera, Cecropis, 479.
——, Cotyle, 479.

tapera, Hirundo, xxxii, xxxiv, xxxvi, xl, xli, xliii, 479.
——, Petrochelidon, 479.
——, Phæoprogne, 479.
——, Progne, xlviii, 437, 479, 488, 490.
Tapere, La, xxxvi.
Tawny-headed Swallow, 515.
tectorum, Chelidon, 9.
thalassina, Chelidon, 175.
——, Herse, 175.
——, Hirundo, xlviii, 175.
——, Petrochelidon, 175.
——, Tachycineta, 175, 191, 196.
thalassinus, Cecropis, 175.
——, Tachycineta, liv, lxvi. 175, 191, 637.
tibialis, Atticora, lv, 499, 501, 517, 520.
——, Microchelidon, lviii, 501.
——, Neochelidon, 501.
——, Petrochelidon, lv, 501.
Timor Cliff-Swallow, 529.
timoriensis, Petrochelidon, lxiv, 523, 529, 593, 598.
torquata, Cotyle, 67.
——, Hirundo, xl, 67.
Tree-Martin, 479.
Tropical Swallow, 279.
typica, Pristoptera, 621.
tytleri, Chelidon, 249.
——, Hirundo, lix, lxiii, lxiv, lxvi, 240, 217, 248, 249, 272.
Tytler's Chimney-Swallow, 249.

unalaschkensis, Hirundo, xl.
urbica, Chelidon, xxxiii, xlvi, xlix, lxiv, 5, 7, 9, 19, 25, 29, 38.
——, Chelidonaria, 5, 9.
——, Hirundo, xxxiv, xxxvi. xxxviii, xxxix, xliii, xlviii, 25.
Uromitus, lvi, 209.

Uromitus filifera, 330.
—— filiferus, 330.
uropygialis, Cotyle, 654.
—— ——, Stelgidopteryx, lviii, lix, 654, 655.

varia, Hirundo, 8.
velocissima, Hirundo, 330.
velox, Hirundo, xli, xliv, xlv.
versicolor, Hirundo, xliv, 439.
vespertina, Hirundo, lxi, 456.
violacea, Cecropis, 440.
——, Hirundo, xl, 439.
Violet Swallow, xxxvii, xl, 139.
Violet-and-Green Swallow, 175.
virescens, Hirundo, xliv.
viridis, Chelidon, 155.
——, Hirundo, xlvii, l, 155.
vulgaris, Chelidon, 9.

Waldenia, lxi, 209.
——, nigrita, lxi, 317.
Western Purple Martin, 455.
Wheat Swallow, xxxvii, 204.
White Swallow, xxxvii.
White-banded Swallow, 495.
White-bellied Purple Martin, 475.
—— Swallow, xxxvii, xl, 155, 195.
White-breasted Swallow, 433.
White-bodied Chimney-Swallow, 311.
White-collared Swallow, xl.
White-gorgeted Swallow, 317.
White-headed Rough-winged Swallow, 623.
White-rumped Cliff-Swallow, 525.
White-throated Swallow, 363.
White-winged Swallow, xxxvii, xl, 139.
whiteleyi, Chelidon, lviii. 25.
Wire-tailed Swallow, xlvi. 327.

zonaris, Chætura, xliv. xlvi.

www.ingramcontent.com/pod-product-compliance
Lightning Source LLC
Chambersburg PA
CBHW032007300426
44117CB00008B/935